# EXCHANGE-TRADED FUNDS IN EUROPE

# EXCHANGE-TRADED FUNDS IN EUROPE

ADAM MARSZK

*Gdansk University of Technology, Faculty of Management and Economics, Gdansk, Poland*

EWA LECHMAN

*Gdansk University of Technology, Faculty of Management and Economics, Gdansk, Poland*

ACADEMIC PRESS

An imprint of Elsevier

Academic Press is an imprint of Elsevier
125 London Wall, London EC2Y 5AS, United Kingdom
525 B Street, Suite 1650, San Diego, CA 92101, United States
50 Hampshire Street, 5th Floor, Cambridge, MA 02139, United States
The Boulevard, Langford Lane, Kidlington, Oxford OX5 1GB, United Kingdom

**Notices**
Knowledge and best practice in this field are constantly changing. As new research and experience broaden
our understanding, changes in research methods, professional practices, or medical treatment may become
necessary.

Practitioners and researchers must always rely on their own experience and knowledge in evaluating and using
any information, methods, compounds, or experiments described herein. In using such information or methods
they should be mindful of their own safety and the safety of others, including parties for whom they have a
professional responsibility.

To the fullest extent of the law, neither the Publisher nor the authors, contributors, or editors, assume any
liability for any injury and/or damage to persons or property as a matter of products liability, negligence or
otherwise, or from any use or operation of any methods, products, instructions, or ideas contained in the
material herein.

**British Library Cataloguing-in-Publication Data**
A catalogue record for this book is available from the British Library

**Library of Congress Cataloging-in-Publication Data**
A catalog record for this book is available from the Library of Congress

ISBN: 978-0-12-813639-3

For Information on all Academic Press publications
visit our website at https://www.elsevier.com/books-and-journals

  Working together
to grow libraries in
developing countries

www.elsevier.com • www.bookaid.org

*Publisher:* Candice Janco
*Acquisition Editor:* J. Scott Bentley
*Editorial Project Manager:* Katerina Zaliva
*Production Project Manager:* Poulouse Joseph
*Cover Designer:* Miles Hitchen

Typeset by MPS Limited, Chennai, India

# Contents

# Foreword

Exchange-traded funds (ETFs) have been around for more than a quarter of a century, yet they continue to be innovative financial products with tremendous growth of market share and assets under management. This innovation also continues to develop new varieties in terms of market coverage and types of traded portfolios. The first and probably the most well-known ETF product in the market is SPDR that tracks S&P 500 and has the largest share and trading activity in the ETF market. It took almost a decade for ETFs to get traction and attract interest among investors from the time of its introduction. Currently, the variety of ETFs is vast not only in terms of the indexes they cover within an asset type (broad index, industry, sectors, international, and country specific, among others), but also the types of assets (equity, fixed-income, commodities), portfolio holdings (physical vs synthetic), and intensity of portfolio management (active vs passive ETFs).

As recently summarized in a *Wall Street Journal* article on October 8, 2018, there are almost a dozen strategies that ETFs follow. The two oldest strategies are a passive strategy, which entails index tracking, and an active strategy, which entails selecting securities to try to outperform a benchmark index or manage downside risk. These are used by many fund types including ETFs, mutual funds, and closed-end funds. More recent and innovative strategies are: smart beta—typically any ETF that weighs holdings differently from market capitalization; factor—index funds and ETFs that weigh portfolio holdings based on security attributes such as size, value, and momentum; multifactor—similar to the factor strategy but also attempts to derive returns by including more than one factor; tilt—slightly overweighs stocks in the index with certain characteristics and may indicate a preferred investing style such as value or growth; quantitative—based on technology and math-driven investment decisions; self-indexed—an ETF product based on an index without licensing fees in an attempt to reduce costs; leveraged and inverse, and inverse leveraged—uses core index holdings in combination with futures or swaps to generate daily multiple returns of an index or sector; thematic—a step beyond industries and sectors to follow market trends; and hedged—indicates some level of risk control, often using short-selling, options, futures, or swaps.

As ETF products and markets continue to grow and develop its complexity, investors need more information resources and education on these products. There is growing literature in academic and practitioner research that tries to shed some light on different aspects of ETFs and their influence on the markets. Earlier studies looked at performance and characteristics of ETFs, such as tracking errors, fees, and flows and compared ETFs to other similar products such as mutual funds and closed-end funds. As ETFs continue gaining a substantial share of the market, investors, practitioners, academics, and regulators alike started to raise questions on the systemic effects of ETFs on underlying securities and markets. This led to the development of a trench of literature that looks at the effects of ETFs on liquidity and volatility of underlying securities and markets, and spillover effects. There are also a few books that detail ETFs' operation and assessment of ETF choices. Some books also provide summaries of academic research on ETFs. However, given the continuing evolution of the ETF markets and products, there is a need for more research and publications, both peer-reviewed and educational.

This book is a good addition to the existing list of publications on ETFs. Main difference of this book from others is that its focus is on European ETF markets, which is second in size after the one in the United States, but relatively less studied or covered by publications in comparison to the US ETF counterparts. Why is covering the European market important? It is a large and growing market, yet has regulatory, organizational, and cultural differences. The book is a combination of educational materials on ETF concepts, functionality (Chapter 2: Exchange-Traded Funds: Concepts and Contexts), and history of European ETF market (Chapter 3: Exchange-Traded Funds Markets in Europe: Development Patterns), as well as providing empirical studies on the determinants of the European ETF market development (Chapter 4: Determinants of the European Exchange-Traded Funds Markets Development) and integration of the European ETF market with the European financial system (Chapter 5: Exchange-Traded Funds and Financial Systems of European Countries: A Growth Factor or Threat to Stability?).

**Dr. Anna Agapova**
*Florida Atlantic University, Boca Raton, FL, United States*

# Acknowledgments

Our book could not have been developed without the support and constructive criticism from a large number of people. We are deeply indebted to all of them and would like to them thank for their intellectual contribution to this work. We are especially grateful for Prof. Krzysztof Jajuga from the CFA Society Poland and Wrocław University of Economics, and the other participants of the seminars of the Department of Economic Sciences at Gdańsk University of Technology for their support and valuable suggestions concerning our research. Our colleagues were a great source of ideas, encouragement, and inspiration and helped us keep things in the right perspective. Prof. Tomasz Miziołek from the University of Łódź provided us with valuable support and his works shaped and directed our thinking and understanding of issues presented throughout the book. We appreciate the enormous help from all the people involved in processing the large datasets that were used in our research, with special thanks to Jan Marszk. We are also grateful to Dr. Anna Agapova from the Florida Atlantic University for the foreword. Last but not least, we express our gratitude to our families for their enormous patience and understanding during the days and nights spent working on the manuscript. They kept us going with this work, which would not be possible without them.

The research presented in this book has been supported by the National Science Centre of Poland (project no. 2015/19/D/HS4/00399). A. Marszk has received support from the Foundation for Polish Science (FNP).

As always, the responsibility for any errors in the book remains our own.

# 1

# Introduction

*We are living through a revolution in the way people invest. Never before have so many different investment products been available to investors at the click of a mouse (. . .).* **Abner (2016)**

## 1.1 BACKGROUND

That there are various forms of investment funds is undeniably a crucial characteristic of the contemporary financial system. By slightly modifying the definitions of a synonymous concept of "investment companies" provided by Abner (2016) and the Investment Company Institute (2017), and without dwelling into unnecessary details, they can be most broadly understood as financial institutions that gather financial resources from either retail and institutional investors and invest them in securities and other assets in order to reach a range of investment aims; investment funds are managed by investment professionals. Despite the relatively long history of some types of investment funds, their position has become significantly strong during the past few decades, boosted by various economic and social changes, and take place in the most advanced economies. Investment funds are a substantially heterogeneous class of financial institutions that, using the most general classification, covers (yet is not limited to) subcategories such as mutual funds, closed-end funds, exchange-traded funds (ETFs), private equity funds, and hedge funds. Moreover, investment funds have a broad range of investment aims, offering exposure to numerous asset classes in many sectors as well as countries and regions. Investment funds are also highly diversified in terms of their other attributes, including their legal form (vastly depending on the country-specific regulations or the structure of the local investment industry) and construction (with specific examples such as umbrella or master-feeder funds). During recent years the development of investment funds can be noticed globally in many dimensions including the two key perspectives: their assets and number. Substantial growth has also occurred in most cases on the country level.

In spite of the substantial and still increasing diversity of investment funds, most people (even in the group of the financial professionals) associate this category of financial institutions exclusively with the mutual funds that generally overshadow other types, such as closed-end funds or ETFs. Mutual funds are available all over the world in the majority of advanced and emerging economies; however, in the poorest countries their availability remains severely limited due to the underdevelopment of the local financial systems. These mutual funds are also the most diversified type of investment funds. The global assets of mutual funds as of the end of 2017 reached a record-high level of $45 trillion, out of which approximately 80% were managed by the United States and European funds, and most of the remaining by the Asia-Pacific institutions—estimations based

*Exchange-Traded Funds in Europe.*
DOI: https://doi.org/10.1016/B978-0-12-813639-3.00001-8

on ETFGI (2018) and Investment Company Institute (2018)—which indicates the high level of the global market's concentration.

Obviously, the focus on mutual funds can be explained by their domination on the global investment funds market. However, it should not be forgotten that this was not always the case. If we consider the United States—the world's largest financial system (and also the biggest investment funds market) that is strongly linked to financial sectors in other countries through a broad array of interdependencies—we may clearly see that, in the early 20th century, closed-end funds were the dominant category and mutual funds had marginal importance mostly due to their later launch (Abner, 2016). However, starting from the stock market crash of 1929, over the next decades the position of closed-end funds sharply declined while, at the same time, mutual funds emerged as the leading institutions in the investment industry. There were some moments of increases in the popularity of closed-end funds yet these were rather short-lived (interestingly, one of the most recent episodes was interrupted by the rise of ETFs). This shows that the structure of the market for investment funds should not be regarded as definite as it has undergone changes, at times sudden and radical; the United States is not unique in this matter as investment fund markets have also evolved in other regions albeit that the exact changes have sometimes significantly differed. Moreover, it means that the leading position of the mutual funds may be threatened by the other categories of investment funds as well as some developments in the financial system. One of the main contestants is ETFs—investment funds that combine the attributes of various categories of financial institutions and products, and offer their users a range of previously unavailable investment possibilities.

The evolution of the investment funds market over the past several years should not be considered without taking into account the events in the global economy, in particular those that affected the global financial system, such as the 2008 financial crisis or the unparalleled spread of information and communication technologies (ICT) with their profound social and economic implications (Lechman, 2015). As emphasized in the opening citation from Abner (2016), technological revolution has in many ways influenced the investment industry, offering alternatives to the most frequently used bank deposits being accessible as probably never before and increasing the competition among providers of various investment services. More generally, ICT has reshaped all aspects of the financial system, starting from the services provided by banks, through to insurance for all dimensions of the financial markets (e.g., processing of transactions, access to information), among many others.

From a slightly different perspective, one of the key trends that shape the investment industries in many countries is the growing popularity of passive investing (indexing). The basic concept of passive investing is to track (replicate) the performance of the selected index (in other words, the performance of a specified market or a segment of it) rather than to try to outperform it. The reason for such strategy being, inter alia, the after-cost advantage in relation to active investing (Malkiel, 2016; Sharpe, 1991). Regardless of the possible objections to such an approach, its increasing popularity in the global investment industry is undeniable. It would be impossible without the introduction of the new category of investment funds that corresponds perfectly to the main assumption of passive investing—ETFs; however, the cause and effect are not so straightforward as, at the same time, the launch of the first ETFs appears to be an offspring of the heated discussion of the possible advantages of indexing.

The rapid expansion of ETFs is one of the key processes that have taken place in the investment industry (yet its pace differs substantially in various regions and countries; in some there are still no such investment funds). Within several years since their launch they have moved from a marginal product, almost unrecognized on a global scale, to a part of the mainstream financial industry. However, they have not lost their "innovative spirit." ETFs can still be labeled as financial innovations as ETFs markets experience continuing innovational activity with the launch of new types of funds, giving more people access to the increasing group of assets and investment strategies. It may be stated that the launch of the first ETF can be regarded as one of the milestones in the global financial history. Such a designation can be explained not only by the broadening of the range of investments available to their users, but also by the emergence of the new segments of the financial system, such as robo-advising, that were impossible or unfeasible to offer before the advent of ETFs. It should, thus, not be surprising that launch of ETFs and development of the ETFs markets are described by Madhavan (2016, p. 3) as a "disruptive innovation to today's asset management industry" and by Abner (2016, p. XVII) as "the most interesting products in the financial industry today." It would, thus, not be an overstatement to regard them (with the usual caution) as a revolution in the financial industry.

The rising popularity of ETFs has resulted in the burgeoning academic literature devoted to this topic, with a vast number of interesting studies that address various aspects of this group of investment funds considered from various perspectives. Most previous studies focused on the key attributes of ETFs as tools for passive investing (e.g., their performance as funds tracking certain indexes) or the ways particular funds affect the related assets. There are obviously also many nonacademic publications that show various dimensions of ETFs, in many cases aimed at educating investors interested in this rather new part of the financial sector. Nevertheless, publications that cover the entire ETFs markets (in certain regions or countries) and the position of ETFs in the financial and economic system (including interdependencies between ETFs and capital markets) are rather rare. Moreover, the issue of the determinants of the development of ETFs markets (e.g., role of new technologies) remains, to large extent, unexplored. We attempt to fill these gaps, following, among others, the earlier stream of research that examined the factors behind the development of the mutual funds industry, with the seminal works of, for example, Klapper, Sulla, and Vittas (2004) or Khorana, Servaes, and Tufano (2005). Our discussion covering the main features of ETFs, their position in the investment industry, and the environment of ETFs markets draws heavily from the excellent books (the list is by no means exhaustive) by Ferri (2009), Gastineau (2010), Hill, Nadig, and Hougan (2015), Abner (2016), and Madhavan (2016).

It must be underlined that in our book we adopt a somewhat different focus and we do not present in detail the general issues that constitute a crucial part of the discussion concerning ETFs such as the advantages and disadvantages of passive investing or indexing (for more details see, for instance, Sharpe, 1991, 2013; Ferri, 2011; Ellis, 2015; Bogle, 2016; Malkiel, 2016; Schneider, 2017; Sialm & Sosner, 2018; for an excellent review of the current state of research on mutual funds see Diltz & Rakowski, 2018). However, we briefly discuss them within the outline of the main features of ETFs and the relationship of these investment funds with the other parts of the economic and financial system.

## 1.2  AIMS AND SCOPES

Our book covers ETFs in European countries. We include in our analysis almost the entire group of these investment funds on the European exchanges (according to the criterion of primary listing; some yet rather insignificant exclusions stem from problematic issues from a methodological perspective). Despite the position of Europe as the world's second-largest ETFs market (in terms of the aggregate assets in the region), most previous academic and nonacademic publications were highly US-centric—this should not be perceived as surprising due the longest history and largest size (in most possible dimensions) of the US ETFs market (the notable exceptions are, e.g., the papers published by the EDHEC-Risk Institute). However, we believe that for many reasons the European region is particularly interesting with regard to this part of the investment funds market and requires a separate and detailed presentation that accounts for some of its distinctive features, including the high heterogeneity of the European ETFs markets, the complicated legal and regulatory environment that experiences dynamic changes—with the crucial role of the law enacted within the European Union (EU)—and the high level of interconnectedness of the European financial systems (again, related to the cooperation within the EU). Another reason that to some extent distinguishes European ETFs markets (yet not all of them) from their counterparts in the other regions is the popularity of certain categories of funds that are absent or rarely available in the United States or Asia-Pacific region, the most notable example probably being derivatives-based ("synthetic") funds.

The key aim of this book is to explore the issues associated with the development of the ETFs markets in Europe between 2004 and 2017. We discuss both theoretical and empirical aspects of these innovative funds, yet, to significantly contribute to the present state of knowledge, more attention is devoted to the presentation of empirical results with this respect. In other words, in what follows, we present an exhaustive empirical study regarding the issues that were almost untouched in previous publications in the field of ETFs.

In the flow of this research, we distinguish three major goals:

- Explaining development patterns of the European ETFs markets (i.e., diffusion of ETFs) and providing predictions for their possible changes in the future.
- Identifying seminal factors that influence the spread of this category of investment funds on regional and country level.
- Examining potential consequences of the diffusion of these financial products for the European financial systems by focusing on the impact on the capital markets and financial stability.

In the empirical part of our analysis we study the development of the European ETFs markets in 12 countries by using data on their assets that were aggregated from the fund-level information. Our study covers France, Germany, Greece, Hungary, Italy, Norway, Poland, Spain, Sweden, Switzerland, Turkey, and the United Kingdom. This approach facilitates the detailed examination of a particular country's achievements in terms of this category of investment funds; assets indicators are broadly used for various types of studies on the investment funds, including the most recent, innovative type of such financial institutions (conducted for both academic and nonacademic purposes). Still, it must be underlined that assets indicators are not the only possible approach; the alternative would be to account for the fundamental attribute of ETFs as funds with shares listed and traded through stock exchanges (and other trading venues) and, consequently, to apply the turnover indicators that more accurately show aspects of the development of the ETFs markets such as their liquidity. However, in the context of our analysis such an approach is hindered by substantial problems with data availability, inconsistencies of the between-country data, and other issues discussed throughout the book.

In our study we consider evidence both in the regional and country-wise perspectives. Nevertheless, we concentrate on the results obtained for the particular countries as using regional-level evidence could lead to misleading conclusions. We consider ETFs to be an example of financial innovations.

## 1.3 STRUCTURE AND CONTENTS

The book comprises six main logically structured parts. This chapter is the introduction. Chapter 2, Exchange-Traded Funds: Concepts and Contexts, presents the theoretical background for the empirical analysis. Chapters 3–5 are empirical and address the empirical aims of the book with the presentation of the results of our analysis; each chapter is supplemented by a case study. Chapter 6, Conclusions and Recommendations, covers the conclusions and recommendations. The final chapter is followed by the Methodological Annex.

The contents and key issues addressed in the consecutive chapters are:

This chapter introduces the context and background of this study and briefly outlines contents of the following chapters.

Chapter 2, Exchange-Traded Funds: Concepts and Contexts, presents the main theoretical issues related to ETFs. It illustrates the nature of this category of investment funds and discusses them in a broader perspective—on the level of ETFs markets rather than single funds. It begins with the discussion of the history and key attributes of ETFs. Various definitions of ETFs are also compared with the aim to identify their key common elements in order to provide the reader with a clear explanation of the book's main subject. Moreover, it explains the mechanisms of the investment funds, focusing on the primary and secondary ETFs markets. Where possible, we avoid detailed discussion of the technical details, for example, transactions in the shares of ETFs as these are covered in a number of previous publications. The chapter also addresses the issue of ETFs as financial innovations, providing justification for such designation, shows the key categories of ETFs, and compares them to, inter alia, mutual funds. Based on the extensive review of both theoretical and empirical literature, it presents a comprehensive overview of the most important determinants that affect the development of ETFs markets considered from various perspectives (e.g., demand and supply side of the ETFs market or, more generally, factors influencing the overall investment funds market); due to their likely substantial role, the discussion puts special emphasis on the new technologies. Finally, it discusses the potential channels through which ETFs may both positively and negatively impact the financial system, in particular its development and stability.

Chapter 3, Exchange-Traded Funds Markets in Europe—Development Patterns, portrays the development of the European ETFs markets with a focus on the past and predicted diffusion of ETFs that is assessed within the innovation diffusion framework by using the logistic growth model. First, the chapter describes the foundations of the adopted approach to the analysis of the ETFs markets, a general overview of ETFs in the European region, as well as some issues that may be considered to be common for most analyzed countries, such as the regulatory environment of ETFs. The second and third parts of the chapter are purely empirical and are devoted to the country-specific analysis of the past and projected diffusion of ETFs. We use the data on the total net assets of ETFs in a particular country extracted from the Lipper's database and some supplementary sources of data. The time period of the analysis is January 2004–August 2017 (subject to data availability and length of the history of European ETFs markets) and it covers 12 European countries, that is, most of the European economies with ETFs listed on the local stock exchanges (country-level data were aggregated from information on a few thousand individual funds); some countries had to be excluded for certain reasons such as problems with the exact country-level classification of the funds.

Chapter 4, Determinants of the European Exchange-Traded Funds Markets Development, sheds light on the determinants of the development of the European ETFs markets. The baseline time period of the analysis is 2004–16 and annual data are used, extracted, above all, from the Lipper's database and the most recent editions of the World Development Indicators, World Federation of Exchanges, Total Economy Database, Global Financial Development Database, IMF Financial Development Index Database, and World Telecommunication/ICT Indicators. The analysis begins with the presentation of the selected indicators that are broadly divided into financial and nonfinancial variables as well as their sources and additional information necessary for a full understanding of the subsequent analysis. In the first part of the chapter, estimated panel models are interpreted in order to investigate the potential determinants of the diffusion of ETFs, starting with the models with a single explanatory variable followed by the models with multiple independent variables (both static and dynamic models are used). In the second part of the chapter, evidence on the country level is provided, that is, based on the country-specific data for the considered European economies. We evaluate exclusively the variables that were recognized (based on the theoretical overview) as potentially influencing the diffusion of ETFs and research methods include country-level correlations and nonparametric techniques. Finally, this chapter presents and compares the results, focusing on the identification of the most important factors that influence the diffusion of ETFs. We also discuss briefly the identified differences between the examined countries, attempting to explain them by referring to the country-specific factors. Additional issues that are covered in the chapter are the empirical role of ICT for the diffusion of ETFs and region-broad decomposition of the changes in the assets of ETFs.

The targets of the final empirical part of the book, Chapter 5, Exchange-Traded Funds and Financial Systems of European Countries: Growth Factor or Threat to Stability?, are twofold. First, it provides insight into the possible influence of ETFs on the various aspects of the financial system's development. Analysis starts with the most general examination of the role played by ETFs as the factor that potentially accelerates or hinders the development of the overall financial systems in Europe; the study is conducted with the use of the financial development indicators published in the IMF Financial Development Index Database. Moreover, we examine the mutual relationships between ETFs markets and the parts of the financial system that (based on the literature review and preceding analysis of the determinants of the diffusion of ETFs) are hypothesized to be most strongly linked: markets for investment funds other than ETFs (exclusively the ones listed on the stock exchanges), stock markets, and bond markets. To this end, data and research methods similar to the ones used in Chapter 4, Determinants of the European Exchange-Traded Funds Markets Development, are used. As for the second aim, mostly with regard to the countries with the most developed ETFs markets, we evaluate the possible impact of ETFs on the stability of the European financial systems by using the Country-Level Index of Financial Stress provided by the European Central Bank and supplementary datasets. Additionally, the chapter briefly portrays one of the potential sources of instability triggered by the diffusion of ETFs: synthetic ETFs.

Chapter 6, Conclusions and Recommendations, briefly summarizes the main empirical findings of our study that are presented in detail in the preceding chapters. It discusses the key trends in the development of the European ETFs markets and provides insight into the factors that affect these processes, either positively or negatively. Moreover, it sheds light on the impact of ETFs on European financial systems. Finally, it discusses the implications of the study for some of the groups that can be influenced by the development of ETFs in Europe, that is, investors, financial companies, and policy makers. The chapter also provides some possible directions for future research.

In the Methodological Annex we present the research methods that were applied in our analysis, with a special focus on the diffusion models that were used to examine the development of the ETFs markets in Europe. Models used to analyze the relationships between ETFs and other parts of the financial systems and economy are also briefly described.

Additionally, in the final sections of Chapters 3–5 we present case studies of the ETFs markets in three European countries (listed in the order they appear in the book): Poland, Italy, and Germany. The choice of these countries for the detailed analysis of the local markets for the innovative funds is not random and has substantial basis. First, we discuss an example of an underdeveloped ETFs market—Poland. Second, we show the market for which clear-cut evaluation is impossible—Italy. Finally, as the third case study, we examine one of the European countries with the most developed ETFs market—Germany. In each case our analysis is aimed at explaining the reasons for the particular market's designation (as "failure," "mixed," or "success" respectively) and provide the reader with a detailed overview.

We are aware of the fact that some readers may find the content of our book surprising. In contrast with previous publications, we focus on some aspects of the ETFs markets that are rarely addressed in strictly financial publications such as the factors that affect the spread of financial innovations or linkages between this category of investment funds and a particular country's financial system. As already mentioned, most publications on ETFs are devoted to their applications and their attributes from the perspective of their user. It does not mean, though, that our book is not addressed to the practitioners and professionals in the financial industry. On the contrary, we believe that the financial audience may be interested in our discussion of, inter alia, the prospected paths of the future development of ETFs, determinants of their diffusion, as well as the influence of ETFs on the global financial system and its segments. All these issues are of utmost significance for the participants of the ETFs markets and other related entities.

## References

Abner, D. (2016). *The ETF handbook. How to value and trade exchange-traded funds* (2nd ed.). John Wiley & Sons.

Bogle, J. C. (2016). The index mutual fund: 40 years of growth, change, and challenge. *Financial Analysts Journal, 72*(1), 9–13.

Diltz, J. F., & Rakowski, D. (2018). Mutual fund research: A perspective on how we have arrived at the current state of academic research on mutual funds. *Managerial Finance, 44*(3), 294–302.

Ellis, C. D. (2015). In defense of active investing. *Financial Analysts Journal, 71*(4), 4–7.

ETFGI. (2018). *ETFGI global ETF and ETP industry highlights – December 2017.*

Ferri, R. A. (2009). *The ETF book: All you need to know about exchange-traded funds* (Updated ed.). John Wiley & Sons.

Ferri, R. A. (2011). *The power of passive investing: More wealth with less work.* John Wiley & Sons.

Gastineau, G. L. (2010). *The exchange-traded funds manual.* John Wiley & Sons.

Hill, J. M., Nadig, D., & Hougan, M. (2015). *A comprehensive guide to exchange-traded funds (ETFs).* CFA Institute Research Foundation.

Investment Company Institute. (2017). *Investment Company Fact Book 2017.*

Investment Company Institute. (2018). *Investment Company Fact Book 2018.*

Khorana, A., Servaes, H., & Tufano, P. (2005). Explaining the size of the mutual fund industry around the world. *Journal of Financial Economics, 78*(1), 145–185.

Klapper, L., Sulla, V., & Vittas, D. (2004). The development of mutual funds around the world. *Emerging Markets Review, 5*(1), 1–38.

Lechman, E. (2015). *ICT diffusion in developing countries: Towards a new concept of technological takeoff.* Springer.

Madhavan, A. N. (2016). *Exchange-traded funds and the new dynamics of investing.* Oxford University Press.

Malkiel, B. G. (2016). *A random walk down wall street: The time-tested strategy for successful investing.* W.W. Norton & Company.

Schneider, D. (2017). *Index funds & ETFs. What they are and how to make them work for you.* The Writingale Publishing.

Sharpe, W. (1991). The arithmetic of active management. *Financial Analysts Journal, 47*(1), 7–9.

Sharpe, W. (2013). The arithmetic of investment expenses. *Financial Analysts Journal, 69*(2), 34–41.

Sialm, C., & Sosner, N. (2018). Taxes, shorting, and active management. *Financial Analysts Journal, 74*(1), 88–107.

# 2

# Exchange-Traded Funds: Concepts and Contexts

## 2.1 EXCHANGE-TRADED FUNDS: EVOLUTION, FEATURES, AND CATEGORIES

Due to their multiple and, to large extent, innovative features, formulating a comprehensive definition of exchange-traded funds (ETFs) is not an easy task. Therefore, we begin this chapter by presenting the most popular definitions of ETFs used by various authors and organizations in order to help the reader understand their most basic distinctive properties. Next, we present the history of ETFs within the context of the leading alternative investment products, that is, mutual funds. Subsequently, we discuss the key features of ETFs, including their mechanisms (rather generally, without technical details, which are relevant mostly for institutions engaged in their creation and distribution). Finally, we look at the increasingly complicated structure of the ETFs markets and we briefly discuss their main categories.

## 2.1.1 Defining Exchange-Traded Funds

Due to their rapid growth, ETFs have become one of the issues studied by international and national financial organizations. Consequently, definitions of ETFs were presented in a significant number of reports and other documents published by these entities; we will refer to some of the most prominent literature. The association of the United States investment companies, the Investment Company Institute (ICI), adopted the following definition of ETFs: "investment companies...whose shares are traded intraday on stock exchanges at market-determined prices" [see, for instance, the "Research Perspective" series published by the ICI (Antoniewicz & Heinrichs, 2014, p. 36)]. A similar explanation was used by the International Monetary Fund (IMF) in its Global Financial Stability Reports in which ETF is defined as "an investment fund traded on stock exchanges. Many of them track an index, such as the S&P 500" [International Monetary Fund (IMF), 2011, p. 139] or in a more recent report: "[a] type of collective investment vehicle traded on an exchange" (IMF, 2015, p. 162). According to the Financial Stability Board (FSB) ETFs are an "investment vehicle that track an index (e.g., S&P 500), trade continuously on exchanges—in contrast with traditional mutual funds...and are redeemable daily" (Financial Stability Board, 2011, p. 1). It may be noted that the definition by FSB seems outdated as currently ETFs are not limited to the index-tracking products. Finally, in the Bank of Canada's publication, ETF was described as "an investment fund that is traded on a stock exchange" (Foucher & Gray, 2014, p. 37).

Despite the increasing significance of ETFs, from the perspective of both their users and entire financial systems, the amount of research on this topic, published either as books or journal articles, is still notwithstanding. Nonetheless, it seems to be rapidly growing, especially in the past few years. In the next paragraph we cite definitions suggested in some of the most influential articles and books about ETFs which are often referred to by the other authors (the list is by no means exhaustive). We limit the presentation to the texts published since 2008 onwards, that is, in the period when ETFs have been gaining an increasingly stronger position on financial markets, in particular in the United States.[1]

In one of the chronologically first broadly cited books about ETFs from this period, they are defined as "baskets of securities that are traded, like individual stocks, through a brokerage firm on a stock exchange" (Ferri, 2009, p. xvii). One year later, in the second edition of his ground-breaking book, G. Gastineau suggested a similar approach to explain the foundation of ETFs by defining them as products which can be traded "throughout the day at market-determined prices that are close to the intraday value of an underlying portfolio or index" (Gastineau, 2010, p. 2). In the book published by the CFA Institute, ETFs are described in a two-part definition as "hybrid investment products, with many of the investment features of mutual funds married to the trading features of common stocks" (Hill, Nadig, & Hougan, 2015, p. 2). In their analysis of the potential risks of financial innovations, other authors defined ETFs as alternative form of investment which replicate an index basket in order to track market indexes (Diaz-Rainey & Ibikunle, 2012). According to Madhavan (2016, p. 3), ETF is "an investment vehicle that trades intraday and seeks to replicate the performance of a specific index...a vehicle for investors to gain their desired exposures." In the second edition of his *ETF Handbook*, Abner (2016, p. xvii) did not provide one single definition of ETFs, but instead started the Introduction by stating that ETFs are "[I]n the same way that Lego building blocks are used by both children and adults to make creations of all sizes, ETFs are the portfolio building blocks of the modern age, usable by investors of all sizes and for a variety of portfolio demands."

Finally, we look briefly at definitions formulated by some of the entities which are probably most interested in the correct evaluation of the ETFs market, that is, multinational financial companies that manage such funds. The largest provider of ETFs in Europe in terms of the managed assets (Deutsche Bank, 2017b), BlackRock, stated that ETFs are "open-end index funds that provide daily portfolio transparency, are listed and traded on exchanges like stocks" (BlackRock, 2011, p. 4). In the research paper supported by the second-largest provider, Lyxor, ETF is defined as "a 'basket' of securities—each ETF share represents a series of ownership stakes in the underlying basket of stocks or bonds held by the ETF" (Hanouna, Moussawi, & Agarwal, 2017, p. 4). Finally, the third-biggest provider, Deutsche Bank (2017b, p. 64), distinguished between the definition of the United States and European ETFs by stating that they are "fund structures that issue shares that are traded on an exchange much the same way as equities."

The variety of definitions outlined shows that ETFs are denominated in a number of ways. For simplicity, in this book, we have labeled ETFs predominantly as "financial products" or "investment funds" (particularly when

---

[1]Due to high heterogeneity of the publications about ETFs (especially journal articles), our review of the literature is highly scattered—we discuss the key publications with regard to the specific issues rather than jointly in one separate section.

they are discussed in the context of mutual funds or other similar investment companies) even though they may also be considered to be "investment companies," "securities," "investment vehicles," and many others which clearly shows their complicated nature (for more on this topic, see Section 2.1.3). We decided not to present our definition, which would at best raise doubts as in the case of other explanations (e.g., due to word selection), but rather list their key attributes. This approach can be helpful in evaluating whether the considered financial products are in fact ETFs. Concerning the vast majority of ETFs these common attributes are:

- legal and trading form of equity security
- listing on a stock exchange
- high trading and pricing frequency
- returns linked to some benchmark
- the name of the product includes "ETF"

As for key competing types of investment funds (or investment companies as we use both terms interchangeably) mutual funds and closed-end funds, we adopt the terminological approach (including definitions) of the ICI [Investment Company Institute (ICI), 2017]. Consequently, we use the term "mutual fund" as a synonym for "open-end fund." Mutual fund is defined as "an investment vehicle that offers investors professional money management and diversified investment opportunities" (ICI, 2017, p. 275); its key feature is the readiness to buy back its shares or create them (i.e., "open-end" structure). There are two differences between open- and closed-end funds:

1. Closed-end funds have a fixed number of shares.
2. Their shares are traded on stock exchanges (analogically to shares of listed companies or ETFs).

Other financial terms used in this chapter are explained as they appear.

## 2.1.2 History of Exchange-Traded Funds

ETFs are one of the most recently launched types of financial products, especially in the category of investment funds. The history of ETFs is incomparably shorter than open-end (mutual) or closed-end funds. Interestingly (when we look at the current structure of the global investment industry), both appeared first in Europe rather than in the United States. We present, first, a brief overview of the history of investment funds, second, the background of the launch of the first ETFs, and, third, the history of ETFs (for a brief summary see Table 2.1).

Historically, the first financial products bearing some similarity to modern mutual funds can be traced back to as far as the second half of the 18th century in the Netherlands when a new type of financial product was created in order to broaden investing possibilities of investors with limited means (Rouwenhorst, 2004). Many other similar investment companies were developed in the 19th century, initially in Europe, but by the end of that century their expansion in the United States began. The history of mutual funds in their modern structure in the United States started in 1924 with the launch of the Massachusetts Investors Trust and another similar fund by State Street later in the same year (Ferri, 2009). It initiated the increasing assets of mutual funds accompanied by their growing diversity (e.g., the first funds investing partially into bonds were launched in 1928); it was, though, interrupted by stock market crashes or economic slowdowns. In the long-term perspective, growth of the market was boosted by the establishment of Securities and Exchange Commission (SEC) in 1934 and two legal acts, the Securities Act of 1933 and the Investment Company Act of 1940 (Ferri, 2009). More than 200 years after their introduction, mutual funds are globally the biggest group of investment companies both in terms of assets and their number, and the US market is much larger than any other in the world (ICI, 2017).

The first closed-end fund in the United States was launched in 1893 (The Boston Personal Property Trust) but in England they had already gained some popularity a few decades earlier (Abner, 2016). Closed-end funds became very popular during the US stock market boom in the 1920s (they highly outnumbered mutual funds) because their shares could be purchased even by investors with small amounts of investable capital. Improper regulation of the US closed-end funds market contributed to some extent to the stock market crash of 1929. After the crash, the reputation of closed-end funds worsened significantly and they lost their market share to mutual funds (Abner, 2016). Since then, closed-end funds remain on the margin of the investment industry. The brief revival of this category (e.g., in the United States) in the 1980s was soon interrupted by the appearance of ETFs.

The prehistory of ETFs begins during the late 1980s after the market crash on October 19, 1987 (labeled Black Monday) when the limitations of the available financial products (e.g., closed-end funds) became apparent to

TABLE 2.1    Milestones in the Global History of Exchange-Traded Funds (ETFs) and Other Investment Companies

| Year | Event |
|------|-------|
| 1774 | First investment trust similar to modern-day mutual funds founded in the Netherlands |
| 1893 | First closed-end funds launched in the United States |
| 1924 | First mutual funds launched in the United States |
| 1929 | Stock market crash |
| 1940 | Investment Company Act—key legislation concerning US investment companies |
| 1987 | Black Monday |
| 1990 | World's first ETF launched in Canada, on the Toronto Stock Exchange |
| 1993 | First ETF in the United States—SPDR S&P 500 Trust |
| 1995 | First ETF outside North America—Nikkei 300 Stock Index Listed Fund in Japan |
| 1999 | First ETF in Europe—iShares SMI ETF (CH) in Switzerland |
| 1999 | First ETF in Asia-Pacific (ex-Japan)—Tracker Fund of Hong Kong ETF in Hong Kong |
| 2000 | First fixed-income ETF—iShares Core Canadian Universe Bond Index ETF Units in Canada |
| 2002 | First ETF in Latin America—iShares NAFTRAC in Mexico |
| 2003 | World's first ETCs |
| 2005 | ProShares launches first US inverse and leveraged ETFs |
| 2006 | World's first ETNs |
| 2007 | Actively managed ETF launched in the United States |
| 2008 | Global financial crisis |
| 2016 | Hybrids of mutual fund and ETF, exchange-traded managed funds, launched in the United States |

*ETCs*, Exchange-traded commodities; *ETNs*, exchange-traded notes.

more sophisticated participants of the US financial markets (Ferri, 2009). However, discussions concerning the need for new products that could facilitate tracking the returns of some benchmarks (i.e., passive investing, indexing, or benchmarking) rather than trying to outperform it (i.e., active investing) had already started a few decades earlier. These discussions were a direct result of the intensive debate about the advantages of such a strategy popularized in *A Random Walk Down Wall Street* by Malkiel (2016, first edition in 1973), supported by the arguments of Samuelson (1974) and Ellis (1975). It led to the launch of the first index fund (index funds are a subcategory of mutual funds that aim to track selected indexes) in 1975 by the Vanguard Group (Bogle, 2016). Debate on passive investing continues; further important publications about the benefits of indexing include Fama and French (2010) and Sharpe (1991b, 2013)

The foundation for the discussion was laid by research on the modern portfolio theory. The seminal papers which suggested the framework of portfolio analysis based on returns, variances (standard deviations), and covariances (correlation coefficients) of the considered assets and underlined the importance of diversification were published by Markowitz (1952, 1959). For his input to the theory of economics he was awarded the Nobel Memorial Prize in Economic Sciences in 1990 (Nobel Prize in Economics). The concepts of Markowitz and other pioneers of the portfolio theory were later expanded by other economists who created the foundations of the capital market models such as the single factor model by Sharpe, another winner of the Nobel Prize in Economics (Sharpe, 1961, 1963). An even larger role was played by the probably most recognized capital asset pricing model (CAPM), suggested approximately at the same time by Sharpe (1964), Lintner (1965, 1969), and Mossin (1966); see an overview in the Sharpe's Nobel lecture (Sharpe, 1991a) as well as Treynor who did not publish his papers on this topic in any book or journal and is, therefore, often omitted from this list of pioneers (French, 2003). Many other types of models derived from the baseline CAPM or developed independently were suggested over the next few decades. Among others, these include zero-beta CAPM (Black, 1972), arbitrage pricing theory (Ross, 1976), CAPM with transaction costs (Levy, 1978), or the Fama—French three-factor model (Fama & French, 1993). However, despite the burgeoning theoretical and empirical framework and critical view of CAPM among many academics and practitioners (see up-to-date detailed overview of this discussion in Fernandez, 2017), it remains the foundation of the modern investment analysis due to, for instance, its relative simplicity and common sense assumptions.

It should be added that another, related field of finance which provided further arguments for the idea of indexing was the research on the efficiency of capital markets (see, for instance, the seminal papers by Fama, 1965, 1970). Any evidence for the strong form of the market efficiency may be viewed as a support for the use of index financial products such as basic ETFs (the broad discussion of the efficient market hypotheses, their tests and implications lie outside the scope of this book).

The first financial products that can be regarded as a direct predecessor of ETFs were the shares launched by the American Stock Exchange and the Philadelphia Stock Exchange that offered returns linked to the equity market without the need to purchase individual stocks. The objections of the regulatory authorities precluded, though, listing them on the stock exchange (Foucher & Gray, 2014). The second close ancestor of ETFs was SuperTrust, based on the S&P 500 index and launched in December 1992 (Ferri, 2009). It combined the features of mutual and closed-end funds and had many attributes of ETFs. However, its history ended soon due to the prespecified maturity of 3 years and clearly less advantageous features than offered by the first ETF that was launched soon after (e.g., SuperTrust required a larger minimum investment sum).

On January 22, 1993, State Street Global Advisors launched SPDR S&P 500 Trust on the American Stock Exchange which over the years has become the largest ETF in the world; today, under the name "SPDR S&P 500 Trust" [with the informal name—"spider" (Elton, Gruber, Comer, & Li, 2002)[2]] it is traded on various exchanges (its primary is NYSE Arca; its well-known ticker is "SPY"). However, the US financial institutions may not de facto be called the absolute innovators as the first-ever ETF was launched a few years earlier in Canada in March 1990 and it was admitted to trading on the Toronto Stock Exchange (Foucher & Gray, 2014). The full name of the world's first ETF was "Toronto Stock Exchange Index Participation" (or TIP) and it remained listed in its initial form until 2000 when it was partially liquidated and converted into the shares of the new fund (Gastineau, 2010); after some further evolution, it currently trades as iShares S&P/TSX 60 Index ETF (exchange's ticker "XIU").

Initially, the number of ETFs available worldwide remained very low. After Canada and the United States, Japan was the next country where ETFs were launched (and the first outside North America). Nomura Nikkei 300 Stock Index Listed Fund was launched in April 1995. It tracks the Nikkei 300 index and remains listed and is managed by Nomura Asset Management. For the final years of the 20th century, it was the only investment fund of its kind in Japan.

A more significant evolution of the ETFs market took place in the United States and led to the domination of this country in the global ETFs landscape. In April 1995, the fund currently known as "SPDR S&P MidCap 400 ETF" was launched by State Street Global Advisors and was the second US-listed ETF (Hill et al., 2015). The number of US ETFs started growing when new companies decided to enter the market. In 1996, Morgan Stanley together with Barclays Global Investors introduced 13 World Equity Benchmark Series (WEBS) which tracked international benchmarks, that is, indexes of equity markets in countries outside the United States such as Australia (Gastineau, 2010); WEBS are currently known as iShares and managed by BlackRock. WEBS created the links between the still rather limited industry and the financial markets in various countries.

The ETFs market in the United States continued to expand with the launch of new types of funds, tracking not only broad market or blue-chip indexes (such as Dow Jones Industrial Average) but also industry-sector indexes such as the Select Sector SPDR launched by State Street Global Advisors in 1998 and iShares by Barclays Global Investors in 2000 (Gastineau, 2010; Crigger, 2017). Another important event was the market entry of the next soon-to-become giant of the ETFs industry, Vanguard, with its Vanguard Index Participation Equity Receipts in 2001. In 2002 PowerShares in its debut on the ETFs market offered an innovative solution by introducing funds tracking quant-based indexes in contrast with the previously used indexes of the broadly recognized index providers and were aimed at achieving higher returns (Hill et al., 2015); these funds were the pioneers in what has become labeled "enhanced indexing" ETFs. Their launch may be regarded as the first step toward the current diversity of the ETFs industry with funds offering multiple approaches concerning the rate of return in relation to the benchmark.

---

[2]For consistency and in order to enable the reader finding current data about the presented funds, in the whole book (unless stated otherwise) we use their current names (full or shortened) extracted from the Lipper's database; in some cases they are accompanied by their tickers. In case of delisted funds we use the name from Lipper's, which is usually the final name under which they were traded, or (if the fund is no longer included in the Lipper's database) the name is extracted from other sources.

Despite the apparent development, the ETFs industry in the United States and other countries by the end of the 1990s consisted exclusively of equity ETFs. It changed in 2000 with the inception of the first fixed-income (also called "bond") fund (iShares Core Canadian Universe Bond Index ETF Units), followed in 2001 by the first commodity fund, both launched in Canada (BlackRock, 2011). Canada may, therefore, again be called the key ETF innovator. The growth of the new segment was spurred, though, by the launch of the new types of funds in the United States. The history of the fixed-income segment of the US ETFs market started with the launch of four funds in 2002 and currently managed by BlackRock under the "iShares" label. Over the next few years they have become the second-largest group in terms of assets. The development of the commodity segment started when the first US commodity ETF, SPDR Gold Shares, was launched in November 2004 by State Street Global Advisors (Rompotis, 2016b). SPDR Gold Shares (its ticker is simply "GLD") offers returns based on the prices of gold (held physically by the fund) and its assets have quickly risen; soon it became one of the largest ETFs in the world with approximately $36 billion of assets at the end of September 2017.

With the launch of the first ETFs on various stock exchanges, they have slowly started gaining attention of investors not only in the United States, Canada, and Japan. In the Asia-Pacific region The Stock Exchange of Hong Kong was the first of the major stock exchanges (apart from the Japanese) with ETFs admitted to trading which took place in 1999 with the launch of Tracker Fund of Hong Kong ETF (Hill et al., 2015). It should be added, though, that in 1997 a fund classified currently in the Lipper's database as an ETF was started in New Zealand, but in most publications it is not included in the discussed category with the noteworthy exception of BlackRock (2011) in which it is mentioned as the first global ETF in history (i.e., global in terms of the offered exposure).

Similar confusion can be observed in case of the European market. According to the Lipper's database and the fund's reports, the first ETF in Europe was the fund known now as iShares SMI ETF (CH) launched in October 1999 and listed on the Swiss stock exchange. Nonetheless, other sources indicate that the introduction of ETFs took place in 2000 when the funds under their initial names "iShares DJ STOXX 50" and "iShares DJ Euro STOXX 50" (their current names do not include "DJ") became listed in Germany, followed soon by similar funds in the United Kingdom (Miziołek, 2013; Hill et al., 2015; Abner, 2016).[3] However, this issue seems difficult to clarify due to the lack of detailed data on the European market prior to 2000.

In other regions, the number and assets of ETFs have remained very low (e.g., there are almost no such funds in Africa), with the notable exception of South Africa and some Latin American countries, for example, in Mexico where in 2002 iShares NAFTRAC was launched as the first ETF in Latin America (BlackRock, 2011).

Over the next few years, the category of ETFs began to become more complicated not only in terms of the classes of tracked assets (e.g., currencies or real estate) but also the method of returns calculation and its relation to the benchmark. Among the most important events, the introduction of two categories is particularly worth mentioning: geared (inverse and leveraged) as well as active funds. Once again, the significant development of these groups started when they became available in the United States. ProShares was the first company in the United States to launch inverse and leveraged funds in mid-2006 which quickly became a noticeable segment of the ETFs market (Hill et al., 2015). Even more importantly, the increasing number of funds offered returns which deviated from the benchmarks (i.e., they were no longer passive) to some extent in an attempt to attract clients of similar mutual funds (the trend which was started by the already mentioned funds of PowerShares in 2002). The most fundamental modification was observed with the launch of actively managed ETFs: the first short-lived fund appeared in 2007, but was closed due to the global financial crisis and failure of its provider, Bear Stearns (Ferri, 2009). In early 2016, after long negotiations with SEC, Eaton Vance Management introduced the first exchange-traded managed funds (ETMFs) which combine features of actively managed ETFs and mutual (open-end) funds (Madhavan, 2016). This may be regarded as a symbolic moment in the evolution of ETFs; they were initially funds which started as an alternative to mutual funds and, throughout the years, proponents of ETFs have always stressed their benefits in relation to the traditional funds. Moreover, it can also be perceived as an important moment for the entire investment industry as it proves that the differences between various categories of financial products have become increasingly blurred.

---

[3]Lipper's databases include a few ETFs listed in Europe with earlier inception dates in 2000, listed for example, in the United Kingdom, France, or Sweden, but the inception date of the fund may differ from the date when its trading began. Consequently, in order to avoid focusing on the secondary issues, we may regard both 1999 and 2000 as the initial years of the history of ETFs in Europe, without specifying an exact date.

### 2.1.3 Mechanisms and Structure of Exchange-Traded Funds

In order to understand the mechanisms of ETFs, it is necessary to distinguish between primary and secondary ETFs markets analogically to the markets for the other listed securities such as stocks or bonds (we present the usual architecture, in practice it may differ in some rare cases; for exact descriptions the documents of the fund should be scrutinized). Despite similar labels, the key functions of the primary ETFs market differ significantly from those of the stock or bond market through which funds flow between the security's issuer and its buyers. In case of ETFs, the main activity on the primary market is the creation and redemption of the fund's shares—the distinctive feature that makes them unique in the financial sector and one of the reasons of their accruing success (Charupat & Miu, 2013). The secondary market is accessed by investors who wish to buy or sell shares of ETFs or conduct any related transactions. Next we provide more details on both the mechanisms and structure of usual ETFs.

The decision to create a new ETF is made by the sponsoring company. In many reports the term "fund provider" is used which seems to better capture the role of this entity; due to its direct or indirect responsibilities it may also be called fund manager or fund trustee (Deloitte, 2009). We will use all these terms interchangeably (even though in some specific cases they may be not fully overlapping). It is usually one of the large financial corporations such as BlackRock, State Street Global Advisors, and Vanguard, or their regional and national subsidiaries. The second key participants of the primary market are authorized participants (APs). The third, and less significant, entity is a custodial bank which is responsible for the technical side of the creation and redemption, that is, physically holding the securities and keeping all necessary records of the transactions (Deloitte, 2009; Ferri, 2009; Wiandt & McClatchy, 2002).

Full activity of an ETF begins after the provider obtains all the necessary permissions from the financial regulators and the fund fulfills the exchange's listing requirements. The fund's provider enters agreements with one or more APs[4] which will take part in the creation and redemption of its shares. Initial public offering (IPO) involves issuance of the fund's shares on the primary market. These shares are bought by the APs in order to distribute them on the secondary market (Abner, 2016). This process, in contrast with bonds or equities, is continuous—new shares of ETFs may be created at any time after the full launch of the fund (under the conditions established between the provider and APs). Another difference between the primary equity and ETFs market is the redemption of the fund's shares which, to some degree, are similar to the buy back of a company's shares yet much more frequent and common. APs are not compensated by the fund's provider (in fact they are required to pay the creation/redemption fee to the provider) and they gain their profits from transactions with the other participants of the secondary market (Antoniewicz & Heinrichs, 2014).

Creation and redemption of an ETF's shares due to its uniqueness may seem complicated to less sophisticated investors (or simply investors unfamiliar with these innovative financial products) yet scrupulous analysis proves that they consist of a few rather simple steps (see Fig. 2.1).

The creation of the fund's shares takes place at the beginning of its full operation and numerous times afterwards (especially in the largest and most liquid funds). If APs want to create the fund's shares (which can be later sold to investors on the secondary market), they need to contact the provider. In order to receive the shares, APs are required to deliver certain securities to the provider (an AP can either buy or borrow them on the market and it is not important for the course or outcome of the whole process) in exchange it obtains a specified number of shares (Hill et al., 2015). The list of required securities (called the "creation basket") is specified daily by the fund's provider and is usually close to the list of the underlying (i.e., tracked) assets. The exact expected portfolio also depends on the tracking mechanism used by the provider (for more details see the discussion of replication methods in the further part of this section). The provider of the fund specifies the exact proportions of securities in the creation basket; for instance, in case of a fund's tracking returns of the stock market's index they are usually equal to the weights applied for the calculation of the index. The delivery of securities may be supplemented by cash (again, it depends on the exact rules adopted by the sponsoring company). The creation basket is also used to calculate the net asset value (NAV) of the fund's shares which is computed using the prices of the assets included in the basket with the liabilities

---

[4]A report published by the ICI shows that in the United States the average number of independent entities acting as APs of the ETFs is 34 and larger funds (i.e., with more assets under management) tend to have more such agreements (Antoniewicz & Heinrichs, 2014). Newer funds usually have less APs simply due to lower size in the initial stages of their operation. In most cases, APs are authorized to act on the primary market of all funds offered by a certain provider, unless they face some restrictions on participating in the market for the specific underlying assets.

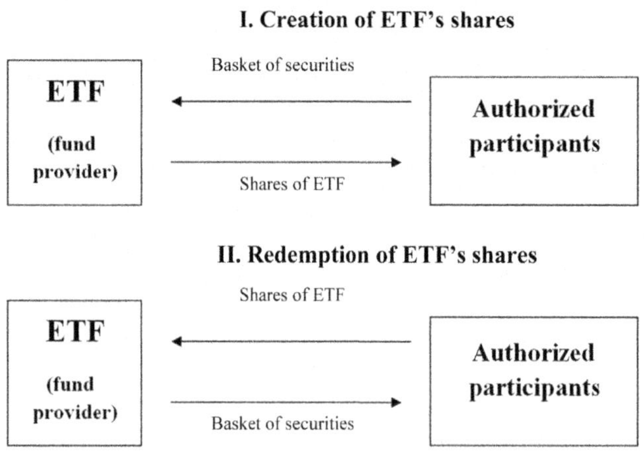

**I. Creation of ETF's shares**

**II. Redemption of ETF's shares**

**FIGURE 2.1**   Primary ETFs market: General design of creation and redemption. *ETFs,* Exchange-traded funds.

subtracted. NAV serves as the reference point in the transactions on both primary and secondary markets. In the case of the former, it determines the value of the assets required to create the shares and in case of the latter it can be used to gauge the deviations of the prices of the fund's shares from their NAV and, even more importantly, from the prices of the tracked assets. To sum up, during the creation process in its most basic form, APs exchange baskets of securities (explicitly specified) for the fund's shares of equal value (total value calculated as the number of shares multiplied by their NAV). Intensity of such transactions depends on the activity on the secondary market which means, above all, the demand and supply of the fund's shares that is closely observed by its APs.

The fund's provider declares its benchmark. In the case of the most basic ETFs it is simply some kind of index (e.g., describing behavior of the stock or bond market) either introduced by a well-known provider or (rarely) proprietary; choice of the index should be identified with the selection of the tracked assets (also called underlying assets). It, however, becomes more complicated in funds that are not passive; see the classification of ETFs presented in Section 2.1.4.

The redemption of the fund's shares is the exact reverse of the creation process. If APs wish to reduce their inventory of the ETF's shares (due to, e.g., decreasing demand on the secondary market), they can notify the fund's provider and exchange the shares for the basket of the securities and, in some infrequent cases, depending on the exact provisions of the fund, cash (Wiandt & McClatchy, 2002; Ferri, 2009; Hill et al., 2015). Value of these securities should be equal to the value of the fund's shares that are to be redeemed (i.e., their NAV). The basket used during the redemption process is called the "redemption basket" and it is usually identical to the creation basket. Some discrepancies are possible depending on the provider's policy—managers of the fund may modify the redemption basket in order to limit or increase its allocation to selected assets.

Creation and redemption, the basic mechanisms on the primary ETFs market, are often labeled as "in-kind" transfer as it involves an exchange of one type of security (fund's shares) for another type of security (e.g., stocks) or, less often, other assets (e.g., commodities). The use of cash is typically limited to rounding off the entire sum or in cases of small holdings (Abner, 2016). In-kind creation and redemption are unique for ETFs and have important consequences for the fund's features (e.g., its performance as a tool for passive investing); they also facilitate avoiding additional costs in some countries (e.g., they allow for favorable taxation of investments in ETFs in the United States). However, in-kind transfers are not present in all types of ETFs with the notable exception being "synthetic" funds with a considerably different internal structure which offers investors similar benefits achieved in other ways. It should also be added that a custodial bank is responsible for the actual transfer of the fund's shares and other assets, based on the agreements between providers and APs (Ferri, 2009).

The exact course of the creation (as well redemption) of shares, especially with regard to the composition of the creation and redemption basket, is influenced by the tracking mechanism used by the fund's provider, that is, whether it employs a full or optimized replication (there is also synthetic replication, which will be discussed separately). Full replication is the most simple and usually the most expensive method. As its name suggests, it involves a purchase of all securities in the proportions equal to the ones used in the tracked index (Ramaswamy, 2011); full replication is applied usually for highly liquid indexes such as S&P 500 (Nikbakht, Pareti, & Spieler,

2016). Optimized replication is used usually in case of indexes for which full replication is either too expensive or simply impossible due to, for example, liquidity limitations (especially on the bond markets). It is achieved by selecting some smaller groups of assets within the index which most closely mimic its rates of return; the downside being potentially larger deviations than in the case of full replication (Hill et al., 2015).

Creating or redeeming only one or a few shares of an ETF in a particular transaction would be too expensive and time-consuming for all entities involved. Therefore, operations between the fund's provider and APs are conducted in much larger amounts, called "creation units," that is, some multiple of the fund's shares required by the provider from the APs (actually it is also the multiple of the creation or redemption baskets, depending on the transaction's type). Creation units consist usually of 50,000 shares (depending on the fund).

It should be added that on some exchanges APs are also market-makers on the market for the fund's shares. This means that they are broker-dealers and provide clients with bid and ask quotations (BlackRock, 2017); their exact role depends, inter alia, on whether the particular market is quote or order driven. However, from the reverse perspective, not all market-makers engage in the activities typical for APs. Finally, we should note that the process of the in-kind creation and redemption of the ETF's shares (in exchange for portfolios of selected assets) resembles in some ways the mechanisms observable in commodity trading, for example, one of the creators of the first US ETF wanted to design them like warehouse receipts (Gastineau, 2010).

One of the significant features taken into account by the investors who decide to use ETFs as tools for passive investing is their tracking error, usually lower than for the comparable alternative investment products—mutual funds, and in particular index funds (we will present a detailed comparison separately). In the ETFs industry tracking error is usually defined as the annualized standard deviation of the daily differences between the performance of the fund and the tracked assets, in other words, its benchmark (Nikbakht et al., 2016). Three other similar measures are (for more details see Charupat & Miu, 2013):

1. The average absolute difference between the rates of return on ETF and rates of return on the tracked assets.
2. The root-mean-square deviation of the rates of return on ETF from the rates of return on the tracked assets.
3. The standard error of the regression of the rates of return on ETF on the rates of return on the tracked assets.

Generally, tracking error shows how well certain fund follows the returns of the tracked assets. For instance, for ETF tracking the returns of the S&P 500 index, tracking error is calculated using the difference between returns on the fund's shares and returns on S&P500. The lower the tracking error, the more positive should be the evaluation of the fund and its managers (at least in terms of their tracking commitment; investors may decide to limit their holdings of a certain fund due to other reasons).

Another analogous concept is tracking difference which is simply the difference between the returns on the fund's shares and returns of the benchmark (Madhavan, 2016). Tracking difference, thus, shows the relative performance of the fund versus its benchmark over a selected time period. As a result, tracking error shows the consistency of the fund with regard to tracking whereas tracking difference focuses exclusively on its performance. Both metrics, therefore, have different applications. Tracking error is valuable for investors using ETFs in hedging strategies, whereas tracking difference is useful for investors who wish to evaluate long-term deviations between the fund's return and its benchmark.

Determinants of the tracking errors of ETFs have, in recent years, been an intensively studied topic. Shin and Soydemir (2010) claimed that changes in the exchange rates are one of the sources of the tracking error. Buetow and Henderson (2012), cited in Yiannaki (2015), showed that tracking errors of ETFs have two main sources: (1) efficiency of the fund's management and (2) fluctuations of prices of the shares in relation to their NAV. Qadan and Yagil (2012) examined the USA's domestic equity ETFs and concluded that tracking error and the daily volatility of the shares of ETF are positively correlated. Charupat and Miu (2013) listed factors that influence the tracking errors of ETFs as management fees (positively related, i.e., higher expense ratios lead, ceteris paribus, to higher tracking errors); transaction costs; dividend yields of the tracked stocks; and cash holdings (also positive association). Other factors are linked to the replication method and modified returns of some funds. According to Chen, Chen, and Frijns (2017), who analyzed New Zealand funds, the tracking errors of ETFs depend on the characteristics of the fund and the composition and volatility of the tracked index.

Arbitrage activity of the APs keeps the tracking error and difference of ETFs low in most cases. One exception is the deviations caused by institutional factors such as differences in the approaches toward the valuation of the assets between the fund's provider and the provider of its benchmark that may lead to some inconsistencies. Arbitrage in this context is based on the relationship between primary and secondary ETFs markets as well as the market for the underlying (tracked) assets. For various reasons the market price of the fund's shares may deviate from its NAV which is based on the prices of the underlying assets; such divergences provide an opportunity for the APs to gain profits from the arbitrage operations (Ben-David, Franzoni, & Moussawi, 2017). If APs notice that the price of the fund's shares on the secondary market is lower than their NAV,[5] they can purchase the shares and exchange them for the assets included in the redemption basket. For the opposite case, that is, when prices of the shares exceed their NAV, APs can use the underlying assets (specified in the creation basket) and exchange them for the fund's shares. As a consequence, APs receive either underpriced assets or the fund's shares which may be sold on the secondary market and generate profit. Market-wide effect is the upward pressure on the prices of the underpriced assets or shares and downward pressure on the overpriced ones which limits the deviations between market prices of the fund's shares and their NAVs.

Despite the importance of the arbitrage activity underlined in many academic or professional publications, it should be emphasized that the possibility to gain arbitrage profits by APs is severely restricted by the market efficiency and applicable costs—trading expenses[6] or fees charged by the managing company (Charupat & Miu, 2013; Gastineau, 2010). If the transaction costs are higher than potential profits, then the arbitrage will not be undertaken and mispricing will persist. Arbitrage opportunities may also be severely limited in the case of funds which track securities listed on foreign markets or the securities that are infrequently traded and, therefore, difficult to value (Lettau & Madhavan, 2018). Various aspects of the arbitrage were verified in the studies of Caginalp, DeSantis, and Sayrak (2014), Charteris, Chau, Gavriilidis, and Kallinterakis (2014), Hilliard (2014), Aditya and Desai (2015), Kalfa Baş and Eren Sarıoğlu (2015), Swathy (2015), Broman (2016), Kreis, Licht, and Useche (2016), Badenhorst (2017), Caginalp and DeSantis (2017), Kreis and Licht (2018), and Piccotti (2018); one of the most in-depth analyses was conducted by Petajisto (2017) who found substantial evidence for the mispricing. We discuss the issue of arbitrage on the ETFs markets in the context of the impact of ETFs on the tracked assets. Finally, it should be added that APs usually generate profits through transactions on the secondary market and most movements on the primary market result from their inventory management activity. Scarce empirical research confirms very limited primary market turnover for most funds. Lettau and Madhavan (2018) cite the ICI statistics (for the US market as of 2014) according to which the primary turnover is approximately 25% of the secondary market trading.

The architecture we have presented here (including the purchase of the tracked assets or at least some optimized basket, supplemented by cash) is applied in most funds and they are labeled as "physical" ETFs. They may be contrasted with synthetic ETFs that have fundamentally different tracking mechanisms. Synthetic funds do not replicate the returns of the tracked assets by holding them in their portfolio—and creating or redeeming shares based on the delivery or request of securities by the APs—but rather through the swap contracts which include an exchange of some agreed-upon cash flows (based on returns of selected assets). Forwards or options are used less often (Kosev & Williams, 2011). As a result, synthetic funds do not apply in-kind creation and redemption, but rather in-cash exchange, that is, transfer of fund's shares in exchange for cash (Ben-David et al., 2017). Some ETFs combine the features of physical and synthetic funds. To complete the comparison of physical and synthetic ETFs, it should be added that regardless of the fund's structure, the dividends received on the stocks held by the fund, directly from the companies or through swap payments may be distributed to the holders of the fund's shares (such funds sometimes add "Dist" to their name) or reinvested (the extension of the fund's name may include "Acc").

The main advantage of synthetic funds (in other words the key motivation of providers to launch such a product) is the ability to decrease the tracking error in relation to the physical ETFs (Kosev & Williams, 2011). Empirical research on this topic, which takes into consideration the costs of each method of replication, is inconclusive (Mateus & Rahmani, 2017; Maurer & Williams, 2015; Meinhardt, Mueller, & Schoene, 2015). However, the undisputable advantage of synthetic ETFs is that they can offer exposure to asset classes which may be difficult or impossible to obtain using physical replication (such as currencies or commodities or even equities and bonds in the case of countries with limited convertibility of the local currency).

Investors considering buying shares of synthetic ETFs should bear in mind their radically different operational model than applied in physical funds. Consequently, synthetic funds expose their users to different types of risks

---

[5]The fund's provider in most cases publishes indicative net asset values or intraday indicative value frequently during trading hours in order to facilitate arbitrage operations (Lettau & Madhavan, 2018). However, due to some technical issues APs often prefer to use their proprietary models and data sources (Madhavan, 2016).

[6]Trading costs and arbitrage mechanisms in single country equity ETFs were examined recently by Zaremba and Andreu (2018) who concluded that trading costs substantially reduce the potential profits in real-life conditions. Other studies on the trading costs of ETFs include Marshall, Nguyen, and Visaltanachoti (2013) and Ivanov (2016).

than physical funds. The type of risk most characteristic for synthetic funds is counterparty risk which has been covered by many theoretical and empirical publications and is one of the most intensively discussed issues concerning synthetic funds (see, e.g., Amenc, Ducoulombier, Goltz, & Tang, 2012; Diaz-Rainey & Ibikunle, 2012; European Fund and Asset Management Association, 2011; Hurlin, Iseli, Perignon, & Yeung, 2014; Kosev & Williams, 2011; Marszk, 2016; Maurer & Williams, 2015). Counterparty is understood in this context as the side of the swap contract other than the fund's provider, while the possible risk is the possibility that it will not fulfill its contractual obligations. However, scarce empirical research on this topic proves that the actual level of this risk is much lower than suggested in the theoretical works, particularly in Europe due to the high degree of collateralization required by the law (for more on this topic see the discussion in Section 2.4). Moreover, it should be remembered that physical funds may also expose investors to counterparty risk if the fund uses security lending, particularly frequent among equity ETFs (Blocher & Whaley, 2016). Another problem with synthetic ETFs is their possible low transparency resulting from the application of derivatives which may hinder proper evaluation of their risks (again, this issue is examined in Section 2.4).

Synthetic ETFs are used mostly in Europe and to some extent in Asia; they are much less common in the United States (BlackRock, 2017) and even in Europe their number has been decreasing over the past few years since the intensive debate about the potential threats of the synthetic funds was initiated in the late 2000s (see Section 5.3.3).

In case of the transactions on the secondary ETFs markets, there are no significant differences between physical and synthetic funds; see Fig. 2.2 for an overview of the basic mechanisms. Investors (both retail and institutional, with the exception of APs who also operate on the primary market) buy or sell the shares of ETFs through their brokerage accounts, paying any necessary commission (Hill et al., 2015). The details of the process depend on the organization of trading on certain exchange or other trading venue; therefore, we will not discuss them in detail but rather merely outline the fundamentals. The other side of the transactions are usually APs (or other entities acting as market-makers) as they have the easiest access to the shares of ETFs and may engage in operations on the primary market when they wish to manage their inventories. Of course, it is also possible that transactions take place between two investors who have opposite views on the preferred position in the fund's shares. Depending on the structure of the local investment industry (often shaped by past events and trends in the financial system) and regulations, shares of the funds are traded above all on the exchanges (sometimes on segments designated particularly for ETFs and similar securities) or on over-the-counter (OTC) trading venues. Technically, in a less abstract perspective, secondary market transactions take place in three key ways: on exchanges on which ETFs are listed (such as NYSE Arca, London Stock Exchange, and Xetra among many others), privately off the publicly available exchanges (i.e., in dark pools), and on other trading platforms (Antoniewicz & Heinrichs, 2014). Secondary market participants may short the shares of ETFs and conduct all other types of transactions allowed by the regulators for the listed securities.

Transactions on the secondary market may, in some part, be arbitrage-motivated in relation to the fund's NAV, which is similar to the ones conducted by APs between primary and secondary markets (Ben-David et al., 2017). Market-makers or traders may attempt to profit from differences between the prices of the fund's shares and underlying assets (or other linked tradable assets) by taking relevant positions and waiting for the disappearance of these deviations. However, the deviations may increase, thus, leading to losses. In contrast with the actions of APs, such operations are not pure arbitrage yet they may have comparable effects on the prices of the affected securities.

Results of the research conducted for the ICI using data on the US ETFs market show that trading on the secondary ETFs market is much more intensive than on the primary market. The exact proportions depend on the type of tracked assets (and their liquidity); for fixed-income ETFs the relative value of creations and redemptions is slightly higher than in the case of, for example, equity ETFs, but still much lower than the value

FIGURE 2.2 Secondary ETFs market: General design. *ETFs*, Exchange-traded funds.

of trades on the secondary market (Antoniewicz & Heinrichs, 2014). Moreover, for most funds transactions on the primary market take place less often than on a daily basis. These outcomes suggest that the role of the primary market in ensuring the liquidity of the fund's share may be overstated due to typically minimal activity of its participants.

Examination of the other empirical research and reports by financial institutions shows that the issue of liquidity of ETFs (to be more precise—the liquidity of the shares of ETFs) is even more complicated. Marshall, Nguyen, and Visaltanachoti (2018) claimed that the measurement of the liquidity of ETFs is a complicated and rarely discussed issue. Liquidity of the ETF's shares and tracked assets are strongly interrelated. Golub et al. (2013) described the three layers of the ETF's liquidity as (1) displayed liquidity (observed within the transactions on the trading venues), (2) reserve liquidity (it is not displayed yet can be supplied by market makers), and (3) primary market liquidity (liquidity of the underlying basket of assets). Higher liquidity of the underlying assets means that arbitrage activity is easier and less expensive; consequently, shares of ETFs also become more liquid (Ben-David et al., 2017). This means that evaluation of the ETFs market's liquidity should focus on the liquidity of the underlying assets rather than the liquidity of the shares of ETFs as the former depends mostly on the actions of APs and similar entities. Moreover, according to Lettau and Madhavan (2018), due to the generally much greater activity on the secondary ETFs markets in relation to the primary ones, liquidity of the shares of ETFs is usually higher than in the case of the underlying assets. The issue of liquidity in the context of linked assets is discussed in more detail in Section 2.4. In order to supplement the presentation of the determinants of the ETF's liquidity factors, it should be added that it is improved by active markets for the derivatives based on ETFs: options and futures (Madhavan, 2016).

### 2.1.4 Approaches to the Classification of Exchange-Traded Funds

The first classification of ETFs which we will discuss is based on the asset classes tracked by the funds. Accordingly, the key categories are

1. Equity ETFs
2. Fixed-income (bond) ETFs
3. Commodity ETFs
4. Mixed-asset ETFs
5. Other and alternative ETFs (currency, real estate, money market, volatility, etc.)

Equity ETFs were the first, and for many years the only, group of ETFs. Despite the introduction of the other categories, they still remain the largest (in all perspectives including assets, turnover, etc.) and in many countries are the only available type of ETFs. The category of equity funds is highly heterogeneous and many subcategories may be distinguished. For example, the following classifications may be used (Cameron, 2015; Deutsche Bank, 2017a):

1. Geographical:
    a. All-world or all-world excluding the United States (or global): funds tracking the major equity markets, both developed and emerging, with the US market included or excluded.
    b. Developed markets: funds tracking one or more equity market/s in the developed countries (e.g., United States or United Kingdom).
    c. Emerging markets: funds tracking one or more equity market/s in emerging economies (e.g., China).
2. By reference to the covered part of the economy:
    a. Broad market: funds tracking entire domestic equity market or its significant part such as the largest listed companies (e.g., S&P 500 in the United States).
    b. Sector: funds tracking selected industries which may be further divided into
        i. consumer discretionary
        ii. consumer staples
        iii. energy
        iv. financials
        v. health care
        vi. industrials
        vii. information technology
        viii. materials

    **ix.** real estate (we discuss them within the "other and alternative ETFs" category)
    **x.** telecommunication services
    **xi.** utilities
    **xii.** other sectors

**3.** By capitalization of the companies whose shares are tracked by the fund, which usually means that such funds track indexes that cover companies of the selected market size (therefore classification of the companies is not performed by the fund; instead it depends on the index provider's evaluation):
    **a.** large cap (italization)
    **b.** mid cap (italization)
    **c.** small cap (italization)

**4.** By the "style" of the tracked index (or selected stocks), that is, the criteria that applies to some specified relation between the attributes of the company's equities and its fundamental features:
    **a.** Dividend: funds tracking stocks that regularly pay dividends and have the highest dividend yields.
    **b.** Value: funds tracking stocks that seem cheap in relation to their fundamentals (which usually means, e.g., low P/BV and P/E ratio).
    **c.** Growth: funds tracking stocks that are predicted to experience the above-average growth of their earnings.
    **d.** Blend: funds tracking some combination of value and growth stocks.

**5.** By the "theme" of the fund which applies to some rather unique groups of equity funds such as:
    **a.** Clean environment: funds tracking stocks of companies that in some way contribute to the environmental protection (e.g., through low carbon dioxide footprint or conservation of water resources).
    **b.** Shariah: funds tracking indexes that include only companies whose operations comply with the shariah principles.

**6.** Other division methods, for example, by the strategy concerning the declared returns or by the modification of the tracked indexes; for more details see the outline of geared and enhanced indexing ETFs discussed next.

It should be emphasized that the subcategories listed are not fully mutually exclusive which means that certain funds may be included in different categories by various data providers; moreover, certain funds may simultaneously be evaluated according to, for example, geographic (and be thus regarded as, e.g., an emerging market ETF) and capitalization criterion (and be labeled also as, e.g., mid cap ETF). In practice, one of the most popular approaches which links two different classification criteria is the "Morningstar style box" whose name stems from the financial company which introduced this approach in 1992 (Morningstar, 2005). It uses a nine-square grid based on three types of style (vale, blend, and growth) and three groups of capitalization (large, mid, and small). As a result, ETFs (or other funds or stocks) can be included in one of the nine subcategories. Yet another complication to this classification method is introduced by the currency-hedged ETFs: funds with exposure to foreign assets that employ derivatives in order to hedge against changes in the exchange rates. These, thus, provide investors with exposure to foreign assets, although with minimized currency risk (Abner, 2016; Shank & Vianna, 2016).

Fixed-income funds are the second-oldest and also the second-largest group of ETFs (yet significantly smaller than the equity subcategory); due to predominance of bonds as tracked assets they are also labeled bond ETFs (we discuss the marginal group of money-market funds separately as an example of alternative ETFs). They offer exposure to various types of fixed-income instruments, above all US treasury notes or bonds and fixed-income securities issued by the financial and nonfinancial corporations. In countries other than the United States (particularly in the less-advanced economies) the size of the fixed-income segment of the ETFs market is severely limited due to the lack of liquid secondary markets for sovereign and corporate fixed-income securities (Fulkerson, Jordan, & Travis, 2017). Here we list the subcategories of fixed-income ETFs which they may be divided into—the list is simplified in relation to much more complicated group of equity ETFs analogically to equity funds; it is based on Cameron (2015) and classification of Deutsche Bank (2017a):

**1.** Corporate bonds: funds tracking selected groups of bonds issued by companies in developed economies; they may be further divided according to, for instance, the maturity or rating of the tracked bonds.

**2.** Sovereign bonds: funds tracking indexes selected groups of bonds issued by governments of developed economies. The two key groups of sovereign bonds ETFs are:
    **a.** Fixed-coupon: funds tracking bonds that have prespecified coupon rates.
    **b.** Inflation-linked (or inflation-protected): funds tracking bonds whose coupon rates are reset at some points in time order to account for the inflation rate.

**3.** Overall: funds tracking both corporate and sovereign bonds issued by developed countries entities.

4. Strategy: for details see the outline of geared ETFs.
5. Emerging markets bonds: funds tracking selected groups of corporate bonds, sovereign bonds (issued by governments) or both, issued by companies or governments of emerging countries—they are regarded as a separate category due to the different attributes of the securities issued in emerging markets (e.g., in most cases their credit rating is lower).
6. Other, rare types such as covered bond ETFs or credit/CDS ETFs.

Companies which launch and manage fixed-income ETFs encounter problems which are absent in the case of equity funds, mostly due to the limited market access in case-fixed of income securities (Murphy, 2017). In contrast with most equities, the majority of bonds are traded off the exchanges (i.e., OTC) whereas shares of fixed-income ETFs are traded mostly on exchanges or similar venues. Moreover, full replication is rarely achievable for funds tracking fixed-income instruments due to the high cost of trading in the illiquid bond markets. Consequently, most funds apply some type of optimized replication approach, that is, they purchase only some representatives of the tracked bond market (Meziani, 2016; Golub, Ferconi, Madhavan, & Ulitsky, 2018). Another problem is linked with the illiquidity of the bond markets which hinders the pricing of bonds and, consequently, calculation of the fund's NAV. Market prices cannot be used for most bonds as they are inaccurate or outdated which means that bond-pricing models are necessary (Hill et al., 2015). However, they are based on a variety of assumptions and can lead to diverse results. In the case of different models or assumptions (or even different data processing methods) applied by the fund's sponsor in comparison to the index provider, the tracking error may arise simply due to technical factors. This issue should be taken into account in the evaluation of the tracking performance of fixed-income ETFs.

Nevertheless, despite the described stipulations, the launch of fixed-income ETFs undeniably gave their users more ways to invest into this class of assets. What is equally or even more important, the distinguishing feature of fixed-income ETFs is their very low cost (among the lowest in the whole ETFs industry). Fixed-income ETFs are also applied for additional reasons; for instance, some institutional investors decided that it may be safer to trade the shares of ETFs instead of bonds after the turmoil on the conventional trading facilities in the aftermath of the Lehman Brother's default (Murphy, 2017). Relative benefits of bond ETFs in comparison to investing in the bond themselves include lower trading costs, higher transparency, and less frequent transactions being required to maintain the desired portfolio's maturity (Lettau & Madhavan, 2018). However, it should not be forgotten that fixed-income ETFs (this applies also to similar mutual funds) may be not be regarded as perfect substitutes of the direct investments into fixed-income securities: fixed-income ETFs do not guarantee principal protection and their results may differ significantly from the returns on single bonds (or similar instruments) due to, for instance, necessary reinvestments (Hill et al., 2015).

Commodity ETFs are the funds that track one or more commodities—such as gold (Wang, Hussain, & Ahmed, 2010)—or, in the case of funds that may also be regarded as a subcategory of equity ETFs, the companies that produce certain commodity (Cameron, 2015; Jensen, Johnson, & Washer, 2018). Due to severe complications and costs linked with the physical holding of the tracked commodities, most commodity ETFs employ the synthetic structure. There are, though, some exceptions (usually in the case of older funds), among them the global leader of this category, SPDR Gold Shares. Commodity ETFs should not be confused with exchange-traded commodities (ETCs) which also track the prices of commodities but have an entirely different structure; above all, ETCs are debt securities, not equities like ETFs (or, more precisely, securities which closely resemble equities).

The final category of the well-established ETFs and, in fact an extension of the three groups discussed, are mixed-assets ETFs. Mixed-asset (or "multi-asset") ETFs are funds simultaneously tracking assets from various classes (e.g., equities, bonds, commodities, or cash); sometimes they also track assets from various countries or regions. They are not one of the major ETF categories in terms of managed assets or turnover, but they are appreciated by some investors who are interested in their built-in diversification.

ETFs markets, especially in the United States, consist of a number of the other categories of ETFs, less popular and often much more complicated than the leading equity, fixed-income or commodity funds; they offer access to niche asset classes. The ETFs landscape undergoes ceaseless transformation and new categories (or new types of funds within certain categories) are introduced almost each year. There are four main categories of these funds, labeled together as "other" or "alternative" (to the more conventional) ETFs: currency, real estate, money-market, and volatility. This list is by no means exhaustive as the geared or nonpassive funds presented next (or other even more recent types of funds) may also be regarded as other or alternative ETFs (some examples of the new alternative funds, not discussed here due to their scarcity, are private equity or hedge funds ETFs).

Currency ETFs aim to track the movements of one or more currencies by employing futures contracts or making foreign cash deposits (Cameron, 2015). Due to many complications encountered in creating and managing such funds, these are very rare and investors who wish to gain currency market exposure more frequently use currency ETCs or exchange-traded notes (ETNs). According to the Deutsche Bank (2017a), there were no currency ETFs domiciled in Europe as of end of 2016; however, a detailed analysis shows that this conclusion may be not fully accurate (see the discussion on the UK ETFs market in Section 3.2).

Money-market ETFs may be considered a subcategory of fixed-income funds or as a separate group (we chose the second approach, following, e.g., Lipper's database, as the fixed-income category is dominated by bond funds). These are funds that manage portfolios composed mostly of short-term cash equivalents (very liquid and with high ratings), including commercial papers, certificates of deposit, or short-term sovereign securities, usually the US treasury bills (Madhavan, 2016). The assets of money-market ETFs are minimal not only in comparison to their mutual funds competitors, but also when compared to the other similar categories of ETFs.

Real-estate ETFs are funds that hold shares of real-estate investment trusts (REITs; a distinctive type of company that generates profits from the commercial real estate (such as hotels or offices as well as apartment buildings or warehouses) and distributes most of the profits among shareholders in the form of dividends). It means that they offer returns based on the income generated from the real-estate market. Most real-estate funds hold shares of several REITs in their portfolios for diversification purposes.

Volatility ETFs are a very narrow group of funds. In fact they can be regarded as a subcategory of equity funds as their returns are strictly related to the attributes of the equity market (Deutsche Bank, 2017a). In the United States volatility ETFs were launched in 2009, a few years after the introduction of volatility futures and option contracts (Bhansali & Harris, 2018). Most volatility ETFs worldwide are linked to VIX, that is, the Chicago Board Options Exchange Volatility Index that measures the expected volatility of the S&P 500 implied by the options contracts on this index (Hill et al., 2015). Futures on VIX are the basis for volatility ETFs and the returns on these funds depend on the changes in the expected volatility of S&P 500 (which influences the prices of VIX futures); additional gain or loss is derived from the rolling (closing and entering new futures contracts) necessary in order to maintain the declared exposure (some funds even include the rolling profits as their aim). However, as explicitly explained by Bessembinder (2018), the concept of the "roll yield" is often misunderstood as it is not linked with any actual cash flows. Deutsche Bank's directory of European-listed ETFs (2017a) includes only one volatility fund.

The second possible classification of ETFs refers to the method of the return's calculation, that is, whether they offer simply the closest-possible replication of the benchmark's return (plain-vanilla funds) or some modification. ETFs with modified returns attracted considerable attention in some countries, for example, South Korea where they contributed substantially to the development of the ETFs market. Funds with modified returns may generally be labeled as "geared" ETFs and, more specifically, we distinguish three groups of geared ETFs:

1. Leveraged ETFs
2. Inverse ETFs
3. Inverse-leveraged ETFs

Next we briefly discuss the main categories of geared ETFs; descriptions are based on an overview presented in Hill et al. (2015). For more detailed discussion, see the book by Charupat and Miu (2016) which is entirely dedicated to this topic.

Leveraged funds aim to provide their users with the positive multiple of the selected benchmark's performance, for example, multiplier of 2 or 3 which means that return on the benchmarks is multiplied by 2 or 3 (Aguilar, Bianco, Milliken, & Spieler, 2016; Leung & Santoli, 2016). Their benchmark may be, for example, stock or bond market index. Inverse funds offer investors the reverse of the benchmark's return (e.g., −2% instead of 2%). They are labeled informally as "bear" funds as their rates of return are positive if the underlying market is in decline (Murphy, 2013). Inverse-leveraged funds (also called leveraged-inverse funds) provide a combination of inverse and leveraged performance, for example, with the multiplier of −2 or −3.

It should be added that distinctions outlined here, by definition, do not apply to funds other than passive as they are based strictly on the benchmark's return. Moreover, the funds whose rates of return are modified in some way declared in advance and advertised by the provider and other interested companies remain a source of controversy. It is caused by misunderstandings among investors who are often attracted by their names, leading to unfulfilled expectations of obtaining magnified or inverse returns on the particular benchmarks. Geared funds offer modification of the return for a single day which over a longer period will lead to deviations from the weekly or monthly return due to compounding of the daily results (Hill et al., 2015; March-Dallas, Daigler,

Mishra, & Prakash, 2018; Tang, Xu, & Yang, 2014; Tsalikis & Papadopoulos, 2018). The exact impact of the compounding effect depends on the trend and volatility of the benchmark's return (number of reversals); the interest paid (Jarrow, 2010) as well as management factors (Shum & Kang, 2013). In the case of downward or upward trends the return on the geared fund will be higher than the sum of the benchmark's performance, thus, generating higher gain or lower loss for the investors with a long position in a certain fund. Frequent reversals of the trend will have opposite effect. Results of empirical research show that geared ETFs tend to be used by the other types of investors than funds without modified returns—one of the key groups of investors of geared ETFs are short-term contrarian speculators (see the analysis of the US market in Jiang & Yan, 2016).

The third way to categorize ETFs is to divide them according to their relation to the benchmark. Generally, three main groups may be distinguished:

1. Passive ETFs
2. Enhanced indexing ETFs
3. Active ETFs

The oldest and the most established group is passive ETFs that most closely follow the initial idea of ETFs as cheap indexing tools. Passive funds are simply constructed as investment solutions that attempt to track the benchmark's performance as closely as possible, that is, minimize the tracking error. Their key features have been presented already.

Enhanced indexing (some other names include "factor," "smart beta," "strategic beta," or "semi-active"; in the past they were also called "quantitative investing") ETFs are the intermediate category between passive and active funds. The first funds of this type were launched in the United States in the early 2000s (Meziani, 2016). The attribute that distinguishes enhanced indexing ETFs from passive funds is the use of modified weighting schemes, for example, factor-based schemes (Nikbakht et al., 2016). In contrast with passive funds which adopt a market-capitalization weighting scheme (as in tracked indexes), enhanced indexing funds attempt to modify the weights of the particular assets held in their portfolios by identifying one or multiple factor/s important for the rates of return (e.g., high growth of dividends, low volatility, or high dividend yields) or some investment theme by, for example, using different definitions of the subsectors (Amenc, Goltz, & Le Sourd, 2017; Hill et al., 2015; Lettau & Madhavan, 2018). In other words, enhanced indexing funds aim to generate returns superior to the benchmark by using a systemic approach for selection and rebalancing of securities. It is important to note that this approach is predefined and declared by the fund's manager which distinguishes them from conventional active investment strategies used by, for instance, active ETFs or mutual funds (Deutsche Bank, 2015). The vast majority of enhanced indexing funds operate in the equity ETFs category and some of the most common approaches include tracking equal-weighted indexes, volatility-weighted indexes, focusing on the stocks with the lowest variance, or with some other attributes; style equity funds (e.g., dividend or value) may also be regarded as the part of this category (Deutsche Bank, 2017b). One of the alternative names of this category, smart beta funds, refers to the mainstream capital market models such as CAPM. Smart beta funds attempt to skillfully select securities with betas different than one (one would mean that their expected returns move one-to-one with the returns expected on the market, i.e., their benchmark) in order to outperform the fully passive approach.

Extending the enhanced indexing approach to asset classes other than equities has proven to be difficult due to limitations of the underlying markets such as their lower efficiency which hinders determining and implementing semi-active strategies (Hill et al., 2015). Regardless of the limitations, some pioneering smart beta bond or commodity ETFs were launched; commodity enhanced indexing ETFs attempt to benefit from modifying the weights or adopting particular strategies regarding the management of futures contracts.

Enhanced indexing ETFs have gained much popularity in recent years and have become one of the fastest growing categories of ETFs as evidenced by their rapidly increasing assets. For example, in Europe they have reached €43 billion by the end of 2016 (Morningstar, 2017).

Active (actively managed) ETFs have radically different aims than the simple and most popular passive ETFs; they do not declare to track the returns of specific assets (follow the benchmark) but rather outperform them. On the downside, it means that they may underperform the benchmark (Nikbakht et al., 2016). In contrast with enhanced indexing funds, the composition of their portfolios does not adhere to some predetermined rules and they are not representatives of some predefined market segment. Moreover, they less often apply diversification rules (Deutsche Bank, 2015). Managers of active funds can at their discretion invest in assets which are not covered by the benchmark within the limits of the fund's policy. Due to the lack of a benchmark there is no arbitrage mechanism for active ETFs. According to Madhavan (2016), active funds based on the equity or bond markets may be divided into three broad groups, according to the applied investment strategy:

1. Fundamental strategies that involve the selection of securities, timing, and similar decisions.
2. Screening of securities which entails deviations from the market-capitalization weighting by including or excluding securities according to predefined criteria (e.g., selecting only shariah-compliant companies).
3. Quantitative strategies (also labeled model-based strategies), for example focusing on certain factors that are assessed as determining the rates of return.

According to Sherrill and Upton (2018), active ETFs and active mutual funds may to some extent be regarded as substitutes and the differences between those two categories of investment funds can be noted mostly with regard to their taxation and liquidity.

The most recent innovation in the ETFs industry is ETMFs (Madhavan, 2016). These are a financial product which should be classified somewhere on the borderline between active ETFs and traditional mutual funds, that is, funds with an open-end structure. In 2014, the key US financial supervision authority—the SEC—allowed creating funds relieved from certain regulations. ETMFs are traded on exchanges similar to typical ETFs, but they are less transparent. It should be noted that they are still very new financial products with minimal assets in comparison to the other investment funds and, therefore, their future development is very difficult to predict. According to the Lipper's database, in September 2017 there were eight such funds in the so far only US market, and their cumulated assets reached only approximately $58 million.

Investors who wish to gain access to the features offered by ETFs may also use derivatives options (both call and put) or futures on ETFs which provide investors with access to even more complicated and diversified investment strategies (Cameron, 2015). The variety of options contracts on ETFs is available, principally for the largest ETFs such as SPY; they combine features of well-recognized index and stock options and include both European and American style as well as cash or physically settled options depending on the ETF (Tirado, 2016). This type of ETF-based derivative has become popular in certain countries; one of the strongest proofs is the size of the turnover of ETF options which in the United States exceeded 122 million contracts in September 2017. In comparison, the turnover of stock index options in the United States was at about 58 million contracts (data derived from the database of the World Federation of Exchanges). Investors may utilize options on ETFs in a number of strategies and tactical approaches (Madhavan, 2016), for instance, in order to achieve asymmetric returns; they may also be used by APs or market-makers (or other providers of ETFs market liquidity) with the aim of hedging or cost reduction. Futures on ETFs are much less popular but are available in some Asian or European countries. For instance, a number of ETF futures were launched on the Eurex Exchange (based on iShares and db-xtrackers ETFs) together with similar options contracts (Eurex, 2016, 2017).

## 2.1.5 Exchange-Traded Funds as Financial Innovations

In the final part of this section we briefly address the complicated issue of ETFs as an example of financial innovations (we often refer to ETFs as "innovative" funds or products throughout the book). Justifying using such a designation is a difficult task due to ambiguity concerning the term "financial innovation" (here used both as a noun, i.e., understood as the result and the innovatory process itself). There are a number of concepts of financial innovation; some of them may seem partially contradictory. For brevity, we present only selected definitions formulated during the past 30 years when the current structure of the financial system was being shaped.

The winner of a Noble prize, Miller for his 1986 seminal paper on financial innovations, listed the major novelties of the time such as Eurobonds, options, financial futures, money-market funds, or home-equity loans (Miller, 1986, p. 459); some of the innovations mentioned by Miller never gained significant popularity, but most became major elements of the modern financial system. Miller did not present a straightforward definition of financial innovations but rather explained them as "unforecastable" improvements, sometimes available for many years until the right environment stimulates their growth. Allen and Gale (1989, p. 229) understand financial innovation as the introduction of new securities with novel features which seems a similar concept to Miller's if we consider the list he presented.

Some of the most popular (i.e., most frequently cited) definitions refer to the concepts introduced by Schumpeter. According to Diaz-Rainey and Ibikunle (2012, p. 55) financial innovation is "the creation and diffusion of new financial instruments, technologies, institutions and markets." Lerner and Tufano (2011, p. 6) formulated a similar definition by viewing financial innovation dynamically as "the act of creating and then popularizing new financial instruments, as well as new financial technologies, institutions and markets"—an identical definition can be found in, for example, Tufano (2003). Gennaioli, Shleifer, and Vishny (2012) regard financial innovations as the result, that is, new securities that offer the cash flows demanded by investors; such cash flows are extracted from existing projects or more risky securities. Frame and White (2012) group financial innovations into (1) new products or services; (2) new production processes; and (3) new organizational forms. They define financial innovations as examples of products and services, etc. that can reduce risks and costs or in other ways better satisfy the demands of the participants of the financial system.

Despite these terminological problems regarding the conceptualization of financial innovations, the designation of ETFs as an example of such products (instruments, companies, etc., depending on the exact concept) is widespread in various types of publications addressed to both professionals and academics. We present a few examples.

In of the first broadly cited publications about ETFs, Deville (2008) stated that ETFs are highly successful financial innovations and compared the growth of their popularity to that of financial futures. Gastineau (2010, pp. 1−2) presented first the motivation for the creation of ETFs in a way similar to other milestones in human history by using the example of fire; then (pp. 17−18) he continued this discussion by referring to the general aspects of financial innovation and assessing the probability of their success as high. Agapova (2011) discussed ETFs in a comparative perspective by contrasting their innovative features with conventional funds. In the report published by the ICI (Antoniewicz & Heinrichs, 2014, p. 2) ETFs are called "one of the most successful financial innovations in recent years." Schoenfeld in the "Foreword" in Hill et al. (2015, p. X) stated that ETFs are innovative financial vehicles and compared their launch (and generally the growth of indexing) to a revolution. Yet another term used to describe ETFs is innovative financial products; treating ETFs as both financial vehicles and products confirms, again, their complicated nature. Madhavan (2016, p. 3) juxtaposed innovative funds with financial innovations popular before the financial crisis and labeled ETFs as a genuine financial innovation, adding that they may have the power to significantly disrupt the asset management industry. A very positive attitude toward ETFs may also be noticed in Amenc et al. (2017, p. 16) where they are called "perhaps one of the greatest financial innovations of recent years."

In other recent publications, ETFs are simply classified as innovations, usually with no further justifications which confirms that such a view has been broadly accepted and causes no notable controversies. Blocher and Whaley (2016) consider ETFs to be an innovation in asset management. Hill (2016) analyzed the evolution of ETFs as a further development in the field of indexing and used the term "product innovation" to define these funds. Jiang and Yan (2016) labeled ETFs as financial innovations but stressed the significant difference between regular (i.e., with nonmodified returns) and geared funds (in their terminology: "levered" ETFs). Dannhauser (2017) used the term "innovation" in the title of a research article concerning the impact of ETFs on the underlying assets (in this case: corporate bonds) and referred to the studies on financial innovations. Ben-David et al. (2017) regard ETFs as financial innovations and mention "innovations within innovations," such as active funds which are a further extension and modification of the initial concept.

## 2.2 EXCHANGE-TRADED FUNDS AND COMPETING INVESTMENT ALTERNATIVES: A COMPARISON

ETFs may be compared to various types of financial products and instruments depending on the adopted perspective to their exact classification within the financial system. We start this section by presenting a detailed comparison of ETFs with mutual funds (i.e., open-end funds), which is the most common approach both in the theoretical and empirical literature. We also identify the key risks of ETFs for their users in this context. In order to broaden the picture and account for various potential applications of ETFs, we present comparisons with other alternative solutions by referring to various key features of ETFs:

- ETFs as funds traded on stock exchanges and other trading venues, that is, ETFs versus closed-end funds.
- ETFs as tools for passive investing, mostly tracking indexes of the stock markets, that is, ETFs versus selected derivatives (certain types of futures contracts); and ETFs considered to be alternative investments, that is, ETFs versus hedge funds.

Finally, we discuss other similar products that belong to the group of exchange-traded products (ETPs): ETNs, ETCs, and others of minimal market significance, typical for certain countries, for example, exchange-traded vehicles (ETVs).

Prior to the detailed discussion, it needs to be stressed that there are some risks of ETFs of investors common for all contexts in the subsequent paragraphs. They include (Hill et al., 2015):

1. Unfamiliarity with these innovative funds, that is, their return and risk profile, basic features and mechanisms, and specific risks posed by more complicated types such as synthetic, foreign equity, or commodity funds. It may also refer to funds with modified returns (e.g., leveraged ETFs) whose name and declared aim may be misleading for less sophisticated investors.
2. Higher than expected costs of investing resulting not from fees paid to the fund's sponsor, but rather to a brokerage company or financial professionals who assist in the investment decisions. These costs may elevate the expe/nses linked with ETFs and should be considered in the comparison between various investment solutions.

## 2.2.1 Exchange-Traded Funds versus Mutual Funds

Since their launch, ETFs are considered to be an alternative to certain types of mutual funds. For many years until recently, any comparison between these innovative and conventional funds focused on showing the differences between ETFs and index funds, that is, mutual funds that aim to track selected indexes, usually of the stock markets (Agapova, 2011). The reason for this choice is simple—equity ETFs that track the key stock market indexes (with the aims similar to index funds) were the first and still are by far the largest group. The development of the new types of innovative funds (e.g., fixed income or commodity) means that any discussion of this kind should be conducted from a broader perspective. In other words, ETFs may now be considered an alternative for almost entire category of mutual funds (exceptions include, e.g., the money-market segment in which the position of ETFs is negligible). Consequently, we concentrate on a comparison between ETFs and index funds, but we extend our outline to ETFs or mutual funds at large.

In spite of a number of differences (for an overview see Table 2.2), it should be remembered that ETFs and mutual funds have a number of shared features that include (Hill et al., 2015):

- They give investors access to ownership of the proportional interest in the pooled assets and can be used in similar investment strategies.
- They are managed by professional investment advisers working for a financial institution.
- Investing into them requires bearing various fees.

Investors who wish to buy or sell shares of ETFs usually conduct such transactions with the intermediation of stock brokers (i.e., through their brokerage accounts) and rarely interact with the fund's provider (this is the responsibility of the APs). In case of mutual funds, the basic mechanism is radically different. Mutual fund's units are not traded on stock exchanges. Even though the units of mutual funds may be sold by financial advisers or wealth management companies (or many other types of entities which are also present on the ETFs market), the transaction takes place in fact between the investor and the fund as cash in exchange for the fund's units. Mutual funds sell its units and stand ready to redeem them at the investor's request. This leads to another difference: managers of mutual funds use the resources gathered from investors to conduct trades on various markets, whereas in case of ETFs it is usually the key and unique responsibility of the APs (the fund's providers announce the composition of the creation or redemption basket). In ETFs, the creation and redemption transactions are conducted between the APs and sponsors whereas in mutual funds they take place directly between each investor and the fund. This difference stems from the dual structure of the ETFs market, with two distinct segments.

The distribution channel of ETFs results in their relative advantage over mutual funds in terms of accessibility—investors can access these innovative funds by purchasing only one share. The variety of ETFs traded on the main exchanges is very high and the product range continues to expand as proven by the large number of available categories, such as commodity funds or funds tracking foreign equity markets or sovereign bonds. It means that even investors with limited means and experience can access a very large number of assets and investing strategies through their brokerage accounts. For instance, without incurring considerable costs they may add exposure to foreign stocks to their portfolio by buying on the local exchange shares of ETF based on the stocks of companies listed in other countries. The costs of comparable mutual funds are usually higher and their accessibility more limited by, for example, high required minimum value of investment (entry barriers). Moreover, brokerage accounts usually give investors the opportunity to purchase shares listed abroad which means that ETFs listed on the foreign exchanges (in other countries) may be accessed without significant barriers (of course, trading costs may be considerably higher); investing in units of mutual funds registered abroad is linked with more serious barriers (Cameron, 2015).

**TABLE 2.2**  Exchange-Traded Funds (ETFs) and Mutual Funds: A Comparison of Key Features

| Feature | ETFs | Mutual Funds |
|---|---|---|
| Distribution | Exchange or similar | Unavailable through stock exchanges; distributed through other channels |
| Structure of the market | Two segments: primary and secondary | Unified—only one segment |
| Pricing of the units | Price on the primary market determined by the fund; price on the secondary market depends on the price on the primary market and interaction of demand and supply | Determined by the fund |
| Portfolio (basket) transparency | Composition usually published daily | Composition usually published monthly or quarterly |
| Total investing costs | Usually lower in than their mutual funds counterparts due to lower management fees | Usually higher than in ETFs |
| Tracking errors and differences | Usually kept lower than in mutual funds due to the arbitrage mechanism | Usually higher than in ETFs |
| Derivatives | Available (options and futures) | Not available |

*Own elaboration based on Wiandt, J., & McClatchy, W. (2002). Exchange traded funds. John Wiley & Sons; Miffre, J. (2007). Country-specific ETFs: An efficient approach to global asset allocation. Journal of Asset Management, 8(2), 112–122 (Miffre, 2007); Ferri, R.A. (2009). The ETF book: All you need to know about exchange-traded funds (Updated edition). John Wiley & Sons; Anderson, S.C., Born, J., & Schnusenberg, O. (2010). Closed-end funds, exchange-traded funds, and hedge funds. Springer (Anderson, Born, & Schnusenberg, 2010); Gastineau, G.L. (2010). The exchange-traded funds manual (2nd ed.). John Wiley & Sons; Agapova, A. (2011). Conventional mutual index funds versus exchange-traded funds. Journal of Financial Markets, 14, 323–343; Charupat, N., & Miu, P. (2013). Recent developments in exchange-traded fund literature: Pricing efficiency, tracking ability, and effects on underlying securities. Managerial Finance, 39(5), 427–443; Murphy, J.J. (2013). Trading with intermarket analysis: A visual approach to beating the financial markets using exchange-traded funds. John Wiley & Sons; Cameron, R. (2015). ETFs exchange traded funds: Everything to know about trading exchanges traded funds. Amazon; Hill, J.M., Nadig, D., & Hougan, M. (2015). A comprehensive guide to exchange-traded funds (ETFs). CFA Institute Research Foundation; Abner, D. (2016). The ETF handbook. How to value and trade exchange-traded funds (2nd ed.). John Wiley & Sons; Madhavan, A.N. (2016). Exchange-traded funds and the new dynamics of investing. Oxford University Press; Nikbakht, F., Pareti, K., & Spieler A.C. (2016). Exchange-traded funds. In H.K. Baker, G. Filbeck, & H. Kiymaz (Eds.), Mutual funds and exchange-traded funds: Building blocks to wealth (pp. 153–168). Oxford University Press; Investment Company Institute (ICI). (2017). Investment company fact book 2017; Chang, C.-L., McAleer, M., & Wang, C.-H. (2018). An econometric analysis of ETF and ETF futures in financial and energy markets using generated regressors. International Journal of Financial Studies, 6(1), 2 (Chang, McAleer, & Wang, 2018); Farinella, J., & Kubicki, R. (2018). The performance of exchange traded funds and mutual funds. Journal of Accounting & Finance, 18(4), 44–55 (Farinella & Kubicki, 2018); Lettau, M., & Madhavan, A. (2018). Exchange-traded funds 101 for economists. Journal of Economic Perspectives, 32(1), 135–154.*

Shares of ETFs may be sold short (i.e., both a long and short position may be taken), lent, bought and sold on the margin, or used in many other investment strategies which are not available in the case of mutual funds (Murphy, 2013; Hill et al., 2015; Lettau & Madhavan, 2018). Furthermore, these transactions may be conducted much more frequently than typical operations involving units of mutual funds, that is, at any moment during the trading hours which further expands the array of strategies available to users of ETFs and facilitates prompter responses to any events on the financial markets or in an entire economy, not limited to the ones related to the domestic markets (through, e.g., withdrawal from the fund or shortening its shares).

Apart from the differences in the distribution mechanisms, ETFs and mutual funds utilize significantly varying pricing procedures (Ferri, 2009; Gastineau, 2010). Shares of ETFs are valued once a day by the managing company (or indicated entity) which calculates their NAV. It is required for the correct functioning of the creation and redemption mechanism as it is the binding price in transactions between the fund's sponsor and APs. However, there is also a second (yet highly related) way the shares of ETFs are valued. Within the course of transactions conducted on the stock exchange or another platform where shares of ETFs are listed and traded; this price depends, thus, on the interaction of the demand for the ETF's shares and their supply and its importance is stressed by the fact that most investors use only the secondary market because the activity on the primary market is limited to the APs. This means that there are, in fact, two prices of the fund's shares: one determined using NAV (used on the primary market) and second resulting from the interaction of demand and supply on the secondary market. The second type of price is determined continuously during trading hours (Hill et al., 2015). Any significant deviations between those two types of prices should be prevented by the arbitrage mechanism. Units of mutual funds are priced by the fund (again, not necessarily directly by the managing company as calculations may be made by some other party and then released by the fund), analogically to the ETFs primary market, and this is the only and binding price for all entities which interact with the fund (i.e., there is no separate primary and secondary market price). In other words, when investors buy or redeem the units of mutual funds, the total value of the transaction between the client and managing company is calculated using the announced NAV.

Tracking error and tracking difference are important indicators that are applied to evaluate the results of ETFs, (see Section 2.1.3) in particular strictly passive funds that are aimed at mirroring the performance of the benchmark. An arbitrage mechanism unique for ETFs leads to lower deviations from their benchmark than in comparable mutual funds which may be perceived as one of the key relative benefits of ETFs. It is possible due to the other comparative advantages of the innovative funds—that is, more frequent valuation and higher transparency of their holdings—which, in turn, are both strongly linked to the basic feature of ETFs as funds with shares listed on stock exchanges. Lack of an arbitrage mechanism in the case of mutual funds tends to make their tracking errors and differences higher. It should be underlined that exact comparisons should be made on a case-by-case basis for ETFs and mutual funds tracking the same indexes as, due to various factors, some ETFs may also experience worse tracking accuracy.

Tracking cost (cost of tracking for the funds which focus on mirroring the performance of their benchmarks, i.e., passive or partially passive, e.g., enhanced indexing funds) or, more generally, the cost of investing in various funds (including active ones) is another indicator which should be taken into account when comparing ETFs and mutual funds. It may be used to compare various investment products, usually in addition to the tracking error or difference when passive funds are considered. A useful indicator which may be employed for such evaluation is total expense ratio or simply expense ratio, provided in most directories and rankings of either ETFs or mutual funds. Expense ratio is the fee charged by the management company to run the fund and is expressed as a percentage of its assets and disclosed by the fund in its reports (Madhavan, 2016; ICI, 2017). According to the ICI report (ICI, 2017) on the US ETFs and mutual funds, the simple average expense ratio of equity mutual funds in 2016 was 1.28% and for bond mutual funds it was 0.94% (for index equity mutual funds it was 0.63%; there is no data for index bond mutual funds). For ETFs it was 0.52% for index equity ETFs and 0.31% for index bond ETFs (for active equity ETFs it was 0.87%; there is no data for the entire equity or bond ETF category).[7] In the case of Europe, in 2016 the weighted average expense ratio of ETFs was 0.31%, including 0.26% for index bond ETFs (MacManus & Lee, 2017).

The presented data on the expense ratios prove that costs of typical ETFs are lower than the costs of mutual funds (Chen, Estes, & Pratt, 2018). The key reason is the passive nature of most ETFs which reduces costs linked with the portfolio adjustment (position management, etc.). However, even when funds with comparable aims are considered in the other categories—that is, active funds are included, ETFs tend to be cheaper because of the lower marketing, distribution, or accounting expenses (Cameron, 2015). As Lettau and Madhavan (2018) explain, the cost advantage of ETFs results from the dual structure of their markets; trading on the secondary market does not necessarily cause transactions on the primary market, thus, limiting the cost that arises in mutual funds in the case of the withdrawal of investors. They also underline that costs of ETFs are typically lower than those of active mutual funds and, yet, higher in relation to the index mutual funds.

We discuss the main costs for the ETF investors next by focusing on the explicit costs; however, the implicit ones such as bid-ask spreads should also be considered (as in all investment decisions). It should be noted, again, that final investment decisions should depend on a case-by-case assessment. Generally, Pace, Hili, and Grima (2016) emphasize the need to focus on the transactions costs (including expense ratios) rather than considering solely rates of return.

The three main elements of the total cost of ETF investments are trading costs, management fees, and taxes (Ferri, 2009); we skip taxes in our discussion due to their highly country-specific nature—for more information on this topic see, for example, Malkiel (2016) or Meziani (2016); the results of empirical research are inconclusive; see, for instance, the seminal paper by Poterba and Shoven (2002). When compared with mutual funds, trading costs are typical exclusively for ETFs due to their distribution method whereas management fees are common for both types of investment funds. Therefore, trading costs increase the relative cost of ETFs, but, at the same time, they may still be more favorable to much lower management fees (and higher tax efficiency). The other reason is the lack of sales load fees paid by investors in mutual funds to financial professionals who are compensated in this way for their services and they can be a significant percentage of the total cost for the investors. According to ICI (2017), the usual solution is front-end sales loads paid at the time of the purchase whose average value in the United States was c. 1% in 2016.

Trading costs are all expenses linked with buying and selling the shares of ETFs through brokerage accounts which should be added to the market price in order to calculate the total cost of the transaction. Their most

---

[7]The results are different for asset-weighted averages as the investors tend to allocate relatively more assets to the least expensive funds. For the exact results see ICI (2017). Interestingly, the asset-weighted average expense ratios for index equity mutual funds are significantly lower than for index equity ETFs (0.09% vs 0.23%).

obvious part are usually brokerage commissions paid per each transaction, but the most important implicit cost, the spread—that is, the difference between the bid (selling) and ask (buying) price—should also be considered. The exact value of trading costs depends on a number of factors such as the frequency of trades and sum of each investment; the flexibility offered by continuous trading of ETFs may in some cases be detrimental to investors who trade too often while the values of their transactions are low (Gavriilidis, Gregoriou, & Kallinterakis, 2017). In such scenarios, relative costs of ETFs tend to be higher than mutual funds. It should be added that investors who buy ETFs with the assistance of financial professionals incur different expenses than trading costs. They usually pay an asset-based fee directly which covers the costs of distribution, accounting, and maintenance services and may be compared to sales load fees in mutual funds (ICI, 2017).

Management fees (indicated by the expense ratios) are charged as a percentage of the managed assets in both ETFs and mutual funds (Abner, 2016); apart from the costs of managing the fund's assets (such as costs of transactions or required legal, accounting or custody services), they consist of marketing expenses (increasing over the recent years due to growing competition) and index licensing costs (fees paid to the publishers of the indexes tracked by ETFs whose names are often used in the names of the funds). For ETFs they are in the vast majority significantly lower than in mutual funds which offer similar exposure due to the fundamental features of the innovative funds. One of the reasons is usually the difference in the treatment of the costs linked with the entry and exit of the investors in the fund; in mutual funds they are paid by all remaining shareholders, but in ETFs they are paid only by the investor because of the in-kind creation and redemption of the shares. These costs may include cash drag and trading costs incurred in particular when these flows are unexpectedly high (Gastineau, 2010; Hill et al., 2015; Madhavan, 2016). Another cause is the lack of distribution and record-keeping costs in ETFs related to the transactions with the fund's shareholders, i.e., ETFs do not interact directly with their individual customers (only with APs or similar entities) and these costs are incurred by the brokerage companies (they influence thus the trading costs).

One of the main benefits of ETFs is their higher transparency as the composition of their portfolios is usually published daily at the beginning of the trading day (Hill et al., 2015) whereas most mutual funds disclose this information only monthly or quarterly. The more frequent publication of the ETF's holdings facilitates a more accurate evaluation of their risk/return profile (e.g., whether the fund's managers have conducted transactions which deviate from the stated targets) as well as conducing arbitrage transactions on both primary and secondary markets which compresses their tracking error in the case of passive funds. Transparency of the fund's portfolio is particularly significant for the more complicated ETFs which use derivatives (synthetic ETFs) or employ active strategies. There are, though, some exceptions from the regularly updated holding data in the ETFs sector. Due to an exemptive relief from the market regulator, one of the largest US providers of ETFs, Vanguard, discloses its portfolios much less often, that is, monthly (Crigger, 2017). This apparent lack of transparency is less important in the case of the most popular, passive ETFs as the composition of the underlying assets can be checked with the index providers or via other sources.

Another relative benefit of ETFs is the availability of derivatives based on the shares of ETFs (analogically to equity or fixed income derivatives). Such products cannot be offered for units of mutual funds due to the different distribution procedures, that is, lack of open trading. Options or, much less common, futures on ETFs provide investors with a broader range of possible investment strategies and give easier access to using leverage (Cameron, 2015).

Passive ETFs resemble most closely index mutual funds, but the much newer category of fully or partially active ETFs should more correctly be compared with the other types of mutual funds. Relative benefits of active ETFs in this context are, however, rather similar to the ones discussed: higher transparency (more frequent publication of the holdings and their NAV), higher liquidity of their shares (in comparison to the units of mutual funds), as well as lower costs and tax savings in some countries, for example, in the United States (Securities and Exchange Commission, 2004; Nikbakht et al., 2016). However, in the perspective of active investing one of the key advantages of typical ETFs, that is, lower tracking error and difference, becomes less important or even insignificant. It should be added that many active mutual funds invest into ETFs for various reasons, for example, tactical purposes (Madhavan, 2016; Sherrill, Shirley, & Stark, 2017). Moreover, the advantages of active ETFs (higher transparency, liquidity, etc.) may be regarded as rather insignificant by some investors who are more interested in obtaining returns higher than the benchmark and adopt a longer holding perspective. This explains, to some extent, the continuing popularity of traditional active funds.

As already noted, despite the significant relative advantages of ETFs (regardless whether passive or active funds are considered), there are still some areas in which mutual funds have a stronger position. It also means

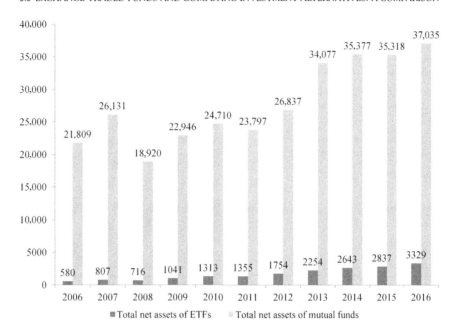

FIGURE 2.3   Total net assets of the world's mutual funds and ETFs. Year-end data for 2006–16 (billion USD). *ETFs*, Exchange-traded funds. *Source: Own elaboration based on Deutsche Bank (2017b).* European monthly ETF market review synthetic equity & index strategy; *ETFGI (2017)*. ETFGI global ETF and ETP industry highlights—December 2016; *Investment Company Institute (ICI). (2017).* Investment company fact book 2017.

that the complete disappearance of mutual funds is highly improbable, even in the countries with most developed ETFs markets. Some of the benefits of mutual funds include (Baker, Filbeck, & Kiymaz, 2016):

- Prohibition to use ETFs in many retirement and pension plans.
- A much broader selection of active mutual funds than similar ETFs, preferred by some investors over the passive investing solutions; active ETFs are still very new products and it is difficult to assess whether they will become part of the mainstream investment industry.
- A much higher recognition of the attributes of mutual funds than ETFs (the return and risk profile), even among some more experienced investors and regulators.

Another relative benefit of mutual funds suggested by Huang and Guedj (2009) is that they provide insurance for more some risk-averse investors who want protection from the liquidity shocks (due to the less frequent trading). It must also be added that differences between ETFs and mutual funds can, in some cases, become blurred, for example, the example of active mutual funds that allocate large share of their portfolio to ETFs (Sherrill et al., 2017).

Based on an extensive literature review, Charupat and Miu (2013) concluded that ETFs are more efficient for a certain groups of investors: long-term and institutional investors subject to lower trading costs, and tax-sensitive investors. Nonetheless, index mutual funds are more advantageous for short-term and retail investors subject to higher trading costs and investors with some specific retirement accounts (specific in terms of taxation, i.e., lowered or deferred).

The exact evaluation of the relative advantages and disadvantages of ETFs and mutual funds depends to a large extent on the country- or region-specific factors and we will discuss some of these issues concerning the European investment funds in Chapter 3, Exchange-Traded Funds Markets in Europe—Development Patterns. However, it may be noted that in all regions mutual funds remain the largest category of investment funds and dominate the investment industry; the role of ETFs has, however, been rapidly increasing over recent years. Fig. 2.3 shows the main trend in the cumulated assets of mutual funds and ETFs listed on all exchanges in the world starting from the mid-2000s when innovative funds began to expand quickly on a global scale. It confirms the rapidly rising assets of ETFs which increased from c. $580 billion in 2006 to more than $3 trillion in 2017 which translates for a growth from c. 2.59% to 8.25% in the total global market for mutual funds and ETFs. Consequently, it means that the assets of innovative funds have grown much more significantly than the assets of the traditional funds. Nevertheless, the assets of mutual funds have also increased, despite significant fluctuations during the turmoil in the global financial system in 2008 and 2011 as the rebound was very quick and substantial.

**TABLE 2.3**  Exchange-Traded Funds (ETFs) and Closed-End Funds: A Comparison

| Feature | ETFs | Closed-End Funds |
|---|---|---|
| Trading venue | Exchange or similar | Exchange or similar |
| Pricing of the units | Price on the primary market determined by the fund; price on the secondary market depends on the price on the primary market and interaction of demand and supply | Similar to ETFs |
| Tracking cost and difference | Usually kept lower than in closed-end funds due to the arbitrage mechanism; shares may trade at a premium or discount | Usually higher than in ETFs; shares usually trade at a discount |
| Portfolio (basket) transparency | Composition usually published daily | Composition usually published monthly or quarterly |
| Number of shares outstanding | Changing (increasing due to creation, decreasing due to redemptions) | Fixed (usually) |
| Product range | Broad and increasing | Limited |
| Investment profile | Mostly passive funds, growing number of enhanced indexing or active funds | Exclusively active funds |

*Based on Value Line. The differences between mutual funds, closed-end funds, and ETFs. (2010). <http://www.valueline.com/Tools/Educational_Articles/Funds/ The_Differences_Between_Mutual_Funds,_Closed-End_Funds,_and_ETFs.aspx> Accessed 10.07.17; Morningstar. Closed-end funds vs. mutual funds and ETFs. (2012). <https://www.fidelity.com/learning-center/investment-products/closed-end-funds/cefs-mutual-funds-etfs> Accessed 10.07.17; Abner, D. (2016). The ETF handbook. How to value and trade exchange-traded funds (2nd ed.). John Wiley & Sons; Baker, H.K., Filbeck, G., & Kiymaz, H. (2016). Mutual funds and related investment vehicles: An overview. In H. K. Baker, G. Filbeck, & H. Kiymaz (Eds.), Mutual funds and exchange-traded funds: Building blocks to wealth (pp. 3—20). Oxford University Press; Wang, J. (2016). Close-end funds. In H.K. Baker, G. Filbeck, & H. Kiymaz (Eds.), Mutual funds and exchange-traded funds: Building blocks to wealth (pp. 119—136). Oxford University Press.*

## 2.2.2 Exchange-Traded Funds Versus Closed-End Funds

From the perspective of their distribution and trading scheme, ETFs resemble another category of investment funds: closed-end funds (see Table 2.3). Even though both have primary and secondary markets, they share more features with regard to the secondary market. On secondary market shares of ETFs and closed-end funds are traded continuously on exchanges or similar venues (including OTC markets) at prices determined by the interaction of demand and supply (Baker et al., 2016; Morningstar, 2012). It means that, from the perspective of an investor, both types of securities are distributed through brokers. Market participants may also conduct various operations typical for stocks, such as shorting the fund's shares.

Apart from apparent similarities, there are a number of significant differences, most of them being the relative advantages of ETFs whose launch and development led to a decreasing role of closed-end funds, for example, in the United States. It should be remembered, however, that in many countries there were no closed-end funds or their position was negligible even before the introduction of ETFs due to various, often country-specific factors.

In contrast with the continuous issuance of ETFs' shares (within the creation and redemption mechanism) the shares of closed-end funds are issued once during the IPO and their number is fixed (Abner, 2016). However, in some cases additional public offerings are possible (Baker et al., 2016). This means that activity on the primary markets is much more limited than on their ETF counterparts. Another effect is no or limited possibility to increase the range of the fund's operation in the case of high interest among potential users. Shares of closed-end funds are not redeemed but they may be withdrawn in the case of the fund's liquidation. Managers of closed-end funds directly invest cash received from their clients (proceeds from the sale of shares during the IPO), but there is no intermediate role for the APs.

From the perspective of the key parameters used to evaluate the fund's usefulness in the investor's portfolio it should be noted that premiums and discounts (positive or negative differences between market price and NAV) of the closed-end funds units and, consequently, their tracking errors and differences are usually larger than in case of ETFs (Morningstar, 2012; Value Line, 2010); shares of closed-end funds usually trade at a discount (Baker et al., 2016).[8] The reason for this is the lack of the arbitrage mechanism typical of the innovative funds that limits significant deviations from NAV. Another important difference and, at the same time, the second key reason for

---

[8]The literature on the possible causes of the closed-end funds' discount is very rich. It has been called "closed-end funds discount puzzles" and attracted considerable attention [for a detailed overview see Wang (2016)]. Two broad frameworks addressing this issue explain the reason of the discount as: (1) irrational behavior of the small investors who are the main group of participants of the closed-end funds market; or (2) trade-off between the contribution of managers and managerial extraction of rents. The discount results from the lack of value of the managerial contribution. Potential sources of such contribution include ability of managers, transformation of liquidity, or use of leverage (Wang, 2016).

the discrepancies between the market price and NAV is the transparency of the holdings in the two categories. The composition of the ETFs' holdings is disclosed daily whereas closed-end funds resemble mutual funds in this aspect and publish the list of the managed assets much less frequently (typically monthly).

Finally, the range of asset classes tracked by ETFs is much larger than in the rather limited category of closed-end funds (Value Line, 2010). Differences are caused by various limitations imposed on the older category which hinder or preclude the establishment of, for instance, commodity funds. Nevertheless, closed-end funds may still invest in less liquid assets than mutual funds which give them a relative advantage over this group (Baker et al., 2016). Some closed-end funds offer leveraged returns, like certain ETFs, yet they are reached in a radically different way by, for example, issuing debt or preferred shares (prohibited in the case of ETFs). The advantage of closed-end funds when compared to ETFs (analogically to mutual funds) is broader access to active funds; in fact closed-end funds should be perceived as active investing solutions (Morningstar, 2012).

The relative advantages of ETFs in comparison to closed-end funds were proven in the study by Harper, Madura, and Schnusenberg (2006). Substitution between ETFs and closed-end funds was verified empirically by Barnhart and Rosenstein (2010) who proved that the launch of ETFs led to an increased discount of the closed-end funds as well as a decline of their turnover, that is, more established products lost their market share to the innovative ones. However, there are also some studies that provide evidence for the relative benefits of the closed-end funds in comparison to ETFs. Chang and Krueger (2012) as well as Chang, Ragan, and Witte (2013) showed that in spite of the substantially lower expenses of ETFs, their performance (after deducting the expenses) is generally worse than in the case of closed-end funds. In a more recent study of fixed income funds, the results of the comparison of ETFs and closed-end funds are mixed (Chang, Krueger, & Witte, 2015).

It should be added that the third important category of investment funds which may also be regarded as a competitor of ETFs are unit investment trusts (UITs). UITs share attributes of both mutual and closed-end funds: they issue shares which may redeemed by investors (like mutual funds) but their number is limited (like closed-end funds); their shares (legally "units") are sometimes traded on secondary markets like either closed-end funds or ETFs (ICI, 2017). The unique feature of most UITs is the lack of an investment manager and the fixed composition of their portfolio (established at their launch). As this structure of the investment company is characteristic exclusively for the Unites States (and even in there its role is minimal and has been decreasing over the past several years), we do not discuss it.

## 2.2.3 Exchange-Traded Funds Versus Other Financial Products

Analysis of the similarities and differences between ETFs and derivatives (here limited to the most popular group, i.e., tracking stock indexes) led to the proposal of one of the most interesting approaches to analyze the role of innovative funds. According to Gastineau (2010), the most useful way to analyze trades on equity and linked derivatives markets is to use the arbitrage complex approach. This consists of (groups of) financial instruments that are based on the common basket of the underlying assets; in the case of ETFs the key arbitrage complex is called the "equity index arbitrage complex" (underlying is a stock market index). This may be divided into three categories: traditional security positions (such as ETFs); symmetric derivatives (such as stock index futures or index swaps); and convex instruments (such as stock index options). They may be considered within one complex as there are some (usually very small) arbitrage profits which may be gained when their price relationships become distorted. However, what is even more important is that the market activity should diminish any significant deviations of their prices from the level suggested by the equilibrium relationship. This means that modern financial markets focus on the arbitrage complexes whose growth is further boosted by an increase in the volume of trading and decreasing costs of trading (an example of a positive feedback loop).

Due to the highest level of their similarity we concentrate our discussion on the comparison of ETFs with stock index futures (it may be extended by accounting for the specific features of stock index options or swaps); by focusing on stock index funds we omit nonpassive and nonequity ETFs albeit that they are the minor part of the total ETFs markets. ETFs and stock index futures have a few common applications. The first and most established is short- or long-term risk management, mostly by large institutional investors (Amenc, Goltz, & Grigoriu, 2010; Gastineau, 2010). The choice between ETFs and futures in this context is based on a cost analysis and selected time perspective. According to Gastineau (2010), futures are more beneficial for short-term applications as using ETFs is linked with relatively higher trading or management fees which are a larger burden in the short-term (see the discussion about the costs of ETFs) whereas ETFs have more advantages in the longer term as they do not require rolling, that is, entering new contracts after the previous ones mature. Other fields in which ETFs and futures may be considered substitutes have developed due to the legal and regulatory changes imposed in the aftermath of the 2008 global financial crisis which increased the costs and constraints linked with the use of derivatives and boosted the comparative benefits of, among others, ETFs (Arnold & Lesné, 2015).

Apart from the similar applications, other common features of ETFs and stock index futures are intraday continuous pricing, high or very high liquidity, large number of market participants, and similar trading venues, exchanges, or competing facilities (Arnold & Lesné, 2015).

There are, however, a number of differences between ETFs and stock index futures (Arnold & Lesné, 2015; BlackRock, 2015; CME Group, 2016; Madhavan, Marchioni, Li, & Du, 2014). The main advantages of futures in comparison to innovative funds can be observed in these features: lower required capital (only a margin needs to be posted to enter a position in futures whereas ETFs require full payment); more possibilities to use leverage (usually very high multiples); or short sales. According to Madhavan et al. (2014), two of the key benefits of ETFs versus stock index futures are their low transaction costs and lack of mispricing which is typical for futures contracts within the timeframe of their rolling moment. Other relative benefits are operational simplicity (e.g., less problematic pricing for investors), a much broader product range (not limited to stock market indexes or similar indexes), minimal position management required prior to exiting, open-ended structure (i.e., no predefined maturity), and easier management of foreign investments (futures require managing the foreign exchange component).

A final comparative analysis of ETFs is possible if we consider them to be a part of the broadly regarded group of alternative investments such as real estate, private equity, hedge funds, and commodities due to the uniqueness of their features in relation to the other investment funds (mutual and closed-end funds) or passive investing tools (index derivatives), and the fact that they offer exposure to some of the other types of alternative assets (e.g., in currency or real-estate ETFs). We, therefore, briefly compare ETFs to their closest counterparts in the landscape of alternative investments, that is, hedge funds, and such a comparison is an extension of the discussion regarding relative advantages when ETFs are contrasted with mutual funds.

The comparison between ETFs and hedge funds should cover only active ETFs due to the active nature of the hedge funds (the basic idea of hedge funds means that there are no passive hedge funds). The key relative benefit of ETFs is their lower cost (hedge funds declare to offer higher returns which should justify larger expenses; results of the very extensive research on this topic is mixed and its discussion is outside the scope of this book). Other advantages of ETFs include higher transparency (it may, however, be a problem in some strategies as the behavior of the fund may be followed by other market participants and in such cases hedge funds will be more beneficial) and lower tax burden (resulting from, e.g., lower turnover). However, in most countries (above all in the United States) hedge funds are subject to less strict regulations regarding their holdings and strategies and they may, thus, offer investors some relative benefits, particularly in the case of funds that provide exposure to alternative assets (including real estate, private equity, or commodities). Hedge funds are able to have highly concentrated portfolios (of course, this can be detrimental for investors seeking diversification, yet it is advantageous in the presented context), use much higher leverage (not the multiples of two or three as in leveraged ETFs, but even several) which may be combined with shorting (again with more opportunities than available for ETFs) and holding highly illiquid assets (particularly the ones which are not publicly traded).

## 2.2.4 Exchange-Traded Products

For the first several years of the ETFs market its structure was rather simple. The vast majority of ETFs were rather simple equity products tracking well-known stock market indexes. It became more complicated when new types of products were launched, beginning with the sector funds. Over the next few years the complexity of the ETFs market, especially in the United States, increased considerably and investors have gained access to funds with exposure to numerous types of assets with returns calculated using various algorithms. However, it is often unnoticed by investors or analysts that the expansion of ETFs led to the emergence of other similar innovative financial products, labeled together with ETFs as ETPs. Even though ETFs remain the largest group of ETPs (in all dimensions: their number, managed assets, and turnover), other products gained limited popularity in some market niches.

Chronologically, the most recent type of ETPs other than ETFs is ETNs which were launched in the United States in 2006 by Barclays Bank (Ferri, 2009). The name of the new products was "iPath ETNs" and their returns were linked mostly to selected indexes of the commodity market. First ETNs are still listed on the NYSE Arca exchange and are among the largest in the world in terms of assets. The selection of the new products' name (very similar to ETFs which were already well-established in the United States) was clearly marketing-backed; it was an attempt to profit from the quickly growing popularity of ETFs.

Despite some similarities between ETFs and ETNs (e.g., similar applications or listing/trading on stock exchanges), a more careful evaluation of ETNs shows significant differences (Ferri, 2009). Many, especially less sophisticated, investors seem, however, not to pay any attention to it and regard them as simply a subcategory of ETFs (a similar problem applies to the other ETPs which are clearly overshadowed by the undeniable domination of ETFs). In contrast with the funds, notes are not equities which offer returns linked to certain benchmarks through holding a specific basket of securities (in physical funds) or entering derivative contracts (in synthetic funds) but they are debt securities, that is, bonds issued by the bank and listed on a stock exchange (Diavatopoulos, Geman, Thukral, & Wright, 2014; Rakowski, Shirley, & Stark, 2017; Wright, Diavatopoulos, & Felton, 2010). An additional yet very minor group of ETNs are ETFs backed by bank loans (Lettau & Madhavan, 2018). ETNs utilize synthetic replication (Deutsche Bank, 2010). As a result, they may expose their users to risks absent in ETFs or caused by different factors; nevertheless, they also offer certain relative advantages. The notes are typically characterized by lower tracking errors and costs when used for, for example, hedging which comes at the expense of potentially dealing with the credit risk of the issuing company (the rare event of its default or credit-downgrade could lead to significant losses) and counterparty risk (also very limited due to, e.g., regulations) (Ferri, 2009; Financial Industry Regulatory Authority, 2012; Hill et al., 2015). As of 2016 year-end, the global assets of ETNs reached approximately $30 billion (Deutsche Bank, 2017a; ETFGI, 2017).

Another parallel group of ETPs are ETCs. The first ETC was introduced in Australia in 2003 by ETFS Metal Securities Australia Ltd. and its current name is slightly misleading, "ETFS Physical Gold." The next year they were launched in Europe: the pioneer was again the subsidiary of ETF Securities with "Gold Bullion Securities ETC" listed in Germany and the United Kingdom. They share most of the features of ETNs and the detailed differences regarding their structure or mechanisms seem irrelevant from the point of view of most investors or the factors of market development as well as systemic impact. The distinction between ETCs and ETNs is even more blurred on certain markets such as one of the world's largest regulated trading platforms for ETNs and ETCs, the German Xetra. According to Xetra's documents, the only difference between those two types of financial products lies in the tracked categories of assets: ETCs track prices of commodities and commodity indexes whereas ETNs follow noncommodity assets or indexes, that is, reflecting changes in currencies, volatility, stock prices (with modifications such as short or leveraged return), or interest rates (Xetra, 2016). The benefits and risks of ETCs are very similar to the ones presented in the preceding paragraphs for ETNs; more information on of their key attributes, that is, pricing efficiency, is provided by Dorfleitner, Gerl, and Gerer (2018). In order to complete the presentation of these products it is necessary to add that there is one group of ETCs that differs substantially from the other and from ETNs, that is, physical ETCs that purchase tracked assets instead of employing derivatives (Deutsche Bank, 2010). The first ETCs, most of which still trade, had such a structure. Total assets of ETCs in 2016 were approximately $27 billion (Deutsche Bank, 2017a; ETFGI, 2017).

The last presented category is ETVs. Even though the cumulated assets of ETVs are much higher than those of ETNs and ETCs—$94 billion in 2016 (Deutsche Bank, 2017a; ETFGI, 2017)—their significance is significantly limited as they are used exclusively in the United States. Due to legal reasons they are structured as grantor trusts and offer exposure to commodities or currencies; the rest of their attributes is similar to the other types of ETPs (Deutsche Bank, 2015). Legally, some of the US funds which are broadly viewed as commodity ETFs are in fact ETVs (e.g., the biggest fund in the United States and in the world is SPDR Gold Shares). Consequently, in order to avoid unnecessary confusion, we henceforth do not use this category.

In some reports other types of ETPs are mentioned, for instance, exchange-traded instruments (BlackRock, 2017), but they are simply the categories of the products presented in this section only labeled differently to account for the attributes of the particular market (e.g., United States). We will, thus, not refer to them in our analysis. In our approach ETPs market consists of three groups: ETFs, ETNs, and ETCs. Bearing in mind the generally common attributes of ETNs and ETCs, the key distinction is between the most popular ETFs and all other categories of ETPs, with negligible significance on a global scale.

## 2.3 FACTORS INFLUENCING THE DEVELOPMENT OF EXCHANGE-TRADED FUNDS MARKETS

This section constitutes the theoretical foundation for the detailed analysis of the factors that influence the development of the European ETFs markets. It should be underlined that the extended evaluation of the factors that impact the emergence and growth of ETFs constitutes a novelty in the literature. Such attempts (either theoretical or empirical) are scarce and fragmented; most research concerning ETFs is limited to the evaluation of particular applications of these funds and assessing whether using them facilitates achieving the assumed goals, or focuses on their impact on the underlying securities. As noted in the final part of this section, such studies concentrate mainly on what may be labeled as "microeconomic" factors. In our research we are interested in the broader context of the ETFs market development.

In order to present a comprehensive overview of the most important determinants of the development of ETFs markets, it is necessary to begin at the micro level and refer once again to their benefits for users, either retail or institutional. This perspective may be labeled as a "demand" approach as it concentrates on the factors that influence the interest of investors in ETFs and purchases of their shares instead of other financial products. Khorana, Servaes, and Tufano (2005) considered as the demand-side factors the attributes of the potential retail investors and the factors that can affect them, including the length of the local market's history, its size, sophistication, wealth and access to information of the customers, as well as pension policy.

After discussing the demand factors we present determinants of the "supply" side of the ETFs market, that is, various processes that lead to the creation of ETFs by their providers and facilitate the distribution of their shares among market participants. In other words, a supply approach focuses on the competitive dynamics of the ETFs markets. According to Khorana et al. (2005), supply-side factors convey attributes of the financial sector that could affect the speed of adoption of the investment funds. In their study devoted to the development of mutual funds they examined these factors (Khorana et al., 2005, p. 148): "bank concentration, restrictions placed on banks to enter the securities business, the number of distribution channels available for funds, the presence of an explicit deposit insurance system for banks, and the time and cost to set up a new fund."

We believe that both the demand and supply sides should be carefully evaluated as even the highest awareness of attributes of innovative funds among financial markets' participants and their willingness to invest in the shares of ETFs may not materialize in the case of substantial barriers hindering the launch of ETFs or making them relatively expensive and, thus, unable to compete with alternative choices such as mutual funds or derivatives.

We discuss three groups of determinants separately from the other demand and supply factors:

1. The development of financial markets and other linked macroeconomic factors (presented prior to the outline of the other factors as the hypothesized significant determinant).
2. New technologies (after the evaluation of the other factors as they influence to some extent all of them and it is necessary to firstly present the relevant context).
3. The impacts of governmental actions which is a rather separate and highly heterogeneous factor observed only in some countries.

In the final part of this section we present a different and broader approach to the examined issues as we discuss the factors that affect the development of the investment funds market to which ETFs belong.

It must be emphasized that regulatory issues are mostly omitted in our discussion due to the substantial differences between various regions and countries. We address them with regard to European ETFs markets in our overview of the legal environment in Section 3.1.


## 2.3.1 Development of Financial Markets and Other Linked Macroeconomic Factors

At the beginning of this chapter we presented the mechanisms and attributes of various categories of ETFs. Even a very basic analysis of the way ETFs are created reveals that they are inextricably connected to the other parts of the financial system, in particular financial markets. What is more, the typical structure of the ETFs market should also be considered; the dominant category of ETFs are funds tracking stock market indexes (followed by the bond funds yet with substantially lower market share) which proves that the most important segments of the financial markets to be considered are stock and bond markets (with emphasis on the former).

We supplement the outline in this Section by presenting the role of related parts of the financial sector and entire economy: banking sector and general economic trends.

The correct course of the ETF's shares creation and redemption process depends on the correctly functioning markets for the underlying assets, usually stocks or bonds; it applies also to other assets held by the funds (not necessarily the tracked assets as it may concern not only physical funds but also synthetic ones which may hold significantly different securities as the collateral in the swap contracts). This means that these markets should be highly liquid and large enough in order to facilitate operations of the entities such as APs or other market participants without significant disruptions of the prices or turnover, particularly in the context of the arbitrage mechanism. Moreover, apart from the impact on the processes linked with the functioning of the innovative funds, the adequate development of the linked financial markets (mostly equity sector) should also be perceived as one of the determinants influencing the relative competitiveness of ETFs in comparison to the alternative financial products: mutual funds, closed-end funds, stock index derivatives, or hedge funds. For instance, taking into account the key competing category, that is, mutual funds, the level of the development of the linked financial markets impacts the cost advantage of ETFs (conducting transactions necessary for proper functioning of the innovative funds at low cost and without significant time delays). In the largest group of ETFs, that is, passive funds, it influences the level of tracking error and tracking difference, in particular the possibility to keep them at low levels. To sum up, a sufficient level of the equity or bond market development may be perceived as necessary for the launch of ETFs by the financial institutions which consider the potential interest in their products resulting from the offered features and their further development due to the demand from the investors seeking the comparative benefits of these funds.

In addition to the factors which influence the rather technical aspects of the individual ETFs and their entire market, the development of the ETFs market (mostly on the demand side) depends on the general trends in the profitability (e.g., returns in the recent periods) and volatility on the equity and bond markets. It should be underlined that the basic concept of ETFs as tracking instruments means that they follow the parallel parameters of the mirrored markets. This means that, for example, unfavorable conditions on the equity market (e.g., depressed returns, increased volatility) and withdrawal of investors will strongly impact the demand for the ETFs with exposure to the equities.

If we focus on the impact of the other macroeconomic trends on ETFs market development, it should not be forgotten that the changes on the equity market are at least to some extent dependent on the overall economic conditions (both domestic and global; one notable example is the rate of economic growth), including changes in the financial system not limited to the financial markets. In most economies, apart from the financial markets (whose role differs substantially between countries), the largest part of the financial system is the banking sector. Banks and other similar financial institutions are a part of the ETF landscape due to their role in providing access to the financial services such as brokerage accounts, which enable the transactions in the shares of ETFs, or asset management services which involve the use of ETFs in the portfolio management. More generally, the higher level of banking sector development in a given country may be associated with more widespread use of financial services which may result in the increase of the financial system's assets and availability of resources that may be invested in the shares of ETFs.

The examination of the potential factors that affect the development of the ETFs markets should not necessarily be limited to the national level. One of the factors that can potentially influence the development and structure of particular ETFs markets is the relative differences in the performance and risk management of funds domiciled in various countries, as concluded by Yiannaki (2015) using the example of ETFs in Luxembourg and Ireland.

## 2.3.2 Demand-Side Factors

We start our discussion concerning demand-side development factors by stressing that the growing demand for ETFs, is linked to the deep change taking place in the investment industry, labeled the "rise of passive investing" (Ben-David et al., 2017). The growing popularity of passive funds started in the 1970s and 1980s with the launch of passive mutual funds (in other words, new indexing tools). The reasons for this trend still remain a topic of intensive discussion—see the in-depth overview in Ben-David et al. (2017). Some explanations presented in the literature include:

- A more common belief among investors about market efficiency which led to preference of cheaper passive funds that offer similar or even superior results to the active funds. At the same time, they may be used to gain inexpensive exposure to the selected common risk factors.
- Disappearance of arbitrage opportunities which are used by managers of active funds in order to generate profits superior to their benchmarks—created, for example, by the actions of retail investors who create noise in prices of securities (Stambaugh, 2014). Again, this explanation is based on the assumed improved market efficiency.
- Possibility to limit the investors' exposure to some economic shocks—such as prices of the stocks of the companies which suffer most significantly due to such events should be relatively lower (Bond & Garcia, 2016).

Tracing the evolution of the groups of investors who entered the ETFs market at various stages of its development (using the most advanced example of the United States) provides some hints for the proper analysis of the changing demand and underlying factors—see the discussion in Hill et al. (2015). In its very early phase, in the early- and mid-1990s, innovative funds were first used by early-adopters, that is, sophisticated investors, mostly financial institutions which focused on ETFs' trading possibilities, including hedge funds (which later, to some extent, became one of the casualties of the quick growth of the new investment funds). These early-adopters selected ETFs over more established instruments such as futures due to their higher liquidity and, more importantly, easier access to international markets through ETFs tracking international indexes. This nascent stage may be compared to the very first years of the mobile phones industry when such phones were bought by rather affluent young people following the technological trends. Over the next few years, starting from the late-1990s and early 2000s ETFs left the market niche and became a mainstream investment product that has been adopted by all the key groups of investors: financial institutions, financial advisers and, indicating the growing awareness of their availability and attributes, by retail investors (directly or through financial professionals). The range of applications of ETFs has become much broader and started to include, for example, both short-term speculation and long-term investing, and shifting exposure to asset classes. It should be added that similar changes could be observed on the providers' side of the ETFs market: first managers of the new funds were mostly representatives of the companies which were already established in the indexing industry (e.g., State Street), but over the next few years ETFs have been launched and managed by increasingly more companies from the mutual funds industry, not only from its indexing subsector but often associated rather with active investment products.

It is noted, then, that the first and main group of users of ETFs are financial institutions rather than other entities; the European ETFs market is not an exception as shown in Chapter 3, Exchange-Traded Funds Markets in Europe: Development Patterns—retail investors owned only about 10%−15% of the total assets as of 2016 (Abner, 2016; Amenc et al., 2017). This means that the demand-side factors of the ETFs market development are strongly linked to the institutional segment of the financial markets and entire financial system. The applications of ETFs by institutional investors have changed since the early years of the innovative funds. In the beginning they were used with a short-term focus (e.g., in managing the portfolio during changes on the managerial positions) but new applications have emerged and have become part of the baseline investment strategy, with increasingly more funds allocated for longer time periods. New sources of the growing demand for ETFs from institutions are pension funds, insurance companies, foundations, or endowments as well as more types of hedge funds. Moreover, ETFs have become popular—this trend can be expected to continue—in the group of market participants who represent the middle-way between the retail and institutional sector, that is, financial advisers who include ETFs in their retirement and wealth management strategies. It should be underlined, however, that we have discussed trends in the demand for ETFs using mainly the example of the US market (Hill et al., 2015) and the investment industry in other regions may have a different structure and experience other tendencies. The US market is the largest in the world and dominates the global ETFs industry and, therefore, most strongly influences its situation. We analyze the European market separately in the empirical Chapters 3 and 4. Finally, it should be added that the rising popularity encompasses various categories of ETFs. For example, in the United States bond ETFs are increasingly more popular among pension funds due to, for example, low cost and transparency, and hedge funds, for example, as a way to invest cash (Lettau & Madhavan, 2018).

The fact that retail investors lag behind institutional investors in the adoption of ETFs has been addressed by some authors. However, before continuing the discussion on this issue, it should be stressed that among the other factors which shape the demand for innovative financial products such as ETFs, some are difficult or even impossible to quantify and the demand from retail investors seems to belong to this category. J.Y. Campbell stated in 2006 (quoted by Gastineau, 2010, p. 17) that adoption of innovation among retail users may be slowed down by lack of advertising and education of households as well as insufficient patent protection in the case of financial products. What seems even more important for the diffusion of innovations, "naïve" households (i.e., unaware of the benefits offered by the new products and services) tend to lag behind with regard to their adoption which leads to benefits for "sophisticated" households, called "cross-subsidy" by Campbell. Profits from the cross-subsidy paradoxically slows down the diffusion of financial innovations as sophisticated households delay the adoption of the most recent solutions due to the potential costs of foregone benefits. According to Gastineau, similar processes may be observed in the investment industry between the users of mutual funds and ETFs.

Despite some barriers to demand from retail investors and their low share in the total assets of ETFs, the use of innovative funds among individuals is expected to grow and to some degree shape the overall development of the ETFs market (Hill et al., 2015). Retail investors are attracted by the increasing diversity of ETFs (for instance, in terms of the offered exposure to asset classes) as well as marketing actions that raise the awareness of individuals regarding possible applications of innovative funds. An additional but increasingly significant reason is the growing availability of digital advisory (e.g., robo-advisers) and similar services (we discuss them separately).

## 2.3.3 Supply-Side Factors

We begin our discussion of the supply-side ETFs market development factors by considering the most practical side of the process that is linked to the motivations of various entities which participate in the key decisions regarding innovative funds. A very important factor that influences the supply side of the market and the potential for its development are issues linked with the distribution of the ETFs' shares and their accounting treatment (Hill et al., 2015). In the United States some barriers to the distribution of shares of ETFs in the past had been caused by regulatory limitations. For example, US insurance companies had been reluctant to invest in innovative funds because bond ETFs could not be treated in their books as bonds which led to necessary capital charges and decreased their usefulness; after legal changes that solved this issue the popularity of bond ETFs among insurance companies has surged. Another reason was the lack of fee payments from the fund's sponsor to financial advisers for using them, typical for mutual funds which meant that advisers had been financially motivated to use mutual funds instead of ETFs. This changed to some extent after the introduction of partially similar compensation agreement in ETFs, that is, distribution fees paid by managers who build portfolios of ETFs for brokers for assets flowing to their portfolios. It should be added this solution is still rather rare. Another important consideration is that the distribution fees in ETFs are externalized (Lettau & Madhavan, 2018) which makes them attractive for financial advisors who are paid directly by the client based on the amount of assets under management (an increasingly common model worldwide) as costs such as distribution or accounting fess of the funds are not included in their expense ratios. The issue of the compensations in the asset management industry remains a source of continuing discussions and controversies. Due to its highly region- or country-specific nature we do not discuss the issues of regulations or compensations in more detail; we address it with regard to European ETFs markets in our overview of the legal environment in Section 3.1.

Within the discussion regarding the supply-side perspective of the ETFs market development we also refer to the supply-side theory of financial innovations by Awrey (2012) who contested the conventional demand-side approach. In Awrey's critique, neglecting the evaluation of factors such as response to the actions undertaken by regulators contributed to the growth of systemic risk which became clearly visible during the global financial crisis of 2008. In the supply-side theory, the key undertaken issue concerns the motivation of financial intermediaries to innovate. These motivations should not be limited to the potential profits as the possible gains are prone to be quickly diminished within the course of the innovation's diffusion due to the actions of imitators. Profits of innovators in the financial system cannot be usually protected by intellectual property rights like in other industries. Awrey suggests two explanations of the financial innovation activity (apart from the demand-driven decisions): mitigation of the regulatory requirements and recreation of monopolistic conditions. The latter strategy may be conducted via two versions. The first involves artificial boosting of the diffusion's rate by capitalizing on the short-term approach of many investors. The second version is based on the increasing complexity of the offered products or services by applying new technologies or advances in the financial theory, making them more opaque and, thus, more difficult to imitate which prevents their commoditization.

To substantiate his approach which is radically different from previous studies, Awrey presents a few case studies, showing the application of the supply-side theory to the analysis of the financial sector, among them synthetic ETFs. According to Awrey, the growth of the popularity of synthetic ETFs observed in some regions particularly up to 2011 had partially been caused by the incentives of the financial institutions acting as counterparties in swap contracts. Such contracts are used to obtain the desired exposure and involve the exchange of some agreed-on returns. They also include, in some cases (known as "unfunded synthetic ETFs") transfer of the collateral from the swap's counterparty to the fund's sponsor. Some swap counterparties took advantage of the synthetic funds and utilized them to remove unwanted assets from their balance sheets by providing them as collateral (in extreme scenarios synthetic ETFs became a "dumping ground"). A further supply-side explanation of the development of synthetic ETFs is linked with their complicated and sometimes opaque structure which makes their launch and management difficult, thus, discouraging competing financial institutions from entering the market and contending with more established providers.

Another, interesting and unique supply-side approach to the development of ETFs markets (limited to conventional passive funds) was suggested by Blocher and Whaley (2016) who refer to the works of, inter alia, Rochet and Tirole (2002, 2006) and Parker and Van Alstyne (2005). They showed that ETFs follow a two-sided market model, with a common platform that is used to match the two sides of the transactions; a well-known example of such a model includes companies in the "share economy," for example, Uber (another cited analogous to ETFs is

Facebook). In the case of the ETFs market, the funds themselves are a common platform that links retail broker-age holdings of securities with the institutional borrowers of securities. Purchase of the fund's shares means that investors have increasingly standardized holdings. Providers of ETFs gather these assets and lend them to insti-tutional borrowers (large financial institutions which otherwise could have problems with assembling such secu-rities) in order to generate profits that may be used to compensate the providers for the decreasing fees paid by the clients; the long-term effect may be the possibility to decrease the management fees to zero or even make them negative and, consequently, increase the relative advantage of ETFs in comparison to, for example, mutual funds. As a result, Blocher and Whaley state that incentives of the funds' providers must be taken into account in the evaluation of the factors influencing the development of ETFs markets it is necessary to take into account the incentive of the funds' providers to keep more assets in the portfolios which can be lend profitably. The results of their empirical research (based on 2009–13 data from the US market) prove that the growth of ETFs' assets is driven by the ratio of lending fees to expense ratios which confirms the two-sided market model. Moreover, they suggested that lending revenues should be disclosed to the clients of ETFs as one of the factors influencing decision-making.

The development of the ETFs markets may also be examined from the perspective of the factors that determine the liquidations of the funds bearing in mind that closure of the particular funds does not necessarily mean that the ETFs market becomes smaller—investors may decide to opt for some other innovative funds (obviously, they may incur some costs linked with taxes or searching for a new substitute fund). According to Sherrill and Stark (2018), the primary determinants of the fund's liquidation are insufficient assets under management and fund inflows as well as factors linked with its inception, that is, the initial size, position of the provider (i.e., competi-tion on the ETFs market), and popularity of the fund's objectives among investors. This means that the decisions to liquidate ETFs depend both on fund-specific and external factors. In a similar manner, Oztekin (2018) exam-ined the factors that affect inflows and outflows of particular ETFs. Competition on the ETFs markets was also studied by Box, Davis, and Fuller (2017) whose findings imply that liquidity and activity on the primary ETFs markets may be negatively affected (with regard to individual funds) by the entry of new funds. Moreover, they claimed that launching new funds did not influence the management fees.

## 2.3.4 New Technologies and Exchange-Traded Funds

Within the broad array of the factors which influence the development of ETFs markets, a special role belongs to the new technologies, particularly information and communication technologies (ICT). This is observed both on the demand and supply side of the market for innovative funds and its significance has been confirmed in previous research; see, for example, Lechman and Marszk (2015).

The role of ICT in the diffusion of financial innovations was underlined even before the widely observed spread of the Internet and other similar services. One notable example from the early-1990s is W. Sharpe's Nobel prize lecture in which he stated that financial innovation has to large extent been facilitated by "the remarkable advances in computation and communication technology" (Sharpe, 1991a, p. 506). Another factor mentioned by Sharpe is growing global competition (i.e., decreasing monopoly power in both the private and public sectors) and new theoretical developments in the financial economics such as CAPM and its extensions. Obviously, state-ments by Sharpe could not be directly referred to as ETFs as this market had de facto not yet appeared in 1991 (the first ETFs had been launched in Canada about 1 year earlier).

The broad adoption of ICT, which can also be labeled as "diffusion"—in a manner similar to other innovations (including financial ones such as ETFs and we use this term in the further parts of the book)—influences the development of ETFs markets above all through the links between the innovative funds and other parts of the financial system, especially financial markets. As Lettau and Madhavan (2018) observed the management of index portfolios that usually consist of a large number of securities was costly before the development of elec-tronic trading systems. Consequently, the spread of the new technologies may be considered one of the funda-mental factors that initiated and boosted, firstly the market for index mutual funds and, secondly, the market for the even more innovative category, that is, ETFs.

On the demand side of the ETFs market, diffusion of ICT is one of the determinants of their relative benefits available to investors. The decreasing importance of the partially physical (open-outcry) trading venues and growing role of electronic systems is one of the key factors shaping the ETFs markets resulting from the rising usage of the new technologies (Madhavan, 2016) in a process labeled the "voice to electronic" (Hendershott & Madhavan, 2015). Trading and settlement processes are increasingly computerized and automated which has a number of advantageous effects for investors (Calamia, Deville, & Riva, 2013; Hendershott, Jones, & Menkveld, 2011; Lechman & Marszk, 2015; Schmiedel, Malkamäki, & Tarkka, 2006), such as:

- Lowering the trading costs which are a substantial part of the total costs of investing in ETFs.
- An improved pricing mechanism regarding the shares of ETFs and increased information-linked advantage of ETFs due to quicker and broader access to continuously updated data sources about the stock markets.
- A lower tracking error for passive funds due to a more efficient arbitrage mechanism.

As Shiller (2012) noted, the increased application of the new technologies in the stock operations affected above all the flows of information—and this should be perceived as the fundamental effect—rather than the speed of buying and selling of the securities. For a recent in-depth overview of the economic effects of the advanced systems of electronic trading see Menkveld (2016).

On the supply side, the adoption of ICT affects the decisions of companies which consider launching or further extensions of their ETF range as well as the actions of institutions which act as APs. Most generally, as in the basic supply-side theory, they influence the potential profits for these companies to be generated by participating actively in the ETFs market. Costs of the basic operations of the innovative funds may be lowered by transferring securities using technologically advanced systems; it also applies to the duration of the creation and redemption processes whose timeliness may be scrutinized by actual and potential clients (Schmiedel et al., 2006). It should be stressed that the adoption of ICT is of particular importance in the case of funds listed on more than one trading platform, especially in multiple countries, as well as funds that offer exposure to foreign assets. Timely and cost-efficient functioning of such ETFs requires an even higher level of ICT diffusion; furthermore, new technologies need to be adopted in more than one country (Calamia et al., 2013). Substantial challenges which may be partially alleviated by the ICT adoption are linked with the funds offering exposure to emerging markets (Blitz & Huij, 2012).

One of the most recent yet already highly significant developments in the investment industry facilitated by the adoption of ICT are services labeled "robo-advising." The basic concept of robo-advising was defined by Szpringer (2017, p. 173) as automated investment advisory services that support asset management by employing special sophisticated software; it facilitates automation of many conventional wealth management processes. Another name used to describe such services is "digital advisory" yet it should be underlined that it can cover more types of services than robo-advising (the latter is, though, most strongly associated with this category). The three basic types of portfolio management services offered to the users of robo-advising are (Madhavan, 2016): (1) model-based portfolio solutions (determined using questionnaires for clients); (2) portfolio rebalancing; and (3) optimization of the portfolio for the taxation purposes. Development of robo-advice services may be considered as one of the demand-side factors of the ETFs market development as it increases the group of investors who may gain access to, at least partially, personalized advisory services by being available even to customers with limited means, thus, with no access to conventional comparable services offered by, for example, private banking (Szpringer, 2017). Moreover, using robo-advising is beneficial for retail clients as it facilitates avoiding some of the cognitive errors and biases discussed in the burgeoning theoretical and empirical literature in the behavioral finance field (Madhavan, 2016), such as home bias, that is, overallocation of funds to the domestic assets. Robo-advising is also usually cheaper for such investors due to the compensation structure being different than those in the traditional advisory and asset management services.

Another important technological change not limited to the financial applications is linked with the developments in data sciences, briefly called "big data," that is, access to very complex datasets (Madhavan, 2016). Such data are gathered from numerous sources (for example, social media) and analyzed with sophisticated methods. In the investment industry they may be applied to offer highly personalized services as well as marketing campaigns targeted at precisely determined groups of potential clients. Moreover, big data solutions may offer new insight into the managers of the funds. It should be underlined that the exact impact of big data on the ETFs markets and entire financial systems still remains to be determined. Currently, it seems to be too early due to its short history.

## 2.3.5 Public Policies and Exchange-Traded Funds

In most countries the primary determinants of the ETFs market development are identified within the private sector. As a result, up to this point we have not considered any potential impact of the public sector (with the brief exception of some legal issues). In some countries, though, actions undertaken directly by the authorities seem to strongly influence the processes on the ETFs market. The growth of innovative funds may be boosted by the government's attempts to privatize state-owned enterprises (in India); in other cases, the mere launch of first ETF was the part of certain governmental strategy (in Japan). We will shortly discuss both countries which in the early 2017 were labeled by Bloomberg as the world's fastest growing ETFs markets (Shah & Ramarathinam, 2017). However, the influence of the governmental actions should not be dismissed in case of other countries. According to Lettau and Madhavan (2018) ETFs began their global growth in the 1990s when they were perceived as a possible way to increase the stability of the financial markets (in the aftermath of the 1987 crash) without affecting the turnover of individual stocks; a similar reaction could be observed after the 2008 global financial crisis when banks with decreased balance sheets started using ETFs in the place of futures or swap contracts.

In our presentation of the history of the global ETFs market we indicated Japan as the first country apart from Canada and the United States where innovative funds became listed. Nomura Nikkei 300 Stock Index Listed Fund was launched in 1995, but for a few years it was the only ETF listed in this country and played a marginal role. Its inception was carefully prepared by the Japanese financial authorities (e.g., necessary laws had been passed) and the pressure to be among the world's first ETFs markets was not coincidental; the new fund was supposed to exert an anticipated impact on the local financial markets. The new fund tracked Nikkei 300 index which was much less popular than the leading Nikkei 225 and, thus, was expected to affect the trading structure by diminishing the turnover of futures based on Nikkei 225 which, in the opinion of the originators, were too strongly impacting the cash market (Osaki, 2001). This did not happen and the significant development of the Japanese ETFs market started much later with the launch of funds tracking Nikkei 225 and TOPIX (Abner, 2016). However, the whole story shows clearly how ETFs markets may start developing simply due to certain governmental actions (motivated in various ways). It should be underlined that it was not the only example when the Japanese authorities attempted to use ETFs to reach their aims (most recently by Bank of Japan). We discuss the other actions briefly in the context of the role of ETFs in the financial system.

In India, a rather unusual ETF was launched in 2014 (named "CPSE ETF") and it became one of the tools in the governmental privatization strategy. In its portfolio it holds stocks of 10 state-owned companies in the energy sector including Coal India Ltd. (Shah & Ramarathinam, 2017). As a result, it does not offer applications typical for ETFs. For instance it cannot be perceived as a diversified investment solution. Moreover, it is not tracking a certain well-known index, but rather specific Nifty CPSE that was created to serve as a benchmark for this state-tailored fund. Shares of CPSE ETF are bought by both public institutions (e.g., state-run agencies) and private investors (it seems that only in the latter case transactions serve the official purpose of the fund). The Indian example shows that the creation of ETFs may be a consequence of governmental plans not necessarily linked with the financial sector and it may include an establishment of unusual types of funds which nevertheless may be in high demand among market participants.

The examples of Japan and India prove that actions of authorities, undertaken in order to reach certain aims, may directly influence the demand and/or supply side of the ETFs markets, even when the private sector is not involved or its role is reactive. In the case of Japan, the government created an environment in which ETFs could be launched by lifting barriers (supply side). In India, it influenced both the supply (launch of new ETFs with distinctive structures) and demand side (encouraging various entities to purchase the shares of the new fund). However, the story of the Japanese market in the mid-1990s suggests that government attempts can be unsuccessful if they do not respond to the actual market trends. It should be added that various elements of the economic policies can indirectly affect the ETFs market if they influence the major macroeconomic indicators (such as economic growth rate and its components) or the economic condition of various sectors (or even individual companies). As such linkages constitute well-recognized factors, extensively discussed in the literature, we skip their analysis. Their impact cannot be perceived as ETF-specific, thus, their influence on the development of ETFs markets (either in absolute terms or market shares defined in various ways) is similar to the other segments of the financial system.

### 2.3.6 Determinants of the Development of the Investment Funds Markets

Determinants of the development of the ETFs markets may also be considered in a different framework than the one presented so far. ETFs are a category of investment funds and, therefore, the factors that influence the entire investment funds industry may also be regarded as impacting the spread of its innovative category.

However, adopting such a perspective is to some extent problematic as the previous theoretical and empirical publications in this field concentrated, either explicitly or implicitly, on the development of the mutual funds due to the relatively much shorter history and smaller assets of ETFs. Consequently, referring them directly to the ETFs markets may be questionable as the attributes of ETFs and mutual funds (or closed-end funds) are in some ways substantially different (for instance, in contrast with mutual funds, shares of ETFs are listed and traded on exchanges, with some profound implications). Nevertheless, we discuss selected issues, focusing on the factors that are linked to the development of the markets at large rather than the fund-level ones; the reason for this is related to the main focus of our book: we are interested in examining the factors that affect the development of the entire ETFs markets in European countries. It must be added that we do not distinguish between determinants of the development of investment funds and the ones that affect mutual funds; we label all as factors of the investment funds market development. We also do not discuss the adopted measures of development as they are relatively irrelevant for our study (we analyze a different type of investment fund).

Factors that influence the development of the investment funds markets are classified according to various criteria. We follow the classification suggested by Perez (2012) who divided them into three broad groups: economic (further split into micro- and macroeconomic), socio-psychological, and regulation and taxation. For a more detailed discussion on the classification of the factors of the development of investment funds markets (including presentation of approaches based on various criteria) see Stańczak-Strumiłło (2013) and Miziołek (2016). The outline of the factors is derived from the discussion in Borowski (2011), Perez (2012), and Stańczak-Strumiłło (2013).

The first group of determinants are the microeconomic factors, that is, the ones linked above all to the returns of the funds, their persistency, and the costs incurred by investors. This is probably the most intensively researched group with numerous studies conducted on various markets, time periods, and categories of funds— for an overview of the seminal papers see Perez (2012). We conduct macro-level analysis in the empirical sections and, therefore, omit the further discussion of microeconomic category as it lies outside the scope of this book; there are several studies devoted to this aspect of the ETFs markets—see the publications cited in Sections 2.1 and 2.2. Moreover, we intend to analyze the entire European ETFs industry over the past several years, therefore, fund-level analysis would be unfeasible—using it would be possible in the case of the analysis of a single or a few carefully defined segments of the ETFs markets, but in the case of a few thousand funds listed on several markets, it would be methodologically incorrect considering the extreme heterogeneity of the sample. We do, however, consider one of the factors that is included in some lists of microeconomic factors, that is, the propensity to save (see, e.g., classification of Borowski, 2011). Nevertheless in the presented classification by Perez (2012), it is included in the socio-psychological and we discuss it accordingly.

Macroeconomic factors are the group of factors of utmost importance in the context of our research on the European ETFs markets. They are generally linked to the economic situation of a certain country that affects the condition of the financial sector. The latter influences the prices of financial instruments and the structure of the financial markets. Moreover, the macroeconomic situation impacts the income and wealth of the population that are both demand- and supply-side factors of the development of the investment funds markets. On the demand side, it may be stated that income and wealth of the society are among the main factors of the demand for the investments in the investment funds. On the supply side they affect the investment funds market's infrastructure and the presence of qualified financial professionals.

In order to facilitate the empirical analysis of the macroeconomic factors it is necessary to identify the exact variables whose impact may be verified. Three groups of key determinants included in this category are: (1) the level and rate of economic development and, partially overlapping, the level of the society's income and wealth; (2) the level of the development of financial markets; and (3) the prices of financial instruments. Our outline of these factors is rather concise as we already discussed most of them in the specific context of the ETFs market development. It should be noted that these factors are to some extent interlinked, see, for instance, the analysis of the relationships between financial and economic development in Chapter 5, Exchange-Traded Funds and Financial Systems of European Countries: Growth Factor or Threat to Stability?

Economic development (its level and rate of change) is one of the most basic factors that shape the conditions of various markets and is not limited to the market for investment funds. By taking into consideration the economic development in the study of the factors that affect investment funds industry, a variety of other determinants are also covered, that is, the ones that influence the process of economic development. However, their discussion lies outside the scope of this book. It is not sufficient to focus exclusively on the impact of economic development in the discussed context as such an analysis would be too general; the additional problem is related to the use of various indicators in the relative dimension, for example, expressed as a share of the local GDP; however, using rate of economic growth is more feasible.

The development of the financial markets or, generally, the development of the financial system, is the second key subcategory. We have already shown their significance in the context of ETFs markets. As far as the entire investment funds markets are concerned, Stańczak-Strumiłło (2013, p. 84) explained that there are three key consequences of the development of the financial systems: (1) increasing assets and number of investment funds; (2) growing number of transactions conducted by the investment funds; and (3) international expansion of investment funds. An important issue in this context is the structure of the financial system which is classified according to the dominant form of the savings allocation. According to Demirgüç-Kunt and Levine (1999) and Levine (2002) two basic categories that can be distinguished are bank-based and market-based financial systems. In the former, companies tend to use above all the external sources of financing linked to the banking sector, usually bank loans. Such loans are provided by large universal banks that dominate the financial system; the role of the capital markets is relatively irrelevant. On the contrary, in the latter, in addition to banks that usually are also the largest financial institutions, the position of capital markets is substantial as they are an important way of transferring the excess supplies of funds to the entities seeking sources of funding. In the context of the investment funds markets, Stańczak-Strumiłło (2013) noticed that market-based financial systems are more beneficial for the development of such financial institutions as investors tend to invest in various financial instruments rather than limit themselves to the bank deposits (as is common in the bank-based systems). Another channel through which a financial system may give further impetus to the development of an investments funds market is the increased competition between the financial institutions.

The third subcategory of fundamental macroeconomic determinants is the price of financial instruments. However, they are in fact usually considered within the analysis of the microeconomic factors as they affect the parameters of investment funds that are examined within that subcategory, such as returns of the funds.

Apart from the key macroeconomic determinants there are also some supplementary ones that are characterized by rather an indirect association with the mutual funds. They include, inter alia, inflation and interest rates.

Increased inflation in certain countries may lead to changes in the preferences of the investors who opt to invest in financial assets other than money (e.g., units of investment funds). However, the impact of inflation on the development of the investment funds market is not clear-cut; high inflation may be detrimental to its growth due to the decline in the real returns obtained by the investors who, consequently, decide to switch to other investment choices. Inflation may also influence the structure of the investment funds market in terms of the offered exposure of the funds, for example, between equity and fixed income funds (Borowski, 2011). The influence of interest rates on investment funds is indirect and, as in the case of inflation, ambiguous (Borowski, 2011). To simplify, we consider the scenario of decreasing interest rates. If the correlation between interest rates and propensity to save (a factor presented in the socio-psychological category) is positive, then declining interest rates could have negative effects on the investment funds market due to the lower supply of savings in the economy. Nevertheless, a positive impact may also occur—lower interest rates could reduce the relative attractiveness of bank deposits and spur the demand for investment choices with potentially higher returns such as investment funds.

Finally, as Stańczak-Strumiłło (2013) noted, effectiveness of a country's pension system is an additional macroeconomic factor; however, it seems difficult to empirically quantify and investigate its impact. It may exert some influence through channels such as the excess supply of savings that may be directed to investment funds or the inclusion of investment funds as one of the possibilities to gather means for pension benefits.

The second broad group of determinants of the investment funds market development is socio-psychological factors. They include, among others, the propensity to save [in some classifications it is a macroeconomic factor (Borowski, 2011)], level of investors' knowledge (or, more broadly, level of their education, i.e., financial literacy in the field of finance), trust of investors toward investment funds, and other psychological or similar attributes of investors that affect their financial decisions (e.g., customs or cultural factors). It needs to be emphasized that all these determinants are highly interlinked, for instance as Perez (2012, p. 247) observed, the amount of savings at the disposal of investors influences their behavior with regard to investment decisions. Despite its micro- and macroeconomic nature, propensity to save is included in this category due to the complicated bundle of its economic and noneconomic determinants (Stańczak-Strumiłło, 2013). Moreover, one stipulation is necessary; as Müller and Weber (2010) noted, the linkages between financial education and development of investment funds are straightforward as growth of active funds can be attributed to the lack of financial sophistication; however, the results of their research led to opposite conclusions. Due to their mostly qualitative nature we do not consider socio-psychological factors in our evaluation of the development of the European ETFs markets, the only exception being the propensity to save that we approximate with the gross savings rate. There are, undeniably, substantial differences between these two variables, yet data of the sufficient frequency are not available in case of the former variable.

The third and final category covers regulation and taxation issues that apply either to the overall financial sector (including the financial markets) or specifically to the investment funds industry. The important aspects include, but are not limited to, the country's legal and judicial system and their efficiency, as discussed by, for example, Lorizio and Gurrieri (2014), regulation concerning the functioning of the investment funds, protection of the rights of investors, and taxation rules concerning both the investment funds and individual investors. The relationship between taxation rules and development of investment funds is one of the most extensively studied topics in this field—for an overview see Stańczak-Strumiłło (2013, p. 79). According to Perez (2012, pp. 282−7), by and large the results of empirical studies confirm that stricter rules on the functioning of the financial markets and financial institutions support the development of the investment funds markets (due to, e.g., higher trust of investors); however, they may exert some negative impact by increasing the entry barriers and limiting the competition between funds. Borowski (2011) divided regulation and taxation factors further into local and international regulations (the latter includes, e.g., international regulation that govern the financial system and investment funds in particular). This group of factors is highly region- or country-specific, therefore we address it with regard to the European financial system in Section 3.1. Due to the similarity of the relevant regulation in most countries in our sample, we do not test the role of variables from this category in our empirical study.

There are also other possible factors of the development of the investment funds markets that cannot be classified in any of the groups presented in the preceding paragraphs such as technological and political determinants as these were already described with regard to ETFs.

Factors of the investment funds markets development were verified empirically in a number of studies whose authors adopted substantially heterogeneous approaches to this subject. We discuss the selected papers in this field all of which covered mutual funds.

In one of the seminal (and first) papers that addressed the issue of determinants of the investment funds markets development, Fernando, Klapper, Sulla, and Vittas (2003) (a later version of the paper was published as Klapper, Sulla, & Vittas, 2004) investigated 40 countries at various levels of economic development over the 1992−98 period. They identified the following universal factors that contributed to the growth of assets of investment funds: higher development of capital markets, market-based structure of particular financial system, higher market returns and liquidity, and lower volatility. In high-income countries, additional factors were trade openness and substantial share of high-tech exports; in middle-income countries they included income per capita and a strong banking system. Moreover, the importance of some determinants such as legal origin and restrictions on other categories of financial products varied depending on the type of fund.

Khorana et al. (2005) examined the investment funds markets in 56 countries using data on the 1996−2001 time period and identified several positive and negative development factors. They considered assets of mutual funds in relation to the country's assets of primary domestic securities (equities, bonds, bank loans) as the primary indicator of investment funds market development. The following factors were concluded to have a positive impact (positive relationship): more strict regulation, better protection of shareholders rights, higher GDP per capita, a more educated population, longer history of the investment funds market, and a higher proportion of defined contribution pension funds in the pension system. On the contrary, the barriers (negative relationship) include: higher trading costs and barriers to entry.

In the study covering more than 50,000 funds in 20 countries, Ramos (2009) unveiled the positive role of competition and contestability (e.g., fewer entry barriers) for the development of the investment funds industry. Varga (2010) analyzed the Brazilian investment funds and concluded that, in contrast with the other studies, most economic and legal determinants were not significant in case of that country; the only important determinants were financial market innovation and market risk. Ioana, Alin, and Lenuţa (2012) studied the Romanian investment funds market uncovering, inter alia, the positive impact of foreign direct investments. Ferreira, Keswani, Miguel, and Ramos (2013) adopted a slightly different approach as they investigated the determinants of the funds' performance in 27 countries. The results of their study imply that following country-level variables affects the performance of funds (i.e., indirectly the size of the investment funds markets): liquidity of the stock markets and strength of legal institutions. Lemeshko and Rejnuš (2014) studied 11 countries in Central and Eastern Europe confirming most of the findings of previous research on the investment funds industries in that region. Dragotă, Tatu-Cornea, and Tulbure (2016) evaluated 38 heterogeneous investment funds markets over 1996−2009, focusing on the socio-cultural rather than economic or legal factors of their development. Their findings show the positive relationship between assets of investment funds and certain variables: perception of happiness, freedom of choice, and preference of individuals toward private ownership. Khodayari and Sanoubar (2016) examined the impact of ICT adoption on the assets of mutual funds in the highly heterogeneous group of eight countries (member-states of the D-8 Organization for Economic Cooperation) over 1999–2014 with the application of panel models. The results of their study did not provide conclusive evidence on the relationship between the spread of new technologies and the growth of the mutual funds industry. Filip (2017) studied the Polish investment funds market and concluded that its development was driven by the upward trend in the prices of equities as well as favorable changes in the regulations.

Apart from these theoretical and empirical studies devoted to the development of the investment funds market, an additional, slightly more specific approach in the context of our discussion can be found in Miziołek (2016) who analyzed the factors that influence the development of the index funds markets. They were classified into three categories:

- Microeconomic: rates of returns of the passive funds in relation to the active funds (in other words, whether active funds over- or underperform the benchmark) and the parallel relation concerning their costs, transparency, and benefits linked to the diversification of the portfolio.
- Socio-psychological: investors' knowledge and awareness concerning index funds.
- Legal: regulations concerning this segment of the investment funds market, in particular in the field of investors' protection.

## 2.4 IMPACT OF EXCHANGE-TRADED FUNDS ON THE DEVELOPMENT AND STABILITY OF FINANCIAL SYSTEMS

The rapid expansion of ETFs, envisioned by their growing assets and turnover as well as the diversity of this financial category elicited a discussion concerning their potential impact on local and global financial systems with a special focus on financial stability. The first reports devoted to this topic were published in 2010 when the intensive activity of ETFs markets could no longer be ignored and the lessons learnt during the 2008 financial crisis substantiated a lack of trust toward relatively new financial products which were not fully understood by the investing public. As a result, the potential threats of ETFs were examined by regulatory institutions. This discussion continued over the next few years when it was spurred by some unusual events on financial markets with the assumed participation of ETFs.

In this section we outline the most important effects of ETFs on financial stability. However, we do not want to limit our analysis to the issue of a financial system's stability as it would considerably underestimate the depth of the potential transformation caused by these products, by some considered to be one of the almost unambiguously positive examples of financial innovations as they facilitate access of a broad group of investors to various low-cost investment solutions (Szpringer, 2017). We present various hypothesized or observed relationships between ETFs and other parts of the financial system by referring to both theoretical and empirical literature. It should be noted that, among several parts of the financial system, ETFs are most strongly linked to equity markets which is a natural consequence of their form (equity securities), prevailing category of tracked assets (stock market indexes), and, to some extent, trading location (stock exchanges or similar trading venues). This discussion will be continued with regard to the empirical study in Chapter 5, Exchange-Traded Funds and Financial Systems of European Countries: Growth Factor or Threat to Stability? in which we investigate the outlined relationships in the context of European ETFs markets.

### 2.4.1 Key Issues

Before presenting the potential impact of ETFs on the financial markets, we continue briefly the discussion about the advantages and disadvantages of ETFs in comparison to similar financial products (for more details see Section 2.2). Within the perspective of the asset management industry, one of the effects of the development of the ETFs markets is the increased concentration in terms of the share of the stock markets owned by the largest investment companies (Ben-David, Franzoni, Moussawi, & Sedunov, 2016; Ben-David et al., 2017); in the United States it has increased almost fivefold since 1980. Growing concentration is caused by the economies of scale in the passive funds in which, due to their fundamental attributes, the increasing size of assets brings more significant cost reductions than in active funds. This explanation is consistent with the supply approach of the ETFs market development suggested by Blocher and Whaley (2016). Ben-David et al. (2016) stated that higher concentration results in the increased volatility of the securities tracked by the fund due to nonfundamental reasons, for instance, departure of key managers, changes in the fund's policy, or even breakdowns of a company's computer system. The impact of such events in a more diversified investment industry is less serious.

One of the key potential threats posed by ETFs to specific parts or the entire financial system is the possibility of shock propagation (shock transmission) from the ETFs market to the markets for underlying assets. Obviously, the transmission of shocks in the reverse direction (e.g., from the stock market to the market for equity ETFs) is also possible yet it should not be regarded as an unexpected effect as it would simply be a consequence of the arbitrage mechanism which should be taken into account by the users of innovative funds. An actual example is the transmission of the volatility from the Chinese market to the US ETFs with the relevant exposure—see the analysis in Rompotis (2016a). To state it differently, the evaluation should focus exclusively on the nonfundamental shocks, that is, sudden changes in the prices or turnover (more broadly: liquidity) that are not linked to the economic processes affecting the underlying assets but are the consequence of the fluctuating demand for the shares of ETFs. It means, for example, that they were not caused by changes in the consumer demand or monetary policy.

The mechanisms of the transmission of shocks from the ETFs market to the markets for underlying assets are explained in various ways. We present two key approaches; for a more detailed discussion see the overview of the current research in Ben-David et al. (2017).

The first approach focuses on the short-termism of the increasing number of market participants conducting transactions in shares of ETFs. This means that ETFs are used by such investors to make short-term directional bets. In the case of market turbulence, in particular significant price declines, short-term investors rapidly exit the market which contributes to the further decrease of the prices of both shares of ETFs and underlying securities.

The second explanation concentrates on volatility. In this approach the effect of the demand shock on the ETFs market is the increased deviation of the prices of the shares of ETFs from their NAV which may transpose to the market for the underlying assets if its liquidity is limited. In other words, as Pan and Zeng (2017) explained, transmission of shock may occur when shares of ETFs are liquid, but the underlying assets are illiquid. Using the example of bond ETFs, they stated that this liquidity mismatch can lead to the breakdown in the correct trajectory of the arbitrage process caused by the withdrawal of APs who have a dual role, that is, participation in the creation and redemption of the ETFs shares as well as dealers on the bond market. Their withdrawal may be motivated by the inventory management decisions. Similar in-kind conceptualization of the shock transmission mechanism is presented by Cespa and Foucault (2014).

Various aspects of the possible shock propagation linked to ETFs were verified in a number of empirical studies and we discuss the best-known cases from the US equity market separately. Most of these studies focused on the issue of volatility. Mazza (2012) showed that introduction and expansion of ETFs in the global financial industry cannot be associated with substantial increases of either volatility or correlations on the equity markets; on the contrary, investors may benefit from using ETFs in their portfolios during the periods of macroeconomic uncertainty. Krause and Tse (2013) concluded via analysis of the sample of United States and Canadian listed equity ETFs and the markets for the underlying securities that volatility feedback is bidirectional.

Yavas and Rezayat (2016) studied spillovers of volatility between United States and European ETFs and stock markets in emerging economies and found confirming evidence in the case of some countries. Xu and Yin (2017) showed that both in the cases of monthly and daily data, trading volume of ETFs tracking the S&P 500 index is a main factor of the underlying index volatility. Chen and Do (2018) confirmed spillover effects between ETFs with exposure to precious metals and the price indexes of tracked assets with regard to both the returns and volatilities. Rompotis (2018) studied US equity ETFs with the emerging markets exposure and concluded that there is a high degree of comovement between the US market and the markets for the underlying equities. In the case of a rather unique category of ETFs, that is, volatility ETFs, the results of the analysis of Białkowski, Dang, and Wei (2016) imply that money flow to such funds do not increase the market instability in the periods of the market downturn. In a different perspective, according to Malamud (2015), transmission of shocks may be intensified by the increased activity on the primary ETFs markets.

The most famous example of possible shock propagation inflicted by ETFs is the "Flash Crash" that took place on the US equity market on May 6, 2010 and led to considerable negative publicity about innovative funds. However, results of careful studies about the real reasons and course of the crash conducted in its aftermath present mixed conclusions, some being partially contradictory. We present in detail this incident, its causes and implications as it is one of the most substantial events in the history of the global ETFs market. Soon after its occurrence it was used as an example of the potential threats posed by ETFs to the stability of the financial systems in the reports published by organizations such as IMF or the Bank for International Settlements (IMF, 2011; Ramaswamy, 2011).

The Flash Crash took place in the late afternoon on May 6, 2010 when the main US stock market indexes declined significantly with no preceding signals. Dow Jones Industrial Average noted the sharpest intraday decline in the history of its calculation which was followed by a very quick upsurge 20 minutes later (Madhavan, 2012); another key index of the US stock market, S&P 500, declined by c. 6% (Ben-David, Franzoni, & Moussawi, 2012). One of the features that distinguished this breakdown from others observed in the past and made it unique in the history of the United States (and at the same time also global) financial markets was the breakdown in prices of stock of many companies which suddenly were traded at historically lowest levels. Despite the cancellation of the transactions conducted at the artificially deflated prices, the Flash Crash led to substantial losses for many market participants, for example, liquidity providers and retail investors. What is important in the context of our topic is that some of the most significant declines of both prices and liquidity were observed for the shares of ETFs (and other ETPs, although we will skip them in the further discussion due to their low share in the total ETPs market). Moreover, ETFs were accused of contributing to aggravating the declines.

According to the report published by the US financial supervision bodies, Commodity Futures Trading Commission and SEC a few months after the 2010 crash (in September 2010), the beginning of the decline of the indexes can be traced back to large transactions conducted by one of the financial institutions on the S&P 500 futures market which led to breakdown of its liquidity (Commodity Futures Trading Commission & Securities and Exchange Commission, 2010). This decline was accompanied by similar process on the market for the shares of the largest ETF, that is, S&P 500 SPDR. Decreases of liquidity occurred in the market environment characterized by the increasing volatility of the entire US equity market which was a result of the nervousness inclined by the news from Europe and, therefore, many of the explanations of the Flash Crash linked its occurrence to the events in Europe and the developing debt crisis. The large sale of the S&P 500 futures contract was made in order to hedge an equity position and it was conducted using an automated execution algorithm. It triggered further sales and contributed to the emergence of the liquidity crisis on the markets for both stock index futures and individual stocks.

It is, therefore, necessary to evaluate the role of ETFs (particularly S&P 500 SPDR) in the Flash Crash of 2010. The basic explanation is related to the arbitrage mechanisms of ETFs. In this case arbitrage may be understood in two ways: firstly, most conventionally, as the fundamental process occurring in ETFs (due to their creation and redemption method) and, secondly, in relation to one of the alternative financial products, that is, stock index futures (see the description of the equity index arbitrage complex in Section 2.2.3.). As a result, the initial decline in the liquidity on the futures market could have been transposed to the ETFs market (consistent with the second concept). In the second stage, due to the arbitrage between ETFs and the underlying stocks, the liquidity shock could have been transmitted from ETFs market to the stock market (Ben-David et al., 2012). These and other possible explanations were verified empirically in various studies; we present results of the two selected (highly representative) comprehensive studies. Additionally, an interesting discussion of the early evidence on the ETFs during the Flash Crash of 2010 can be found in Borkovec, Domowitz, Serbin, and Yegerman (2010) who concluded that the extreme decline of the liquidity of the shares of ETFs and failed price discovery mechanism were the key explanations of the crash.

According to the study by Ben-David et al. (2012), who tested these two potential arbitrage relations, the activity of arbitrageurs in both categories contributed to the shock propagation from the futures market through the ETFs market to the stock market. Moreover, they suggested that the negative role of ETFs was aggravated by the high-frequency trading that was responsible for a significant share of the arbitrage operations and contributed to the nonfundamental volatility.

In one of the most in-depth studies of the event in 2010, Madhavan (2012) showed that the securities with the highest fragmentation of their market structure prior to the event were most strongly affected by the Flash Crash. Fragmentation refers to both quotes and volumes and it means that there were many platforms on which particular security was traded; no single one was dominant. The level of fragmentation was much higher than in the past which explained why there had been no such events previously. However, the explanation suggested for ETFs is a bit different as their turnover was less fragmented which means that they should not have been strongly impacted. In the case of innovative funds, the main reason for their role in the Flash Crash was the distortion between the prices of their shares and the prices of the tracked securities which disrupted the arbitrage mechanism. Deviations between the prices of the underlying securities and prices of the ETFs shares were caused by the limitations imposed on the up and down prices of the securities ("circuit breakers") which hindered the pricing of the ETFs shares. To sum up, Madhavan's explanation is a bit different than the one suggested by Ben-David, Franzoni, and Moussawi; it was not the arbitrage process itself that was responsible for the contribution of ETFs to the Flash Crash, but rather regulatory barriers to its correct course. Furthermore, Madhavan (2016) stated, referring also to the next Flash Crash in 2015, that ETFs should not be regarded as responsible for either of those events as the key disruptive factor was the fragmentation of the equity market. Abner (2016) formulated similar statements based on the results of his analysis and stressed the importance of countermeasures undertaken by both regulators and investors.

In the United States, Flash Crash resulted in the adoption of new rules by the SEC regarding extreme market conditions which require halting trades of securities that experience significant rapid changes in volatility; they apply also to the ETFs (Ben-David et al., 2017). Their worth was checked during the next event similar to the broadly recognized first Flash Crash, yet of different magnitude—in some aspects larger (e.g., influence on ETFs due to their much larger assets and turnover compared to 2010), in others less serious. It was observed 5 years later, on August 24, 2015 (there were other, less important analogous events taking place between 2010 and 2015 and more on this topic can be found in, for example, Abner, 2016). Substantial declines in the prices of the ETFs shares were preceded by decreases on the futures market. From the ETFs market they were transmitted to the stock market (several stocks of large companies). The second Flash Crash was not limited to ETFs, but also affected other US-traded equities while foreign-listed ETFs or foreign equity markets did not experience such changes (Madhavan, 2016). According to Madhavan (2016) the reasons for the clash were again rooted in the structure of the US equity market. In spite of the fact that ETFs were once more at the center of the crash, as Abner (2016) observed, the event in 2015 did not result in publications warning about the risks posed by ETFs but rather showed that ETFs became an integral part of the financial markets. Moreover, it proves that the mechanisms of, for instance, the arbitrage linked to ETFs need to be continuously improved by the regulators and market participants in order to prevent further disruptions.

Apart from the shock propagation, another possible effect of the ETFs market development for the linked segments of the financial system is the decline in the serial dependence of the returns on the tracked indexes on major financial markets (e.g., in the United States or Japan) which became negative since the 2000s (Baltussen, Da, & van Bekkum, 2018). This change seems to be significantly associated with the increased utilization of passive funds (both ETFs and mutual funds) as well as index futures. The key mechanism behind the reversal of the indexes' serial dependence is the index arbitrage (e.g., in ETFs conducted by APs). Increasing negative serial dependence of these returns is a sign of considerable price movements that may cause additional costs for many active investors, for example, financial institutions that act as providers of ETFs. This, in turn, may lead to lower demand for ETFs and weakening of the discussed linkages.

In the cross-sectional perspective, according to Sullivan and Xiong (2012) who focused on the US market, growing popularity of various forms of index trading, including passive ETFs, has in the recent years led to the higher cross-sectional trading commonality and, as a result, higher correlation of the returns on equities. The broader consequence of this trend is the growth of systemic market risk and, as a linked effect, decreased risk diversification opportunities. Diversification benefits in the financial system may also be reduced by the possible contagion between passive ETFs (Neves, Fernandes, & Martins, 2017).

Yet another possible negative consequence of the increasing popularity of index investing (not only in ETFs) is the higher risk of market crashes caused by the growing number of investors who adjust their exposure to the indexes based on their past results, that is, increasing allocation to passive investment products in the periods of continued positive returns, and decreasing their allocation after the period of negative returns (Wurgler, 2011). It may also boost the creation of market bubbles. The rise of the passive investing is also expected to influence the corporate investment and financing decisions through, for instance, the impact on the models used for capital budgeting.

ETFs may also negatively influence the informational efficiency (price informativeness) of the individual securities by affecting their supply and number of informed traders who are interested in trading them (Israeli, Lee, & Sridharan, 2017). The ownership of the securities by the fund is shown to increase their trading costs and decrease the benefits from information acquisition. The channel of transmission is the lock-up of individual shares in the portfolios of the funds which can no longer be used in transactions based on the firm-specific information. According to the cited study, an increase in ETF ownership of the underlying shares of one percentage point leads to 1.6% growth of the average bid-ask spreads of these shares in the following year. Other research which confirms the negative impact of ETFs is Da and Shive (2018) who claimed that stocks tracked by ETFs tend to exhibit higher comovements of their returns which means that they are influenced to a higher degree by information regarding the entire index rather than being company-specific. However, Bansal, McKeon, and

Svetina (2013) showed by using the sample of US-listed ETFs that the introduction of the first ETFs with exposure to certain stocks tends on average to increase the short-selling activity of such equities, in particular if there had been substantial constraints to short-sale transactions for a given security (defined generally as inability to fulfill all demand for shorting). The launch of further funds has less significant results. Overall, they concluded that the introduction of ETFs contributes to the price efficiency of the tracked securities. Bhattacharya and O'Hara (2018) claimed that in the case of the illiquid markets for the underlying assets, activities of ETFs increase their informational efficiency on the aggregate level albeit in the case of individual assets their prices may be distorted; moreover, speculation may be exacerbated across markets.

The next fundamental issue is the impact of ETFs on the liquidity of the financial markets. Some authors claim that ETFs negatively influence the liquidity of tracked assets by various mechanisms such as increased market segmentation (Piccotti, 2018), decreased activity of APs in some scenarios (Pan & Zeng, 2017), or crowding-out in case of bond ETFs, that is flow of the liquidity from bonds to ETFs tracking their returns (Dannhauser, 2017). Czauderna, Riedel, and Wagner (2015) used a measure of stock market illiquidity based on the differences in the prices of an index and shares of respective ETFs, showing the bidirectional relation between such defined illiquidity and market returns.

Nevertheless, a number of studies support the opposite view and their results prove that the development of ETFs markets boosts the liquidity of the tracked securities rather than limiting it—see, some of the most recent studies by Glosten, Nallareddy, and Zou (2016), Li and Zhu (2016), Madhavan (2016), Madhavan and Sobczyk (2016), Wermers and Xue (2015). According to Richie and Madura (2007) the creation of ETFs tracking certain equities can increase their liquidity, in particular in the case of ones with a lower weight in the tracked index. De Winne, Gresse, and Platten (2014), who analyzed the funds traded on the Euronext exchange, stated that the introduction of ETFs leads to the decline in spreads of the stocks that form the tracked index due to the activities of liquidity providers. The exact mechanism can be explained as related to the decrease in the two elements of spreads, the order imbalance and order processing cost. On a broader scale, it means that the launch of ETFs can result in arbitrage between the markets for the tracked assets and shares of ETFs that improve the risk-bearing capacity of the stock markets and provides buying and selling support to order imbalances. The role of liquidity providers seems particularly important in the periods of low liquidity.

Ben-David et al. (2017) note that the mechanisms of the potential positive impact of ETFs on the liquidity of the underlying assets stem from the benefits of the arbitrage mechanism and can be referred to as stylized facts about the influence of ETFs recognized in the research:

1. Improvement in the transmission of systemic information between ETFs and the underlying securities due to the trading activity.
2. Faster incorporation of information by prices of stocks in the portfolios of ETFs.
3. Movements of the prices of ETFs' shares inflicted by informed trades are more significant than the ones caused by noise traders.
4. Utilization of the shares of ETFs by traders to act on new information in case of constraints on the short sale of the tracked securities, thus, improving market efficiency.

Agarwal, Hanouna, Moussawi, and Stahel (2017) claimed that the comovement of liquidity in contrast with the comovement of returns mentioned earlier can be observed between ETFs and the tracked assets, and it seems to be increasing over the past few years. Consequently, it may be stated that the impact of ETFs on the liquidity of the underlying assets may not be unambiguously assessed as either positive or negative.

Potentially negative or positive effects of ETFs may be also be viewed in a slightly different perspective, that is, with regard to the impact on the corporate governance procedures of the companies whose stocks are composed of the portfolios of ETFs (Ben-David et al., 2017). Bradley and Litan (2011) stated that smaller companies may be reluctant to admit for listing on the stock exchanges as they try to avoid becoming a minor part of the large ETF's portfolio based on the assumption that prices of individual stocks of smaller companies are driven by the prices of ETFs that track them; this may slow down the development of equity markets. However, the results of empirical research show that this type of risk may be severely overstated (Appel, Gormley, & Keim, 2016). An increase in the share of a company's equity owned by ETFs (or other passive funds) can be positively linked to improvements in areas such as the number of independent directors, takeover defenses, or equality of voting rights.

The potential negative impact seems to be moderated, or even reversed, particularly in the case of certain funds who adopt countermeasures. The world's largest provider of ETFs, State Street Global Advisors, decided in 2017 to more significantly influence the corporate governance of the companies whose stocks it holds as managed assets (Crigger, 2017). For instance, in order to support gender diversity on the managerial level it objected to the re-election of board members if only men held directorship positions.

Finally, cross-listing of ETFs, that is, listing of the shares of certain funds on more than one stock exchange (here we focus on the case of exchanges located in various countries), or launch of ETFs with exposure to the foreign assets, provides investors with many opportunities, including broader access to various financial products (sometimes unavailable on the local market) as well as easier and often cheaper possibilities to gain foreign exposure. However, it may also lead to the emergence of some threats for financial stability. The unintended consequence of the cross-listed or foreign-exposure ETFs may be increased risk of contagion (understood here as in Claessens & Forbes, 2001) and transmission of shocks between various markets, sometimes in distant locations. Transmission mechanisms may involve the transactions concerning particular assets required within the process of the creation or redemption of the ETFs' shares. Potential threats are more substantial in the case of flows between markets which operate in different and uncoordinated regulatory environments. Nevertheless, the development of the funds which link various countries cannot be regarded unequivocally negative, as, apart from the benefits for individual investors, it may also result in some positive changes in the entire financial system and economy, related to the higher financial openness, including more rapid capital growth and increased factor productivity—see the discussion in Bekaert, Harvey, and Lundblad (2011).

In order to supplement our discussion, it needs to be added that one of the more recent possible impacts of ETFs on the financial system can be observed with regard to the actions undertaken by the Japanese central bank, the Bank of Japan. Purchases of the shares of ETFs are a part of its monetary policy, that is, program of quantitative easing (Abner, 2016). The stated aim of the operations involving shares of ETFs is to facilitate the functioning of the money market (Bank of Japan, 2017a) yet the actual purpose appears supporting the prices of the Japanese equities as purchases of the shares of ETFs are made mostly in the periods in the falling stock markets. Therefore, considering it to be a part of the monetary policy is rather dubious. The program covers exclusively the funds with exposure to some prespecified indexes of the Japanese stock market and transactions in the shares of ETFs are conducted by the appointed trust bank. An additional program (even less related to the monetary policy) is aimed at supporting certain groups of companies through purchases of the shares of funds that hold their stocks (Bank of Japan, 2017b). It should be emphasized that the presented application of ETFs for the aims of the monetary policy is still quite recent and Japan is the only country in which it is utilized. Moreover, its effects are still unclear and remain to be assessed in the future. Some preliminary studies were already conducted (see, e.g., Fueda-Samikawa & Takano, 2017; Nangle & Yates, 2017; Petrov, 2018; Shirai, 2018) and their conclusions are mixed with regard to both ETFs and stock markets.

Evaluation of threats linked with the diffusion of ETFs may lead to the next question concerning their regulation and other required policy responses. Such discussion constitutes yet another possible topic, but we decided to omit it from our book. However, we present selected issues regarding the European financial industry in Chapter 3, Exchange-Traded Funds Markets in Europe—Development Patterns, and Chapter 5, Exchange-Traded Funds and Financial Systems of European Countries: Growth Factor or Threat to Stability? Despite their relatively short history, ETFs seem to be already past the initial stage of the market development in which, as W. Sharpe stated (1991a, p. 506) the "forces of competition are able to regulate a market" and imposing any regulations is premature.

## 2.4.2 Risks Posed by Special Categories of Exchange-Traded Funds

Other possibly disruptive impacts of innovative funds on financial systems or the entire economy are linked to some special categories of ETFs; we present selected issues related to commodity, geared, and, more generally, synthetic ETFs.

Some potentially negative effects of ETFs may be caused by the funds tracking returns on commodities, that is, commodity ETFs; it should be added that the negative impact may also involve other similar ETPs such as ETCs. Initially, the vast majority of the commodity ETFs tracked the returns on precious metals, mostly gold or silver. However, over recent years new types of commodity ETFs or, even more often, ETCs have been launched tracking returns on goods such as cocoa, coffee, cotton, corn, wheat, and other agricultural commodities as well as sources of energy (above all crude oil, natural gas, and gasoline) and industrial metals (copper, aluminum, etc.); even more interesting developments include livestock ETCs based on prices of cattle or lean hogs (Deutsche Bank, 2017a). Commodity ETFs and ETCs were indicated by some authors as the sources of the growing volatility of the commodity markets, much stronger than suggested by the shifts in the fundamental factors in the real economy (see, e.g., Ramaswamy, 2011; Rubino, 2011; Diaz-Rainey & Ibikunle, 2012; Corbet & Twomey, 2014; Foucher & Gray, 2014). This trend is not expected to exert significant consequences for most commodity markets tracked by such funds as precious metals are currently usually transacted for investment purposes. Nonetheless, increased speculation on the markets for basic commodities boosted by the development of linked ETFs or ETCs may have substantial economic and social consequences (e.g., magnified inflation), yet are still difficult to assess due to the rather low assets of these financial products. Golub et al. (2013) claimed that commodity ETPs may influence the commodity markets positively by increasing their liquidity and efficiency of the price discovery.

Viewed in a different perspective, another result of the expansion of commodity ETPs may be changes in the application of capital in the entire economy which is forwarded from the real economy to the financial sector, thus, influencing its productivity and other parameters. According to Shank and Vianna (2016), similar effects can be observed in the case of the currency-hedged ETFs that may lead to the financialization of the economy, above all with regard to the currency markets, they stated that the application of currency-hedged ETFs to protect against the currency risk could have itself become one of the sources of the exchange rates' volatility.

Another threat to financial systems is posed by a special category of ETFs distinguished in terms of their relation to benchmarks; that is, geared ETFs (leveraged, inversed, or both) due to their distinctive construction (Madhavan, 2016). Geared funds need to use some types of derivatives in order to provide magnified or inverse returns as they usually enter swap contracts (total return swaps). The terms of these contracts require their daily rebalancing and increasing or reducing the exposure of the fund (Aguilar et al., 2016). Daily changes are unique for geared funds (other types of synthetic ETFs do not face such requirements). The effect of rebalancing has been shown to be nonlinear which means that such funds generate trades of a much higher value than could be expected from merely changes in the benchmark (Cheng & Madhavan, 2009). Rebalancing operations are conducted by the end of trading day and hedging activity of the fund's counterparties in the swap contracts may influence liquidity and volatility on the markets for tracked assets, especially on more niche markets (such as small capitalization stocks) and during times of higher volatility. Geared funds may, therefore, aggregate the magnitude of volatility and impact the prices of the tracked assets. It should be stressed, however, that the empirical evidence on these effects is mixed (Madhavan, 2016), for instance Li and Zhao (2014) concluded that leveraged ETFs do not increase the price volatility of the underlying equities. Trainor (2010, p. 215) claimed that it is "a spurious coincidence." However, results of the study of the Canadian ETFs by Charupat and Miu (2011) confirm the contribution of geared funds to market volatility. Shum, Hejazi, Haryanto, and Rodier (2015) stated that the most impact of geared ETFs can be observed during the most volatile days.

The potential effects of geared ETFs may also be considered within another framework. According to Jiang and Yan (2016), the development of regular ETFs may be regarded as an attempt to create "information insensitive" innovative securities which could be used to decrease the magnitude of adverse selection and increase market liquidity. This notion applies to passive, index-tracking funds whose returns should be more liquid than the stocks composing the index and less influenced by the company-specific information. However, the consequences of the geared ETFs could be opposite as they increase information sensitivity. They may facilitate short-term speculation with the use of leverage. Jiang and Yan (2016) showed that the turnover on the geared ETFs market is several times higher than in the case of regular (plain-vanilla) funds; taking into account the leverage, the actual difference is even higher. Geared funds seem to attract mostly short-term investors (the average holding period is c. 3 days) who are not discouraged by the relatively higher costs of the trades, that is, larger price impact and higher bid-ask spreads than in the case of regular ETFs. Moreover, higher trading costs mean that the potential for arbitrage is more limited which leads to increased tracking errors. Some further differences between the investors in regular and geared ETFs were noticed such as buyers of the geared funds' shares tending to invest in funds which performed poorly in the previous few months whereas in the case of regular ETFs the correlation between funds' returns and flows is positive.

Synthetic ETFs considered as an entire category (not limited to the geared funds discussed in the preceding paragraphs) are a special group of innovative funds that may negatively influence financial systems in various ways. Due to their popularity (yet decreasing) in Europe this category deserves particular attention. The main difference between physical and synthetic funds is the use of derivatives (usually swaps) for obtaining the stated exposure by synthetic ETFs. Three main types of risk associated with synthetic ETFs are leverage/inverse tracking risks (already presented), counterparty risk, and collateral risk (IMF, 2015). We discuss counterparty and collateral risk together as they are strongly interrelated.

Counterparty risk (or, more precisely, counterparty credit risk) may be defined as the risk of the default of the counterparty in the swap contract or its failure to deliver the contracted returns to the fund's provider (Amenc, Ducoulombier, Goltz, & Le Sourd, 2015; Aguilar et al., 2016; Awrey, 2012; Ramaswamy, 2011). In order to be protected from such an event, funds must adhere to the rules regarding the maximum allowed exposure to one counterparty which often includes fully- or even over-collateralizing such exposure by holding diversified collateral which consists of chosen securities. In the case of the counterparty's default, collateral needs to be sold on the market or used to generate tracking returns in order to maintain the desired exposure and avoid losses. It may be difficult, for example, when the liquidity of collateral is low; in some scenarios the return on the collateral will be too low to cover the necessary costs. These and similar threats may be regarded as collateral risk.

Considerable risk applies to the special case when the same financial institution (usually a large financial corporation) is both the fund's sponsor and counterparty in the swap contract (Aggarwal & Schofield, 2014; Awrey, 2012). In the case of its default investors may suffer significant losses, but, even more importantly, it may threaten the stability of the financial system in one or more than one country. Yet another risk may arise when the swap's counterparty uses such contracts to finance illiquid assets, resulting in the mismatch of liquidity between its short-term liabilities and long-term financing. In the scenario of large redemptions of the fund's shares it may cause considerable problems for the financial institution and, consequently, may lead to systemic threats. Finally, this combination causes clear conflict of interest. The threat resulting from such situation, with the dual role of one institution, has recently been significantly mitigated due to various regulatory measures regarding, for instance, the limitation of the exposure to one counterparty in the swap contract, full or even higher level of collateralization, selecting and publishing the list of authorized counterparties, or posting collateral with an independent custodian.

Another important risk associated with synthetic funds (but not limited to this category of ETFs) is their insufficient transparency and disclosure regarding, for instance, counterparties of the derivatives contracts, quality of the collateral, or composition of the reference basket in the case of complex ETFs (Aggarwal & Schofield, 2014). Lack of transparency is even more problematic in the case of ETFs tracking assets from foreign markets or funds with shares cross-listed in multiple countries as it may pose a potential threat for entities from many, sometimes physically distant, locations. Any kind of ambiguity regarding key attributes of the funds hinders the correct evaluation of their risk for investors and regulatory authorities (as well as financial institutions engaged in their distribution and trading) which may lead to, for example, excessive risk taking. Taking into account the main topic of this book, we discuss the issue of European synthetic funds in more detail in Chapter 5, Exchange-Traded Funds and Financial Systems of European Countries: Growth Factor or Threat to Stability? and evaluate their impact.

Counterparty and collateral risks presented in the preceding paragraphs are, however, not limited to synthetic funds (as suggested incorrectly in some publications). Profits from lending operations have become another source of profits for the providers of physical funds, in some cases generating higher returns than usually very low management fees (Blocher & Whaley, 2016). This means that funds (and, consequently, the owners of their shares) are exposed to the risk of the delay (or decline) of the borrower to transfer the borrowed assets during the time when funds need them in order to deliver them to the APs (i.e., during the shares redemption). Related types of the risk (also leading to possible delays or failures in the settlement procedure) is the "operational shorting" by APs, that is, delaying the delivery of the creation basket to the fund's provider even though the fund's shares are already distributed among investors (Ben-David et al., 2017; Evans, Moussawi, Pagano, & Sedunov, 2017). Widespread occurrence of these risks may have system-broad consequences and increase the level of financial stress. However, Madhavan (2016) stressed that this issue still remains to be fully empirically verified and the level of counterparty and collateral risk is probably overstated (Madhavan presented these types of risk in the section of his book entitled "Common Myths"). As Golub et al. (2013) noted, in the case of the prudent execution of the lending operations (with the robust risk controls) they may not only generate additional profits for the investors in the shares of ETFs, but also lead to some benefits for entire markets such as higher liquidity.

Another specific category of ETFs that may pose additional types of risk (not discussed until recently) to the financial system are volatility ETFs. As Bhansali and Harris (2018) observed, the rapid increase of the popularity of various correlated short volatility strategies, including leveraged short volatility ETFs (above all with exposure to the VIX index), may lead to substantial threats to the financial stability in case of the unexpected upsurge in the volatility due to, for example, changes in the monetary policy or macro events. Furthermore, assets of the stabilizing strategies are much lower than those of the strategies based on VIX, that is, volatility-contingent. However, we do not discuss the issue of volatility ETFs and the possible risks for the European financial system in more detail as they are categorically almost absent from European markets; obviously, in the case of the financial crisis in the United States triggered by this type of ETFs, the European financial system will most probably also be affected yet the probability and severity of this threat is difficult to assess. The events from early February 2018 showed that potential threats inflicted by volatility ETFs should not be dismissed as marginal and possible only in a distant perspective (Mizio≥ek, 2018). Severe declines of the US stock market indexes (linked to increased possibility of the increases in the interest rates) led to the dramatic increase of the VIX index. As a result, the prices of the shares of the short volatility ETFs and ETNs declined, in some cases so significantly that they led to the liquidation of certain ETPs. One of the consequences of this event were the calls of BlackRock, the leading global provider of ETFs, to introduce regulations on specifically this category of ETPs motivated by their behavior during the turmoil on the financial markets that differs from the other groups of ETPs. The issue of ETFs with VIX exposure was also addressed from a different perspective by Chen, Lee, and Hsu (2017).

### 2.4.3 Impact of Financial Innovations on the Financial System and Economy

Potential consequences of ETFs may be viewed within the broader discussion regarding the impact of financial innovations on the financial system and entire economy. Such an approach can help in identifying potential effects which may not be obvious when focusing only on ETFs. We begin by presenting the concepts underlining the negative economic effects of (certain) financial innovations, then, as a counterbalance, we switch to the positive views; finally, we discuss more balanced approaches. Generally, despite the growing attention devoted to these issues, as Shiller (2012) acknowledged, the significance of financial innovations remains understated. Moreover, Dembinski (2017) emphasized that financial innovations, boosted by technological progress, were one of the main forces influencing the financial industry in recent decades, with both positive and negative effects linked to this relationship.

Discussion about the economic effects of financial innovations has intensified in the aftermath of the global financial crisis of 2008 when the negative role of some innovative financial products was undeniable. However, some statements seemed to be too critical, for example, former FED chairmen P. Volcker argued in 2009 that the biggest innovation in the financial industry in the past 20 years was an ATM and there was no proof of the positive contribution of financial innovation to the economic growth. In a similar manner, P. Krugman claimed in 2007 that recent financial innovations spread confusion and promoted irresponsible risk taking, bringing wealth only to their creators; both were cited by Allen (2012, pp. 493–494).

A more extended negative view of financial innovations is particularly notable in the concepts of "innovation-fragility" and "negative innovations." In the innovation-fragility approach the development of financial innovations with high leverage or complicated built-in risks may at some point lead to the instability of the financial system and, consequently, the entire economy if their users suddenly become aware of the mistakes in their previous risk evaluation (i.e., underestimation of its level) and mass withdrawals occur (Gennaioli et al., 2012). Negative effects may be exacerbated by, for example, agency issues. According to Lerner and Tufano (2011) "negative financial innovations" are financial products or services, usually with complicated and opaque features which cause negative changes in the financial system such as the outbreak of the 2008 global financial crisis with the significant role of certain financial products linked to the housing market (Henderson & Pearson, 2011).

Interestingly, Schöler, Skiera, and Tellis (2014) showed that participants of the financial markets perceive financial innovations as profitable, even in the light of their possible contribution to financial turmoil. Moreover, they analyzed the cumulative abnormal stock market returns to financial innovations and found evidence that they are higher in recessions (than in expansions) and positively related to the riskiness and radicalness of the innovation while negatively to their complexity.

The opposite views of the economic role of financial innovations, that is, more optimistic and stressing their positive impact, seem to be wider spread in the literature even after the global financial crisis which undeniably revealed some serious risks of the new financial products. In the traditional "innovation-growth" view, financial innovations are one of the sources of economic growth by influencing both financial and real (i.e., nonfinancial) sectors of the economy as the broader positive effects of financial innovations are reduction of transaction costs, increased market efficiency, and improved risk sharing (Beck, Chen, Chen, & Song, 2016). The exact mechanisms which are indicated as the transmission channels encompass various economic entities and include (Beck et al., 2016; Laeven, Levine, & Michalopoulos, 2015; Lerner & Tufano, 2011):

- New choices in investment and consumption for households, facilitated by, for example, new financing methods.
- Easier and cheaper access to financing for companies, both private and state-owned.
- Smoothening of the business cycle due to reduced volatility of consumption.

Apart from these areas of impact included in the traditional innovation-growth approach, a few other mechanisms with positive influences were suggested (Allen & Gale, 1999; Hsu, Tian, & Xu, 2014; Laeven et al., 2015; Lerner & Tufano, 2011; Low, Tee, Si-Roei, & Ghazali, 2015):

- Boosting entrepreneurial activity.
- Boosting the innovation activity of companies from real sectors, particularly due to development of the stock markets.
- More rapid development of the high-tech companies (due to easier access to financing though financial markets).
- Contribution to the transformation of the economy into a knowledge-based economy.

It should be stressed that the two broad views presented are not necessarily contradictory. This idea was probably expressed most accurately by Diaz-Rainey and Ibikunle (2012) who stated that each financial innovation should be regarded as a "double-edged sword"—exactly the same innovative product or service may have a very different impact on the financial system and economy under varying circumstances; the exact effects will be influenced by a large number of determinants (such as the regulatory environment) and are difficult to predict.

The impact of financial innovations cannot be limited to their strictly economic consequences. Examples of certain innovations in the financial sector prove that they can also influence some aspects of social development or the natural environment. In the first group, some notable examples include crowd-funding or social impact bonds that offer new opportunities for the members of capitalistic societies using them—for more on this topic see Shiller (2013). In the latter category, in recent decades a number of new financial solutions have emerged that allow reaching environmental aims by applying financial tools such as debt-for-nature swaps; this and other examples are discussed in Allen (2012).

# References

Abner, D. (2016). *The ETF handbook. How to value and trade exchange-traded funds* (2nd ed.). John Wiley & Sons.

Aditya, G., & Desai, R. (2015). Pricing efficiency and price discovery of Indian equity ETFs. *The Journal of Index Investing, 6*(3), 67−79.

Agapova, A. (2011). Conventional mutual index funds versus exchange-traded funds. *Journal of Financial Markets, 14*, 323−343.

Agarwal, V., Hanouna, P., Moussawi, R., & Stahel, C. (2017). Do ETFs increase the commonality in liquidity of underlying stocks. In: *Fifth annual conference on financial market regulation.*

Aggarwal, R., & Schofield, L. (2014). The growth of global ETFs and regulatory challenges. In J. Kose, A. K. Makhija, & S. P. Ferris (Eds.), *Advances in financial economics* (pp. 77−102). Emerald Group Publishing Limited.

Aguilar, B., Bianco, M., Milliken, C., & Spieler, A. C. (2016). Leveraged and inverse exchange-traded funds. In H. K. Baker, G. Filbeck, & H. Kiymaz (Eds.), *Mutual funds and exchange-traded funds: Building blocks to wealth* (pp. 169−194). Oxford University Press.

Allen, F. (2012). Trends in financial innovation and their welfare impact: An overview. *European Financial Management, 18*(4), 493−514.

Allen, F., & Gale, D. (1989). Optimal security design. *Review of Financial Studies, 1*(3), 229−263.

Allen, F., & Gale, D. (1999). Diversity of opinion and financing of new technologies. *Journal of Financial Intermediation, 8*, 68−89.

Amenc, N., Ducoulombier, F., Goltz, F., & Le Sourd, V. (2015). *The EDHEC European ETF Survey 2014.* Nice: EDHEC-Risk Institute.

Amenc, N., Ducoulombier, F., Goltz, F., & Tang, L. (2012). *What are the risks of European ETFs?* EDHEC-Risk Institute.

Amenc, N., Goltz, F., & Grigoriu, A. (2010). Risk control through dynamic core-satellite portfolios of ETFs: Applications to absolute return funds and tactical asset allocation. *Journal of Alternative Investments, 13*(2), 47−57.

Amenc, N., Goltz, F., & Le Sourd, V. (2017). *The EDHEC European ETF and smart beta survey.* EDHEC-Risk Institute.

Anderson, S. C., Born, J., & Schnusenberg, O. (2010). *Closed-end funds, exchange-traded funds, and hedge funds.* Springer.

Antoniewicz, R., & Heinrichs, J. (2014). Understanding exchange-traded funds: How ETFs work. *ICI Research Perspective, 20*(5), 1−20.

Appel, I. R., Gormley, T. A., & Keim, D. B. (2016). Passive investors, not passive owners. *Journal of Financial Economics, 121*(1), 111−141.

Arnold, M., & Lesné, A. (2015). *The changing landscape for beta replication—Comparing futures and ETFs for equity index exposure.* State Street Global Advisors.

Awrey, D. (2012). Toward a supply-side theory of financial innovation. *Journal of Comparative Economics, 41*(2), 401−419.

Badenhorst, W. M. (2017). Premiums and discounts of exchanged-traded funds. *South African Journal of Accounting Research, 31*(3), 212−222.

Baker, H. K., Filbeck, G., & Kiymaz, H. (2016). Mutual funds and related investment vehicles: An overview. In H. K. Baker, G. Filbeck, & H. Kiymaz (Eds.), *Mutual funds and exchange-traded funds: Building blocks to wealth* (pp. 3−20). Oxford University Press.

Baltussen, G., Da, Z., & van Bekkum, S. (2018). Indexing and stock market serial dependence around the world. *Journal of Financial Economics,* in press.

Bank of Japan. *Principal terms and conditions for purchases of ETFs and J-REITs.* (2017a). <https://www.boj.or.jp/en/mopo/measures/term_cond/yoryo85.htm/> Accessed 02.09.18.

Bank of Japan. *Special rules for purchases of ETFs to support firms proactively investing in physical and human capital.* (2017b). <https://www.boj.or.jp/en/mopo/measures/term_cond/yoryo91.htm/> Accessed 02.09.18.

Bansal, N., McKeon, R., & Svetina, M. (2013). Short-sale constraints and securities lending by exchange-traded funds. *Managerial Finance, 39*(5), 444−456.

Barnhart, S. W., & Rosenstein, S. (2010). Exchange-traded fund introductions and closed-end fund discounts and volume. *Financial Review, 45* (4), 973–994.

Beck, T., Chen, T., Chen, L., & Song, F. M. (2016). Financial innovation: The bright and the dark sides. *Journal of Banking & Finance, 72*, 28–51.

Bekaert, G., Harvey, C. R., & Lundblad, C. (2011). Financial openness and productivity. *World Development, 39*, 1–19.

Ben-David, I., Franzoni, F. A., & Moussawi, R. (2012). *ETFs, arbitrage, and contagion.* <https://www.rsm.nl/fileadmin/home/ Department_of_Finance__VG5_/LQ5/Franzoni.pdf> Accessed 18.07.17.

Ben-David, I., Franzoni, F. A., & Moussawi, R. (2017). Exchange traded funds. *Annual Review of Financial Economics, 9*, 169–189.

Ben-David, I., Franzoni, F.A., Moussawi, R., & Sedunov, J. (2016). The Granular Nature of Large Institutional Investors. In: *NBER working paper, 22247.*

Bessembinder, H. (2018). The "roll yield" myth. *Financial Analysts Journal, 74*(2), 41–53.

Bhansali, V., & Harris, L. (2018). Everybody's doing it: Short volatility strategies and shadow financial insurers. *Financial Analysts Journal, 74* (2), 12–23.

Bhattacharya, A., & O'Hara, M. (2018). *Can ETFs increase market fragility? Effect of information linkages in ETF markets.* <https://papers.ssrn. com/sol3/papers.cfm?abstract_id = 2740699> Accessed 17.08.18.

Białkowski, J., Dang, H. D., & Wei, X. (2016). Does the tail wag the dog? Evidence from fund flow to VIX ETFs and ETNs. *Journal of Derivatives, 24*(2), 31–47.

Black, F. (1972). Capital market equilibrium with restricted borrowing. *Journal of Business, 45*, 44–454.

BlackRock (2011). *ETF landscape industry review end H1 2011.*

BlackRock (2015). *The art of indexing.*

BlackRock (2017). *A Primer on ETF Primary Trading and the Role of Authorized Participants.*

Blitz, D., & Huij, J. (2012). Evaluating the performance of global emerging markets equity exchange-traded funds. *Emerging Markets Review, 13*, 149–158.

Blocher, J., & Whaley, B. (2016). Two-sided markets in asset management: Exchange-traded funds and securities lending. In: *Vanderbilt Owen Graduate School of Management research paper no. 2474904* (pp. 1–45).

Bogle, J. C. (2016). The index mutual fund: 40 Years of growth, change, and challenge. *Financial Analysts Journal, 72*(1), 9–13.

Bond, P., & García, D. (2016). The equilibrium consequences of indexing. In: *Working paper, University of Washington* (pp. 1–40).

Borkovec, M., Domowitz, I., Serbin, V., & Yegerman, H. (2010). Liquidity and price discovery in exchange-traded funds: One of several possible lessons from the Flash Crash. *The Journal of Index Investing, 1*(2), 24–42.

Borowski, G. (2011). *Rynek funduszy inwestycyjnych w Unii Europejskiej* [Investment funds market in the European Union]. CeDeWu (in Polish).

Box, T., Davis, R., & Fuller, K. (2017). *Fragmentation without competition: When multiple ETFs hold similar portfolios.* <http://www.fmaconfer-ences.org/Boston/FragmentationwithoutCompetition.pdf> Accessed 12.07.17.

Bradley, H., & Litan, R.E. (2011). ETFs and the present danger to capital formation. In: *Ewing Marion Kauffman Foundation research paper.*

Broman, M. S. (2016). Liquidity, style investing and excess comovement of exchange-traded fund returns. *Journal of Financial Markets, 30*, 27–53.

Buetow, G. W., & Henderson, B. J. (2012). An empirical analysis of exchange-traded funds. *Journal of Portfolio Management, 38*(4), 112–127.

Caginalp, G., & DeSantis, M. (2017). Does price efficiency increase with trading volume? Evidence of nonlinearity and power laws in ETFs. *Physica A: Statistical Mechanics and its Applications, 467*, 436–452.

Caginalp, G., DeSantis, M., & Sayrak, A. (2014). The nonlinear price dynamics of US equity ETFs. *Journal of Econometrics, 183*(2), 193–201.

Calamia, A., Deville, L., & Riva, F. (2013). Liquidity in European equity ETFs: What really matters? In *GREDEG working paper series: Vol. 10* (pp. 1–26).

Cameron, R. (2015). *ETFs exchange traded funds: Everything to know about trading exchanges traded funds.* Amazon.

Cespa, G., & Foucault, T. (2014). Illiquidity contagion and liquidity crashes. *Review of Financial Studies, 27*(6), 1615–1660.

Chang, C. E., & Krueger, T. M. (2012). The case for country-specific closed-end funds instead of exchange-traded funds. *International Business Research, 5*(5), 3–7.

Chang, C. E., Krueger, T. M., & Witte, H. D. (2015). Do ETFs outperform CEFs in fixed income investing? *American Journal of Business, 30*(4), 231–246.

Chang, C. E., Ragan, K. P., & Witte, H. D. (2013). ETFs versus CEFs: Performance in international equity investing. *International Journal of Economics and Finance, 5*(12), 79–85.

Chang, C.-L., McAleer, M., & Wang, C.-H. (2018). An econometric analysis of ETF and ETF futures in financial and energy markets using generated regressors. *International Journal of Financial Studies, 6*(1), 2.

Charteris, A., Chau, F., Gavriilidis, K., & Kallinterakis, V. (2014). Premiums, discounts and feedback trading: Evidence from emerging markets' ETFs. *International Review of Financial Analysis, 35*, 80–89.

Charupat, N., & Miu, P. (2011). The pricing and performance of leveraged exchange-traded funds. *Journal of Banking & Finance, 35*(4), 966–977.

Charupat, N., & Miu, P. (2013). Recent developments in exchange-traded fund literature: Pricing efficiency, tracking ability, and effects on underlying securities. *Managerial Finance, 39*(5), 427–443.

Charupat, N., & Miu, P. (2016). *Leveraged exchange-traded funds.* New York: Palgrave Macmillan.

Chen, H., Estes, J., & Pratt, W. (2018). Investing in the healthcare sector: Mutual funds or ETFs. *Managerial Finance, 44*(4), 495–508.

Chen, J., Chen, Y., & Frijns, B. (2017). Evaluating the tracking performance and tracking error of New Zealand exchange traded funds. *Pacific Accounting Review, 29*(3), 443–462.

Chen, J. H., & Do, T. V. T. (2018). Testing leverage and spillover effects in precious metal ETFs. *Theoretical Economics Letters, 8*(03), 197–212.

Chen, M. P., Lee, C. C., & Hsu, Y. C. (2017). Investor sentiment and country exchange traded funds: Does economic freedom matter? *The North American Journal of Economics and Finance, 42*, 285–299.

Cheng, M., & Madhavan, A. (2009). The dynamics of leveraged and inverse exchange-traded funds. *Journal of Investment Management, 7*(4), 43–62.

Claessens, S., & Forbes, K. (2001). *International financial contagion.* Springer.

CME Group (2016). *The big picture: A cost comparison of futures and ETFs.*

Commodity Futures Trading Commission, Securities and Exchange Commission (2010). *Findings regarding the market events of May 6*, 2010.

Corbet, S., & Twomey, C. (2014). Have exchange traded funds influenced commodity market volatility? *International Journal of Economics and Financial Issues, 4*(2), 323−335.

Crigger, L. (2017). How the big three got so big. In: *ETF report*.

Czauderna, K., Riedel, C., & Wagner, N. (2015). Liquidity and conditional market returns: Evidence from German exchange traded funds. *Economic Modelling, 51*, 454−459.

Da, Z., & Shive, S. (2018). Exchange traded funds and asset return correlations. *European Financial Management, 24*(1), 136−168.

Dannhauser, C. D. (2017). The impact of innovation: Evidence from corporate bond exchange-traded funds (ETFs). *Journal of Financial Economics, 125*(3), 537−560.

De Winne, R., Gresse, C., & Platten, I. (2014). Liquidity and risk sharing benefits from opening an ETF market with liquidity providers: Evidence from the CAC 40 index. *International Review of Financial Analysis, 34*, 31−43.

Deloitte. (2009). *Exchange-traded funds: Challenging the dominance of mutual funds?* Deloitte Services LP.

Dembinski, P. H. (2017). *Ethics and responsibility in finance*. Routledge.

Demirgüç-Kunt, A., & Levine, R. (1999). Bank-based and market-based financial systems: Cross country comparisons. In: *World Bank policy research working paper, Vol. 2143* (pp. 2−10).

Deutsche Bank (2010). *The race for assets in the European commodity exchange-traded products space.*

Deutsche Bank (2015). *ETF annual review & outlook 2015.*

Deutsche Bank (2017a). *Europe ETF + quarterly directory.*

Deutsche Bank (2017b). *European monthly ETF market review synthetic equity & index strategy.*

Deville, L. (2008). Exchange traded funds: History, trading and research. In M. Doumpos, P. Pardalos, & C. Zopounidis (Eds.), *Handbook of financial engineering* (pp. 67−98). Springer.

Diavatopoulos, D., Geman, H., Thukral, L., & Wright, C. (2014). Mispricing and trading profits in exchange-traded notes. *The Journal of Investing, 23*(1), 67−78.

Diaz-Rainey, I., & Ibikunle, G. (2012). A taxonomy of the 'dark side' of financial innovation: The cases of high frequency trading and exchange traded funds. *International Journal of Entrepreneurship and Innovation Management, 16*(1), 51−72.

Dorfleitner, G., Gerl, A., & Gerer, J. (2018). The pricing efficiency of exchange-traded commodities. *Review of Managerial Science, 12*(1), 255−284.

Dragotă, I. M., Tatu-Cornea, D., & Tulbure, N. (2016). Determinants of development of the mutual fund industry: A socio-cultural approach. *Prague Economic Papers, 25*(4), 476−493.

Ellis, C. D. (1975). The Loser's Game. *Financial Analysts Journal, 31*(4), 19−26.

Elton, E. J., Gruber, M. J., Comer, G., & Li, K. (2002). Spiders: Where are the bugs? *The Journal of Business, 75*(3), 453−472.

ETFGI (2017). *ETFGI global ETF and ETP industry highlights—December 2016.*

Eurex (2016). *Futures and options on iShares ETFs at Eurex Exchange.*

Eurex (2017). *Exchange traded funds derivatives: Introduction of futures on the db x-trackers Harvest CSI300 ETF.*

European Fund and Asset Management Association (2011). *EFAMA's submission to ESMA on issues related to exchange traded funds (ETFs).*

Evans, R. E., Moussawi, R., Pagano, M. S., & Sedunov, J. (2017). ETF Failures-to-Deliver: Naked short-selling or operational shorting? In: *Working paper, Villanova University.*

Fama, E. F. (1965). The behavior of stock-market prices. *The Journal of Business, 38*(1), 34−105.

Fama, E. F. (1970). Efficient capital markets: A review of theory and empirical work. *The Journal of Finance, 25*(2), 383−417.

Fama, E. F., & French, K. R. (1993). Common risk factors in the returns on stocks and bonds. *Journal of Financial Economics, 33*(1), 3−56.

Fama, E. F., & French, K. R. (2010). Luck versus skill in the cross-section of mutual fund returns. *The Journal of Finance, 65*(5), 1915−1947.

Farinella, J., & Kubicki, R. (2018). The performance of exchange traded funds and mutual funds. *Journal of Accounting & Finance, 18*(4), 44−55.

Fernandez, P. (2017). *Valuation and common sense* (6th ed.).

Fernando, D., Klapper, L. F., Sulla, V., & Vittas, D. (2003). The global growth of mutual funds. In: *The World Bank policy research working paper, Vol. 3055* (pp. 1−44).

Ferreira, M. A., Keswani, A., Miguel, A. F., & Ramos, S. B. (2013). The determinants of mutual fund performance: A cross-country study. *Review of Finance, 17*(2), 483−525.

Ferri, R. A. (2009). *The ETF book: All you need to know about exchange-traded funds. Updated edition.* John Wiley & Sons.

Filip, D. (2017). Market conditions of mutual funds functioning in Poland. *Central European Review of Economics & Finance, 17*(1), 65−81.

Financial Industry Regulatory Authority. (2012). *Investor alerts exchange-traded notes—Avoid unpleasant surprises.* <http://www.finra.org/investors/alerts/exchange-traded-notes-avoid-surprises> Accessed 20.09.17.

Financial Stability Board. (2011). *Potential financial stability issues arising from recent trends in exchange-traded funds (ETFs).*

Foucher, I., & Gray, K. (2014). Exchange-traded funds: Evolution of benefits, vulnerabilities and risks. In: *Bank of Canada Financial System review, December 2014* (pp. 37−46).

Frame, S. W., & White, L. J. (2012). Technological change, financial innovation, and diffusion in banking. In A. N. Berger, P. Molyneux, & J. O. S. Wilson (Eds.), *The Oxford handbook of banking.* Oxford University Press.

French, C. W. (2003). The Treynor capital asset pricing model. *Journal of Investment Management, 1*(2), 60−72.

Fueda-Samikawa, I., & Takano, T. (2017). *BOJ's ETF purchases expanding steadily—How long will the BOJ hold risky assets with no maturity?* Japan Center for Economic Research. <https://www.jcer.or.jp/eng/pdf/170706_report(eng).pdf> Accessed 12.09.18.

Fulkerson, J. A., Jordan, S. D., & Travis, D. H. (2017). Bond ETF arbitrage strategies and daily cash flow. *The Journal of Fixed Income, 27*(1), 49−65.

Gastineau, G. L. (2010). *The exchange-traded funds manual* (2nd ed.). John Wiley & Sons.

Gavriilidis, K., Gregoriou, G. N., & Kallinterakis, V. (2017). Exchange-traded funds: Do they promote or depress noise trading? In F. Economou, K. Gavriilidis, G. N. Gregoriou, & V. Kallinterakis (Eds.), *Handbook of investors' behavior during financial crises* (pp. 335−361). Academic Press.

Gennaioli, N., Shleifer, A., & Vishny, R. W. (2012). Neglected risks, financial innovation and financial fragility. *Journal of Financial Economics*, 104(3), 452−468.

Glosten, L. R., Nallareddy, S., & Zou, Y. (2016). ETF activity and informational efficiency of underlying securities. In *Columbia Business School Research Paper No. 16-71*.

Golub, B., Novick, B., Madhavan, A., Shapiro, I., Walters, K., & Ferconi, M. (2013). *Exchange-traded products: Overview, benefits and myths*. *BlackRock Viewpoint*.

Golub, B. W., Ferconi, M., Madhavan, A., & Ulitsky, A. (2018). Factor-based optimisation and the creation/redemption mechanism of fixed income exchange-traded funds. *International Journal of Financial Engineering and Risk Management*, 2(4), 335−350.

Hanouna, P., Moussawi, R., & Agarwal, V. (2017). Investigating the correlation between ETFs and their underlying securities. In *ETF Research Academy Research Summary, June 2017* (pp. 3−10).

Harper, J. T., Madura, J., & Schnusenberg, O. (2006). Performance comparison between exchange-traded funds and closed-end country funds. *Journal of International Financial Markets, Institutions and Money*, 16(2), 104−122.

Hendershott, T., Jones, C. M., & Menkveld, A. J. (2011). Does algorithmic trading improve liquidity? *The Journal of Finance*, 66(1), 1−33.

Hendershott, T., & Madhavan, A. (2015). Click or call? Auction versus search in the over-the-counter market. *The Journal of Finance*, 70(1), 419−447.

Henderson, B., & Pearson, N. (2011). The dark side of financial innovation: A case study of the pricing of a retail financial product. *Journal of Financial Economics*, 100, 227−247.

Hill, J. M. (2016). The evolution and success of index strategies in ETFs. *Financial Analysts Journal*, 72(5), 8−13.

Hill, J. M., Nadig, D., & Hougan, M. (2015). *A comprehensive guide to exchange-traded funds (ETFs)*. CFA Institute Research Foundation.

Hilliard, J. (2014). Premiums and discounts in ETFs: An analysis of the arbitrage mechanism in domestic and international funds. *Global Finance Journal*, 25(2), 90−107.

Hsu, P., Tian, X., & Xu, Y. (2014). Financial development and innovation: Cross-country evidence. *Journal of Financial Economics*, 112(1), 116−135.

Huang, J. C., & Guedj, I. (2009). Are ETFs replacing index mutual funds? In *AFA 2009 San Francisco meetings paper*.

Hurlin, C., Iseli, G., Perignon, C., & Yeung, S. (2014). The collateral risk of ETFs. In *Universite de Geneve working paper series, 8* (pp. 1−48).

International Monetary Fund (IMF). (2011). Global financial stability report: Durable financial stability. Getting there from here. *World Economic and Financial Surveys*, 1−139.

International Monetary Fund (IMF). (2015). Global financial stability report: Navigating monetary policy challenges and managing risks. *World Economic and Financial Surveys*, 1−162.

Investment Company Institute (ICI). (2017). *Investment company fact book 2017*.

Ioana, R., Alin, N. I., & Lenuţa, C. U. M. (2012). Main determinants of the mutual funds dynamics in Romania before and after the financial crisis. *"Ovidius" University Annals, Economic Sciences Series*, XII(2), 1347−1352.

Israeli, D., Lee, C. M. C., & Sridharan, S. A. (2017). Is there a dark side to exchange traded funds? An information perspective. *Review of Accounting Studies*, 22(3), 1048−1083.

Ivanov, S. I. (2016). Analysis of ETF bid-ask spread components. *The Quarterly Review of Economics and Finance*, 61, 249−259.

Jarrow, R. A. (2010). Understanding the risk of leveraged ETFs. *Finance Research Letters*, 7(3), 135−139.

Jensen, G. R., Johnson, R. R., & Washer, K. M. (2018). All that's gold does not glitter. *Financial Analyst Journal*, 74(1), 59−76.

Jiang, W., & Yan, H. (2016). *Financial innovation, investor behavior, and arbitrage: Implications from the ETF market*. <https://ssrn.com/abstract = 2023142> Accessed 02.05.18.

Kalfa Baş, N., & Eren Sarıoğlu, S. (2015). Tracking ability and pricing efficiency of exchange traded funds: Evidence from Borsa Istanbul. *Business & Economics Research Journal*, 6(1), 19−34.

Khodayari, P., & Sanoubar, N. (2016). The impact of information and communication technology on the assets of mutual funds in D-8 countries. *International Journal of Contemporary Applied Sciences*, 3(10), 11−19.

Khorana, A., Servaes, H., & Tufano, P. (2005). Explaining the size of the mutual fund industry around the world. *Journal of Financial Economics*, 78(1), 145−185.

Klapper, L., Sulla, V., & Vittas, D. (2004). The development of mutual funds around the world. *Emerging Markets Review*, 5(1), 1−38.

Kosev, M., & Williams, T. (2011). Exchange-traded funds. *Reserve Bank of Australia Bulletin, March Quarter*, 51−60.

Krause, T., & Tse, Y. (2013). Volatility and return spillovers in Canadian and US industry ETFs. *International Review of Economics & Finance*, 25, 244−259.

Kreis, Y., & Licht, J. W. (2018). Trading on ETF mispricings. *Managerial Finance*, 44(3), 357−373.

Kreis, Y., Licht, J. W., & Useche, A. J. (2016). Efficiencies in Latin American ETFs. *Cuadernos de Administración*, 29(53), 7−48.

Laeven, L., Levine, R., & Michalopoulos, S. (2015). Financial innovation and endogenous growth. *Journal of Financial Intermediation*, 24(1), 1−24.

Lechman, E., & Marszk, A. (2015). ICT technologies and financial innovations: The case of exchange traded funds in Brazil, Japan, Mexico, South Korea and the United States. *Technological Forecasting and Social Change*, 99, 355−376.

Lemeshko, O., & Rejnuš, O. (2014). *Determinants of mutual fund industry development in countries of central and eastern Europe. European financial systems 2014. Proceedings of the 11th international scientific conference* (pp. 372−379). Brno: Masaryk University, 2014.

Lerner, J., & Tufano, P. (2011). The consequences of financial innovation: A counterfactual research agenda. *Annual Review of Financial Economics*, 3, 41−85.

Lettau, M., & Madhavan, A. (2018). Exchange-traded funds 101 for economists. *Journal of Economic Perspectives*, 32(1), 135−154.

Leung, T., & Santoli, M. (2016). *Leveraged exchange-traded funds: Price dynamics and options valuation*. Springer.

Levine, R. (2002). Bank-based or market-based financial systems: Which is better? *Journal of Financial Intermediation*, 11, 398−428.

Levy, H. (1978). Equilibrium in an imperfect market: A constraint on the number of securities in a portfolio. *American Economic Review*, 68, 643−658.

Li, F. W., & Zhu, Q. (2016). *Synthetic shorting with ETFs*. <https://papers.ssrn.com/sol3/papers.cfm?abstract_id = 2836518> Accessed 15.11.17.

Li, M., & Zhao, X. (2014). Impact of leveraged ETF trading on the market quality of component stocks. *The North American Journal of Economics and Finance, 28*, 90–108.

Lintner, J. (1965). The valuation of risk assets and the selection of risky investments in stock portfolios and capital budgets. *Review of Economics and Statistics, 47*, 13–37.

Lintner, J. (1969). The aggregation of investors' diverse judgements and preferences in purely competitive markets. *Journal of Financial and Quantitative Analysis, 4*, 346–382.

Lorizio, M., & Gurrieri, A. R. (2014). Efficiency of justice and economic systems. *Procedia Economics and Finance, 17*, 104–112.

Low, S.-W., Tee, L.-T., Si-Roei, K., & Ghazali, N. A. (2015). The link between financial development and knowledge-based economy—Evidence from emerging markets. *Journal of Economic Cooperation and Development, 36*(1), 51–88.

MacManus, Ch, & Lee, J. (2017). The growth of ETFs in Europe. *Performance Magazine, 22*, 1–8.

Madhavan, A. N. (2012). Exchange-traded funds, market structure, and the flash crash. *Financial Analysts Journal, 68*(4), 20–35.

Madhavan, A. N. (2016). *Exchange-traded funds and the new dynamics of investing.* Oxford University Press.

Madhavan, A. N., Marchioni, U., Li, W., & Du, D. Y. (2014). Equity ETFs versus index futures: A comparison for fully funded investors. *The Journal of Index Investing, 5*(2), 66–75.

Madhavan, A. N., & Sobczyk, A. (2016). Price dynamics and liquidity of exchange-traded funds. *Journal of Investment Management, 14*(2), 1–17.

Malamud, S. (2015). A dynamic equilibrium model of ETFs. In *Swiss finance institute research paper no. 15-37.*

Malkiel, B. G. (2016). *A random walk down Wall Street: The time-tested strategy for successful investing.* W.W. Norton & Company.

Markowitz, H. (1952). Portfolio selection. *The Journal of Finance, 7*(1), 77–91.

Markowitz, H. (1959). *Portfolio selection: Efficient diversification of investments.* Yale University Press.

March-Dallas, S., Daigler, R., Mishra, S., & Prakash, A. (2018). Exchange traded funds: Leverage and liquidity. *Applied Economics, 50*(37), 4054–4073.

Marshall, B. R., Nguyen, N. H., & Visaltanachoti, N. (2013). ETF arbitrage: Intraday evidence. *Journal of Banking & Finance, 37*(9), 3486–3498.

Marshall, B. R., Nguyen, N. H., & Visaltanachoti, N. (2018). Do liquidity proxies measure liquidity accurately in ETFs? *Journal of International Financial Markets, Institutions and Money, 55*, 94–111.

Marszk, A. (2016). Complexity of innovative financial products: The case of synthetic exchange traded funds in Europe. *Financial Sciences, 2*(27), 49–64.

Mateus, C., & Rahmani, Y. (2017). Physical versus synthetic exchange traded funds. Which one replicates better? *Journal of Mathematical Finance, 7*(04), 975–989.

Maurer, F., & Williams, S. O. (2015). Physically versus synthetically replicated trackers. Is there a difference in terms of risk? *Journal of Applied Business Research, 31*(1), 131–146.

Mazza, D. B. (2012). Do ETFs increase correlations? *The Journal of Index Investing, 3*(1), 45–51.

Meinhardt, C., Mueller, S., & Schoene, S. (2015). Physical and synthetic exchange-traded funds: The good, the bad, or the ugly? *The Journal of Investing, 24*(2), 35–44.

Menkveld, A. J. (2016). The economics of high-frequency trading: Taking stock. *Annual Review of Financial Economics, 8*, 1–24.

Meziani, A. S. (2016). *Exchange-traded funds: Investment practices and tactical approaches.* Palgrave Macmillan.

Miffre, J. (2007). Country-specific ETFs: An efficient approach to global asset allocation. *Journal of Asset Management, 8*(2), 112–122.

Miller, M. (1986). Financial innovation: The last twenty years and the next. *Journal of Financial and Quantitative Analysis, 21*(4), 459–471.

Miziołek, T. (2013). *Pasywne zarządzanie portfelem inwestycyjnym—indeksowe fundusze inwestycyjne i fundusze ETF. Ocena efektywności zarządzania na przykładzie akcyjnych funduszy ETF rynków wschodzących [Passive portfolio management—Index mutual funds and ETFs. Evaluation of the management's effectiveness using the example of equity emerging markets ETFs].* Lodz University Press (in Polish).

Miziołek, T. (2016). Europejski rynek indeksowych funduszy inwestycyjnych i determinanty jego rozwoju [European market for index investment funds and determinants of its development]. *Annales Universitatis Mariae Curie-Skłodowska, sectio H—Oeconomia, 50*(4), 325–338. (in Polish).

Miziołek, T. (2018). *Echa załamania na amerykańskich giełdach na rynku funduszy ETF i instrumentów typu ETP [Echoes of the crash on the US stock exchanges on the ETFs and ETPs markets].* <http://www.etf.com.pl/Aktualnosci-Swiat/Echa-zalamania-na-amerykanskich-gieldach-na-rynku-funduszy-ETF-i-instrumentow-typu-ETP> Accessed 2.09.18.

Morningstar (2005). *Fact sheet: The Morningstar equity style box.*

Morningstar (2012). *Closed-end funds vs. mutual funds and ETFs.* <https://www.fidelity.com/learning-center/investment-products/closed-end-funds/cefs-mutual-funds-etfs> Accessed 10.07.17.

Morningstar (2017). *A guided tour of the European ETF marketplace.*

Mossin, J. (1966). Equilibrium in a capital asset market. *Econometrica, 35*, 768–783.

Müller, S., & Weber, M. (2010). Financial literacy and mutual fund investments: Who buys actively managed funds? *Schmalenbach Business Review, 62*(2), 126–153.

Murphy, C. (2017). 15 Years of bond ETF history in a nutshell. In: *ETF Report, October 2017* (pp. 24–26).

Murphy, J. J. (2013). *Trading with intermarket analysis: A visual approach to beating the financial markets using exchange-traded funds.* John Wiley & Sons.

Nangle, T., & Yates, A. (2017). *Quantifying the effect of the Bank of Japan's equity purchases.* <https://voxeu.org/article/quantifying-effect-bank-japan-s-equity-purchases> Accessed 22.08.18.

Neves, E., Fernandes, C., & Martins, P. (2017). Are ETFs the right diversification vehicles? New evidences for critical investment periods. In *XXVII Jornadas Hispano-Lusas de gestão científica*, Spain-Universidade de Alicante-Benidorm.

Nikbakht, F., Pareti, K., & Spieler, A. C. (2016). Exchange-traded funds. In H. K. Baker, G. Filbeck, & H. Kiymaz (Eds.), *Mutual funds and exchange-traded funds: Building blocks to wealth* (pp. 153–168). Oxford University Press.

Osaki, S. (2001). The development of exchange-traded funds (ETFs) in Japan. *Capital Research Journal, 4*(3), 45–51.

Oztekin, A. (2018). Information fusion-based meta-classification predictive modeling for ETF performance. *Information Systems Frontiers, 20*(2), 223–238.

Pace, D., Hili, J., & Grima, S. (2016). *Active versus passive investing: An empirical study on the US and European mutual funds and ETFs. Contemporary issues in bank financial management* (pp. 1–35). Emerald Group Publishing Limited.

Pan, K., & Zeng, Y. (2017). ETF arbitrage under liquidity mismatch. In: *Fourth annual conference on financial market regulation*.

Parker, G. G., & Van Alstyne, M. W. (2005). Two-sided network effects: A theory of information product design. *Management Science, 51*, 1494–1504.

Perez, K. (2012). *Fundusze inwestycyjne. Rodzaje, zasady funkcjonowania, efektywność. [Investment funds. Categories, rules of operations, effectiveness]*. Wolters Kluwer Business Publishing House (in Polish).

Petajisto, A. (2017). Inefficiencies in the pricing of exchange-traded funds. *Financial Analysts Journal, 73*(1), 24–54.

Petrov, A. (2018). *ETFs in monetary policy case study: Bank of Japan*. State Street Global Advisors.

Piccotti, L. R. (2018). ETF premiums and liquidity segmentation. *Financial Review, 53*, 117–152.

Poterba, J. M., & Shoven, J. B. (2002). Exchange-traded funds: A new investment option for taxable investors. *American Economic Review, 92*(2), 422–427.

Qadan, M., & Yagil, J. (2012). On the dynamics of tracking indices by exchange traded funds in the presence of high volatility. *Managerial Finance, 38*(9), 804–832.

Rakowski, D., Shirley, S. E., & Stark, J. R. (2017). Tail-risk hedging, dividend chasing, and investment constraints: The use of exchange-traded notes by mutual funds. *Journal of Empirical Finance, 44*, 91–107.

Ramaswamy, S. (2011). Market structures and systematic risks of exchange-traded funds. *BIS Working Papers, 343*, 1–13.

Ramos, S. B. (2009). The size and structure of the world mutual fund industry. *European Financial Management, 15*(1), 145–180.

Richie, N., & Madura, J. (2007). Impact of the QQQ on liquidity and risk of the underlying stocks. *The Quarterly Review of Economics and Finance, 47*(3), 411–421.

Rochet, J.-C., & Tirole, J. (2002). Cooperation among competitors: Some economics of payment card associations. *The RAND Journal of Economics, 33*(4), 549–570.

Rochet, J.-C., & Tirole, J. (2006). Two-sided markets: A progress report. *The RAND Journal of Economics, 37*(3), 645–667.

Rompotis, G. G. (2016a). The effects of the Chinese stock crisis on the US exchange-traded funds market. *The Journal of Trading, 11*(4), 33–55.

Rompotis, G. G. (2016b). Physical versus futures-based replication: The case of commodity ETFs. *The Journal of Index Investing, 7*(2), 16–37.

Rompotis, G. G. (2018). Spillover effects between US ETFs and emerging stock markets. *Global Business and Economics Review, 20*(3), 327–372.

Ross, S. (1976). Arbitrage theory of capital asset pricing. *Journal of Economic Theory, 13*, 341–360.

Rouwenhorst, K. G. (2004). The origins of mutual funds. In *Yale ICF working paper, 04-48* (pp. 1–31).

Rubino, J. (2011). Emerging threat funds? *CFA Magazine, 22*(5), 30–33.

Samuelson, P. A. (1974). Challenge to judgment. *The Journal of Portfolio Management, 1*(1), 17–19.

Schmiedel, H., Malkamäki, M., & Tarkka, J. (2006). Economies of scale and technological development in securities depository and settlement systems. *Journal of Banking & Finance, 30*(6), 1783–1806.

Schöler, L., Skiera, B., & Tellis, G. J. (2014). Stock market returns to financial innovations before and during the financial crisis in the United States and Europe. *Journal of Product Innovation Management, 31*(5), 973–986.

Securities and Exchange Commission (2004). *SEC concept release: Actively managed exchange-traded funds*.

Shah, A. & Ramarathinam, A. (2017). Indian ETF market doubles in three years to $4 billion. *Mint, 9.03.2017*, pp. 7.

Shank, C. A., & Vianna, A. C. (2016). Are US-Dollar-Hedged-ETF investors aggressive on exchange rates? A panel VAR approach. *Research in International Business and Finance, 38*, 430–438.

Sharpe, W. (1961). *Portfolio analysis based on a simplified model of the relationships among securities* (PhD dissertation). University of California.

Sharpe, W. (1963). A simplified model for portfolio analysis. *Management Science, 9*, 277–293.

Sharpe, W. (1964). Capital asset prices: A theory of market equilibrium under conditions of risk. *The Journal of Finance, 19*(3), 425–442.

Sharpe, W. (1991a). Capital asset prices with and without negative holdings. *The Journal of Finance, 46*(2), 489–509.

Sharpe, W. (1991b). The arithmetic of active management. *Financial Analysts Journal, 47*(1), 7–9.

Sharpe, W. (2013). The arithmetic of investment expenses. *Financial Analysts Journal, 69*(2), 34–41.

Sherrill, D. E., Shirley, S. E., & Stark, J. R. (2017). Actively managed mutual funds holding passive investments: What do ETF positions tell us about mutual fund ability? *Journal of Banking & Finance, 76*, 48–64.

Sherrill, D. E., & Stark, J. R. (2018). ETF liquidation determinants. *Journal of Empirical Finance, 48*, 357–373.

Sherrill, D. E., & Upton, K. (2018). Actively managed ETFs vs actively managed mutual funds. *Managerial Finance, 44*(3), 303–325.

Shiller, R. J. (2012). *Finance and the good society*. Princeton University Press.

Shiller, R. J. (2013). Capitalism and financial innovation. *Financial Analysts Journal, 69*(1), 21–25.

Shin, S., & Soydemir, G. (2010). Exchange-traded funds, persistence in tracking errors and information dissemination. *Journal of Multinational Financial Management, 20*(4-5), 214–234.

Shirai, S. (2018). Bank of Japan's exchange-traded fund purchases as an unprecedented monetary easing policy. *Asian Development Bank Institute Working Paper Series, 865*, 1–20.

Shum, P., Hejazi, W., Haryanto, E., & Rodier, A. (2015). Intraday share price volatility and leveraged ETF rebalancing. *Review of Finance, 20*(6), 2379–2409.

Shum, P. M., & Kang, J. (2013). Leveraged and inverse ETF performance during the financial crisis. *Managerial Finance, 39*(5), 476–508.

Stambaugh, R. F. (2014). Investment noise and trends. *The Journal of Finance, 69*(4), 1415–1453.

Stańczak-Strumiłło, K. (2013). *Uwarunkowania rozwoju funduszy inwestycyjnych w Polsce [Determinants of the investment funds development in Poland]*. Difin (in Polish).

Sullivan, R. N., & Xiong, J. X. (2012). How index trading increases market vulnerability. *Financial Analysts Journal, 68*(2), 70–84.

Swathy, M. (2015). An empirical analysis on pricing efficiency of exchange traded funds in India. *International Journal of Engineering and Management Sciences, 6*(2), 68–72.

Szpringer, W. (2017). *Nowe technologie a sektor finansowy [New technologies and financial sector]*. Poltext Publishing House (in Polish).

Tang, H., Xu, X. E., & Yang, Z. (2014). Can international LETFs deliver their promised exposure to foreign markets? *Journal of International Financial Markets, Institutions and Money, 31*, 30–74.

Tirado, F. (2016). *Why options? ETF Report, August 2016* (pp. 22–27).

Trainor, W. J. (2010). Do leveraged ETFs increase volatility. *Technology and Investment, 1*(03), 215–220.

Tsalikis, G., & Papadopoulos, S. (2018). Assessing the performance of American and European leveraged exchange traded funds. *Investment Management and Financial Innovations, 15*(2), 165–182.

Tufano, P. (2003). Financial innovation. In G. Constantinides, M. Harris, & R. Stulz (Eds.), *Handbook of the economics of finance (volume 1a: Corporate finance)* (pp. 307–336). Elsevier.

Value Line (2010). *The differences between mutual funds, closed-end funds, and ETFs*. <http://www.valueline.com/Tools/Educational_Articles/Funds/The_Differences_Between_Mutual_Funds,_Closed-End_Funds,_and_ETFs.aspx> Accessed 10.07.17.

Varga, G. (2010). *The growth and size of the Brazilian mutual fund industry*. <https://papers.ssrn.com/sol3/papers.cfm?abstract_id = 1571553> Accessed 20.08.18.

Wang, J. (2016). Close-end funds. In H. K. Baker, G. Filbeck, & H. Kiymaz (Eds.), *Mutual funds and exchange-traded funds: Building blocks to wealth* (pp. 119–136). Oxford University Press.

Wang, L., Hussain, I., & Ahmed, A. (2010). Gold exchange traded funds: Current developments and future prospects in China. *Asian Social Science, 6*(7), 119.

Wermers, R., & Xue, J. (2015). *The role of ETFs in intraday price discovery*. ETF Research Academy.

Wiandt, J., & McClatchy, W. (2002). *Exchange traded funds*. John Wiley & Sons.

Wright, C., Diavatopoulos, D., & Felton, J. (2010). Exchange-traded notes: An introduction. *The Journal of Index Investing, 1*(1), 164–175.

Wurgler, J. (2011). On the economic consequences of index-linked investing. In W. T. Allen, R. Khurana, J. Lorsch, & G. Rosenfeld (Eds.), *Challenges to business in the twenty-first century: The way forward*. American Academy of Arts and Sciences.

Xetra (2016). *Xetra: The leading trading platform for ETCs & ETNs.*

Xu, L., & Yin, X. (2017). Exchange traded funds and stock market volatility. *International Review of Finance, 17*(4), 525–560.

Yavas, B. F., & Rezayat, F. (2016). Country ETF returns and volatility spillovers in emerging stock markets, Europe and USA. *International Journal of Emerging Markets, 11*(3), 419–437.

Yiannaki, S. M. (2015). ETFs performance Europe—A good start or not? *Procedia Economics and Finance, 30*, 955–966.

Zaremba, A., & Andreu, L. (2018). Paper profits or real money? Trading costs and stock market anomalies in country ETFs. *International Review of Financial Analysis, 56*, 181–192.

# Exchange-Traded Funds Markets in Europe: Development Patterns

## 3.1 INTRODUCTION

### 3.1.1 Development of Exchange-Traded Funds Markets: Approaches to the Analysis and Time Period of the Analysis

Before we discuss the results of the preliminary analysis of the European exchange-traded funds (ETFs) markets with a focus on the general information about the entire region, it is necessary to present our approach to the examination of the ETFs market development and to explain which countries are included in our research sample and which are omitted for various reasons; this discussion is extended in the Methodological annex.

The conceptualization of the development of the ETFs markets is not straightforward as many different approaches may be adopted depending on the specific aspect of the market for innovative funds which is regarded as the most substantial. It may, therefore, refer not only to the assets managed by the funds (as the indicator of the market's size) or turnover of their shares (another indicator of the size and, with some stipulations, an indicator of the market's liquidity), but also, in some cases, to the number of funds listed (or domiciled), net cash flows to the funds (or sales of their shares), and other indicators. An important selection criteria is the feature of ETFs which is considered to be the most crucial as it frames the analysis, that is, whether they are regarded above all as investment funds or rather as financial instruments, etc. In Chapter 2, Exchange-Traded Funds: Concepts and Contexts, we focused mainly on the attributes of ETFs as alternatives to conventional investment funds, in particular mutual funds. We pursue further this approach which means that we juxtapose

ETFs with mutual funds; closed-end funds are omitted due to their much less significant role on most considered markets (in terms of, e.g., assets). As a result, it is necessary to take into account mostly the indicators based on assets. Finally, a terminological remark is necessary as two terms are used interchangeably in the remainder of the book, *ETFs market development* and *ETFs diffusion*, as they can be regarded as synonyms—diffusion of the innovative funds is understood in the context of the general concept of diffusion discussed in the Methodological annex.

For reasons outlined next, throughout our analysis we focus on the results obtained with the use of indicators based on assets as the most correct in the context of the European region. The most relevant indicator is linked to the concept of NAV and is labeled as "total net assets," that is, market value of the fund's assets with liabilities deducted. Another way of calculation is, thus, to multiply the NAV per share by the number of fund's shares outstanding. For conciseness, we henceforth use the term "assets" of the funds. As *total assets of ETFs on a certain market (certain country) we understand the sum of the assets of all ETFs on this market, classified according to the location of their primary listing*.

In our approach, the development of ETFs markets (i.e., diffusion of ETFs) is measured with the *total value of assets of ETFs in a certain country*. All values are expressed in US dollars which facilitates between-country comparisons as well as analysis with regard to the regions other than Europe. This means, however, that the obtained results are to some extent influenced by fluctuations in exchange rates. Nevertheless, for the exchange rates in most of the countries considered in our research (in most cases EUR vs USD) the variability was limited, particularly in the period of the most rapid growth of the assets of ETFs. This means that using values expressed in, for example, EUR would not contribute to a better understanding of the investigated processes and would limit the possibility to compare our results to the ones published in other books, articles, and reports, etc., as apart from the ones exclusively covering European markets, most of them provide values in US dollars. In order to more fully understand this approach, it should be noted that there are two main elements that affect the values of the fund's assets: (1) net cash flows to the fund (differences between inflows and outflows of cash to the fund); and (2) changes in the market values of the securities (or other assets, e.g., commodities) held in its portfolio.

An alternative approach could focus on the relative position of the innovative funds on a specific market which consists of both innovative and conventional financial products; it could be applied to ETFs and the main alternative category of investment funds, that is, mutual funds. The development of ETFs markets would, thus, be measured in terms of percentage market share of the assets of ETFs in the total assets of mutual funds and ETFs in a particular country. However, the dominant approach in our research is based on the total values of assets of ETFs rather than their market shares. The main reason is rather straightforward—data availability. Data on the assets of mutual funds for the majority of the considered time period may be obtained with quarterly frequency whereas we use monthly data on ETFs; retrieving monthly data on mutual funds using the method applied by us in the case ETFs was impossible due to the technical and financial limitations and serious data gaps.

*Primary listing* is defined by Deutsche Bank (2017a, p. 55) as the listing on the primary exchange which in most cases constitutes the first (oldest) listing. In other words, it is the location where a certain fund becomes available for trading for the first time. Primary exchange usually is the exchange with the highest turnover of the particular fund's shares. Each fund has only one place of primary listing. We use the Lipper's primary listing classification of individual funds in order to calculate the values of assets for the selected European countries. Therefore, under the term "European ETFs" we understand funds with their primary listing in one of the European countries; we do not classify them according to their domicile as such a decision may be motivated purely by legal or tax reasons; see, e.g., the discussion regarding Ireland and Luxembourg in this section.

The dataset on the assets of European ETFs was created using monthly observations on individual funds extracted from the Lipper's database and available through the Thomson Reuters Eikon platform. Aggregate values for a particular country in a given month were calculated as the *sum of assets of all ETFs that were primary listed in that country*. It means that we use the classification of funds provided by Lipper, both in terms of their primary listing locations and their benchmarks (i.e., underlying assets). Lipper's database covers the entire European investment funds industry and comparisons of our aggregated values to the ones available from other sources proves the high level of their consistency. In the case of unavailable monthly observations of the certain fund's assets in the Lipper's database—a very rare situation yet sometimes noticed, caused by, e.g., political and economic turmoil as in Greece in 2010—we fill the gaps by estimating the missing values as means of neighboring ones. The other, more complicated approach could be chosen and the effects were preliminary tested, yet the differences appear to be insignificant in the vast majority of cases. In addition to the Lipper's database, ETFGI (2016, 2017) publications were used in order to obtain data on the global annual assets of ETFs.

There are, though, some stipulations which concern measures based on assets and limit their usefulness as the indicators of the ETFs market development. One of the most crucial weaknesses is the fact that changes in the values of assets of the funds depend (apart from the impact of creations and redemptions) on the fluctuations in the market prices of the assets in their portfolio. This means that they may decline substantially only due to the worsening of the situation on the benchmarked financial or nonfinancial market, even without significant withdrawals of investors. In the opposite scenario, the assets of the funds may increase significantly, even though there is no substantial activity in terms of the demand for its shares which may hinder the proper evaluation of the market development. It should be stressed, however, that this problem is common for all types of competing investment funds and is not limited to ETFs. Another problem with the market-based valuation was mentioned in the context of the discussion regarding the tracking ability of passive ETFs; in the case of funds investing in illiquid assets (e.g., many categories of bonds), the entity responsible for the valuation of the fund's shares must use valuation models and make assumptions that may differ considerably from the ones applied by the provider of the benchmark (see Chapter 2, Exchange-Traded Funds: Concepts and Contexts). However, regardless of the outlined problems, the more substantial weaknesses of the other approaches justify the application of assets-based indicators.

Applying indicators based on *turnover* is another method of analyzing the development of ETFs markets that we use to supplement our approach. Base turnover indicator is the value of the turnover of the shares of all ETFs listed in a certain country in a selected time period. Analogically to assets, for comparability purposes we use data expressed in US dollars. In order to calculate this indicator, we gathered data on the turnover on all stock exchanges in a particular country and usually there is only one such marketplace; however, in some countries the market structure is more fragmented and turnover is divided among two or more exchanges. It should be emphasized that in the case of turnover indicators it is to a large extent impossible (due to the way data are gathered and distributed) to take into account solely turnover of the shares of funds that are primary listed in certain country as statistics cover all types of funds, regardless of their primary listing location. Moreover, such a distinction is irrelevant when using turnover indicators as it means a fundamentally different approach to setting the boundaries of the ETFs market. In the case of assets indicators, the analyzed market unit is the specific country and ETFs primary listed on the exchanges in this country are included, whereas in the case of turnover indicators the market unit is stock exchanges in a given country. In most cases the discrepancies will be not substantial as the largest ETFs are usually primary listed and most actively traded on the same exchanges. For less-developed markets the differences may be more significant. For instance, there may be only a few funds primary listed in such a country (or even none), but more funds are traded on local exchanges as a consequence of the cross-listing.

Additional turnover measures which may be employed to describe ETFs market from the trading perspective are the number of ETFs' shares traded or number of transactions on a particular stock exchange. Their usefulness is, though, severely limited as they neglect the value aspect of the transactions. They may be used together with data on the values to calculate, for instance, the average value of transactions in ETF shares conducted on the stock exchange.

For two key reasons we evaluate exclusively data on the transactions conducted on the secondary ETFs markets. Firstly, access to information about the operations on the primary market is limited as they are actually a subject of agreement between the fund's sponsor and APs. Other entities are never or rarely involved, apart from the technical side of the operations. Secondly, and even more importantly, is the fact that such transactions are dependent on events taking place on the secondary market, for example, the creation of the fund's shares results from the demand observed by the AP. Consequently, actions observed on the secondary market may be perceived as indicators of the development of both parts of the ETFs market.

It should be noted that transaction data on the turnover of European-listed funds may be considerably misleading because reporting many such trades has not been obligatory until the inception of the new European Union rules in January 2018, that is, Markets in Financial Instruments Directive (MiFID) II. The previous rules did not require reporting over-the-counter transactions that account for about 70% of European trades in the shares of ETFs according to Bloomberg (Edde & Vaghela, 2017) or two-thirds according to other estimations (Fuhr, 2015). Another problem is the lack of data on trades made across the exchanges which should change with the introduction of consolidated reporting. A further stipulation, raised by Golub et al. (2013) is the lack of information on the "reserve" liquidity, that is, provided by the market makers. As a result, historical ETFs turnover data should be analyzed with caution. Nevertheless, turnover indicators may still give useful insight into the key trends and should not be disregarded.

When ETFs are considered above all as the group of investment funds being a substitute for the more-established mutual funds, the usefulness of the turnover indicators is severely limited as the units of mutual funds are not traded on exchanges which means no turnover measure can be calculated. It should be added that turnover measures are most relevant when ETFs are compared to derivatives with similar exposure or to simply investing in the underlying (tracked) assets instead of using other instruments (particularly in case of equity funds). They may also be applied to comparisons between ETFs and closed-end funds as listing of the shares on exchanges is their common feature.

The distinction between primary and secondary markets, problems with unreported transactions, and no turnover measures for mutual funds become insignificant if the assets of funds are considered as they show the development of both parts of the ETFs market and are unaffected by the missing turnover data. Furthermore, values of assets are reported both for ETFs and mutual funds. A common problem for both turnover and asset data is possible distortions in the evaluation of the individual fund's and entire market's development, linked with the valuation based on market prices.

Despite these limitations, data on turnover was extracted from the monthly reports published by the World Federation of Exchanges (WFE) and, in the case of missing observations for certain countries or time periods, it was supplemented by various documents issued by the local stock exchanges (e.g., monthly and annual reports, their websites, etc.) as well as our own estimations for individual data breaks such as in the case of missing data for only 1 month in the particular year, made by calculating averages of the neighboring values. In the reports by WFE, the value of each transaction is counted from one side only, that is there is no double counting for both purchase and sale.

Apart from assets and turnover, a few additional indicators may be used to more accurately analyze various aspects of the ETFs market—we mention just a few. The number of funds is basically the number of ETFs according to some criterion, for instance, offered by a certain provider or listed in particular country. The applicability of this indicator is limited without simultaneously referring to data on assets or turnover, but it gives some insight into the market's structure. Data on the number of funds listed in particular countries used in our research was extracted from the sources analogous to the ones used in case of the turnover; for market-broad statistics the reports by ETFGI (2016, 2017) were used in order to avoid possible double counting.

Another common measure is cash flows which may be further divided into inflows, outflows and, most importantly, net flows (i.e., difference between inflows and outflows to the funds); sometimes another similar term, that is, "net sales," is used yet it is slightly misleading with reference to ETFs and is more appropriate for, e.g., mutual fund. According to ICI (2017) net cash flow is the amount of cash that flows in or out of investment funds, calculated as the difference between purchases of shares and redemption of shares; in the case of ETFs, these transactions take place on the primary market. Various forms of cash flows indicators may be employed to evaluate the interest of investors in particular funds, segment of the market, or, on a broader scale, to compare the preferences of investors toward various types of investment funds, for example, ETFs versus mutual funds. Nevertheless, their applicability depends on the time frame of the analysis. They show quite accurately short-term switching between various types of funds, but in the long term using them to assess the development of ETFs markets may lead to questionable conclusions. For example, large inflows to a certain fund (or funds) which were preceded by similarly substantial outflows would result in small net flows and not disclose the real intensive activity. Consequently, asset indicators are more reliable for long-term analysis because the fund's assets are, in some part, created by the build-up of net flows (another element is the change in market prices of assets in the portfolio); in shorter terms more robust conclusions in such cases can be drawn from the values of the turnover. Another limitation is the high variability of the flows values which hinders their use in the analysis with many econometric methods. We rarely refer to the cash flows indicators.

Apart from the number of funds and cash flows, other infrequently used indicators which show to some extent certain aspects of the ETFs market development are the number of investors holding the shares of ETFs, number of new launches and closures of funds, volatility of the funds' shares prices, or the number of providers. We do not mention indicators such as average assets per fund because they are derived from baseline measures.

*The time period of our base analysis* (unless stated otherwise) *is January 2004—August 2017*. Before 2004, ETFs markets in most analyzed countries were nonexistent or the assets of primary listed funds were very low, but starting from 2004, some interesting trends can be observed. However, the period of rapid growth started a bit later. The selection of the end of this time period was subjected to data availability as no complete information about assets could be extracted for September 2017 or later months at the time when our database was prepared. In the analysis of the diffusion of ETFs (ETFs markets development) in Europe we use monthly observations for calculations; however, in the subsequent chapters, the annual dataset is mainly utilized because other examined indicators could not be retrieved with monthly frequency. This choice may be perceived as a trade-off: applying daily or weekly observations could possibly contribute to a better understanding of the ETFs markets development (ETFs diffusion) but may introduce more volatility; using annual (or even quarterly) data could simplify the analysis, but it might mask some valuable conclusions that can be reached from an evaluation of within-year changes. In some parts of the study we consider either shorter or longer time periods depending on the data availability in certain context.

### 3.1.2 Examined Exchange-Traded Funds Markets: List of Countries and Selection Criteria

After the discussion concerning the selection and application of the various ETFs market development indicators, we need to explain the reasons behind the choice of the analyzed countries. The basic criterion for our preliminary list was very simple—we selected only the countries in Europe with any sign of local ETFs market activity (members and nonmembers of the European Union (EU), with a few exceptions there are no European ETFs markets outside the EU, so we include mostly EU member states). However, for various reasons, some additional revisions had to be made which limited the list of countries which could be robustly analyzed and we will outline these revisions. As a result, the final list of 12 analyzed countries was created which includes:

1. France
2. Germany
3. Greece
4. Hungary
5. Italy
6. Norway
7. Poland
8. Spain
9. Sweden
10. Switzerland
11. Turkey
12. United Kingdom

Nine of these countries are members of the EU (France, Germany, Greece, Hungary, Italy, Poland, Spain, Sweden, and United Kingdom, with the last country having been in the procedure of exiting the EU) and the three remaining countries (Norway, Switzerland, and Turkey) have strong economic ties to the EU and have adapted in some ways their legal systems to the EU rules.

The first revision concerns one of the major European ETFs markets, that is, in France. In order to facilitate a meaningful analysis of the market trends and development determinants, etc., we decided that all funds primary listed at the European multi-country exchange Euronext are included in the statistics for France. This decision does not affect significantly the results of the research; the size of the local ETFs markets in Euronext's countries other than France (in terms of primary listings) is rather small, with the exception of the Netherlands. The structure of the Euronext's assets of ETFs by the country of primary listing as of end of 2016 was following:

1. France: $78.69 billion; Euronext Paris
2. Netherlands $3.26 billion; Euronext Amsterdam
3. Belgium $97.03 million; Euronext Brussels
4. Portugal $49.24 million; Euronext Lisbon

It should be noted that this data is based on approximations as an accurate division of the assets (or turnover) between the four countries is difficult to evaluate due to the very high level of integration of the four segments, with most instruments that can be traded through venues located in all countries.

The second revision concerns four Baltic and Nordic countries, Latvia, Lithuania, Finland, and Iceland, which are not included in our analysis due to two reasons:

1. They are (together with a few other marketplaces) parts of the same stock exchange group—OMX Nordic Exchange (Nasdaq Nordic). To some extent their situation is similar to the one presented for Euronext yet their total assets of ETFs are much smaller.
2. The key reason is that there are some unclear classifications of the funds in the Lipper's database with regard to these countries. A closer evaluation shows that most funds, which are labeled as ETFs by Lipper and assigned to these markets, are in fact open-end funds which hinders proper analysis.

A special comment regarding country-specific data is necessary for Sweden. Similarly to the other selected countries, we analyze data about assets of ETFs which are designated by Lipper as primary listed in this country. However, for the reasons identical to the countries mentioned (the Swedish stock exchange also belongs to the same conglomerate), detailed analysis concerning other indicators is impossible. Despite our stipulations, we decided not to omit this country in the analysis concerning assets due to the much larger assets of Swedish funds than in case of the other segments of the OMX Nordic Exchange and, consequently, the higher significance of this market on a regional scale.

A third modification of the list of countries is made with regard to a non-EU country, that is, Russia. Funds primary listed in Russia are not included in our research due to the weak institutional links between Russian and EU financial systems which means that this country should be regarded as separate entity in relation to the EU countries which are our main area of interest. Another reason for exclusion of the Russian market is its unusual structure; the turnover of local ETFs is negligible as most investors prefer to purchase foreign ETFs through Russian mutual funds (Tarassov, 2017). Despite some apparent similarities in this issue, another non-EU state, that is, Turkey, is among the analyzed countries as its links with the EU are much more substantial. It is, for example, a part of the EU-Turkey Customs Union. Two other analyzed non-EU countries (Norway and Switzerland) are member states of the European Free Trade Association (EFTA) and have even stronger links.

A fourth, minor revision, refers to the scarce funds that are classified by Lipper as domiciled in Jersey; in order to clarify our analysis, we do not separate Jersey's funds from the other primary listed in the United Kingdom. Another, relatively more significant issue must be mentioned in this context: the vast majority of ETFs in the United Kingdom and Italy are listed on the stock exchanges that are a part of the London Stock Exchange Group (LSEG), that is, London Stock Exchange (LSE) and Borsa Italiana. This means that, at least in terms of the assets, these two ETFs markets may to a large extent be considered jointly and the division of assets is a matter of some assumptions (made by Lipper). As a result, particularly in the case of Italy, we extensively also discuss turnover data (see Section 4.4).

Furthermore, we do not include in our analysis countries where ETFs were incepted at some point, but not launched for sale on the local stock exchange or no data on assets could be obtained by the end of 2016 (according to Lipper), that is, Bulgaria (according to the Deutsche Bank's database at the end of 2016 there was one fund listed in Bulgaria with total assets of €13 million), Cyprus, Romania, and Slovenia (similarly to the other cases, we take into account only primary listing locations). This list shows that there are some countries where the development of the ETFs market may potentially begin in the near future as some of the key steps were already made.

The final issue regarding the selection of countries requires more detailed explanation; it also serves as an introduction to the presentation of the overview of the European ETFs market. Our analysis does not cover two countries with unique states of ETFs markets: Luxembourg and Ireland. In order to understand the reasons for their distinctiveness, it is necessary to take into account the legal issues linked with the European ETFs, above all the possibility to offer funds in several countries (discussed later) and the fact that some countries offer favorable conditions for such investments. Some of the benefits of using Ireland as the place of the domicile for the providers of funds include (O'Sullivan, Cunniff, Harrington, & Murphy, 2011; Yiannaki, 2015): very limited tax burdens (applying both to the managing company and investors), developed regulatory infrastructure aimed at attracting providers of investment funds, and governmental treaties regulating introduction of Ireland domiciled funds on foreign markets (not only in the EU). Luxembourg is chosen for similar reasons which include (apart from the already listed) (Association of the Luxembourg Fund Industry, 2013): political and economic stability, competitive legal and regulatory framework, and a developed legal, technological, etc., environment surrounding the financial industry.

For these reasons outlined, Ireland and Luxembourg are selected by many of the largest financial companies operating in Europe as their headquarters (at least in legal terms). Due to the very high level of standardization and EU-level common regulations, funds domiciled in Luxembourg or Ireland may be easily offered in other countries of the EU. This means, however, that it is very difficult to analyze the actual level of the ETFs market development in those two countries as it would require to unambiguously determine which funds are listed primary on the local exchanges and which should be included in the lists for other countries. For instance, as of 2016 year-end, according to WFE there were approximately 120 funds listed on the Luxembourg Stock Exchange (this includes cross-listings); Deutsche Bank's reports provide no such data, and in the Lipper's database there are 15 funds with values of assets available. In case of Ireland the differences are even more substantial. This issue becomes even more confusing when we look at the statistics concerning the numbers and assets of domiciled funds.

In order to more accurately discuss the source of these differences, we may refer to the Deutsche Bank's database on the ETFs domiciled in Europe (Deutsche Bank, 2017b, 2017c). It should be remembered that in our analysis of the ETFs markets development (diffusion of ETFs) presented in this chapter we use a different definition of European funds classified by the country of their primary listing according to the Lipper's database rather than the country of their domicile. Moreover, it is necessary to add that, despite these differences, we use Deutsche Bank's database as the source of data on certain attributes of the aggregated European ETFs market in the general discussion in this section, e.g., its structure framed in terms of providers, exposure, and total expense ratios. In these aspects, particularly on a regional scale, the differences between categorization by country by domicile and primary listing become insignificant, with the exception of the country-level lists.

Another source of potential discrepancies lies in the exchange rate; Deutsche Bank's reports on the European ETFs provide data in Euros while we use US dollars to facilitate comparisons between various countries and regions. The next possible reason is the classification of financial products and utilized data sources which differ to some extent, yet not significantly. There are also some differences in the considered lists of countries, e.g., Deutsche Bank does not distinctively include Russia (which is omitted in our research), Poland, and Turkey in the main list of European countries—Russia is classified as a part of BRIC and both Poland and Turkey are in the EMEA (Europe, Middle East, and Africa) categories. These discrepancies are mostly irrelevant in the context of the aggregate European statistics due to the minimal development of ETFs markets in these countries (in all studied dimensions).

Discrepancies between the approach of the Deutsche Bank and our method of the ETFs market development's analysis can be presented most evidently by referring to the general data on the assets as of end of December 2016. According to the Deutsche Bank, the total assets of 1507 ETFs domiciled in European countries were at $555 billion. Ireland and Luxembourg were two European leaders in terms of the domiciled funds (see the detailed breakdown in Fig. 3.1): at the end of 2016 there were ETFs with more than $306 billion of assets domiciled in Ireland, and with about $86 billion in Luxembourg, meaning that more than the half of European funds was managed by companies legally established in those two countries. When we look at the largest European ETFs markets (in terms of our basic approach; see Fig. 3.5) there were only 117 funds domiciled in Germany (with $53 billion of assets) and only one in the United Kingdom with low assets (with the addition of 9 more funds in Jersey); the position of France as a place of ETFs' domicile was much stronger as there were 308 funds with approximately $80 billion of assets.

### 3.1.3 Overview of the European Exchange-Traded Funds Markets

As of end of 2016, the total assets of European ETFs by primary listing locations of funds (in our baseline approach) were estimated at $544 billion, that is, almost the same value as in the Deutsche Bank's database.

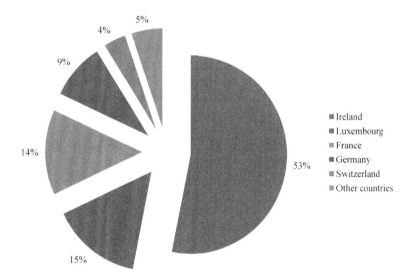

**FIGURE 3.1** Structure of the European ETFs market; assets of European ETFs by the country of domicile. 2016, year-end data. *ETF*, Exchange-traded fund. Source: *Own estimations based on Deutsche Bank (2017c)*. Europe ETF + quarterly directory.

**TABLE 3.1**    Assets of the European Exchange-Traded Funds by Country of Primary Listing. Detailed List. End of August 2017

| Country | Assets (mln USD) | Assets (% of the aggregate European market) | Assets (% of local GDP) | Assets (mln USD)—end of 2016 |
|---|---|---|---|---|
| United Kingdom | 312,100.05 | 45.017 | 9.35 | 252,295.32 |
| Germany | 188,704.77 | 27.219 | 4.25 | 148,911.99 |
| France | 111,308.56 | 16.055 | 3.29 | 78,762.55 |
| Switzerland | 73,298.87 | 10.573 | 8.12 | 54,396.83 |
| Sweden | 3471.64 | 0.501 | 0.57 | 2868.18 |
| Italy | 2344.36 | 0.338 | 0.10 | 1241.35 |
| Spain | 1821.54 | 0.263 | 0.11 | 1414.89 |
| Norway | 135.97 | 0.020 | 0.04 | 128.74 |
| Turkey | 48.55 | 0.007 | <0.01 | 40.11 |
| Poland | 32.07 | 0.005 | <0.01 | 21.03 |
| Greece | 16.03 | 0.002 | <0.01 | 15.86 |
| Hungary | 6.08 | 0.001 | 0.01 | 13.86 |
| Total | 693,288.48 | 100 | – | 540,110.71 |

*Note*: Data for assets as a % of local GDP as of end of December 2016.
In italics values as of end of 2016.
*Own estimations.*

According to ETFGI (2017), there were 1560 European ETFs, also very similar to the count of the Deutsche Bank. However, the structure of the market in terms of division of assets between countries differs considerably as will be shown in detail; see Fig. 3.5 and Table 3.1. What is important, though, in this context is the fact that all funds primary listed in Europe are domiciled in one of the countries of this region; there are no ETFs domiciled outside Europe, for example, in some off-shore locations. This fact may to a large extent be explained by the legal requirements concerning the introduction of funds to the European financial markets. The dominant group of funds is structured according to the rules that require European domicile (Bush, Lee, Ferguson, & Forstenhausler, 2015).

Next, we scrutinize the key measures of the European ETFs markets and present some key conclusions, starting with the discussion of the trends in the time period 2004−16 (we do not use pre-2004 data due to negligible development of the ETFs markets; data for the entire 2017 was not available during the writing of this book), followed by an in-depth evaluation of its structure in various dimensions. In our analysis we consider the *regional European ETFs market, that is, aggregate of all European ETFs markets.* We use two lists of European ETFs markets: (1) constructed in the course of our study which includes 12 countries; and (2) by Deutsche Bank which is used only in the case of data extracted from the publications prepared by this company.

We begin our discussion by presenting the three chosen key indicators which may be utilized to evaluate the trends in the (regional) European ETFs market development: assets, turnover, and number of funds; discussing most extensively the assets, our fundamental research approach.

We present firstly aggregate assets indicators expressed in US dollars. At the end of 2004, the total assets of the European ETFs amounted to $33.4 billion (see Fig. 3.2). Since 2004 the assets have been increasing quickly, with the average annual growth rate of c. 28%—their growth was most rapid over the period 2005−10 when the average annual growth rate was at c. 44%. For example, in 2009 the value of assets grew by more than 57% compared with the previous year which means that the rebound after the global financial crisis was very substantial; it was the second-highest rate of growth after year 2006 when the record high of 74% was noted. Even in 2008 assets did not decline, but increased by c. 14%. This shows that the growth trend of the European market was to a large extent unaffected by the turmoil on the global financial markets linked with the mortgage-backed securities breakdown and the chain of further events.

The positive trend was interrupted in 2011 when the eurozone debt crisis had a noticeable impact on the European financial systems (including, e.g., declines of the prices of various financial assets) and ETFs markets were not an exception. In 2011, the assets of European innovative funds declined on an annual basis for the first

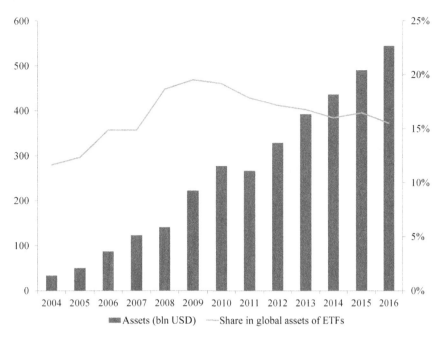

**FIGURE 3.2** Total assets of European ETFs. 2004−16, year-end data. *ETF*, Exchange-traded fund. Source: *Own estimations.*

time since their launch. The level of the decrease was rather small, at only c. 4%, but it still meant a break in the previous trend. In some aspects the year 2011 represents, thus, the "critical point" of the European ETFs markets development as it marked the change of its trajectory (see references to the diffusion concepts). Starting from 2012, the assets of European innovative funds continued to grow, but at much slower rate than pre-2011; the average annual growth rate for the 2012−16 period was at c. 16%. It should be stressed that this apparent slowdown was not caused by, for example, a decrease in the demand from investors. When changes in the values of assets expressed in US dollars are considered, we may notice that, for instance, in 2013 the assets of European ETFs grew by almost $64 billion (the second-highest observed value, after c. $81 billion in 2009). In 2015 and 2016 they increased by c. $54 billion. The reduced rate of growth may be explained referring to the treatment of ETFs as innovations. After 2012, the European ETFs markets entered the stage of slower growth as the financial system became, to a higher degree, saturated with innovative funds. The continuation of the positive trend shows, though, that their diffusion is still far from complete. At the end of 2016, the value of European ETFs reached a record-high level of more than $544 billion which means that in comparison to the end of 2004 the value of their assets increased by c. 1500%, corresponding to $511 billion in dollar terms, that is, almost half a trillion US dollars growth over 13 years.

Assets of European innovative funds may also be compared to the assets of the global ETFs market which consists mostly of the funds listed (and also domiciled, traded, etc.) in three regions: North America (above all in the United States), Asia-Pacific, and Europe. Fig. 3.2 shows the percentage share of the assets of European ETFs in the global value. At the beginning of their rapid growth stage, in 2004, European ETFs accounted for c. 11.7% of the global assets. Six years later, at the 2010 peak-point of the fast expansion phase, they reached the highest share of almost 20%. However, since 2010 the position of European funds began to weaken in comparison to the rest of the world; in 2016 their share in the global assets was at the lowest level since 2007. The most substantial decline was noticed in 2011 (the year that we labeled as the critical point) which can be explained basically. In 2011 the assets of European ETFs fell due to the eurozone crisis whereas the global assets grew slightly. After 2011, the global market continued to grow at a faster rate than the European market due to being fueled by the development of the United States and major Asia-Pacific markets. The weakening of the European position in the context of the global ETFs industry is also linked with the rapid emergence of previously small or even negligibly small ETFs markets in countries such as Australia, and even more importantly, India or in mainland China. In Europe the list of leading countries remains almost intact and no new significant markets have developed, although Italy is potentially the sole exception.

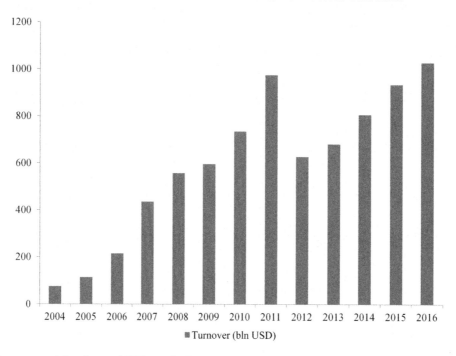

**FIGURE 3.3**  Total turnover of the shares of ETFs on the European stock exchanges. 2004–16, annual data. *ETF*, Exchange-traded fund. Source: *Own estimations.*

The next measure of the European ETFs markets development (conveying slightly different information than assets indicators) is the dollar value of the turnover on the European stock exchanges, shown in Fig. 3.3. As it may be clearly noticed, the period of the rapid growth of the turnover was similar to the one characterized for assets, that is, up to 2010. It proves that 2004–10 was a period of fast expansion of innovative funds in Europe. However, data for 2011 shows a substantial difference between assets and turnover indicators. It was the year of the second-highest turnover of the shares of ETFs on the European stock exchanges in the considered period whereas the value of assets declined for the first time in this time period. It may be, thus, concluded that the intensive activity on the European market was at least to some extent caused by investors who decreased their allocation to ETFs and sold their shares. Another reason was uncertainty inflicted by various economic and political events in the EU, particularly related to the situation of Greece which resulted in an increased number and value of transactions linked with entering or closing positions in ETFs. Interestingly, data on other parts of the financial markets such stock or bond markets (as well as exchange-listed derivatives) do not indicate substantial increases in the turnover in comparison to the previous years; in fact, in Germany and France (according to the reports by the WFE) turnover on both stock and bond markets was significantly lower than in the previous years. It may be, therefore, with considerable caution, interpreted that ETFs were one of the main tools used to react to the dynamically changing economic and political situation. In 2012, the turnover declined significantly to the level comparable with 2009, but over the next few years it has grown rapidly reaching the record-high level of more than a trillion US dollars in 2016. In comparison, turnover for the 12 months of 2004 was only c. $76 billion. This means a 1260% growth over the thirteen-year period, which is lower than in the case of assets, yet is still substantial. This rather basic analysis of the total turnover of ETFs in Europe shows that the overall trend in the value of transactions is shaped by the same factors as assets yet the differences may be noticed, particularly in the times of magnified uncertainty. Due to lack of data on some stock exchanges (not all major marketplaces are members of WFE and data from other sources are inconsistent) we do not evaluate the share of European exchanges in the total global turnover.

The third, yet least substantive, indicator of the ETFs markets development that we present is the total number of innovative funds listed in Europe. To ensure consistency, we use aggregate data on the European and global market from ETFGI; see Fig. 3.4. In contrast with either assets or turnover, the number of funds has been increasing over the entire 2004–16 period. However, the rate of growth slowed down after 2010 for reasons similar to the ones concerning assets. In 2004 there were 113 ETFs listed in Europe and in 2016 their number increased to 1560; each fund is counted only once; due to cross-listing within Europe and (less frequent) listing of funds not

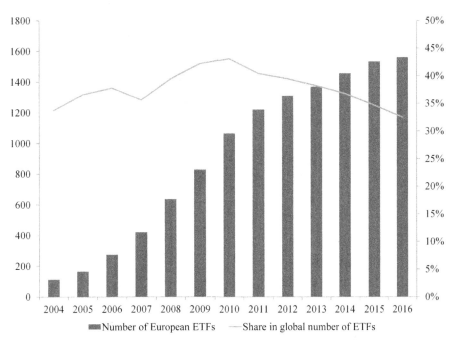

FIGURE 3.4 Total number of European ETFs. 2004–16, year-end data. *ETF*, Exchange-traded fund. Source: *Own estimations.*

primary listed in Europe, the number of actually available funds on some exchanges may even exceed the total European count, e.g., in case of the LSEG. The share of European ETFs in the global number of innovative funds has varied between c. 32% and 43% (average annual value of c. 38%), considerably higher percentage than in terms of assets which means (using a simplistic measure) that European funds are on average smaller than the typical funds in the world. Overall trends in the market share closely resemble the ones observed for assets and it can be assumed that they are shaped by similar determinants. It should be noted, though, that the analysis of the European market in terms of the number of funds may lead to partially misleading conclusions, particularly when it is juxtaposed with other regions; for instance, European markets may seem to be more developed than its United States counterpart due to the larger number of funds in some periods even though the value of their aggregated assets is much lower. The high number of ETFs in Europe is to some extent artificially inflated by the lack of a single market for the innovative funds; in many cases basically the same fund in terms of exposure, provider, and other key attributes is divided into a few separate funds, offered on different exchanges, with varying share classes or currencies (Abner, 2016).

After this presentation of the general trends in the 2004–16 period, we turn our attention to the analysis of the structure of the European ETFs industry in a few selected crucial dimensions; in the analysis by countries we consider exclusively the selected 12 countries. First and foremost, we discuss its structure in our base approach, that is, by assets according to the location of primary listing, starting with the division between countries. Strikingly, the chosen countries may be divided into three groups which consist of almost equal number of economies: "top," "middle," and "bottom" in terms of the assets of the local ETFs.

As Fig. 3.5 distinctively shows, there are four European countries that account for almost the entire assets of the innovative funds primary listed in the region: the United Kingdom, Germany, France, and Switzerland. The regional leader is the United Kingdom as the assets of ETFs in this country are close to half of the aggregate European value. Their value as of the end of August 2017 amounted to more than $312 billion, that is, c. 45% of the total regional market (see Table 3.1 for the detailed allocation). The leading position of the UK ETFs market may be attributed to a number of factors, among them the size of its financial markets and the entire financial sector as one of the most crucial reasons; the United Kingdom is considered to be one of the world's financial centers, with a large number of financial institutions and highly developed financial infrastructure. Germany is directly behind the United Kingdom in this ranking, yet with significantly lower value of assets and share in the regional market, that is, c. $189 billion and 27% correspondingly. Those two countries account together for almost three quarters of the entire European ETFs market. The third and final country with assets exceeding $100 billion was France (the actual value was even lower because statistics for France include also values of assets of three

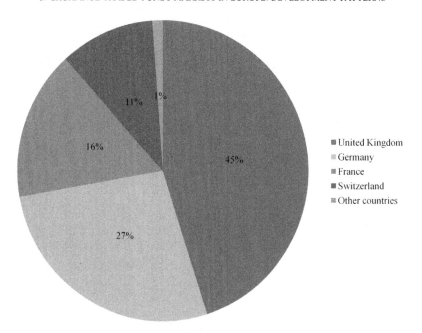

**FIGURE 3.5** Assets of the European ETFs by country of primary listing. End of August 2017. *ETF*, Exchange-traded fund. *Source: Own estimations.*

other much smaller economies). The last country in the top category is Switzerland, with the share exceeding 10%. Switzerland is in many aspects a different case than the other three countries—it is not a member of the EU and its economy is much smaller. However, the high value of the assets of ETFs may be explained by the size of its financial sector and globally leading financial institutions (e.g., banks).

Sweden, Italy, and Spain comprise a "middle" group between the regional leaders in terms of assets and countries that apparently lag behind. The assets of their locally primary listed ETFs are much lower than in the top group and the sum of their shares in the European market merely exceeds 1.1%. However, these values are incomparably higher than for the last group. The position of Italy in this group is particular and should be regarded with caution as data on assets considerably understate the actual level of ETFs market development, e.g., turnover statistics position this country among the European leaders (the reason for this discrepancy is the place of the Italian stock exchange within the LSEG group; see Section 4.4 which is dedicated exclusively to this country). Generally, the three middle countries are economies with some potential for further ETFs market development, yet reaching high values of assets may take several years.

The conclusion that may be drawn from the analysis of the division of assets among countries is the evident prevalence of the most-developed economies. The position of the relatively less-developed countries such as Turkey, Poland, Greece, or Hungary is extremely weak as evidenced by the values of their ETF assets and their share in the aggregate market. The financial systems of these four countries are also comparatively less advanced when juxtaposed with the top or even middle category evidenced by, e.g., bank deposits or stock market capitalization in relation to GDP; naturally, the differences are not so obvious in certain cases. It may, thus, seem that the assets of ETFs tend to be lower in less-developed countries. However, another, fifth country in the "bottom" group, Norway, is an example of a country which does not adhere to these attributes as it has one of the most advanced economies in the world.

Another more convincing, yet only apparently, joint preliminary explanation for the five bottom countries' backwardness with regard to the values of ETFs' assets could be formulated with reference to the size of their economies; one could state that the assets of their ETFs are lower simply because their economies (e.g., in terms of GDP) are smaller than in the case of the three major countries: UK, Germany, and France—for Switzerland such a conclusion would be less valid. We attempt to explicate the factors that influence the development of the European ETFs markets in Chapter 4, Determinants of the European Exchange-Traded Funds Markets Development, yet we may already state that the size of the economy may not be simply regarded as the major determinant of this process and should not be used in such analysis. There is no straightforward relationship implying that in smaller economies the assets of ETFs are lower, whereas in larger economies the assets of innovative funds are higher. For this purpose, we refer to data on the assets of ETFs in relation to GDP (see the fourth column in Table 3.1). It can be clearly noticed that again three groups can be distinguished and, more importantly, that they cover the same countries—there are only some slight changes in the order within each group; the most significant one is second place being Switzerland, with assets of ETFs which reached 8.12% of the local GDP, much more than in Germany or France. It provides, thus, almost exactly the same results as in the neighboring column and confirms the irrelevance of the hypothesis stressing the role of the economy's size.

Before we proceed to the further discussion, it must be emphasized that here we do not attempt to explain in detail the reasons for each country's ETFs market's development position (or its lack). This will be addressed throughout the further parts of the book as this presentation is only introductory.

A comparison of the values of assets at the end of 2016 (see the auxiliary, most-right column in Table 3.1) and 8 months later, at the end of August 2017, supplements the conclusions from the analysis of Fig. 3.2 and confirms that the rapid growth of the regional market's assets continued in 2017. The only country where the assets of innovative funds have declined is the smallest among the studied European ETFs markets, in Hungary. Overall, the rate of growth of aggregate assets of ETFs in Europe has been in the first 8 months of 2017 at the highest level since 2009.

After discussing data on individual countries, we adopt a different perspective to the analysis of the European ETFs market and discuss its structure according to the categories of funds in terms of exposure, followed by the ranking of the largest European-listed funds. For data availability reasons, except for the ranking of the funds, we use data on the underlying asset classes extracted from the Deutsche Bank's reports rather than from our customized database (discrepancies are irrelevant in this context).

Figs. 3.6 and 3.7 show the general layout of the European ETFs markets divided into three groups according to the underlying asset class (i.e., the asset class of the fund's exposure, the one that serves as the benchmark for the fund, usually some type of index). The vast majority of the European ETFs are passive or enhanced indexing funds, the role of active funds is minimal (Deutsche Bank, 2017b) which means that Figs. 3.6 and 3.7 show the tracked classes of assets. As it may be clearly noticed, the largest group of ETFs both in terms of assets and the number of ETFs, are equity funds whose regional market share was at c. 71%. At the end of November 2017 there were more than 1100 such funds primary listed on the European exchanges, compared with 390 funds with exposure to fixed income securities and merely 71 funds that are benchmarked to the prices of commodities or offer other exposure, e.g., multi-class. Presented data confirm that the European ETFs market is very similar in this aspect to its counterparts in, for instance, the United States due to the leading position of the most established equity funds, followed by the bond funds yet with much smaller market share. When we compare November 2017 with 2016 year-end data (Deutsche Bank, 2017b) we can notice the relative strengthening of the position equity market's funds at the expense of the two other groups; the exact market share of equity ETFs has grown

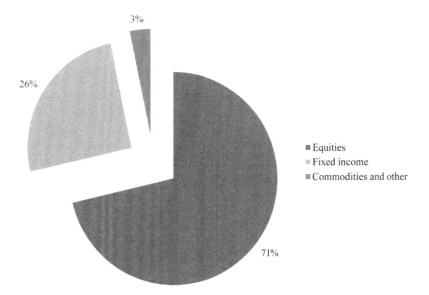

**FIGURE 3.6** Assets of European ETFs by benchmarked asset classes. End of November 2017. *ETF*, Exchange-traded fund. *Source: Own estimations.*

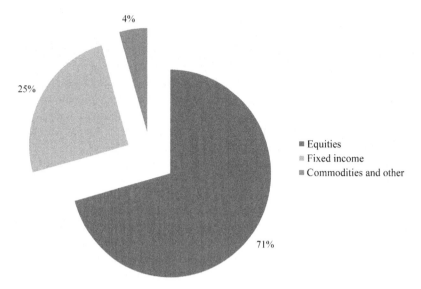

FIGURE 3.7 Number of European ETFs by benchmarked asset classes. End of November 2017. *ETF*, Exchange-traded fund. Source: *Own estimations*.

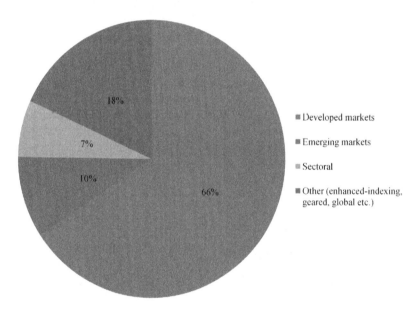

FIGURE 3.8 European equity ETFs—assets by benchmarked equity class. End of November 2017. *ETF*, Exchange-traded fund. Source: *Own estimations*.

from 69.8% to 71.4%, by 1.6%. In absolute terms (values expressed in either EUR or USD) the assets of all three categories have increased over the first 11 months of 2017, but for equity funds this growth has been most substantial, which may be attributed to the significant increases of most global and European stock market indexes over this period.

Figs. 3.8 and 3.9 present the detailed structure of two major categories of ETFs in Europe: equity and bond ETFs. In the case of equity funds, most assets (about two-thirds) are held by ETFs that track the returns of the indexes of stock markets in single developed countries (or their groups). Only 10% track benchmarks of single emerging stock markets (or their groups) and 7% are linked to indexes constructed using the sectoral not country-wise criteria. The remaining 18% of assets are managed by the other types of equity ETFs, mostly enhanced-indexing or geared funds (apart from them, e.g., with global exposure). Even closer scrutiny shows that in the group of the developed markets ETFs merely two types account for c. 60% of the total assets, that is, the ones tracking broad European and US stock indexes (in particular S&P 500). These results can be explained

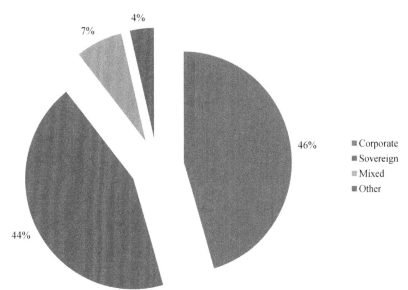

**FIGURE 3.9** European bond ETFs—assets by benchmarked bond class. End of November 2017. *ETF*, Exchange-traded fund. *Source: Own estimations.*

by considering the size and liquidity of the tracked markets as individual European stock markets are relatively small in terms of the turnover and capitalization when compared to the US market; another reason for the high share of broad-European indexes is the considerable level of integration of the stock markets in the EU. What is important, the third place in the category of developed markets ETFs belongs to Japan (c. 8% share). The highest share of an individual European country was noticed for Germany (c. 7%); it shows that European participants of ETFs markets to a large extent use these funds to gain exposure to the foreign equities as they may access the domestic (or other European) markets using different financial products. In the group of emerging markets funds, the most assets were accumulated by ETFs with exposure to the largest economies, that is, BRIC (Brazil, Russia, India, and China; within this group almost half is invested in Chinese-exposure equity funds). Among the sectoral equity ETFs, funds tracking indexes of the financial industry are the leader, followed by real estate and energy funds. In the "other" category, various smart beta or comparable ETFs manage most assets.

The structure of the bond ETFs market is more complicated, with no clear leading group (see Fig. 3.9). the vast majority of the European market is split between funds that offer exposure to corporate and sovereign bonds. Remaining c. 7% belongs to funds that track mixed benchmarks, composed of both groups as well as some more complicated types of bond ETFs (tracking returns on covered bonds, collateralized with some assets, or indexes based on credit default swaps) and money-market ETFs which are not presented separately due to their minimal assets. Most sovereign bond ETFs are connected to fixed coupon securities, ones tracking inflation-linked bonds are rare (Deutsche Bank, 2017c). Some European bond ETFs are geared, similarly to leveraged, short, and other geared equity funds. In terms of the geographical exposure, most funds track bond markets in the developed economies, above all markets for fixed income securities issued by the countries of the eurozone.

Comparison of the total expense ratios (TERs) of European ETFs (Fig. 3.10) shows that bond funds are the most cost-effective and commodity funds may be regarded as the least cost-effective (the very small number of commodity funds means, though, that these results should be interpreted with caution). Providers of the funds have been lowering the costs over recent years, partially as a part of competition between various financial companies. Noticeable differences between weighted and simple averages may be considered, in case of equity and commodity ETFs, as the proof for cost limitation possibilities in the larger funds (economies of scale); however, for bond ETFs smaller funds tend to operate less expensively which may be related to the problems typical for this group such as limited liquidity of the tracked markets (encountered by the larger funds) that may hinder their expansion. These results may not be directly compared with the TERs calculated for the US market due to the varying classification of the funds yet in both regions the observed TERs for ETFs were significantly below 1% and the costs of equity funds were higher than costs of bond funds. Within both categories passive products are the least expensive.

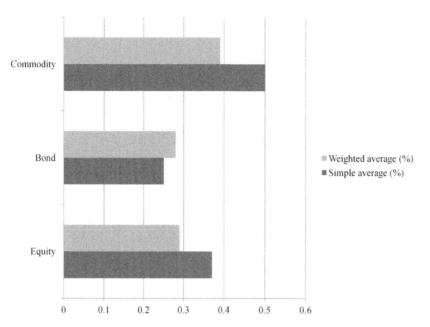

**FIGURE 3.10**    Total expense ratios of European ETFs by the categories of the benchmarked asset classes. End of October 2017.
*Note*: Weighted average, with values of assets applied as weights. Total expense ratio is calculated as total (operating) costs divided by total assets. *ETF*, Exchange-traded fund. Source: *Own estimations*.

Table 3.2 provides the ranking of the 12 largest European ETFs, positioned according to their assets. Each fund accounts for at least 1% of the aggregate assets of European ETFs and their combined share is close to 20% which means that almost one out of five US dollars in the European innovative funds are managed within this relatively small group. Most of the largest ETFs are equity funds; there are only three bond funds on the list which corresponds to the overall structure of the European market, discussed in the preceding paragraphs. Two of the biggest funds offer exposure to the US equity market—they track the S&P 500 index identically to the world's largest ETF, SPDR S&P 500. The third-largest European ETF tracks the MSCI index which covers multiple world's equity markets. Benchmarks based on the European financial markets are relatively less common, only five funds on the list track such indexes, which indicates that funds that attract the most capital from investors are used to gain exposure to the non-European assets; for investment in European assets other financial products are used, not necessarily shares of innovative funds. The largest bond fund on the list is iShares Core Corp Bond UCITS ETF EUR (Dist), with c. $9.4 billion of assets; it tracks the returns of the index which covers corporate bonds in the eurozone. Two remaining bond ETFs on the list offer exposure to emerging markets' bonds.

As it can be noticed in Table 3.2, BlackRock is the provider of most funds (two funds are managed by Vanguard and Lyxor). There are no funds provided by the Deutsche Bank's asset management division (Deutsche AM[1]), even though this company is the second-largest in Europe in terms of managed assets of ETFs (an analysis of the providers is given next). As it is shown later, the Deutsche AM manages ETFs that are on average smaller than the ones offered by BlackRock.

Most of the biggest European ETFs are primary listed on the largest European stock exchange, that is, LSE, and they are domiciled in Ireland. The remaining funds are primary listed in France and Germany are domiciled in that country, identically in the case of the only French fund (both listed and domiciled in that country). What is remarkable is that there are no funds domiciled in Luxembourg on the list even though it is the second most-popular European location for the formal inception of ETFs (see Fig. 3.1). This indicates that this domicile has not only attracted lower aggregated assets (or number) of ETFs, but it is also used by smaller funds than Ireland. In order to emphasize this point, we estimated two basic descriptive statistics for these two domiciles. The average value of assets of ETFs domiciled in Ireland was at the end of 2016 and was more than 115% higher than in Luxembourg; the difference in medians was much smaller, at c. 19%. The largest fund domiciled in Luxembourg (and also the largest one managed by Deutsche AM) was as of end of 2016 db x-trackers Euro Stoxx 50 UCITS

---

[1]Throughout the book we use the name "Deutsche AM." However, it must be noted that during writing, in early 2018, asset management division of Deutsche Bank had begun rebranding to the new name: "DWS."

**TABLE 3.2** 12 Largest European Exchange-Traded Funds (ETFs) in Terms of Assets. End of August 2017

| Fund | Assets (bln USD) | Assets (% of the aggregate European market) | Exposure class | Benchmark | Provider | Primary listing exchange | Domicile | Total expense ratio (%) | Tracking error (%) | Replication method |
|------|------|------|------|------|------|------|------|------|------|------|
| iShares Core S&P 500 UCITS ETF USD (Acc) | 22.95 | 3.31 | Equity US | S&P 500 | BlackRock | London Stock Exchange (UK) | Ireland | 0.07 | 0.18 | Physical |
| Vanguard S&P 500 UCITS ETF | 19.06 | 2.75 | Equity US | S&P 500 | Vanguard | London Stock Exchange (UK) | Ireland | 0.07 | 0.23 | Physical |
| iShares Core MSCI World UCITS ETF USD (Acc) | 10.77 | 1.55 | Equity global | MSCI World | BlackRock | London Stock Exchange (UK) | Ireland | 0.20 | 0.38 | Physical |
| iShares EURO STOXX 50 UCITS (DE) ETF | 10.52 | 1.52 | Equity eurozone | EURO STOXX 50 | BlackRock | Xetra (Germany) | Germany | 0.16 | 1.40 | Physical |
| iShares Core DAX UCITS ETF (DE) | 9.94 | 1.43 | Equity Germany | DAX 30 | BlackRock | Xetra (Germany) | Germany | 0.16 | 0.40 | Physical |
| iShares Core Corp Bond UCITS ETF EUR (Dist) | 9.41 | 1.36 | Bond corporate | Bloomberg Barclays Euro Aggregate Corporate | BlackRock | London Stock Exchange (UK) | Ireland | 0.20 | 0.86 | Physical |
| Lyxor Euro Stoxx 50 (DR) UCITS ETF D-EUR | 8.47 | 1.22 | Equity eurozone | EURO STOXX 50 | Lyxor | Euronext Paris (France) | France | 0.20 | 0.67 | Physical |
| iShares J.P. Morgan $ EM Bond UCITS ETF USD (Dist) | 8.15 | 1.18 | Bond emerging markets | JP Morgan EMBI Global Diversified | BlackRock | London Stock Exchange (UK) | Ireland | 0.45 | 0.91 | Physical |
| iShares S&P 500 UCITS ETF USD (Dist) | 7.56 | 1.09 | Equity US | S&P 500 | BlackRock | London Stock Exchange (UK) | Ireland | 0.07 | 0.20 | Physical |
| iShares Core MSCI EM IMI UCITS ETF USD (Acc) | 6.98 | 1.01 | Equity emerging markets | MSCI Emerging Markets IMI | BlackRock | London Stock Exchange (UK) | Ireland | 0.25 | 1.11 | Physical |
| iShares JP Morgan EM Local Gov Bond UCITS ETF | 6.92 | 1.00 | Bond emerging markets | J.P. Morgan GBI-EM Global Diversified 10% Cap 1% Floor | BlackRock | London Stock Exchange (UK) | Ireland | 0.50 | 4.00 | Physical |
| iShares STOXX Europe 600 UCITS (DE) ETF | 6.91 | 1.00 | Equity Europe | STOXX Europe 600 | BlackRock | Xetra (Germany) | Germany | 0.20 | 1.27 | Physical |

*Notes*: Tracking error for the one-year period April 2017–March 2018, extracted from TrackInsight database. Some common abbreviations are used for the names of the funds by their providers: UCITS—see discussion of the legal structures; Dist—incomes received from assets held by the fund are distributed among shareholders; Acc—incomes are accumulated within the fund; DE—Germany; EM—emerging markets. *UCITS*, Undertakings for Collective Investment in Transferable Securities.

*Own elaboration.*

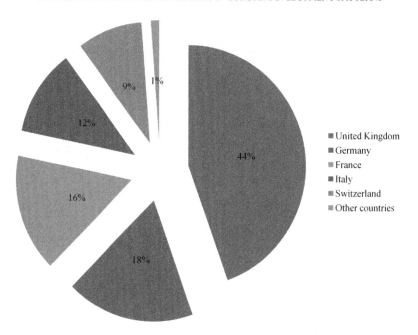

**FIGURE 3.11**    Turnover of the shares of ETFs on the European stock exchanges. 2016, Annual data. *ETF*, Exchange-traded fund. *Source: Own estimations.*

ETF (DR)-1D, with the German Xetra as the place of primary listing; it was, however, c. 12.6% smaller than the last fund in Table 3.2.

Total expense ratios of most of the largest European ETFs are much lower than the average values calculated for the entire market (compare Table 3.2 with Fig. 3.10), with the notable exception of the emerging markets bonds ETFs which confirms the previously discussed conclusions, indicating the problems of the largest funds within this category. The final important conclusion which can be drawn from Table 3.2 refers to the replication methods of the funds. Among the current European leaders there are no synthetic funds which proves the limited role of this replication method, an issue which is covered in more detail in Section 5.3.

After focusing on various indicators of the regional structure based mostly on assets or number of funds, we now focus on another approach to the development of ETFs markets, that is, in terms of the turnover of their shares. We treat this approach as secondary (due to its weaknesses), therefore, we discuss only basic statistics, starting again with the structure of the market divided by countries (countries in which certain stock exchanges are located), followed by the funds' turnover by the benchmarked asset classes.

Identically, as in case of assets, the United Kingdom is the regional leader in terms of turnover of ETFs' shares (see Fig. 3.11). In both cases almost the same market share of close to 45% is observed. The LSE is also the European leader in terms of stock turnover, which is closely linked to the transactions in the shares of ETFs. Germany is directly behind the United Kingdom, yet with a substantially lower share than in case of assets indicators (18% vs 27%) which indicates that large assets of ETFs primary listed in Germany are not necessarily matched by the high turnover of their shares on the German stock exchanges. This conclusion is also proven by the comparison of the absolute values of assets and turnover (compare the last columns in Table 3.1 and second in Table 3.3). For Germany and Switzerland, the ratios of turnover to assets were the lowest among the major European ETFs markets at c. 120% while for the United Kingdom and France they were at c. 180% and 200%, respectively. The share of the third country, France, is almost identical regardless whether we consider assets or turnover; for Switzerland the difference is not very significant—c. 1.5 p.p.

A comparison of the turnover and assets statistics proves that Italy is probably the most interesting case. The value of the assets managed by ETFs that is primary listed in Italy is lower even than in Sweden, but when the turnover of the ETFs' shares is considered Italy is among the leaders in the region, with the share of c. 11.5%. The reason for this apparent discrepancy lies in the structure of the Italian trading facility; the Italian stock exchange is a part of the LSEG together with, inter alia, the LSE (there are no such strong links between any other two markets we consider). Primary listing in Italy is rather uncommon and most such funds manage rather low assets and they are usually some variants of funds listed on the other exchanges. An analysis of the turnover

**TABLE 3.3** Turnover of the Shares of Exchange-Traded Funds on European Stock Exchanges. Detailed List. 2016, Annual Data

| Country | Turnover (mln USD) | Turnover (% of the aggregate European market) |
|---|---|---|
| United Kingdom | 457,522.36 | 44.527 |
| Germany | 183,944.82 | 17.902 |
| France | 162,117.84 | 15.778 |
| Italy | 118,666.73 | 11.549 |
| Switzerland | 93,386.37 | 9.088 |
| Spain | 6657.24 | 0.648 |
| Norway | 4385.65 | 0.427 |
| Turkey | 793.34 | 0.077 |
| Poland | 44.34 | 0.004 |
| Greece | 4.01 | 0.0004 |
| Hungary | 1.50 | 0.0001 |
| Sweden | NA | NA |
| Total | 1,027,524.18 | 100 |

*Note*: NA—data not available.
*Own estimations.*

statistics for Italy proves that despite this apparent weakness (yet mostly in formal terms), this market shows signs of substantial development. We devote Section 4.4 to discuss this issue.

Turnover of the remaining stock exchanges is low (in the case of Spain or Norway a much higher value of turnover compared to the assets in the latter country can to some degree be explained by intensive trading in a very limited number of funds, particularly leveraged ones) or even very low in the countries that also lag behind in terms of assets (apparent discrepancies between values of assets and turnover, and, consequently, very high or low turnover ratios should not be considered on such small markets).

Analysis of the European market's structure with the funds divided according to the benchmarked asset classes, conducted in terms of the assets, showed the prevalence of equity ETFs. When turnover indicators are considered (see Fig. 3.12) the results are highly similar, yet the domination of equity ETFs is even more clear; they are the most intensively traded category of innovative funds and account for c. 77% of the total turnover. Share of bond ETFs seems to be considerably lower in terms of turnover—20% versus 26% when assets are considered. One of the possible explanations is the difference in applications of equity and bond funds; ETFs offering exposure to fixed income securities may be perceived in some aspects as an alternative to the outright purchase of such securities and used for strategies with longer time horizons than in case of equities. Share of commodity ETFs is close to 3% regardless of the measurement approach, which confirms their negligible position. It should be borne in mind that these statistics may be distorted by underreporting of transactions; bond ETFs may possibly be more strongly affected by lack of data than other categories. This is, however, a conjecture which may be confirmed when more detailed data are published due to the adoption of new legislation in Europe.

After presenting European ETFs markets divided country-wise or according to the exposure of the funds, we briefly focus on their structure in terms of one of the key entities, that is, providers. Fig. 3.13 presents the providers that manage ETFs with the most assets. In comparison, Fig. 3.14 shows the percentage market shares of particular providers in terms of the number of funds they offer. Despite the large number of providers (close to 50 as of end of November 2017 (Deutsche Bank, 2017c)), the vast majority of such companies manage assets of ETFs that account for less than 1% of the total market—only 11 providers exceeded this value as shown in Figs. 3.12 and 3.13. We present by name exclusively providers whose share in assets exceeded 3%. This proves the high concentration of the European ETFs industry which seems to persist. The number of providers in Europe has been stable since at least 2014 (see Fuhr, 2015; Deutsche Bank, 2017c). The structure of the market split in terms

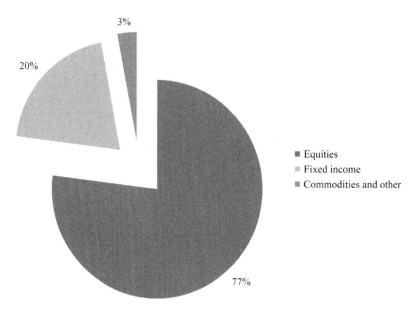

**FIGURE 3.12** Turnover of European ETFs by benchmarked asset classes. November 2017. *ETF*, Exchange-traded fund. *Source: Own estimations.*

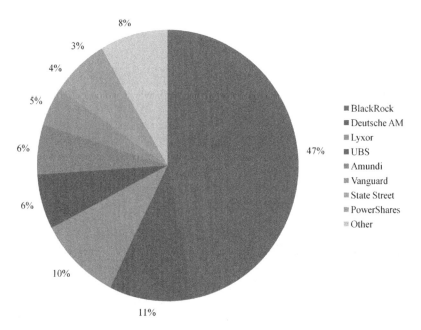

**FIGURE 3.13** Structure of European ETFs markets through assets by funds' providers. End of November 2017. *ETF*, Exchange-traded fund. *Source: Own estimations.*

of the number of funds offered by each provider seems to be more divided than when assets are considered, with a much lower share of the regional leader and relatively higher share of the smallest providers.

According to the values of either assets or number of funds, BlackRock is the European leader followed by the two other major institutions, Deutsche AM and Lyxor. These three companies together account for almost 70% of the assets held by the European ETFs. BlackRock uses almost exclusively the physical replication method for its funds which makes it an exception among the three European market leaders—37% of assets of ETFs managed by Deutsche AM and 62% by Lyxor respectively are held in synthetic funds. Among the five relatively smaller providers listed in Figs. 3.13 and 3.14, Amundi and PowerShares seem to prefer the synthetic structure whereas the others more often use the physical replication. Among the remaining companies with lower values of

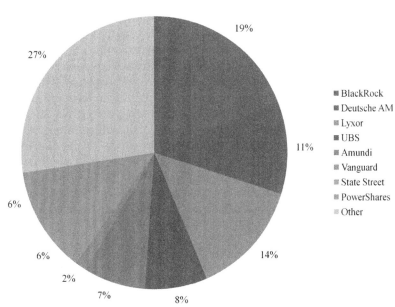

**FIGURE 3.14** Structure of European ETFs markets through number of funds by providers. End of November 2017. *ETF*, Exchange-traded fund. Source: *Own estimations.*

**TABLE 3.4** Profiles of the Three Largest Providers of Exchange-Traded Funds (ETFs) in Europe

| Name of the provider | Trademark name of the offered ETFs | Start of operations in Europe | Short description |
|---|---|---|---|
| BlackRock | iShares | 2000 | The largest provider in Europe and in the world, headquartered in the United States. Its offer of funds is the most diversified in Europe. It is the European leader both in the equity and bond ETFs segment (in the latter it controls c. 66% of the regional assets). Almost all funds comply with the UCITS regulations |
| Deutsche AM | db X-trackers | 2007 | Part of the Deutsche Bank financial group. It offers funds based on all main asset classes but focuses on the equity segment (other types constitute less than 20% of the total assets); all funds comply with the UCITS regulations |
| Lyxor | Lyxor | 1998 | Part of the Société Générale financial group. First provider which launched synthetic funds (until 2012 it had been the only replication method used). Initially focused almost exclusively on equity funds yet in the recent years it expanded its bond funds segment. All funds comply with the UCITS regulations |

*UCITS*, Undertakings for Collective Investment in Transferable Securities.
*Own elaboration based on Deutsche Bank (2017b).* ETF monthly Europe December 2017; *Morningstar (2017).* A guided tour of the European ETF marketplace.

managed assets of ETFs, not listed by name on the figures, the application of synthetic structure is also rather uncommon, with a few exceptions such as ComStage.

Most providers of European ETFs offer similar products, linked to the same benchmarks (in contrast with higher diversity in the United States), an approach which is labeled as the "coffee shop" approach (Fuhr, 2015). A notable example is funds tracking the EURO STOXX 50 index; according to Morningstar (2017) they are offered by 12 different providers and listed on 13 different exchanges. Nevertheless, intensive competition between sponsors of the most popular passive funds (for instance, tracking S&P 500 index) has led to the decline of their TERs and profitability for the managing companies. As a result, in recent years European ETF providers began to higher-margin ETFs other than the passive ones tracking blue-chip or broad stock market indexes (another source of this inclination are the attempts to attract the attention of potential customers). Some of the most popular categories of the higher-margin funds developed by European providers include: enhanced-indexing, currency-hedged or thematic ETFs (Morningstar, 2017). We end the analysis of the European ETFs providers by presenting brief profiles of the three largest ones; see Table 3.4.

The final issue concerning the structure of the European ETFs market which we address is the group of users of innovative funds. In contrast with the US market where retail users constitute a significant group, accounting for almost half of the assets owned, in Europe the role of noninstitutional investors is severely limited as they account for only several percent of the assets. There are no precise estimates (due to problems with exact attribution): according to Abner (2016) the share of retail investors is at c. 15%; Amenc, Goltz, and Le Sourd (2017) cited estimates between 10% and 15%. There are many causes of the apparent underdevelopment of the retail segment of the European ETFs market, among them are: insufficient information about this category of investment funds; lack of awareness of their features (particularly in comparison to the other available financial products); and domination of commercial banks (with lesser role of insurance companies) in the distribution channels of investment funds (with the exception of the United Kingdom where retail market is dominated by independent advisers). Banks prefer traditional funds which are linked with higher margins. Another reason is the technological backwardation of some fund platforms used by the financial advisors which hinders offering ETFs whose distribution is much more technologically demanding due to, e.g., much more frequent trading and pricing (Abner, 2016; Amenc et al., 2017; Morningstar, 2017).

### 3.1.4 Exchange-Traded Funds in Europe: Regulatory Issues

We end this section by outlining some important regulatory issues linked with the European funds. Due to the high unification of the legal environment in the EU, these issues may be discussed at the European level (in some parts of the discussion we refer, though, to the country-specific circumstances as in some cases the EU guidelines may be customized).

One of the distinctive features of the European ETFs market (making it quite unique in comparison to, e.g., its Asia-Pacific counterpart) is its regulatory framework which not only facilitates the creation of funds offered and traded in many countries, but also is in some aspects less restrictive than, e.g., in the United States. We discuss the dominant model of European ETFs' legal structure, followed by an outline of the crucial set of rules which apply to the European financial markets. The regulations presented are a part of the EU legal system which means that they are binding (at least to some extent) for all considered countries (least significantly for Turkey, but the level of ETFs market development in this country is minimal as discussed in Section 3.2). One of the factors that boosted the rapid growth of the European ETFs industry was the legal and regulatory framework which offered solutions aligned with the requirements of the innovative funds' mechanisms.

Legislation concerning the investment funds industry, including the regulations regarding the structure of such funds, was introduced in the EU a few years before the development of the European ETFs started. In contrast, the US regulations were introduced much sooner, a few decades earlier when the needs of this type of fund had not been considered for obvious reasons (Gastineau, 2010). Another difference between US and EU regulations is the continuing evolution of the European legislation in order to accommodate for the changing market conditions, whereas the base US legal document is still the Investment Company Act of 1940. As a consequence, at least from the legal perspective, the development conditions were more favorable in the European region. Their key element is "passporting," that is, facilitating cross-border offering of funds enabled by the model described next. Initially, adoption of common rules in particular countries of the EU was slow due to the vast diversification of the local regulations and necessary changes to be introduced (Gastineau, 2010). However, the final result was a set regulation which is unique on a global scale; there is no other region with such cross-border possibilities (discussion is pending between some Asia-Pacific countries, but is still at an early stage).

There are, however, some other significant discrepancies between the US and European ETFs market that are not limited to the legal issues which may be perceived as relative strengths of the US landscape, that is, more favorable for providers and users of the innovative funds. Fuhr (2015) underlined the importance of the distinction between the homogenous unified US market and the fragmented European one (despite the benefits of the passporting model)—in Europe there are multiple trading facilities, multiple languages, considerably varying tax and regulatory systems, as well as distribution models. According to Abner (2016), the development of the European ETFs market is slowed downed by the considerable fragmentation of trading facilities; turnover in the shares of the European ETFs that are available in multiple countries takes place on many exchanges which causes the problem of multiple currencies in which the values of transactions are expressed as well as separate central counterparties and central securities depositories. Furthermore, in order to manage the imbalances between demand and supply on particular markets, shares of the funds must be transferred between various countries which aggravates the operational costs of ETFs. The key example of transactions leading to such imbalance is the purchase of shares of a particular fund on an exchange in one country and selling them on an exchange in another country (Andagulova, 2015). As Abner (2016) noted, some actions have been undertaken in order to address these issues aimed, in particular, at centralization of the trading settlement. One solution is obtainable through Euroclear Bank (another similar company is Clearstream, part of the Deutsche Börse financial group), a supplier of post-trade services, which provides international central securities depository for ETF trading, thus, linking central counterparties from various countries. Its two main benefits are lack of need of the between-country transfers of shares and the creation of a single, international pool of shares to be used in transactions (Andagulova, 2015). The popularity of such services among the major ETF providers is growing—as of 2017 European ETFs managing c. 35% of the assets were offered using such international services (Fitzpatrick, 2017)—but most funds still use the less efficient model with separate settlement systems. An additional issue emphasized by Abner (2016) is the lack of unified reporting requirements in Europe.

Another problematic issue in Europe emerged after the introduction of UCITS III. In contrast with the US market where the distinction between fund's provider, APs, and other entities involved in the creation and distribution of the fund's shares is clear, in Europe frequently the same financial institutions are engaged in both processes. Moreover, they may also be market makers for the funds which are managed by their direct competitors.

Most European ETFs are structured as Undertakings for Collective Investment in Transferable Securities (UCITS) which allows for their distribution in multiple EU countries. More precisely, every fund structured as UCITS which receives authorization from the regulatory authorities of the country of its domicile (it applies exclusively to the EU countries) may be subsequently distributed not only in EU countries but in all countries which are member states of the European Economic Area, that is, all EU countries and three countries of the EFTA, except for Switzerland (i.e., Iceland, Lichtenstein, and Norway) (Bush et al., 2015). Furthermore, UCITS funds are as well distributed in other countries based on national regulation, mainly Asia-Pacific ones (e.g., Hong Kong) but also in a few South American countries (e.g., Chile), South Africa and, above all (taking into account the discussed topic), in Switzerland. The basic feature of ETFs structured as UCITS is that at least one of their shares is traded throughout the day on at least one stock exchange or other regulated trading facility, with at least one market maker (Fuhr, 2015). One important stipulation concerning UCITS refers to the possibility of country-level modifications of its requirements which means that despite the cross-border distribution opportunities, exact regulations may differ.

Since the introduction of UCITS, its requirements have evolved and successive versions of the initiative have been labeled with numbers from I (first version of UCITS) to V (the latest one as of 2018). Formally, all versions of UCITS are directives of the EU; UCITS I is the original directive and the next documents consist of amendments to the 1985 act. Table 3.5 includes an overview of the main aspects of UCITS I to V; less significant acts introduced during the periods between the main versions of UCITS were omitted. It should be added that consultations concerning UCITS VI started in 2012 yet they have not been concluded and the final form or the terms of its introduction has not been determined; discussion within the EU has rather focused on other elements of the financial system's regulatory landscape such as Alternative Investment Fund Managers Directive (AIFMD) or MiFID (discussed in the final part of this section); for an overview of UCITS VI see, for instance, Muller and Braunstein (2014).

Formally, UCITS-compliant ETFs adhere to the third version of the directive, that is, UCITS III (Deutsche Bank, 2017b). Subsequent versions are extensions of the main directive and they introduce some additional provisions, yet key requirements are listed in the directive published in 2002. Next, we discuss the parts of the UCITS legislation which are most important with reference to ETFs. We mention the requirements of UCITS that apply to ETFs and are not applicable for other types of UCITS-compliant investment funds as they mean that innovative funds are more strictly regulated than, for example, mutual funds.

With regard to ETFs, the key requirements of UCITS refer to the structure of the funds and their holdings. Some of the most significant rules apply to the diversification of the fund's portfolio (BlackRock, 2010; Gastineau, 2010; Amenc, Ducoulombier, Goltz, & Le Sourd, 2015). The "5/10/40" rule requires that UCITS funds that do not track indexes comply with specific investment limits (we discuss general rules and do not present applicable exceptions as they are outside the topic of this chapter):

1. No more than 10% of the fund's total net assets may be invested in money market instruments or transferrable securities issued by particular entity (in the case of deposits the limit is higher, i.e., 20%); however, the limit of 10% may be lowered to no more than 5% if the further requirement in the next point is not met.

**TABLE 3.5**   Selected Main Features of the Undertakings for Collective Investment in Transferable Securities (UCITS) Directives

| Directive | Year of publication | Main features |
|-----------|---------------------|---------------|
| UCITS I | 1985 | Initial directive. Its importance was limited due to restrictions on the asset classes and cross-border marketing barriers |
| UCITS II | None (abandoned in 1998) | Abandoned due to lack of agreement between EU member states |
| UCITS III | 2002 | Key UCITS legislation. Consists of two directives: <br> 1. The Product Directive: increases the range of assets allowed for the funds <br> 2. The Management Directive: introduces the European passport for UCITS funds (and additional requirements for the managing companies regarding, e.g., capitalization or risk management) <br> It created the foundations of the fund structure which has been employed by the emerging European ETFs industry. Apart from cross-border distribution possibilities, one of the main provisions was the allowance to use derivatives (both listed and traded over-the-counter) which resulted in the development of synthetic ETFs, based on swaps, as well as changes in the diversification rules which allowed development of index tracking funds. This version of the directive boosted the development of the European ETFs market also due to the provisions that increased the maximum limits for UCITS funds regarding investments in other UCITS funds (from 5% to 20%) |
| UCITS IV | 2009 | Introduces or amends provisions concerning, for example, cooperation of regulators, passports for managing companies (UCITS fund may be managed by company supervised in other EU country), structures and mergers of the funds. It further simplifies the process of fund's cross-border distribution |
| UCITS V | 2014 | Aligns the UCITS legislation with the AIFMD in areas such as managers' remuneration policies, depositary regimes and administrative sanctions |

*Note:* Publication dates refer to the year in the 'The Official Journal of the European Communities' (for UCITS I and III), 'Official Journal of the European Union' (for UCITS IV and V). Directives came into force at later dates. *EU,* European Union; *ETF,* exchange-traded fund; *AIFMD,* Alternative Investment Fund Managers Directive.
*Own elaboration based on BlackRock (2018). iShares MSCI Poland ETF; Association of the Luxembourg Fund Industry (2013). Luxembourg: The global fund centre; Bush, P., Lee, M., Ferguson, M., & Forstenhausler, M. (2015). European mutual funds. An introduction to UCITS for US asset managers. Ernst & Young LLP; Fuhr, D. (2015). Appendix A. The global footprint of ETFs and ETPs. In J. M. Hill, D. Nadig, & M. Hougan, A comprehensive guide to exchange-traded funds (ETFs) (pp. 160–181). Charlottesville, VA: CFA Institute Research Foundation.*

**2.** The aggregate limit of 40% of the fund's total net assets is imposed on the sum of investments in transferrable securities or money market instruments issued by single entity (e.g., company) which exceed 5% of total net assets each.

**3.** In the case of money market instruments or transferrable securities which are not listed or dealt on some regulated market, the aggregate limit is 10% of the fund's total net assets.

These limits do not apply to securities issued or guaranteed by local or national authorities and some international organizations (Donovan-Smith & Gibson, 2014). For borrowing, the limit is set at 10% of the total net assets; it is stressed that it must be temporary and for liquidity purposes only.

In the case of index-tracking funds, that is, the majority of innovative funds, the UCITS requirements concerning diversification of the holdings are less strict (Gastineau, 2010; Miziołek, 2016). They may hold even up to 20% of the securities issued by single entity and in some cases this limit may be increased to 35%, depending on the composition of the benchmark index (formally in "exceptional market conditions"). There are a number of attributes which must characterize such an index, for instance, sufficient diversification in relation to the underlying strategy, detailed methodology of rebalancing, and management independent from the company which provides certain UCITS fund (Laven Partners, 2011). Special requirements for index-tracking funds facilitate the creation and management of ETFs which offer exposure to capital markets in smaller economies or to some specific segments of the financial markets (e.g., sectoral indexes), regardless of the country. In most cases, ETFs have no significant problems with adhering to the basic diversification rule as they are funds that track rather diversified indexes.

In addition to these requirements outlined, there are also a number of other rules which we present briefly due to the available extensive literature on this subject (see, among others, Jesch et al., 2014; Alshaleel, 2016; Bodellini, 2016; Chance, 2016; Micheler, 2016; Stanton, 2017; Haentjens & de Gioia Carabellese, 2018).

According to UCITS, the frequency of calculation of the NAV of the funds which comply with this directive depends on their type (minimum frequency for certain categories is twice a month) yet this rule does not constitute a severe limitation for ETFs due to their basic mechanisms, with much more frequent calculations. Each fund must prepare and publish two key documents before its launch: prospectus and Key Investor Information (introduced by UCITS IV). Moreover, UCITS-compliant funds are obliged to publish both annual and semi-annual financial reports (the annual report must be audited) as well as a formal risk management policy which needs to be implemented separately from the typical operations (such as portfolio management).

In Chapter 2, Exchange-Traded Funds: Concepts and Contexts, we presented two types of replication methods which may be used by innovative funds: physical (based on the holding of physical assets) and synthetic (in which desired exposure is gained through derivatives, such as swap contracts or futures). The UCITS directive allows both types of replication methods (since UCITS III). There are, however, some rules which apply only to the funds managed within the synthetic structure as they refer to the use of derivatives (the discussion in this paragraph is based on overview in Amenc et al., 2015); it may be stated that the regulations regarding synthetic funds are much stricter which stems from their more complicated structure and operational mechanisms (they also apply to other UCITS-compliant funds which employ derivatives, not necessarily ETFs). What is important is that UCITS allows funds to use derivatives traded either on regulated markets or over-the-counter if they meet certain requirements, such as the limit of 10% of exposure in terms of assets to any individual counterparty being a credit institution (5% in case of other entities) or limitations regarding the liquidity and credit quality of the collateral. Collateral must be sufficiently liquid, valued daily, should have very high credit rating—otherwise special treatment is necessary, that is, it is treated as if its value was lower (haircut is applied); additional limitations apply to the possible use of the collateral. In case it is cash, it may be reinvested exclusively in risk-free assets; other types of collateral may not be re-invested, sold, or pledged.

A further aspect which may be regarded as an advantage offered by the UCITS directive in the context of the development of the European ETFs markets, is the substantial harmonization of the requirements which ensure certain standards of their management (Laven Partners, 2011). As a result, UCITS-compliant funds may be perceived by both retail and institutional investors as more attractive than other types of funds; some financial institutions (particularly in Europe) may be required to invest only in UCITS funds due to their internal regulations.

One of the results of the UCITS regulations may have been observed in the consolidation of the ETFs industry, proven by, for example, the size of the largest European funds, offered in many locations, which gathered substantial assets due to their competitive advantages enabled through the economies of scale (Gastineau, 2010). Table 3.2 shows that TERs of the biggest funds are in most cases much lower than the average values calculated for the entire industry (compare with Fig. 3.10).

An important aspect of the UCITS regulation refers to the regulatory institution responsible for the particular fund's supervision. Most responsibilities are preserved for the regulatory authority in the country of domicile (Bush et al., 2015); this means that the majority of assets of European ETFs are held by funds regulated by the Luxembourgian and Irish financial authorities. Despite the fact that the United Kingdom is the European leader in terms of innovative funds' assets, the minimal number of funds domiciled in this country means that UK regulatory authorities have substantially limited the direct impact on the ETFs market (to some degree a similar situation may be observed in Germany). The regulator in the distribution country (i.e., listing country other than the domicile) conducts the notification procedure and communicates with the regulator in the domicile country.

It should be noted that apart from these UCITS requirements which are common for both ETFs and other types of investment funds, there are also rules established by exchanges which apply exclusively to the funds (and other securities) which are listed on exchanges (Amenc et al., 2015). Each exchange may establish its own requirements yet the main provisions are usually similar. Using the example of Euronext (i.e., one of the main European trading platforms for ETFs), some of the key requirements are (from Amenc et al., 2015 and on the website of Euronext, 2018):

1. There must be at least one liquidity provider for the shares of the fund.
2. The expected market capitalization of the fund must be no lower than €5 million, with at least 25% of the issued shares sold publicly (a lower percentage is acceptable in some scenarios).
3. Disclosure rules: daily submission of the portfolio's composition; computation and publication of the iNAV throughout the trading period.

One of the requirements (although rather simple) for UCITS-compliant ETFs is the obligation to include both terms "UCITS" and "ETF" in its name; funds which do not adhere to the UCITS rules may not use the UCITS designation.

UCITS regulation, despite the benefits for innovative funds (particularly in terms of passporting possibilities), limits the development of certain categories of ETFs, particularly commodity or alternative ETFs. The main reason is the limit imposed on the investments in assets that are not listed or traded on regulated markets (Bush et al., 2015); UCITS-compliant funds may not invest in real estate (generally immovable assets) and physical commodities (Donovan-Smith & Gibson, 2014). Another problem is that the diversification rules prohibit the creation of funds that are in fact tied to only one or only a few assets (such as most commodity or currency ETFs). As a result, providers of such funds apply non-UCITS structures or create other types of ETPs such as ETCs or ETNs (which are not regulated by UCITS as they are not investment funds but rather debt securities). Consequently, the growth of commodity ETFs (such as physical ETFs which offer exposure to prices of gold and some of such funds are among the largest in the world) in Europe is severely limited. Yet another regulatory, UCITS-linked barrier to the development of certain segments of the European ETFs market is the directive's rules concerning borrowing and derivatives.

It should be further noted that in addition to the limitations regarding counterparties of the derivative contracts (and the 10% limit of borrowing), there are two additional restrictions that influence the range of ETFs that may be offered as UCITS funds: prohibition of short selling (with the exception of obtaining short exposure by employing derivatives, subject to the general limitations) and exceeding the leverage of two times the fund's total net assets, e.g., by using derivatives. In other words, the fund is required to be able to cover all its outstanding obligations; with the use of short-term borrowing 210% exposure in terms of the total net assets may be reached (Laven Partners, 2011; BlackRock, 2010, 2015). These rules result in some operational and risk management problems for the geared funds and constitute a limit for some categories, practically forbidding the launch of UCITS-compliant funds with a leverage higher than $\pm 2$.

As stated, UCITS funds must be domiciled in one of the EU countries which means that funds domiciled in other countries of the European Economic Area, say for example Norway, are not allowed to benefit from the advantages of the UCITS structure and are usually traded exclusively on the exchanges in the country of domicile (UCITS-compliant funds may, though, be offered in countries such as Norway). According to the Deutsche Bank's report (Deutsche Bank, 2017c) as of the end of 2016, all five ETFs domiciled in Iceland and Norway were listed exclusively on their stock exchanges; the case of the largest European non-EU ETFs market, that is, in Switzerland, is distinct as this country is not a member of the European Economic Area but the analysis of ETFs domiciled in Switzerland leads to the same conclusions as they are all listed only on the Swiss exchange.

Generally, non-UCITS European funds (of all types, not only ETFs) are structured according to the particular country's legal requirements and may not be offered on other markets (Fuhr, 2011; Riedl, 2017); there are some exceptions with regard to funds formed under the AIFMD which may be used to distribute investment funds labeled as "alternative" in the entire EU region yet exclusively to professional investors [European Fund and Asset Management Association (EFAMA), 2015] or under the local country's regulations—e.g., funds domiciled in offshore locations need to adhere to private placement rules and register separately in each country (Laven Partners, 2011). Almost the entire group of non-UCITS ETFs in Europe consists of funds domiciled in Switzerland, listed exclusively on the Swiss stock exchange, among them equity funds (tracking Swiss stock indexes), commodity funds (above all based on the prices of gold [Morningstar, 2017]) and a few bond funds, again linked to the Swiss fixed income securities. There are also several such funds either domiciled or primary listed in another country chosen for our analysis, that is, Norway. It should be added that all funds that are primary listed in Turkey are not compliant with UCITS as this country is not a member state of the European Economic Area. The total assets of ETFs primary listed in these two countries are, though, negligible in comparison to Switzerland.

According to the estimates by Amenc et al. (2015), non-UCITS ETFs account for less than 5% of the European assets (data as of 2012). Our estimates of the European assets by country of domicile based on the Deutsche Bank's more recent data, presented in Fig. 3.1, show that the share of Swiss-domiciled funds as of end of 2016 was at c. 4% (taking into account several non-UCITS funds domiciled in other countries it adds up to a very similar value as 4 years earlier), that is, a value of c. 5%, and may thus be regarded as the current maximum level of such funds. Their future growth is unlikely due to the observable strong preference toward the UCITS structure among providers. It must be added, in order to clarify this part of the analysis, that the number and assets of UCITS-compliant funds primary listed in Switzerland is much higher.

Despite the prevalence of funds based on UCITS regulations, other types of regulations also serve as a basis for some (yet very limited) number of ETFs. In the context of regulations alternative to UCITS, we mentioned the AIFMD directive. However, it should be stressed that it refers above all to "alternative" funds such as hedge funds, private equity funds, real estate funds, or investment trusts, and are labeled in the directive as "alternative investment funds" (AIFs) and the companies which manage them are labeled as "AIF managers" (AIFMs). As the UK Financial Conduct Authority (2018) noticed, the main focus of this directive is to regulate AIFMs rather than the funds they manage. In a way similar to UCITS, AIFMD introduces the passporting regime for AIFs whose managers wish to distribute them in the entire European Economic Area; it also sets a number of requirements (concerning, e.g., funds' transparency) which must be met by the managers (BlackRock, 2011). There are, however, some considerable limitations in comparison with UCITS. Probably the most severe one is the restriction for the managing company to sell and market AIFs only to professional investors (unless national regulation allows a broader range of potential users; it refers to the very detailed definition of professional client in yet another directive, the MiFID) in comparison to the possibility to offer UCITS funds to retail investors (BlackRock, 2015).

As a result of these limitations, the AIF structure is rarely used by ETFs available in Europe, with the exception of some funds which are domiciled outside Europe, for instance in the United States, yet such funds are rarely primary listed on the European exchanges which means that they play an insignificant role in our analysis. It must be added, though, that the restrictions regarding the "professionalism" of the investor may be circumvented if the purchase is made through a brokerage account, as is typical in the case of innovative funds. There are, however, restrictions imposed on the services provided by brokerage houses stemming from MiFID directive, in some aspects similar in that they are also required to determine the suitability of the offered services for a particular client. The advantage of the AIM structure over the UCITS is less strict regulation regarding, for example, the fund's holdings which means that it may be employed to create funds which are difficult or impossible to manage in line with UCITS.

Apart from the UCITS or, to a lesser extent, AIFMD regulation, another important element of the European ETFs markets' legal environment is the MiFID. This is a further directive of the EU authorities which, most generally, is aimed at harmonization of the regulation concerning investment services in the member states of the European Economic Area which means that, similar to UCITS, it does not apply to Switzerland (Bush et al., 2015). Chronologically, it was introduced after UCITS III and before UCITS IV. As of early 2018, two versions of MiFID have been introduced. The scope of both MiFID I (which came into force in 2007) and MiFID II (a more recent version which came into effect at the beginning of 2018) is very broad. We concentrate, therefore, only on their rules which are most strongly linked to ETFs; particularly on the ones covered by the more recent version of the document. Analogically to UCITS regulations, MiFID applies to countries in the European Economic Area (SEB Bank, 2018).

MiFID I replaced the much earlier EU directive which regulated the investment industry, that is, the Investment Services Directive from 1993. Generally, it applies to all types of financial services and instruments (with some exceptions), activities of financial institutions offering investment services, and their relationships with customers. Such institutions have been required to determine the status of their client, e.g., whether it may be classified as professional (which is an important matter as shown with regard to AIFMD) or the suitability of the investment for the client. Moreover, the scope of information regarding investment which needs to be revealed to the client has been broadened. MiFID has offered new possibilities for the European providers of investment services by facilitating their provision in various countries of the European Economic Area under the license obtained in the home country (SEB Bank, 2018). However, the overall effect of MiFID I on the development of the European ETFs market may be assessed as much less significant than in case of the UCITS regulations as it has not addressed directly this category of investment products, although it has referred to companies involved in, for example, the distribution of their shares.

MiFID II is a complex set of legislations which consists not only of the "base" directive, but includes other legal acts such as the Markets in Financial Instruments Regulation (MiFIR) (Watts, 2018). There are a number of aims which are expected by legislators to be reached with this set of new and updated rules, above all higher transparency of trading in financial instruments and improved protection of investors through, e.g., removal of potential conflicts of interest between asset managers and clients with regard to brokerage operations as well as creation of more transparent and competitive research market (Preece, 2017). It may be added that some of the requirements introduced by these rules are similar to the ones in the earlier US Dodd-Frank's Act (Schumacher, 2018; the full name is "Dodd-Frank Wall Street Reform and Consumer Protection Act"); yet European regulations are more comprehensive.

In the context of the European ETFs markets, one of the most important effects of MiFID II (in fact these rules are outlined in MiFIR which may be considered a key legal document) is the required introduction of European consolidated tape (E&Y, 2014), that is, full disclosure regarding transactions conducted on all types of trading facilities, including over-the-counter venues; it could be beneficial in the evaluation of the European funds' liquidity and prices. According to currently available data, ETFs traded in Europe seem in many cases illiquid due to underreporting (Edde & Vaghela, 2017; Morningstar, 2017). In the previous version of MiFID there was no requirement concerning the shares of innovative funds. In MiFID II shares of ETFs are included in the category of "equity instruments" for which pre-trade and post-trade transparency is obligatory (Busch, 2017) New regulations will also facilitate comparison of turnover in these shares on various exchanges or other trading venues. As Miziołek (2018) showed, already in early 2018 the disclosure of the full turnover of the shares of ETFs uncovered its actual value, much higher than in the previous years. Gomber, Clapham, Lausen, and Panz (2018) discussed potential future scenarios based on the survey conducted among the financial market experts.

Moreover, the requirement to disclose the full cost of investing in conventional funds and other competing financial products, above all the required commissions (Lannoo, 2018), may boost the development of the ETFs markets due to their more advantageous features for the investors. In particular, growth of demand from retail investors is expected (Edde & Vaghela, 2017; Jackson, 2018). Another MiFID II-related change which may boost the development of ETFs markets in Europe is more strict restrictions concerning the commissions paid by managers of (conventional) investment funds to their distributors for the sale of the fund's units, known as "retrocessions" which used to account for a considerable share of the management fee. Under MiFID II payment of such fees will be possible only in certain cases, such as provision of execution-only services (Financial Times, 2018) and banned in case of independent financial advisors or discretionary portfolio managers, including both monetary and nonmonetary benefits (E&Y, 2014). Consequently, one of the advantages of conventional investment funds over ETFs, that is, the preference of the higher-margin products across the entities involved in their distribution will be diminished (Lettau & Madhavan, 2018). Examples of countries which have already introduced such restrictions (e.g., the United Kingdom) may be seen as proof of their positive impact on the preference of ETFs in relation to traditional funds (Financial Times, 2018). Institutional investors may increase their use of the innovative funds due to the recognition of ETFs as securities eligible for hedging under MiFID II, which was not possible in the previous version.

Some financial institutions subjected to MiFID II claim, though, that the requirements concerning the increased transparency are too strict and costly to implement; furthermore they indicate that the higher disclosure of prices may actually lead to decreased liquidity due to withdrawal of market participants which wish to maintain anonymity (Schumacher, 2018). Another potential problem is linked with required evaluation of the investment's suitability for the potential buyer—suitability standards have not been changed, but the number of circumstances when they need to be checked has increased in comparison to the previous version of the directive (E&Y, 2014; Watts, 2018).

To conclude, it is still too early to gauge even the potential influence of the MiFID II regulation on the development of the European ETFs market (as a whole or in specific countries). It may be stated, however, that its impact should be at least non-negative as the prospective benefits seem to outweigh the risks. Moreover, the level of directive's implementation differs significantly across various countries of the European Economic Area—(Kamerling, 2018) share of other countries in the European ETFs market is irrelevant, with the exception of Switzerland which is expected to at least partially adjust its regulations over the next few years (Weber, 2017).

## 3.2 EXCHANGE-TRADED FUNDS DIFFUSION PATTERNS AND DYNAMICS

In the previous section we presented several methodological remarks concerning our approach to the development of the ETFs markets as well as general overview of ETFs in the European region, including outline of some region-broad aspects of their landscape, above all regulatory issues. In this section we focus on the results of the country-specific analysis. Firstly, we discuss the conclusions that may be drawn from the key descriptive statistics for the chosen European ETFs markets which show, among others, their substantial diversity. Secondly, we present and interpret the results of study conducted with the application of innovation diffusion models, that is, our core approach to the analysis of these innovative investment funds (for methodological details see the Methodological annex). It should be stressed that analyses of the diffusion of financial innovations are rare; one of the exceptions is Hull (2016) who applied a model with two classes of agents and provided proof for the spread of ETFs. Finally, we adopt a broader perspective and discuss some interesting results regarding the attributes of the regional ETFs industry, supplemented by the analysis of the combined ETFs markets in the five largest economies in our research sample: France, Germany, Italy, Spain, and the United Kingdom. When discussing either descriptive statistics or results of the estimations of diffusion models, we refer to the most significant features of the ETFs markets in particular countries (our presentation covers issues such as their history, listing and trading venues, structure in terms of the available funds, and their providers). It should be added that ETFs markets in three countries are outlined in much more detail in separate sections in the form of case studies indicating specific growth opportunities and barriers observed in the European innovative funds' sector.

## 3.2.1 Development of Exchange-Traded Funds Markets in Europe: Basic Evidence

Before discussing the basic results obtained for particular countries, we present some conclusions with regard to the European region. Table 3.6 covers the most significant descriptive statistics for the 12 analyzed national ETFs markets calculated for the base period of our analysis, that is, January 2004–August 2017. Evident differences in the number of observations are caused by varying lengths of the local market's history: in only four

**TABLE 3.6** Assets of the European Exchange-Traded Funds (ETFs) by Country of Primary Listing Using Selected Statistics. Period 2004–17, Monthly Data

| Country | No. of obs. | First primary listed ETFs (approximately) | Minimum (mln USD) | Maximum (mln USD) | Average (mln USD) | Average monthly dynamic | Absolute change (mln USD) | Total growth rate (%) |
|---|---|---|---|---|---|---|---|---|
| France | 164 | XII 2000 | 7737.2 (I 2004) | 111,308.6 (VIII 2017) | 47,947.4 | 101.7 | 103,221.1 | 1276.2 |
| Germany | 164 | VII 2002 | 5733.7 (I 2004) | 188,704.8 (VIII 2017) | 83,464.1 | 102.3 | 182,971.1 | 3191.1 |
| Greece | 116 | I 2008 | 13.4 (II 2016) | 223.5 (V 2008) | 54.8 | 97.8 | − 189.6 | − 92.2 |
| Hungary | 128 | I 2007 | 5.3 (VI 2017) | 27.5 (XII 2007) | 14.1 | 99.5 | − 4.8 | − 44.6 |
| Italy | 126 | III 2007 | 1.1 (III 2007) | 2344.4 (VIII 2017) | 934.5 | 106.4 (102.9— excluding IX 2007/X 2007) | 2343.3 | 220,048.3 |
| Norway | 142 | XI 2005 | 8.7 (XI 2005) | 342.1 (III 2010) | 150.2 | 101.9 | 127.3 | 14.7 |
| Poland | 84 | IX 2010 | 12.5 (V 2012) | 98.8 (IV 2011) | 29.4 | 98.8 | − 49.9 | − 60.9 |
| Spain | 140 | I 2006 | 0.75 (I 2006) | 2945.9 (VII 2014) | 1454.9 | 105.7 (101.9— excluding VI 2006/ VII 2006) | 1820.8 | 240,290.6 |
| Sweden | 153 | IX 2004 | 60.9 (II 2005) | 3471.6 (VIII 2017) | 2419.6 | 100.8 | 2667.1 | 331.5 |
| Switzerland | 164 | XII 2002 | 2318.7 (I 2004) | 73,298.8 (VIII 2017) | 29,786.4 | 102.3 | 70,980.1 | 3061.2 |
| Turkey | 153 | XII 2004 | 0.9 (XII 2004) | 229.3 (XII 2007) | 105.6 | 102.6 (100.9— excluding XII 2004/I 2005) | 47.6 | 5245.5 |
| United Kingdom | 164 | IX 2001 | 4945.8 (I 2004) | 312,100.5 (VIII 2017) | 96,529.9 | 102.6 | 307,154.2 | 6210.4 |

*Notes*: The month of first ETF's launch according to the data availability of data on assets in the Lipper's database (refers to the primary listing; ETFs may have been available in particular country at earlier dates within cross-listing—their assets are included in statistics for the country of primary listing only). Average monthly dynamic calculated as geometric mean. For Sweden, data breaks in time series during the beginning of the analyzed period.
*Own calculations.*

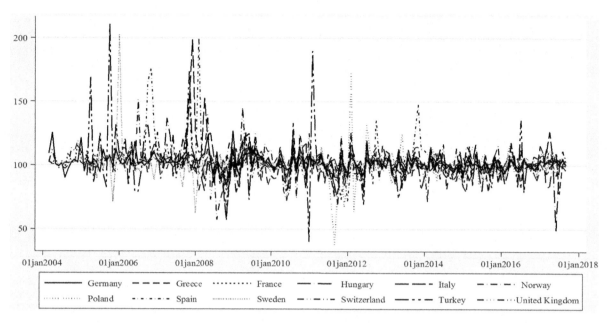

**FIGURE 3.15**  Average monthly dynamics of the changes in the assets of ETFs in European countries. Period 2004–17, monthly data. *Note*: On *Y*-axis—monthly dynamics. Outliers excluded. *ETF*, Exchange-traded fund. Source: *Authors' elaboration.*

countries ETFs have been primary listed since at least start of 2004. Their actual history had started before 2004. As noted in Section 2.1, there is conflicting information concerning the moment of the launch of the first ETF in Europe and its location. Accurate determination of the pioneering fund's identity is hindered by scarce data about European ETFs in the late 1990s and early 2000s. From the perspective of the current research and analysis opportunities, data on the availability of the first observations on the funds' assets in the Lipper database is the key issue; therefore, we use it as an approximate indicator of the market's beginnings. For France we have access to the longest time series in the dataset, starting from December 2000. In comparison, Poland's history of the ETFs market is much shorter and trading in the shares of the first ETF on the local exchange began in September 2010. In all other cases it started before the 2008 global financial crisis, usually before 2007 which indicates that ETFs have been present on those European financial markets for over a decade.

For comparative perspective, the minimum values in Table 3.6 are provided as purely supplementary information as in the vast majority of cases they are simply values that were observed close to the beginning of the analyzed time period. More robust regionwide conclusions may be drawn from the maximum values. The three largest European ETFs markets (United Kingdom, Germany, and France; this group may be extended to include Switzerland) reached the historically highest values of the innovative funds' assets in the last month of the analyzed time period, August 2017, which may be regarded as the peak point in their development. Growth of their assets over time, with some slight deviations, is evidenced in Fig. 3.16. The near absence of declines in the case of the United Kingdom is striking; moreover, it has surpassed the two other countries despite initially lagging behind; in 2009 assets of the UK funds exceeded the French and in 2013 the German ones. The strong upsurge in the final years of the considered time period has made it a distinct regional leader. In case of the smaller markets the development trajectory has been more complicated as they experienced apparent periods of growths and subsequent declines; see Fig. 3.17 for the development paths in Poland, Hungary, and Greece. In those three countries the total net assets of the local ETFs have declined since the launch of the first innovative funds (e.g., in Greece by almost $200 million). When the monthly dynamics of the ETFs market development in the scale of the entire region is considered (see Fig. 3.15 for the average values) it may be clearly noticed that in almost all cases the trajectory of the ETFs market development has become more stable by the end of analyzed time period. Growth rates over the entire period of the local ETFs market's history (different by country) have been highest in Spain and Italy, the countries where ETFs became primary listed later than on the largest markets, but their growth has been very substantial.

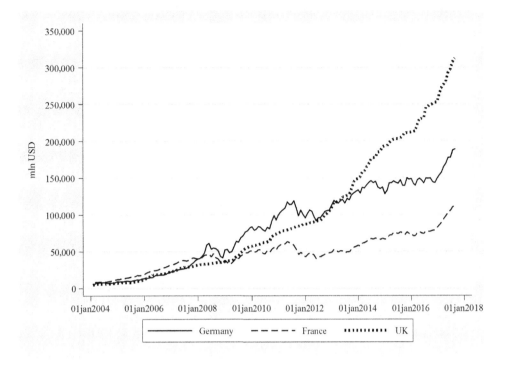

**FIGURE 3.16** Assets of ETFs in Germany, France, and the United Kingdom. Period 2004–17, monthly data. *ETF*, Exchange-traded fund. Source: *Authors' elaboration.*

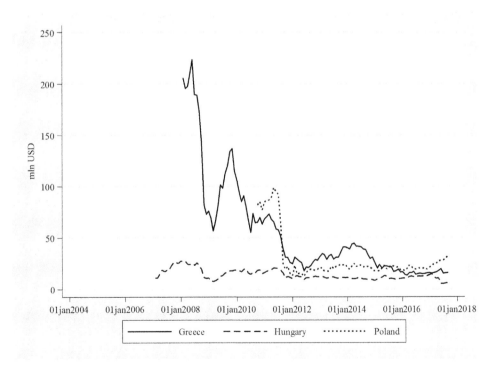

**FIGURE 3.17** Assets of ETFs in Greece, Hungary, and Poland. Period 2004–17, monthly data. *ETF*, Exchange-traded fund. Source: *Authors elaboration.*

In order to ensure clarity of presentation, we discuss key statistics concerning individual ETFs markets by country in alphabetical order as listed in the first row of Table 3.6. This discussion continues with the analysis of diffusion trajectories and an interpretation of the estimates of diffusion models.

France is among the oldest and biggest European ETFs markets; up to 2008 it was the largest one in the region (see Fig. 3.16). The French market grew rapidly between 2004 and 2011, with a temporary slowdown during the 2008 financial crisis. The next reversal of the upward trend occurred in 2011 and may be linked to the debt crisis in the eurozone. French ETFs which had been launched first are also the ones with the most substantial assets. As of end of August 2017 most assets were managed by Lyxor Euro Stoxx 50 (DR) UCITS ETF D-EUR, equity fund tracking the EURO STOXX 50 index; it was the seventh largest fund in Europe, with c. $8.47 billion of assets, launched in February 2001. It is not, however, the most established one as the French second-largest fund, Lyxor CAC 40 (DR) UCITS ETF D-EUR, had been launched several weeks earlier and may be considered the oldest one (with the stipulation concerning availability of data in the Lipper's database). The only primary listing location of ETFs in France is Euronext Paris, part of the Euronext group. An interesting and to some extent unique feature of the French market is prevalence of domestically domiciled funds. As of end of August 2017 c. $91 billion out of the total $111 billion assets were managed by the funds domiciled in France. Most funds (c. 70% in terms of assets) are passive equity ETFs, tracking indexes of the European stock markets (French, such as CAC 40 or joint indexes for eurozone or European countries) offered by the leading European providers such as Lyxor. The base currency of most funds is EUR, with some using other currencies, e.g., USD (mostly linked to non-European stock markets). According to data for the end of the analyzed time period, there were 418 funds primary listed in France (active, i.e., with data about their assets) while the total number of funds traded on Euronext Paris exceeded 800 which indicates that approximately half of ETFs whose shares are traded on the French exchange is primary associated with other market. For a more detailed overview of the trading mechanism of ETFs listed on this stock exchange see De Winne, Gresse, and Platten (2014).

Germany is currently the second-largest ETFs market in Europe, yet between 2008 and 2013 it was the biggest one (before the period of rapid development of ETFs in the United Kingdom). Since 2014 a stagnation of the assets of German ETFs is observed, followed by the next period of quick growth in 2017, common for all three leading European markets (see Fig. 3.16). Three ETFs primary listed in Germany with the highest values of the managed assets are the ones offered by BlackRock under the iShares label, that is, iShares EURO STOXX 50 UCITS (DE) ETF, iShares Core DAX UCITS ETF (DE), and iShares STOXX Europe 600 UCITS (DE) ETF (listed according to their size); they are also one of the most established and all three are passive equity funds domiciled in Germany. Interestingly, when we consider data on funds which had been first in the group of primary listed in Germany (based on data on the funds listed as early as in 2002) it may be noticed that some of them were tracking broad or blue-chip indexes of the local market, while others tracked indexes covering stocks of European companies which operated in sectors such as construction, oil and gas, or household goods. However, over the years the structure of the German market in terms of exposure has become much more conventional. In 2017 approximately $147 billion of the aggregate value of $189 billion were the assets of the passive equity funds with exposure to the main indexes; most of the remaining assets were managed by bond ETFs with three largest ones being SPDR Barclays Emerging Mkts Loc Bd UCITS ETF, PIMCO Euro Short Maturity Source UCITS ETF, and db x-trackers II Eurozn Gov. Bond UCITS ETF (DR) 1C. It should be noted that Deutsche AM, part of the German-headquartered Deutsche Bank's financial corporation, is one the leading providers of innovative funds in Europe.

Close to 99% of the German ETFs (in terms of both assets and their number) are primary listed on Deutsche Börse's electronic trading system, Xetra, with a few funds that have Stuttgart Stock Exchange, Berlin Stock Exchange, or Munich Stock Exchange as their primary listing trading venue. Only about 33% of the funds primary listed in Germany (in terms of assets) are domiciled in that country and most of the assets are held by funds domiciled in either Ireland or Luxembourg. An interesting and, to some extent, paradoxical feature of the German market is the fact that none of the operating Deutsche AM's funds are domiciled in Germany—this domicile is used, however, by Deka Investment GmbH and Commerz Funds Solutions SA, investment management divisions of other German financial corporations. For almost all German ETFs the base currency is EUR. Taking into account data on assets, there were 630 funds on the German market, which is significantly less than more than 1100 funds traded in that country (the explanation is the same as in the case of France). One of the distinctive features of the German market is the presence of other types of exchange-traded products: ETNs and ETCs. We address this issue in a separate discussion concerning German market using a case study in Section 5.4.

After discussing two of the leading European ETFs market, we now turn our attention to two countries that have heavily underdeveloped ETFs market, regardless whether we consider the absolute values of the innovative funds' assets or compare them to the local GDP. The short history of the Greek ETFs market started in January 2008 with the launch of the first and still the largest fund, that is, Alpha ETF FTSE Athex Large Cap Equity UCITS, managed by the local asset management company and tracking the blue-chip index of the Greek stock exchange. However, due to the financial turmoil on the global as well as regional and, particularly, local scale (resulting in, among others, considerable declines of the prices of local equities), the Greek ETFs market has remained in a nascent stage, even in comparison to its starting point (see Fig. 3.17). Since mid-2015 the total assets of Greek ETFs have not exceeded €15 million; problems with this market are clearly envisioned by the fact that the only two funds which had been launched at some point in addition to the pioneering one were discontinued in May 2017. The only listing location is the Athens Stock Exchange and base currency of the funds is in EUR. No other funds were traded on that exchange.

Hungary is the second country which may be characterized as having an almost nonexistent ETFs market and its case is even more evident than Greek. The only Hungarian ETF was launched on the brink of 2006 and 2007, that is, at approximately the same time as in Italy and only several months after Spain. Its underdevelopment is probably best evidenced by the fact that value of the sole Hungarian fund [OTP Tozsden Kereskedett BUX Indexkoveto ETF managed by the division of the local OTP Bank, tracking Hungarian exchange's blue-chip index, with HUF (Hungarian Forint) as the base currency] has never exceeded $30 million (see Fig. 3.17) and its mean value is the lowest in the entire sample (see Table 3.6). It is the only ETF listed and traded on the Budapest Stock Exchange; in the Lipper's database there is one additional fund classified as ETF but it is, in fact, another type of investment fund.

The case of the ETFs market in Italy is probably the most complicated among the analyzed economies and drawing robust conclusions on its main features is not easy. The reason is the small number of funds primary listed despite considerable trading activity as most ETFs traded in Italy have the United Kingdom as their primary listing location and are, consequently, included in assets indicators for that country. Due to its uniqueness in this aspect and other interesting features, we analyze the case of Italy separately in Section 4.4. However, we present here some basic information. Even though, according to the available data, the first primary listed ETFs were launched in Italy in March 2007, the actual start of the market development in this perspective could have been noticed from November 2007, with the introduction of a few funds managed by PowerShares. The size of the Italian market has increased substantially since then (to c. $2.34 billion as of August 2017) yet assets of the Italian ETFs remained very low in relation to the local GDP (at c. 0.1%). Most of the largest Italian ETFs are funds tracking benchmarks of the local equity market yet no fund gathered more than $1 billion of assets—the biggest one is Lyxor FTSE Italia Mid Cap PIR (DR) UCITS ETF D-EUR with c. $650 million. There are no funds domiciled in Italy and all funds primary listed in that country are traded on the Milan Stock Exchange with EUR as their base currency.

In the previous section, Norway was classified in the group of European countries characterized by underdeveloped ETFs markets. It was also stated, though, that is an "outlier" in that category due to the much higher level of economic development than the other included countries. The Norwegian ETFs market is dominated by the one fund which accounts for the vast majority of local assets and is also the pioneer—DNB OBX ETF, managed by DNB Asset Management (division of the Norwegian bank), which tracks the equity index of the Oslo Stock Exchange (the only listing exchange of ETFs in Norway) and it is domiciled in Norway. Other ETFs primary listed in Norway included (most of them are no longer available) funds tracking prices of oil (due to the structure of the local economy) or with geared exposure to the Norwegian equities. In all cases the base currency was NOK. The highest value of assets of Norwegian ETFs was reached in 2010, when at least five ETFs primary listed in that country were available. The number of funds and value of turnover of the shares of ETFs on the Oslo Stock Exchange has fluctuated considerably over the years; the maximum levels of turnover were reached approximately at the time corresponding to the peaks in the values of assets.

The Polish ETFs market is one of the least developed in Europe, regardless of the approach adopted to its analysis (assets, turnover, or number of funds). Since 2010 there has been only one ETF primary listed in Poland with very low total net assets. It is a passive blue-chip equity fund that tracks the index of the Polish stock market, managed by Lyxor, with PLN as the base currency. The strong decline of its assets in mid-2011 was caused by the decisions made by the fund's provider and did not result from any stock market or economy-wide events. In the mid-2017 the assets of the Polish ETF were the largest among the group of the three smallest European ETFs markets (see Fig. 3.17) yet, as in the other two cases, the total growth rate over the considered period was negative (see Table 3.6). For a more detailed analysis of the Polish ETFs market see Section 3.4.

Spain is one of the mid-developed ETFs markets in Europe. ETFs have been primary listed in Spain since 2006 and even though their number is not substantial (at no point in time were there more than 15 active primary listed funds), their maximum assets were close to $3 billion in 2008 and 2014, with the average value over 2006–17 of c. $1.5 billion. The development path of the Spanish ETFs market has been characterized by high variability; similar tendencies have been observed if turnover on the BME Spanish Exchange (the only location of ETF primary listing in Spain) is taken into account. Both assets and turnover declined significantly in the aftermath of the 2008 global financial crisis and the eurozone debt crisis. A rebound which started in 2012 may not be perceived as sustainable reversal of the trend as proven by its decline since 2016. The Spanish ETFs market is unique in at least one aspect. As of March 2018 there are eight funds primary listed on the BME Spanish Exchange and they are the only ETFs listed on that exchange (in August 2017, the last data point in our dataset, there were nine funds, but since then one was liquidated). All funds except one track the blue-chip stock indexes of the Spanish equity market (either IBEX 35 or, in case of Deutsche AM's funds, Solactive Spain 40 Index) and EUR is their base currency. Geared funds (inverse, leveraged, and inverse-leveraged, one of each type) are also available and managed by Lyxor. The largest fund, which accounts for more than half of the aggregated country assets and most turnover, is Lyxor UCITS ETF IBEX35 (DR) D-EUR. It is also the most established ETF in Spain, with the longest history. There are three providers of ETFs in Spain: two of the European leaders, that is, Lyxor and Deutsche AM (their funds are domiciled in France and Luxembourg, respectively), as well as the local provider BBVA Asset Management (its two funds are domiciled in Spain and these are the only European ETFs domiciled in that country). Finally, it should be emphasized that, even though there is only a handful of ETFs that are primary listed in Spain, the number of funds listed and traded at BME Spanish Exchange was in the past much higher, reaching 75 in the peak point in 2012, according to WFE statistics.

Similarly to Spain, Sweden is one of the European ETFs markets which may be classified as being at the mid-level of development—not one of the regional leaders, but characterized by much higher assets in comparison to countries which lag behind. It should be stressed that the Swedish market is the largest in the mid-sized group (which includes Italy), in terms of both average assets in the considered time period (c. $2.5 billion) and the maximum assets reached (c. $3.5 billion at the end of August 2017); see Table 3.6. Data on ETFs primary listed in Sweden is available in the Lipper's database for the period starting from September 2004 which we treat as the beginning of the Swedish market, but one of the funds had been launched in late 2000. Two funds with the longest period of their primary listing in Sweden, according both to the date of their inception and data on their assets are XACT OMXS30 ETF (the oldest one, launched in October 2000, however, data for the period before September 2004 are not included in the Lipper's database) and XACT OMXSB Utdelande; both track stock indexes of the Swedish exchange. The latter was the market leader in terms of assets in most months between September 2004 and the end of 2007 (with the exception of a few months in 2005), but since then the older XACT OMXS30 ETF has become the largest fund together with another fund, XACT Norden 30 (it tracks returns on the 30 most actively traded stocks in the four Nordic countries: Sweden, Norway, Finland, and Denmark) and account for almost two-thirds of the aggregated assets of the Swedish ETFs.

Despite a relatively small number of ETFs primary listed in Sweden (at no time has their number exceeded 20), the Swedish market may be considered to be diversified in terms of the funds offered by providers. Investors have access not only to basic passive equity funds, but also to, for instance, the ones with modified returns—leveraged and inverse-leveraged (the largest Swedish provider of ETFs, Xact Kapitalforvaltning AB, states on its website that they had been first such funds in the world (Xact, 2018)) as well as one bond and one commodity fund. For a few years an active fund with the exposure to Russian equities was offered, but it never accumulated considerable assets (it was delisted in 2015). Total assets of the Swedish ETFs have experienced significant changes, as evidenced by Fig. 3.18, caused by both fund-specific events and global or regional factors (e.g., 2008 financial crisis), yet since 2009 the market has undergone quite stable development. It was, however, interrupted in 2015 albeit followed by a rebound, corresponding to the changes in the indexes tracked by the largest funds also resulting from the closure of a few funds in the mid-2015 (e.g., three funds managed by Swedbank). The only listing location of the Swedish ETFs is OMX Nordic Exchange Stockholm (the name in the Lipper's database; the formal name is NASDAQ Stockholm and it belongs to the global NASDAQ group, so "OMX" was the name used for historical reasons). Swedish ETFs are domiciled either in that country (most of them) or in Luxembourg. SEK is the base currency of all Swedish funds. Analysis of the number of funds traded on the Swedish exchange or their turnover is impeded due to reasons outlined in Section 3.1. Swedish exchange is part of the group of Nordic exchanges.

Switzerland is one of the markets which we included in the group of regional leaders with the average assets of ETFs between 2004 and 2017 at $30 billion and a maximum value close to $73 billion at the end of the analyzed period (see Table 3.6). However, it is the smallest market in this group with substantially lower assets than in, for instance, France (yet still much larger than the markets in the mid-developed category, not to mention the

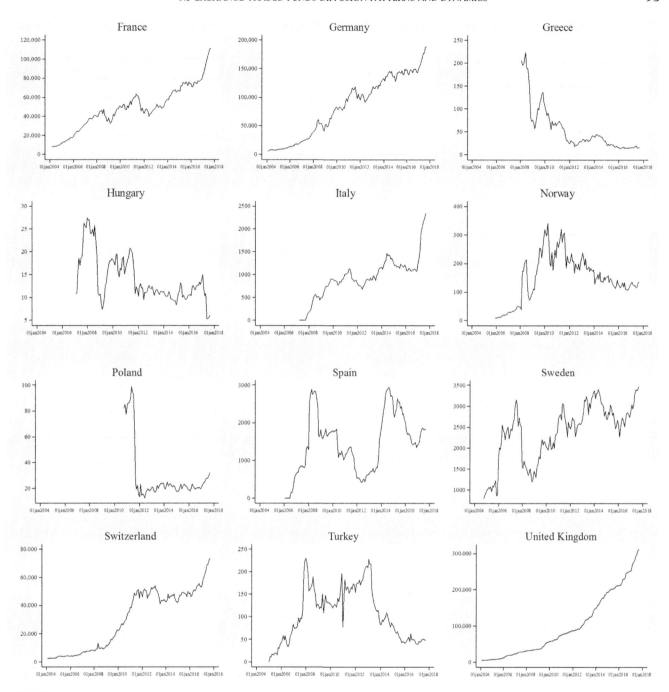

**FIGURE 3.18** Diffusion patterns of assets of European ETFs by country of primary listing. Period 2004−16, monthly data. *ETF*, Exchange-traded fund. Source: *Authors' elaboration.*

countries such as Poland or Hungary). If the size of the local economy is taken into account and assets of ETFs are compared to the GDP, it may be concluded that as of 2016 Switzerland had the second-largest ETFs market in Europe in relative terms, behind only the United Kingdom. When the average value as the % of local GDP for the period 2004−16 is calculated, it may be concluded that Switzerland was the European leader with a mean of c. 4.6% versus c. 3.5% for the United Kingdom. It proves that Switzerland has a large ETFs market in a rather small economy (compared to the biggest ones in Europe). It should be stressed that similarly to the other leading markets, the trajectory of its development has been rather stable with a brief period of noticeable diminishing assets and stagnation between 2013 and 2015, yet followed by a rapid growth, particularly in 2017 (see Fig. 3.18). The aspect that distinguishes Switzerland from other countries in the group of European ETF leaders (or the other countries, in our sample, except Turkey) is the fact that it is not a member of the EU or the European Economic Area which has some important legal consequences with regard to, for example, the UCITS regulation. Nevertheless, within a few years, after the United Kingdom exited the EU, the situation of both countries will be similar in some aspects. Another important consequence is the fact that, taking into account the current market shares of Switzerland and the United Kingdom in the European ETFs market, more than half of European innovative funds' assets will be primary listed outside the EU which may have a potentially serious impact on the regional investment industry (e.g., in the context of regulatory issues) which is currently impossible to assess (as the exact details of the United Kingdom's future relations with the EU are still not fully known).

The Swiss ETFs market consists of two categories of funds classified according to their legal form (there are only a few other funds, e.g., domiciled in the United States with negligible market share): ETFs domiciled in the countries of the EU (mostly structured as UCITS) and ETFs domiciled in Switzerland which are not UCITS-compliant. Considering their assets, assets of funds domiciled in the EEA countries amounted as of end of August 2017 to c. $46 billion (i.e., 63% of the total market) whereas the Swiss-domiciled ETFs managed c. $27 billion (i.e., 37% of the total market). These results show that the Swiss ETFs market is strongly linked to the markets in the EU countries as the distinctive Swiss funds (domiciled and listed exclusively in that country) constitute a minority of the aggregate assets. The total number of ETFs primary listed is substantial, 307 (according to the Lipper's database) as of August 2017, out of which 22 held assets of at least $1 billion; the number of all funds listed at the SIX Swiss Exchange (the key listing venue for ETFs in Switzerland) exceeded 1100 at that point in time, being slightly lower than in Germany and c. 25% lower compared to the United Kingdom. According to the turnover data for 2016, Switzerland was the fifth most active market in Europe (in terms of conducted transactions), behind the other three leading European ETFs markets as well as Italy; data for 2017 gathered from the relevant reports of the WFE and national exchanges shows that Switzerland slightly exceeded Italy. Nevertheless, in relative terms, in relation to the local GDP, turnover of ETFs in Switzerland is by far the highest in Europe and among the highest in the world.

The largest ETF primary listed in Switzerland is iShares Core EURO STOXX 50 UCITS ETF EUR (Acc), with more than $4.7 billion of assets (it tracks EURO STOXX 50 index, similarly to some the Europe's largest ETFs). The other three funds which manage more than $2 billion are two equity funds (one tracks the Swiss equity index and the other stocks of companies in emerging markets) and one commodity fund (tracking the prices of gold by employing physical replication). More than 70% of the Swiss funds (considering their assets) are basic passive equity ETFs, tracking country (usually non-Swiss ones), regional, or global indexes. Commodity ETFs account for c. 22% of the total assets and the third largest group are bond ETFs. Base currencies of Swiss ETFs differ but the most often used one is CHF, and less frequently EUR, GBP or USD. Swiss ETFs are managed by all leading providers of ETFs, among them various subsidiaries of the Swiss financial corporation UBS; the group of the smaller providers includes some Swiss-based companies such as Swisscanto Fondsleitung (provider of the "ZKB" funds) or GAM Investment Management.

The path of the ETFs market development in the next analyzed country, Turkey, resembles the trajectory observed for Norway. After a rapid growth and reaching peak levels of assets (for Turkey it was the second half of 2007), it has undergone a substantial decrease (see Fig. 3.18). Table 3.6 shows that the maximum level of Turkish ETFs' assets was c. $230 million with an average of $106 million. All Turkish ETFs share a number of attributes: they are domiciled in Turkey, their base currency is TRY, and their listing location is Borsa Istanbul. The largest ETFs are not, as in case of most other markets, equity ETFs but rather commodity fund Finans Portfoy Gold ETF and short-term US bond ETF, Finans Portfolio USD Foreign ETF. Their aggregated assets reached $28 billion in August 2017, c. 60% of the total market. The role of funds that track local assets (either stocks or bonds) is recently much less significant, even though during the phase of the Turkish market's expansion they were the largest category. The number of ETFs in Turkey has never exceeded 20 (17 was the highest level) and their turnover followed trends similar to their assets. It may be added that, according to available sources, no funds have been cross-listed on Borsa Istanbul. An interesting feature of the Turkish market was the availability of the world's first ETF tracking Islamic market index, BMD Securities Dow Jones DJIM Turkey ETF, that tracked Dow Jones Islamic Market (DJIM) Turkey (Gozbasi & Erdem, 2010; BMD, 2011) yet it never gathered considerable assets and was apparently closed in early 2016 as no data on assets or share prices is available thereafter.

Finally, we discuss the last country in our sample and, at the same time, the most developed ETFs market in Europe (considering value of the funds' assets) and one of the global leaders, that is, the United Kingdom. At the end of August 2017, the total assets of the British ETFs (i.e., ETFs with the LSE as their primary listing location) exceeded $310 billion, close to 50% of the aggregated regional assets; the average value for the 2004—17 period was close to $100 billion (see Table 3.6). As of 2017 the British ETFs market is the most developed in Europe in almost all considered dimensions: assets in relation to the local GDP (average value is, however, higher for Switzerland), turnover of ETFs on the local exchange, or number of funds listed on the LSE in terms of the primary listed funds. One distinguishing attribute of the British market is the stability of its development as proven by the diffusion paths in Figs 3.16 and 3.18. It is the only country in our sample for which no substantial deviations from the upward trend could be noticed. One of the events which could have been expected to have affected the British ETFs market was the vote on the United Kingdom's leaving the EU (Brexit) in June 2016. There has been, however, no effect observable in relation to the assets of British ETFs; they have, in contrast, grown by c. 35% since the referendum until August 2017. Nonetheless, a significant effect is noted with regard to the transactions in the shares of ETFs as the value of their turnover in June 2016 was the highest in the history of not only the British market, but all European countries and reached c. $51 billion (for comparison, the average value in the United Kingdom for 2016 was at c. $38 billion and a year earlier it was at c. $26 billion). Over the next few months it reversed to the mean level. What is important is that such a surge was not noted with regard to the stock or bond turnover in that country.

The largest British ETFs are also the biggest ones in the entire region. The only listing venue is the LSE. The British market is highly diversified in terms of the available types of funds, their providers, and base currencies. Most funds (when their number or assets are considered) are equity ETFs that track various indexes, mostly broad market or blue-chip covering both European and ex-European markets, but also sectoral; besides them there are geared funds with exposure to equities, bonds or commodities. Equity funds account for c. 63% of the total assets, almost all of the remaining assets are held by bond funds. There are also some alternative ETFs, for instance, money-market funds (yet more assets of the funds in this category are managed by ETFs primary listed in France or Germany); Lipper's database informs about several "other" ETFs whose names suggest that they are currency funds (Deutsche Bank report as of end of 2016 states a lack of such funds domiciled in Europe), but a detailed analysis shows that they are ETCs. BlackRock with its 'iShares' brand of ETFs is the largest provider of British ETFs followed by the other leading managing companies. The base currency of the largest group of British ETFs (in terms of assets) is GBP with its share being approximately 70%; the rest of the market is split almost equally between funds using USD and EUR. Additionally, one fund is denominated in CNY (RMB), that is, CBK CCBI RQFII Money Market UCITS ETF A RMB.

### 3.2.2 Development of Exchange-Traded Funds Markets in Europe: Diffusion Analysis

We have already discussed the diffusion patterns as presented in Fig. 3.18, therefore, we skip the detailed analysis of the observed trends or between-country differences. However, in order to assess the applicability of the diffusion models for the analysis of the ETFs markets in our sample it is necessary to consider the shape of the diffusion patterns, that is, whether they are (at least to some extent) S-shaped-like with the distinguishable three stages of development (see Methodological annex—Method 1). This means that countries where clear decline in the assets of ETFs was observed do not meet this requirement: Greece and Hungary (and Poland).[2] In another group of countries, Norway and Turkey (and, to some degree, Spain) the trajectory is complicated and does not resemble the S-shaped curve. Finally, for the remaining six countries, the diffusion process follows the S-shaped patterns with easily identifiable stages, although growth rates vary among countries examined.

Table 3.7 shows estimates of the diffusion models for each country in our sample. We discuss them in alphabetical order. Methodological issues are discussed in detail in the Methodological annex (see Method 1), hence here we mention only the selected aspects in order to clarify the flow of the analysis. For each country we estimated the following parameters of their ETFs market development observed for the period January 2004–August 2017 ($i$ is the abbreviated name of the country):

$\kappa_i^{ETF}$—ceiling (also called upper asymptote) that shows the limit of growth.
$Tm_i^{ETF}(\beta_i^{ETF})$—midpoint that shows the exact time (in a number of month) when half of the ceiling's level is reached; it may also be expressed as an exact month (e.g., September 2005).
$\alpha_i^{ETF}$—rate of diffusion that may be used to calculate another parameter, specific duration, which is easier to interpret.

---

[2]As in Poland the sharp decline is to high degree "artificial" so we slightly modified the further analysis for this country; see Table 3.7 and the note below the table.

**TABLE 3.7**  Estimates of Diffusion Models of Assets of European Exchange-Traded Funds (ETFs) by Country of Primary Listing. Period 2004—17, Monthly Data

| Country | France | Germany | Greece | Hungary | Italy | Norway |
|---|---|---|---|---|---|---|
| $\kappa_i^{\text{ETF}}$ (ceiling/upper asymptote) | 329,648.5 | 161,833.8 | 136,872,038.7 | 481,471.3 | 1837.9 | 183.1 |
| $Tm_i^{\text{ETF}}(\beta_i^{\text{ETF}})$ (midpoint) | 251 | 79 | − 408 | − 1497 | 99 | 48 |
| | (XI 2024) | (VII 2010) | (n.a.) | (n.a.) | (III 2012) | (XII 2007) |
| $\alpha_i^{\text{ETF}}$ (rate of diffusion) | 0.01 | 0.037 | − 0.03 | − 0.007 | 0.024 | 0.194 |
| $\Delta t_i^{\text{ETF}}$ (specific duration) | 398 | 118 | − 149 | − 670 | 184 | 23 |
| $R^2$ of the model | 0.87 | 0.97 | 0.36 | 0.41 | 0.71 | 0.54 |
| No. of obs. | 164 | 164 | 116 | 128 | 126 | 142 |

| Country | Poland | Spain | Sweden | Switzerland | Turkey | United Kingdom |
|---|---|---|---|---|---|---|
| $\kappa_i^{\text{ETF}}$ (ceiling/upper asymptote) | 740,864.7 | 1626.7 | 3315.8 | 52,184.1 | 120.2 | 563,574.4 |
| $Tm_i^{\text{ETF}}(\beta_i^{\text{ETF}})$ (midpoint) | 2495 | 39 | 26 | 73 | 31 | 161 |
| | | (III 2007) | (II 2006) | (I 2010) | (VII 2006) | (V 2017) |
| $\alpha_i^{\text{ETF}}$ (rate of diffusion) | 0.004 | 0.32 | 0.018 | 0.077 | 0.194 | 0.026 |
| $\Delta t_i^{\text{ETF}}$ (specific duration) | 1030 | 14 | 247 | 57 | 23 | 169 |
| $R^2$ of the model | 0.28 | 0.301 | 0.526 | 0.94 | 0.071 | 0.995 |
| No. of obs. | 73 | 140 | 153 | 164 | 153 | 164 |

*Note*: in italics - misspecifications; for Poland - estimates for data since August 2011 (for details - see Section 3.4).
*Authors' estimates.*

$\Delta t_i^{\text{ETF}}$—specific duration that shows the time needed for the value of the assets of ETFs to grow from 10% to 90% of the ceiling's level (level of upper asymptote, limit of growth).

Values of $R^2$ and the number of observations are also reported for each model.

It must be underlined that the rigid assumption of the applied diffusion model is that the development of the ETFs market follows the S-shaped (sigmoid) trajectory, that is, the growth follows the logistic-type path, along which three stages of diffusion (first and third characterized by slow rate of growth, and the second by quick or exponential growth) may be identified. It may be the case, however, that not all three phases have already been observed and the particular market may still be in the second stage which means that the next one (of saturation) is yet to be reached. In such cases, the estimated ceilings can be much higher than actually observed maximum levels (see, for instance, results for France or the United Kingdom in Table 3.7).

Firstly, we discuss the results obtained for the two largest European ETFs markets, France and Germany. Returned $R^2$ of these models for both countries are very high and there are no apparent misspecifications of any of the estimated parameters. $\kappa_{\text{Fra}}^{\text{ETF}}$ is almost triple as high as the actual final observed value (c. $330 billion vs c. $111 billion) which could imply that ETFs market in this country is still in the second stage of its development, growing exponentially and, thus, this market is far from reaching its saturation. However, the results obtained for France should be interpreted with caution as indicated by $Tm_{\text{Fra}}^{\text{ETF}}$ or $\Delta t_{\text{Fra}}^{\text{ETF}}$ which both refer to very distant points in time (from the perspective of the end of the observed data period, i.e., August 2017). This means that it is difficult to state whether reaching the assets of ETFs implied by $\kappa_{\text{Fra}}^{\text{ETF}}$ is plausible.

The estimates for Germany are less dubious than in the case of the French ETFs market. The estimated parameter $\kappa_{\text{Ger}}^{\text{ETF}}$ is lower than the maximum value of assets observed until August 2017 (the difference is about $28 billion) which could suggest that the acceleration of the ETFs diffusion by the end of the analyzed period is temporary; however, projections discussed in the next section show that further development is highly possible. Regardless of the latter, it may mean that in the case of Germany the ETFs market is approaching the stage of saturation rather than being in the beginning of the rapid expansion. This conclusion is also proven by $Tm_{\text{Ger}}^{\text{ETF}}$ which is estimated at July 2010, and $\Delta t_{\text{Ger}}^{\text{ETF}}$ of 118 months (i.e., about 10 years); both fall within the 2004—17 time period and do not extend in the future, like the estimates in the case of France.

In case of the next two countries presented in Table 3.7, Greece and Hungary, the obtained estimates are apparently misspecifications—note the extremely high levels of $\kappa_{\mathrm{Gre}}^{\mathrm{ETF}}$ and $\kappa_{\mathrm{Hun}}^{\mathrm{ETF}}$ as well as negative values of $Tm_{\mathrm{Gre}}^{\mathrm{ETF}}$, $Tm_{\mathrm{Hun}}^{\mathrm{ETF}}$, $\Delta t_{\mathrm{Gre}}^{\mathrm{ETF}}$, and $\Delta t_{\mathrm{Hun}}^{\mathrm{ETF}}$. In both countries ETFs markets have been in decline over 2004–17 and the trajectory of the changes in the assets of ETFs has not been sigmoid in shape. This implies that diffusion models are not applicable for the analysis of these two markets.

The value of the $\kappa_{\mathrm{Ita}}^{\mathrm{ETF}}$ parameter (for Italy) was estimated at c. \$1.9 billion; similarly to Germany it is lower than \$2.3 billion actually observed by the end of the analyzed period. March 2012 is $Tm_{\mathrm{Ita}}^{\mathrm{ETF}}$ which could imply that the diffusion of ETFs in Italy has already reached the point denoted graphically as the inflection of the logistic curve. However, reaching the levels close to the maximum suggested by estimates of the diffusion model is still quite distant in time as shown by $\Delta t_{\mathrm{Ita}}^{\mathrm{ETF}}$ of 184 months. Interpretation of the results obtained for Italy is hindered by the noticeable deviation of the Italian ETFs market development path from the S-shaped trajectory. Very rapid growth in 2017 is particularly problematic from this perspective as $R^2$ of the model being lower than for France or Germany (0.71) proves validity of such stipulation. Overall, it may be stated that the diffusion of ETFs in Italy has taken place, yet estimates of the diffusion model suggest that the potential of ETFs to evade the local market is limited.

The discussion regarding the graphical evidence (see Fig. 3.18) accentuated the trajectory of the Norwegian ETFs market's development which may not be declared to be S-shaped. A more accurate description would be reverse U-shaped, meaning that employing the diffusion model is bound to be challenging. $\kappa_{\mathrm{Nor}}^{\mathrm{ETF}}$ is \$183 million which is close to the final observed value than the maximum historical levels of more than \$300 million. Even though both $Tm_{\mathrm{Nor}}^{\mathrm{ETF}}$ and $\Delta t_{\mathrm{Nor}}^{\mathrm{ETF}}$ may not be characterized as obvious misspecifications (it should be noted that they are very low compared to respective values estimated for the other countries), it is difficult to regard them as the robust representation of the changes on the Norwegian ETFs market. The high level of the assets' concentration (most are managed by one fund) and substantial variability of both assets and turnover indicate that development of the Norwegian market is highly unstable.

In the case of Poland, misspecifications for all estimated parameters were obtained even though the used time series was revised and the initial period of substantial decline was removed (see the note below Table 3.7). The estimated value of $\kappa_{\mathrm{Pol}}^{\mathrm{ETF}}$ is extremely high; the same applies to the values of $Tm_{\mathrm{Pol}}^{\mathrm{ETF}}$ and $\Delta t_{\mathrm{Pol}}^{\mathrm{ETF}}$; in contrast with the estimates for Greece and Hungary they are positive yet refer to extremely long time periods. As a result, a similar conclusion as in case of the countries already discussed may be formulated, that is, the path of the changes in the assets of ETFs has not been sigmoid in shape and the use of the diffusion model in this case does not result to be informative and conclusive.

The subsequent countries in Table 3.7 are Spain and Sweden, which we discuss jointly as they are both mid-developed European ETFs markets. Not surprisingly, the value of $R^2$ of the model estimated for Spain is much lower than in case of Sweden due to the development trajectory distant from the sigmoid shape generated by the diffusion model. Consequently, estimates for the Spanish market may be dubious. Taking into consideration the estimates of $\kappa_{\mathrm{Spa}}^{\mathrm{ETF}}$ (lower than actual values observed in some months during 2004–17), $Tm_{\mathrm{Spa}}^{\mathrm{ETF}}$ and $\Delta t_{\mathrm{Spa}}^{\mathrm{ETF}}$, probably the only viable conclusion that may be reached is lack of clearly manifested proofs for the diffusion of ETFs. The Sweden interpretation is more comprehensive as, despite some reversals of the trend, a gradual increase in the assets of Swedish ETFs was observed. Estimated $\kappa_{\mathrm{Swe}}^{\mathrm{ETF}}$ is slightly below the maximum value from August 2017 which implies that the Swedish market is already past the phase of rapid development (i.e., past the second stage of logistic growth). $Tm_{\mathrm{Swe}}^{\mathrm{ETF}}$ at February 2006 suggests a similar conclusion and $\Delta t_{\mathrm{Swe}}^{\mathrm{ETF}}$ at approximately 20.5 years (derived from very low rate of diffusion) is consistent with the observed slow, yet sustainable, increase in the assets of Swedish ETFs. It can be also interpreted as evidence for the limited success of ETFs in Sweden.

Apart from the uptake with respect to ETFs market development observed during the last months of the analyzed period, similar to a few other countries (e.g., France), the trajectory of the Swiss market development noticeably resembles S-shaped, with all three stages of diffusion identifiable; therefore, a high $R^2$ of 0.94 was returned. Estimated $\kappa_{\mathrm{Swi}}^{\mathrm{ETF}}$ is lower than the values of assets in the late 2016 and 9 months of 2017. Ignoring that subperiod and focusing on the trends observed prior to it, based on the estimates of $Tm_{\mathrm{Swi}}^{\mathrm{ETF}}$ and $\Delta t_{\mathrm{Swi}}^{\mathrm{ETF}}$ we may state that Swiss ETFs market since at least the mid-2011 has tended to stagnate, without substantial increases in the assets of ETFs. Preceding growth (formally, the second stage of diffusion) was, however, very rapid and apparently the quickest among all leading European ETFs markets.

Even though the values obtained for Turkey should not necessarily be perceived as misspecifications (for instance, $\kappa_{\mathrm{Tur}}^{\mathrm{ETF}}$ has a value similar to the ones observed within the analyzed period, thus, it may be regarded as attainable), the extremely low $R^2$ (at only 0.071; see Table 3.7) means that the diffusion model is not the best way to analyze the Turkish ETFs market. As Fig. 3.18 proves, its development path, similar to the one observed for

Norway, is to some extent reverse U-shaped; or, to be more exact, it is M-shaped, with two emerging peaks and can by no means be described as S-shaped.

Finally, the last analyzed country is the largest European ETFs market, that is, the United Kingdom. Notably, returned $R^2$ of the model for this country is close to 1; the parameter $\kappa_{UK}^{ETF}$ was estimated at c. \$563 billion, the highest level among countries with no misspecifications returned of the estimated models (much higher than the presently achieved level due to the assumed S-shaped diffusion over the entire period). Compared to France, it may be stated that the UK market is still in the phase of very rapid development, without clear signs of saturation of the local investment funds industry with ETFs. However, in contrast to the French market, the implied points in time are much less distant. This conclusion is supported by the value of $Tm_{UK}^{ETF}$, estimated as May 2017. $\Delta t_{UK}^{ETF}$ of 169 months implies that growth to 90% of $\kappa_{UK}^{ETF}$, that is, c. \$507 billion (approximately 62% higher than the maximum observed value, in August 2017), from the level of c. \$56 billion (10% of $\kappa_{UK}^{ETF}$), which was reached in October 2009, it is expected to take c. 14 years and occur in the second half of 2023. Taking into account the estimates for the other large European ETFs market, in Germany, it is evident that the UK market may be denoted as the most developed in the region with the highest penetration of the innovative funds in the local financial system. The high value of $\kappa_{UK}^{ETF}$ implies potential for further growth which is confirmed by the predictions discussed in Section 3.3. Comparison of $\kappa_{UK}^{ETF}$, $\kappa_{Fra}^{ETF}$, and $\kappa_{Ger}^{ETF}$ suggests potential for a change in the ranking of the most developed ETFs markets in Europe as the German market could be overhauled by the French market. Detailed analysis of the predictions (see Section 3.3) indicates, however, that this statement may be too far-reaching and unsubstantiated.

## 3.2.3 Diversity of the European Exchange-Traded Funds Markets

Conclusions from the analysis of both descriptive statistics and estimates of diffusion models as well as discussion of each European ETFs market's attributes indicate a high level of diversity. In our sample we evaluate not only the markets which may be perceived as highly developed, with substantial potential for the future growth, such as Germany or the United Kingdom, but also markets where the assets of ETFs are very low and the periods of their growth were short and unsustainable. Therefore, we focus now on the issue of the European ETFs markets structure in terms of the division of the assets between the countries by applying selected descriptive statistics and coefficients allowing for the analysis of the observed inequalities. This part of the analysis may be regarded as a supplement to the preceding discussion.

Table 3.8 presents an overview of the indicators which may be used to conduct a basic analysis of the inequalities in the geographical structure of the European ETFs markets. The average value of assets of the local ETFs market has been gradually increasing between 2004 and 2017, reaching the level of c. \$97 billion, compared to merely c. \$3 billion at the beginning. Analysis of the smallest market in our sample is biased as in some countries there had been no ETFs in the initial years of the evaluated time period. However, when the final years are taken into account (when ETFs were present in all countries under consideration), it may be noticed that the Hungarian market was the smallest one, with only \$10 million of the assets of locally primary listed funds. Examination of the maximum levels confirms the conclusions which were presented with regard to the country-specific trends. The French market was the largest one (i.e., the most developed in our approach) in the 2004–07 period, during the initial years of the European ETFs industry. Since 2008 and until mid-2013, Germany held the position of the European leader (in the second half of 2012 and first half of 2013 the values of the assets of German and UK ETFs were almost the same). Finally, the United Kingdom is the most recent regional leader, with significant dominance over France and Germany due to rapid growth since 2012.

The next two indicators presented in Table 3.8 are the Gini coefficient and Atkinson index (see Methodological annex—Method 2). In both cases, higher values indicate a more unequal distribution among the analyzed values (here values of assets of ETFs in the analyzed countries); for a graphical representation see Fig. 3.19. It can be clearly noted that both indicators have increased considerably between 2004 and 2017. Looking first at the Gini coefficient, we can see that it has risen from 0.44 to 0.76 (by c. 72%); growth of the Atkinson index has been even more substantial (by c. 150%). However, that apparent increase in the inequality of the distribution of the assets of ETFs has not been gradual. Most of this growth in the disparity took place during the first 4 years of the considered period, between 2004 and 2007 (i.e., before the global financial crisis). This may be explained by the rapid development of the largest ETFs markets (which were also among the first in Europe where ETFs had been launched) while in other European countries innovative funds had been to high degree unrecognized by potential users and their number was scarce. After 2007, the group of the European leading markets has been unchanged yet

**TABLE 3.8** Selected Indicators of the European Exchange-Traded Funds (ETFs) Markets Structure. Period 2004–17

| Year | Average (mln USD) | Minimum (mln USD) | Maximum (mln USD) | Gini coefficient | Atkinson index (for $\varepsilon = 0.5$) |
|------|-------------------|-------------------|-------------------|------------------|------------------------------------------|
| 2004 | 3015.1 | 0.9 (Turkey) | 12,013.5 (France) | 0.44 | 0.25 |
| 2005 | 4395.8 | 9.1 (Norway) | 18,845.6 (France) | 0.53 | 0.35 |
| 2006 | 7948.5 | 28.1 (Norway) | 31,984.9 (France) | 0.58 | 0.39 |
| 2007 | 10,324.2 | 27.5 (Hungary) | 39,659.3 (France) | 0.66 | 0.49 |
| 2008 | 12,318.5 | 10.8 (Hungary) | 52,368.8 (Germany) | 0.69 | 0.52 |
| 2009 | 20,370.9 | 18.3 (Hungary) | 83,236.4 (Germany) | 0.69 | 0.53 |
| 2010 | 29,091.0 | 16.3 (Hungary) | 99,399.7 (Germany) | 0.71 | 0.57 |
| 2011 | 33,869.5 | 10.3 (Hungary) | 95,579.9 (Germany) | 0.72 | 0.59 |
| 2012 | 41,180.3 | 11.8 (Hungary) | 112,991.1 (Germany) | 0.72 | 0.59 |
| 2013 | 48,656.3 | 11.3 (Hungary) | 148,672.4 (United Kingdom) | 0.74 | 0.59 |
| 2014 | 59,589.3 | 8.4 (Hungary) | 193,280.6 (United Kingdom) | 0.75 | 0.61 |
| 2015 | 65,837.3 | 10.5 (Hungary) | 212,144.3 (United Kingdom) | 0.75 | 0.61 |
| 2016 | 77,472.7 | 13.8 (Hungary) | 252,585.5 (United Kingdom) | 0.76 | 0.62 |
| 2017 | 97,229.8 | 6.1 (Hungary) | 312,100 (United Kingdom) | 0.76 | 0.62 |

*Note*: Year-end data for each country are used for calculations, except for 2017 (data as of end of August); zero values (countries with no primary listed ETFs in a given year) are excluded.
*Authors' calculations.*

the distribution has become slightly more equal. It may be stated that in this perspective the structure of the European market has stabilized, with three clearly distinguishable groups of countries and no new countries with primary listed ETFs. Overall, the inequality is still increasing, even though the pace of this process is slow.

### 3.2.4 Exchange-Traded Funds Markets in France, Germany, Italy, Spain, and the United Kingdom: Joint Analysis

In the final part of this section we focus on the ETFs markets in the five largest economies of the EU: France, Germany, Italy, Spain, and the United Kingdom, labeled henceforth as 5-EU, considered jointly. This approach is adopted in order to analyze the regional trends and may be substantiated by the high level of the economic integration of the selected countries which allows their joint analysis. Another reason is their dominance in the

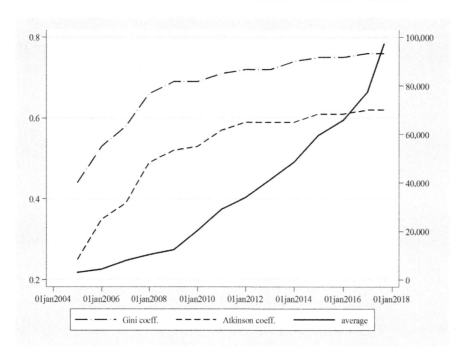

**FIGURE 3.19**  Average values of assets of ETFs in the European countries, Gini coefficients and Atkinson indexes. Period 2004–17.
*Note*: On the left axis are values of Gini coefficient and Atkinson index; on the right axis are average values of assets of ETFs. Year-end data for each country used for calculations, except for 2017 (data as of end of August); zero values (countries with no primary listed ETFs in a given year) excluded. *ETF*, Exchange-traded fund. Source: *Authors' elaboration*.

**TABLE 3.9**  Assets of Exchange-Traded Funds (ETFs) Primary Listed in the Five Largest EU Countries: France, Germany, Italy, Spain, and the United Kingdom (5-EU). Period 2004–17, Monthly Data

|  | No. of obs. | Minimum (mln USD) | Maximum (mln USD) | Average (mln USD) | Average monthly dynamic | Absolute change (mln USD) | Total growth rate (%) |
|---|---|---|---|---|---|---|---|
| 5-EU | 164 | 18,416.7 | 616,279.3 | 229,902.1 | 102.3 | 597,862.6 | 3246.3 |
|  |  | (I 2004) | (VIII 2017) |  |  |  |  |

*Notes*: Average monthly dynamic calculated as geometric mean. *EU*, European Union.
*Own calculations.*

context of the regional market; the share of all other countries is minimal, with the exception of Switzerland. It should be remembered, however, that the 5-EU ETFs market consists above all of the ETFs primary listed in France, Germany, and the United Kingdom, while the share of both Italian and Spanish ETFs is negligible. Following the structure of the analysis applied for the individual countries, we start with the evaluation of the descriptive statistics, followed by the discussion of results obtained using the diffusion model.

Assets of ETFs in the 5-EU countries have grown steadily between January 2004 and August 2017 as indicated by the minimum and maximum values as well as the diffusion pattern (see Table 3.9 and Fig. 3.20). At the beginning of the analyzed period, their value was at c. $18.4 billion and over several years it has risen by c. 2.3% a month to more than $616 billion; the total rate growth was impressive as it exceeded 3000%. Closer scrutiny of the changes in the direction and pace of market development at various moments of this period shows that stages of decline (i.e., decreasing assets of ETFs) were short and rebounds of much stronger strength occurred within a few months. The most serious declines occurred in 2008/09 (during the peak of the global financial crisis) and in 2011/12 among the concerns related to the sovereign debt of some eurozone countries. Very rapid growth could be noticed in late 2016 and first 8 months of 2017, as Fig. 3.18 shows, this was a period of quick increase of the ETFs' assets in all five countries.

Table 3.10 shows the parameters of the diffusion model estimated for the aggregate 5-EU market. Very high value of the model's $R^2$ (c. 0.97) suggests that the obtained results may be used to draw some conclusions about

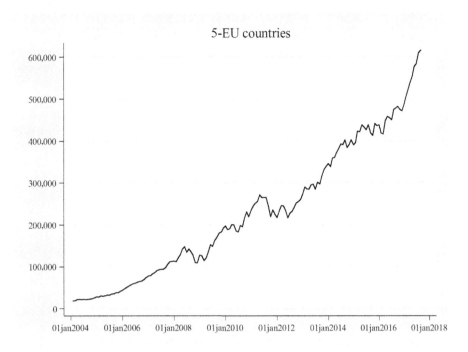

**FIGURE 3.20** Diffusion patterns of assets of ETFs in the 5-EU countries. Period 2004–16, monthly data. *ETF*, Exchange-traded fund; *EU*, European Union. Source: *Authors' elaboration.*

**TABLE 3.10** Estimates of the Diffusion Model of Assets of Exchange-Traded Funds (ETFs) in the 5-EU (5 European Union) Countries. Period 2004–16, Monthly Data

| | $\kappa_i^{ETF}$ **(ceiling/upper asymptote)** | $Tm_i^{ETF}(\beta_i^{ETF})$ **(midpoint)** | $\alpha_i^{ETF}$ **(rate of diffusion)** | $\Delta t_i^{ETF}$ **(specific duration)** | $R^2$ **of the model** | **No. of obs.** |
|---|---|---|---|---|---|---|
| 5-EU countries | 866,637.5 | 139 | 0.022 | 201 | 0.97 | 164 |

*Authors' estimates.*

the analyzed market (taking into account the stage of exponential growth during the final years of the considered time period, the development of the 5-EU market may be characterized as following the logistic trajectory yet still far from the phase of saturation). The parameter $\kappa_{5-EU}^{ETF}$ was estimated at about \$867 billion, which indicates that the assets of the 5-EU ETFs may be even higher if the market development continues and, hence, to be approximated S-shaped trajectory. The midpoint, $Tm_{5-EU}^{ETF}$, was at 139 months (July 2016) which shows that as of the end of the analyzed time period the 5-EU ETFs market is still in the stage of the rapid expansion. Next, the value of $\Delta t_{5-EU}^{ETF}$, that is, specific duration for the 5-EU ETFs markets, may be compared to the country-specific values estimated for the five countries in order to determine the relative pace of the diffusion of ETFs (compare Tables 3.7 and 3.10). For Italy and the United Kingdom the speed of ETFs diffusion has been approximately the same as on the aggregate regional market (this conclusion for the United Kingdom should not be considered as surprising due to the fact the UK ETFs comprise the substantial share of the 5-EU market). In the case of Germany and Spain the pace of diffusion has been much higher and for France significantly lower than for the aggregate 5-EU market. Focusing exclusively on the three largest markets, it means the diffusion of ETFs in Germany proceeded faster than average in the group, while in France it is was below-average, and in the United Kingdom (and Italy) it was neither considerably low nor high.

## 3.3 PROJECTED EXCHANGE-TRADED FUNDS MARKETS DEVELOPMENT

Discussions so far concentrated on the past and current situation in the 12 selected European ETFs markets. However, here we adopt a forward-looking approach and present the results of projections concerning the development of the European ETFs markets (or, more pessimistically, in some cases lack of its displays) obtained using the diffusion models. Consecutive models were estimated separately for each country, based on the arbitrarily imposed values of the upper limits, $\kappa_i^{ETF}$. In order to ensure consistency and comparability of the country-specific models, we adopted a common approach to the setting the values of these parameters; for each market there are five fixed levels of $\kappa_{i,n}^{ETF}$ (the first one is derived from the last observed value, i.e., as of end of August 2017):

**1.** $\kappa_{i,1}^{ETF} = 1.1 \cdot ETF_{2017m8}^i\_\text{assets}$

**2.** $\kappa_{i,2}^{ETF} = 1.25 \cdot \kappa_{i,1}^{ETF}$

**3.** $\kappa_{i,3}^{ETF} = 1.5 \cdot \kappa_{i,2}^{ETF}$

**4.** $\kappa_{i,4}^{ETF} = 1.75 \cdot \kappa_{i,3}^{ETF}$

**5.** $\kappa_{i,5}^{ETF} = 2 \cdot \kappa_{i,4}^{ETF}$

where $i$ is the abbreviated name of the country (i.e., ETFs market) and $n$ is the number of the consecutive level of the upper limit. It is noted that starting from the final empirical level of assets in our dataset, we presume values that grow at an increasing rate, accordingly to the assumptions of the diffusion of innovations framework, that is, before the stage of maturity is reached, innovations should be adopted at a growing rate. Moreover, this facilitates investigation of increasingly more distant upper limits (in time terms). It should be underlined that the application of diffusion models requires making an assumption of the three-staged development path (for details see Methodological annex). Countries are again discussed in alphabetical order. All estimated parameters are presented in Table 3.11. When necessary, we refer to the factors that could affect the further diffusion of ETFs such as overall economic conditions, developments in the financial sector, or other country-specific events. However, a detailed discussion of these issues is presented in Chapter 4, Determinants of the European Exchange-Traded Funds Markets Development.

We start our discussion by outlining the estimates of the parameters returned for France and Germany. The $R^2$ of the estimated models for these two countries are among the highest in the whole analyzed group (behind only the ones obtained for the United Kingdom) which implies their robustness and potential usefulness in formulating predictions concerning the future development of the ETFs markets. Values of the fixed upper limits for France range from $\kappa_{Fra,1}^{ETF}$ at c. \$123 billion to $\kappa_{Fra,5}^{ETF}$ exceeding \$800 billion; for Germany the respective values of $\kappa_{Ger,1}^{ETF}$ and $\kappa_{Ger,5}^{ETF}$ are c. \$208 billion and \$1.36 trillion. As the fourth and fifth projected levels for both countries seem excessively high taking into account the current size of the European or global ETFs market, we focus on levels from one to three. In case of $\kappa_{Fra,1}^{ETF}$ (10% higher than $ETF_{2017m8}^{Fra}\_\text{assets}$) the midpoint should have already been reached in May 2013 yet the value of $\Delta t_{Fra,1}^{ETF}$ shows that 90% of the upper limit will be reached within several years starting from 2017; the same conclusions may be drawn for $\kappa_{Fra,2}^{ETF}$ and $\kappa_{Fra,3}^{ETF}$. Very distant points in time suggested by the specific durations projected for France denote that, despite high values of $R^2$ of the estimated models, these results are highly unreliable and may be regarded as misspecifications. Parameters $\kappa_{Ger,1}^{ETF}$ to $\kappa_{Ger,3}^{ETF}$ are characterized by much lower estimates of midpoints and specific durations (particularly for the first two; for the third level of the predicted upper limit results raise some doubts) which means that reaching them by the German ETFs market may be assessed as more conceivable than in case of its French counterpart. For example, for the level of total assets of c. \$260 billion (i.e., value which was already reached by the UK market in 2017), estimated $Tm_{Ger,2}^{ETF}$ is the month no. 124 (April 2014) and $\Delta t_{Ger,2}^{ETF}$ indicates that growth from 10% to 90% of this value (approximately \$234 billion) is predicted to take about 18 years. As it was noted in Section 3.2.4, the speed of diffusion of ETFs in France over the period 2004−17 has been much lower than in Germany. This conclusion is also supported by the estimates for the least distant future periods presented in Table 3.11. Nevertheless, it may be forecasted that the development of the German market will significantly slow down; comparing $\alpha_{Fra,3}^{ETF}$ to $\alpha_{Ger,3}^{ETF}$ indicates that at some point the French ETFs market will grow more rapidly than its German counterpart.

To sum up, if the historical tendencies persist, our projections imply further substantial development of the German ETFs market over the next few years; in the case of France the outlook is more complicated yet diffusion of ETFs on the local market is highly probable. However, its rate or the approached levels are difficult to predict. Regardless, it may be stated that German ETFs market may reasonably be predicted to remain the second-largest in Europe. It should be emphasized that these countries are two leading economies of the EU and global

**TABLE 3.11** Estimated Parameters of the Exchange-Traded Funds (ETFs) Diffusion for the Selected (Predicted) Values of the Upper Limits

| Country | Upper limit ($\kappa_{i,n}^{\text{ETF}}$) —*fixed* (value of assets of ETFs; mln USD) | $Tm_{i,n}^{\text{ETF}}(\beta_{i,n}^{\text{ETF}})$ (midpoint) — *predicted* | $\alpha_{i,n}^{\text{ETF}}$ (rate of diffusion)—*predicted* | $\Delta t_{i,n}^{\text{ETF}}$ (specific duration)—*predicted* | $R^2$ of the model |
|---|---|---|---|---|---|
| France | 122,439 | 113 (V 2013) | 0.016 | 272 | 0.86 |
| | 153,049 | 143 (XI 2015) | 0.014 | 321 | 0.87 |
| | 229,573 | 200 (VIII 2020) | 0.02 | 365 | 0.82 |
| | 401,754 | 278 (II 2027) | 0.011 | 412 | 0.87 |
| | 803,508 | 369 (IX 2034) | 0.01 | 443 | 0.87 |
| Germany | 207,575 | 101 (V 2012) | 0.026 | 171 | 0.96 |
| | 259,469 | 124 (IV 2014) | 0.021 | 211 | 0.94 |
| | 389,203 | 168 (XII 2017) | 0.017 | 264 | 0.92 |
| | 681,106 | 230 (II 2023) | 0.014 | 309 | 0.91 |
| | 1,362,212 | 303 (III 2029) | 0.013 | 339 | 0.91 |
| Greece | 17 | | Negative parameters returned | | |
| | 22 | | | | |
| | 33 | | | | |
| | 57 | | | | |
| | 115 | | | | |
| Hungary | 6 | | Negative parameters returned | | |
| | 8 | | | | |
| | 13 | | | | |
| | 22 | | | | |
| | 44 | | | | |
| Italy | 2578 | 136 (IV 2015) | 0.018 | 249 | 0.70 |
| | 3223 | 162 (VI 2017) | 0.016 | 282 | 0.70 |
| | 4835 | 212 (VIII 2021) | 0.013 | 325 | 0.70 |
| | 8461 | 279 (III 2027) | 0.012 | 362 | 0.69 |
| | 16,923 | 358 (X 2033) | 0.011 | 387 | 0.69 |
| Norway | 149 | 46 (X 2007) | 0.345 | 13 | 0.53 |
| | 186 | 48 (XII 2007) | 0.189 | 23 | 0.54 |
| | 280 | 72 (XII 2009) | 0.008 | *526—overestimates* | 0.08 |
| | 490 | 283 (VII 2027) | 0.004 | *1020—overestimates* | 0.06 |
| | 981 | *671—overestimates* | 0.003 | *1343—overestimates* | 0.05 |
| Poland | 35 | | Negative parameters returned | | |
| | 44 | 50 (II 2008) | 0.008 | *552—overestimates* | 0.23 |
| | 66 | 162 (VI 2017) | 0.006 | *712—overestimates* | 0.27 |
| | 115 | 328 (IV 2031) | 0.005 | *848—overestimates* | 0.27 |
| | 231 | *532—overestimates* | 0.005 | *939—overestimates* | 0.28 |

*(Continued)*

**TABLE 3.11**   *(Continued)*

| Country | Upper limit ($\kappa_{i,n}^{ETF}$) —*fixed* (value of assets of ETFs; mln USD) | $Tm_{i,n}^{ETF}(\beta_{i,n}^{ETF})$ **(midpoint)** — *predicted* | $\alpha_{i,n}^{ETF}$ **(rate of diffusion)**—*predicted* | $\Delta t_{i,n}^{ETF}$ **(specific duration)**—*predicted* | $R^2$ **of the model** |
|---|---|---|---|---|---|
| Spain | 2003 | 36 (XII 2006) | 0.019 | 227 | 0.141 |
| | 2504 | 65 (V 2009) | 0.012 | 367 | 0.143 |
| | 3756 | 151 (VII 2016) | 0.008 | *533—overestimates* | 0.141 |
| | 6574 | 294 (VI 2028) | 0.006 | *690—overestimates* | 0.139 |
| | 13,149 | *474—overestimates* | 0.006 | *794—overestimates* | 0.139 |
| Sweden | 3818 | 43 (VII 2007) | 0.013 | 342 | 0.522 |
| | 4773 | 86 (II 2011) | 0.009 | 475 | 0.513 |
| | 7160 | 192 (XI 2019) | 0.007 | *655—overestimates* | 0.503 |
| | 12,530 | 357 (X 2033) | 0.005 | *811—overestimates* | 0.490 |
| | 25,060 | *599—overestimates* | 0.005 | *915—overestimates* | 0.49 |
| Switzerland | 80,628 | 107 (XI 2012) | 0.026 | 172 | 0.876 |
| | 100,785 | 130 (X 2014) | 0.021 | 211 | 0.855 |
| | 151,178 | 174 (VI 2018) | 0.017 | 261 | 0.835 |
| | 264,563 | 234 (VI 2023) | 0.015 | 302 | 0.821 |
| | 529,126 | 304 (IV 2029) | 0.013 | 329 | 0.814 |
| Turkey | 53 | | Negative parameters returned | | |
| | 66 | | | | |
| | 100 | | | | |
| | 175 | | | | |
| | 350 | | | | |
| United Kingdom | 343,310 | 125 (V 2014) | 0.034 | 130 | 0.989 |
| | 429,137 | 141 (IX 2014) | 0.029 | 150 | 0.999 |
| | 643,706 | 170 (II 2018) | 0.025 | 177 | 0.999 |
| | 1,126,486 | 209 (V 2021) | 0.022 | 201 | 0.999 |
| | 2,252,972 | 254 (II 2025) | 0.02 | 217 | 0.999 |

*Note:* Misspecifications in italics.
*Authors' estimates.*

economic system, with strong linkages to other countries and regions, which means that the future development of the local ETFs markets may be strongly affected by global events.

As it could have been predicted taking into consideration the observed changes on the ETFs markets in both Greece and Hungary (with noticeable declines over the analyzed time period) and the estimates of the models presented in the preceding section, it is impossible to apply the diffusion models to formulate projections for these countries. Diffusion models assume that the path of the ETFs market development will be S-shaped in form and here it is clearly not the case. This means that, regardless of the assumed fixed level of $\kappa_{Gre}^{ETF}$ or $\kappa_{Hun}^{ETF}$, the returned parameters are negative. To put it differently, it may be concluded that our projections confirm the further expected decline of these markets. In the case of Greece, such results may be explained by referring to the macroeconomic conditions in this country, tracing back to the crisis events which resulted in a strong decline of the local ETFs market between 2008 and 2012. The negligible size of the Hungarian ETFs market, with merely one primary listed fund, means that many, radically different scenarios are possible in the upcoming years. Its closure may lead to the total disappearance of the Hungarian market but, in the opposite scenario, the launch of even a few new funds may lead to its considerable growth (at least in relation to its current state). This means, however, that making any robust projections is impossible.

In the previous sections we included Italy in the middle group of the European ETFs markets, much larger than the group that lags behind yet significantly smaller than the regional leaders. In this section we analyze whether the Italian market can be robustly predicted to come close to the largest ones in Europe. There are no apparent misspecifications for any of the assumed levels of $\kappa_{\text{Ita}}^{\text{ETF}}$ which range from c. \$2.6 billion to \$17 billion and values of $R^2$ of the estimated models are the highest outside the group of the leading countries. However, closer scrutiny of the values of parameters obtained for each $\kappa_{\text{Ita}}^{\text{ETF}}$ shows that they refer to distant points in the future. For instance, in the case of $\kappa_{\text{Ita},1}^{\text{ETF}}$, growth from 10% to 90% of that value of the assets of Italian ETFs (from c. \$258 million to \$2.3 billion) is predicted to require almost 21 years; taking into account the actual moment when the Italian market began its development (since 2008) reaching such level may be assessed as highly uncertain, not to mention any accomplishment of the next upper limits (another reason is the data availability issues described in Section 3.1 that may affect the estimations). It needs to be emphasized, however, that over the last months of the empirical period of 2004—17 the growth of the Italian ETFs market has significantly accelerated. If this trend is sustained in the future, the outlook for this market may change considerably.

Predictions prepared for Norway require particular attention as together with Poland it is the only country in the group of the smallest analyzed ETFs markets for which at least some of the projected diffusion models have not returned negative parameters or misspecifications. Nevertheless, exclusively for $\kappa_{\text{Nor},1}^{\text{ETF}}$ and $\kappa_{\text{Nor},2}^{\text{ETF}}$ (\$149 million and \$186 million) plausible conclusions may be reached due to overestimates for the remaining three levels (extremely high values of specific durations). Predicted rates of diffusion $\alpha_{\text{Nor}}^{\text{ETF}}$ for these levels of $\kappa_{\text{Nor}}^{\text{ETF}}$ are very high and, accordingly, estimates of $\Delta t_{\text{Nor}}^{\text{ETF}}$ are very low. As it may be noticed by checking the values of $Tm_{\text{Nor}}^{\text{ETF}}$, these results must be interpreted with caution as they would mean that projected levels of $\kappa_{\text{Nor}}^{\text{ETF}}$ have already been reached—it is true, but it does not account for the subsequent decline of the Norwegian market. Other reasons of possible distortions were outlined in the preceding section (e.g., high variability). These problems are demonstrated here by the $R^2$ of the respective models of 0.53 and 0.54.

From a technical perspective, results obtained for Poland are to some extent similar to the estimations for Norway. However, in the case of Poland overestimates of $\Delta t_{\text{Pol}}^{\text{ETF}}$ were returned for all levels of $\kappa_{\text{Pol}}^{\text{ETF}}$ (except the first, at \$35 million, for which the values of parameters are negative). The only parameter that could be interpreted is $Tm_{\text{Pol}}^{\text{ETF}}$ yet for $\kappa_{\text{Pol},3}^{\text{ETF}}$ and $\kappa_{\text{Pol},4}^{\text{ETF}}$ it refers to respectively one of the last months in the historical time series and very distant point time (in 2031) suggesting that the diffusion of ETFs in Poland and reaching these levels is marked by high uncertainty. This conclusion is supported by the low values of $R^2$ for all models for Poland. In the case of $\kappa_{\text{Pol},3}^{\text{ETF}}$ (i.e., \$44 million) the midpoint value is February 2008, but $\Delta t_{\text{Pol},2}^{\text{ETF}}$ shows that reaching even that level is projected to take several years. It should be remembered, however, that this is the analysis of one single fund and may not be considered to be plausible as the diffusion of the Polish ETFs may change due to, for example, decisions of this fund's provider (in the extreme scenario of the fund's closure, it may lead to the complete disappearance of the Polish ETFs market).

Spain is the next country (after Italy) in the group of mid-developed ETFs markets. Projected diffusion estimates obtained for this country may be regarded as the least reliable in this group of European countries (compare $R^2$ of models with respective parameters for Italy or Sweden). Only the estimates of $\kappa_{\text{Spa},1}^{\text{ETF}}$ and $\kappa_{\text{Spa},2}^{\text{ETF}}$ are not obvious misspecifications and in both cases the evidence for further diffusion of ETFs is highly unconvincing. One of the factors that may hinder acceleration of the ETFs market development in Spain is the fact that the Spanish exchange is not part of any larger group of exchanges. The examples of both Italy and Sweden (i.e., the two other comparably advanced ETFs markets) show that such cooperation may be able to ensure more sustainable diffusion of ETFs (due to, e.g., easier cross-listing) and more optimistic projections.

Even though in the case of Sweden diffusion models seem to be better fitted to formulate the predictions of the ETFs market development, closer scrutiny of the estimated specific durations shows that only first and second level of $\kappa_{\text{Swe}}^{\text{ETF}}$ allow for some interpretations yet very vague. For both $\kappa_{\text{Swe},1}^{\text{ETF}}$ and $\kappa_{\text{Swe},2}^{\text{ETF}}$ estimated $\Delta t_{\text{Swe}}^{\text{ETF}}$ is very low and $\Delta t_{\text{Swe}}^{\text{ETF}}$ imply an extremely long period before even 90% of the upper limit will be reached (for $\kappa_{\text{Swe},2}^{\text{ETF}}$ growth to that value of assets from 10% of the upper limit is expected to take almost 40 years). It may be, thus, concluded that the future development of the Swedish market is predicted to be very slow and any substantial increases are highly uncertain unless some deep changes take place (one of the possible developments may be linked with cooperation within the NASDAQ group).

Estimates obtained for Switzerland are to some extent inconclusive. At first glance, at least for the lower levels of $\kappa_{\text{Swi}}^{\text{ETF}}$, the results seem to be sensible and refer to not too distant points in time. For instance, growth from 10% to 90% of $\kappa_{\text{Swi},1}^{\text{ETF}}$ (c. \$72 billion) is expected to take approximately 14 years and values of $\Delta t_{\text{Swi}}^{\text{ETF}}$ are close to those obtained for Germany (due to comparable predicted speed of diffusion). This would suggest potential for continued development of the Swiss ETFs market. There is, however, one important stipulation. What is important and underscores the problem with projections for this market, is the comparison of values of $R^2$ of the model discussed in Section 3.2 which refers strictly to the analysis of historical development (0.94) to the respective values for the models applied for projections (between 0.88 and 0.81). It seems that the diffusion framework is more suitable for the analysis of the past development of the Swiss market than its future changes. The reason is the possible saturation of the Swiss financial system with the innovative funds, as concluded previously. This could mean that the Swiss ETFs market requires some significant change that could allow for overcoming the saturation stage and returning to the phase of rapid development. Nevertheless, already very high value of ETFs' assets in relation to the local GDP and the fact that it remains outside the European Economic Area (which can limit the motivation for the European financial companies to domicile or primary list ETFs in this country) may mean that the Swiss ETFs market has approached the limits of its development.

Estimates for the Turkish ETFs market are not discussed for the reasons outlined with regard to Greece and Hungary, that is, lack of noticeable diffusion of the innovative funds in the preceding period and shape of the market development's path. Regardless of the assumed value of $\kappa_{Tur}^{ETF}$, using diffusion models is not possible.

The United Kingdom is the final country in the analyzed group of European economies. One of the most striking findings which may be reached based on information in Table 3.11 is the extremely high level of the $R^2$ for the models estimated for this country, close to 1, which implies that diffusion models are well suited to the predictive analysis of the UK ETFs market. Regardless of the assumed level of $\kappa_{UK}^{ETF}$, estimates of the diffusion parameters indicate projected rapid adoption of the innovative funds in the UK financial system. Estimated midpoints, $Tm_{UK}^{ETF}$, are at points in time in the final years of the historical time period or in the upcoming next few years (between 2014 and 2025). Due to the very high anticipated rate of diffusion (the highest among all considered countries) values of $\Delta t_{UK}^{ETF}$ are on the levels indicating the possibility of reaching very high levels of assets of ETFs over the next few years. Total assets of the UK ETFs could exceed $500 billion in the early 2020s and reach $1 trillion by the end of that decade. Even in the case of a future slowdown, the UK market is bound to remain the largest in the region.

Obviously, these estimates are based on historical data and assumptions of the diffusion models. Among the future uncertainty factors, which may result in less optimistic actual changes, the impact of Brexit is probably most important yet difficult to assess. In the most favorable scenario, in the case of insignificant changes to the British financial system (e.g., legal) its impact will be weak or negligible. In the most pessimistic scenario (rather improbable) a breakdown of the UK ETFs market may take place with funds withdrawing from that market and choosing other listing locations.

In order to sum up our predictions we may formulate three general conclusions regarding the projected development of the European ETFs markets by referring them to the three categories of countries:

1. The *most developed* markets (France, Germany, Switzerland and the United Kingdom) may be predicted to grow even further (assuming no substantial impact of the political events such as leaving the EU; there are, at present, no signs of Brexit negatively influencing the UK ETFs market). Dominance of the UK market is not jeopardized and most probably the German one will still be the second-largest. Interesting changes may take place with regard to the third place in this ranking as the Swiss market may catch up with the currently third-largest French one.
2. In the group of the *mid-developed* markets (Italy, Spain, and Sweden) our projections exhibit some (limited) potential for further development of ETFs. However, none of these markets may reasonably be expected to grow substantially. Reaching levels of development observed for the leading countries is highly improbable.
3. The *least-developed* markets (Greece, Hungary, Norway, Poland, and Turkey) demonstrate no signs of improvement under the scenario of the current trends' continuation. The only exception is Norway (yet the predicted increase is too negligible for this market to converge to the mid-developed group). Obviously, some deep changes in the local financial and economic systems may take place, yet the experiences of the previous years are rather pessimistic and point towards further decline or at least stagnation.

To conclude, our analysis showed that inequalities between the development of the ETFs markets in Europe may in the future grow even further. Furthermore, it confirmed (in addition to the models discussed in the preceding section) that diffusion of the innovations such as ETFs is definitely not uniform, even in the group of regionally leading countries. In Chapter 4, Determinants of the European Exchange-Traded Funds Markets Development, we explore this issue in-depth, both on regional and country-wise levels, with the application of econometric models.

# 3.4 STORY OF FAILURE AND SUCCESS OF EXCHANGE-TRADED FUNDS IN EUROPE: CASE STUDIES (PART I)

The first case study which we consider is the story of ETFs market in a European country where these innovative financial products unambiguously failed to gain any significance: Poland. After presenting briefly the economic conditions in Poland in the period 2010–17 (i.e., since the launch of the first ETFs), we summarize the key trends in the Polish financial system in order to show fully the environment in which ETFs appeared and attempted to compete with other similar financial products. Then we discuss the general patterns observed on the Polish ETFs market and present key information about products available on the local stock exchange. We end our analysis by attempting to identify the key barriers that hindered its development and potential future changes. This case study is supplemented by an analysis of the other part of the global ETFs market which also consists of Polish products, that is, ETFs that manage Polish assets (e.g., stocks of Polish companies) yet are listed on the stock exchanges outside Poland. It explicitly shows that the role of Poland on the global ETFs market is rather insignificant, but the entire outcome is much more positive than when considering exclusively funds listed in Poland. Previous studies on the Polish ETFs market are rather scarce and focused primarily on its history, structure, and the attributes of the Polish ETFs such as their tracking errors; see, for example the studies of (in the chronological order) Chodnicka and Jaworski (2012), Lachowski (2012), Mitrenga (2014), Gierałtowska (2015), and Letkowski (2017), most of these were published in Polish.

The history of ETFs in Poland is much shorter than in any other European country discussed in this chapter. The first ETF on the Warsaw Stock Exchange (WSE; it is the only stock exchange in Poland) was launched in 2010 after a few unsuccessful earlier attempts which can be traced back to 2002 (Chodnicka & Jaworski, 2012; Lachowski, 2012); interestingly the first index fund in Poland was launched in 1997 when the Polish mutual funds market was still in a very early stage of its growth (Miziołek, 2017). In 2010 ETFs were already well-established in most Western European countries. The late launch should not, however, be perceived as a serious obstacle to their growth, which is proven by the examples of other countries, also those outside Europe. Moreover, according to the innovation framework, late adopters of new products obtain certain advantages as they can profit from the experience of the first movers. In Poland, however, we can observe only disadvantages of the late start.

The economic environment of the ETFs market in Poland seems to be undeniably positive. The rate of economic growth (measured in terms of GDP) was positive even during the global financial crisis of 2008 and it has not declined seriously in the post-crisis period (see Fig. 3.12). The levels of public debt and budget deficit have increased, as in most other European countries in this period, but they have not become a burden to the country's economic potential and stayed relatively low when compared to other big economies of the EU. Furthermore, there were no disruptive events (such as defaults of banks or public debt repayment issues) in the Polish financial system in contrast with many other European countries. In fact, the Polish financial system seemed to be almost untouched by the events in the United States or Western and Southern Europe. This does not mean, however, that there were no less or more serious problems in certain parts of the financial system (e.g., serious declines of the stock market prices during the global financial crisis or higher rates of defaults on the currency-denominated mortgage loans, particularly the ones based on the increasingly more expensive Swiss franc), but they have not decreased the overall financial stability (Fig. 3.21).

Despite the rather positive state of the economic and financial system, ETFs in Poland have not developed in any dimension since their launch; in some aspects it may be rather stated that they have weakened their position on the financial markets. The first ETF was launched in 2010, several months after the outbreak of the global financial crisis and during the mounting eurozone debt crisis. The name of the first fund and, in fact, the only one fully linked to the Polish exchange, is Lyxor WIG 20 UCITS ETF'(for brevity we use henceforth the exchange's ticker: ETFW20L). Due to the quite unique (yet not fully unique)[3] situation of the Polish ETFs market (with only one fund listed primarily on the local stock exchange), we scrutinize this fund and analyze its key attributes.

ETFW20L is managed by the Lyxor International Asset Management SAS (i.e., Lyxor) and it is domiciled in Luxembourg (Multi Units Luxembourg, 2017); there are no ETFs domiciled in Poland. It was launched on

---

[3]Among the countries in our sample the only other example with similar ETFs market's structure in terms of primary listing is Hungary, yet we decided to discuss Poland due to its significantly larger economy and financial system. As of the end of 2016 assets of Hungarian ETFs constituted ca. 1.1% of the local GDP whereas in Poland it stands at ca. 0.5%, i.e., the lowest value in the group of analyzed countries which proves the substantial underdevelopment of the Polish ETFs market (additionally, ETFs in Poland have been available for the shortest period in the whole sample).

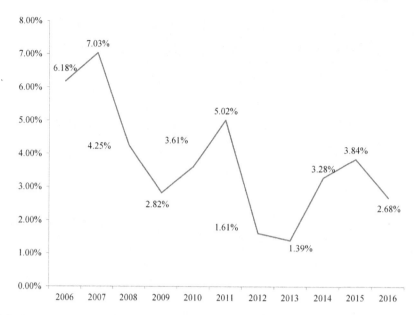

**FIGURE 3.21**  Annual GDP growth rate in Poland during 2006–16 (market prices; constant local currency). Source: *Own elaboration based on World Bank (2017).* World development indicators *(World Bank, 2017).*

February 10, 2010, but due to the necessary notification procedure and obligation to meet the listing requirements, it started trading a few months later, on September 22, 2010 (Lyxor ETF, 2017). The provider of the ETF is represented in Poland by the local subsidiary of the same financial corporation, that is, Société Générale. The fund is a stock-index equity ETF and is legally structured as an UCITS-compliant fund, similarly to the vast majority of the European ETFs. It tracks the returns of the blue-chip index of the WSE, that is, WIG20. WIG20 is based on the prices of the 20 most liquid and largest companies which are listed on the WSE. The index is price-based, therefore, it does not account for the income element of the stock investments (e.g., dividends). However, since 2013, the fund does not pay out the dividends to investors, but rather reinvests them (i.e., they are added to its capitalization) which is one of the sources of the discrepancies between the quotes of the benchmark and ETF (Forsal, 2012). Since then the tracked index is in fact WIG20 TR (total return) as stated in the Lipper's database. The currency of the fund is PLN. It does not engage in securities lending which eliminates this kind of risk for investors.

Despite the strong tendency to withdraw from the synthetic replication observed in the European ETFs industry, some funds remain synthetic-based; ETFW20L is such example as, initially, Lyxor offered only synthetic funds but since 2012 it started switching to physical ones (Morningstar, 2017). It engages in OTC swap contracts with the controlling financial group, Société Générale (Lyxor ETF, 2017), thus it exposes investors to some level of counterparty risk, limited severely by the UCITS regulations.

Assets of ETFW20L declined significantly since their launch in 2010 (see Fig. 3.22) but the very significant decline in the mid-2011 (from the highest level close to $100 million in April 2011 to just c. $20 million in September 2011) was caused by the withdrawal of the seed funds by Lyxor (Miziołek, 2015). Consequently, only the values noted after that initial period fully reflect the changes in the assets caused by activities of investors and results of the tracked benchmark. If they are compared with the changes in WIG20, it can be seen clearly that the only significant growth since the beginning of 2017 was mainly a result of a strong upsurge in the prices on the Polish stock market (see Fig. 3.23) and not by the sudden growth of investors' attention. Interestingly, though, during the severe decline of WIG20 in 2015 investors did not withdraw from ETFW20L; the decrease in the fund's assets was much less substantial than the decline of WIG20. The average value of the ETF's assets for the period September 2011–September 2017 was at c. $21 million and the lowest level of c. $12.5 million was observed in May 2012, that is, during one of the peak points of the eurozone debt crisis (and, accordingly, significant decrease in WIG20; see Fig. 3.23). By the end of September 2017 assets of ETFW20L reached c. 31 mln USD; 1 month earlier it was c. 32 mln USD which was the highest level since the mid-2011, that is, after the seed capital was withdrawn.

ETFW20L is a passive equity fund (i.e., the fundamental type of ETF) aimed at tracking the performance of the domestic (Polish) blue-chip index, therefore, essential parameters to be considered in its evaluation are both

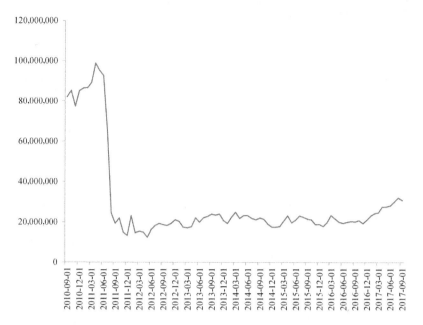

**FIGURE 3.22**    Assets of Lyxor WIG 20 UCITS ETF (ETFW20L) in September 2010–September 2017 (USD). Source: *Own elaboration.*

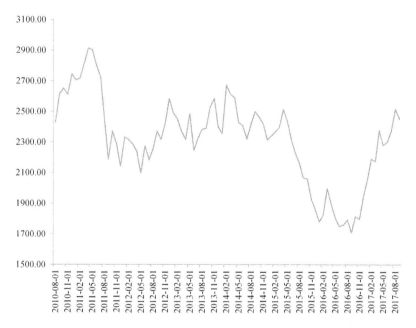

**FIGURE 3.23**    Blue-chip index of the Polish stock market: WIG20. End-of-month values in September 2010–September 2017. Source: *Own elaboration based on the monthly reports of WFE.*

tracking difference and tracking error. According to the September 2017 monthly report published by its provider (Lyxor ETF, 2017), tracking difference for 2016 was calculated as 2.29% (in the preceding years its values were at 2.01% in 2015, 2.74% in 2014, and 3.89% in 2013). More robust conclusions may be reached using the tracking error indicator: in both 2015 and 2016 its calculated value was 0.19% (in 2014 it was 0.24% and in 2013 only 0.03%); according to the fund's prospectus, under normal market conditions it aims to not exceed the tracking error of 0.25% (Multi Units Luxembourg, 2017).[4]

---

[4]According to data acquired through the Lipper's database, the tracking ability of the fund was much poorer. The tracking error of the fund for the one-year period was given as of September 2017 as 2.73%, i.e., considerably higher than in the fund's reports. Most probably it is a result of some unidentifiable error in the selection of the benchmark. Additional parameters (all for the one-year period), alpha of 0.92, beta of 1.58, and correlation coefficient of 82%, support this stipulation (particularly beta substantially above 1, the level expected for a passive fund).

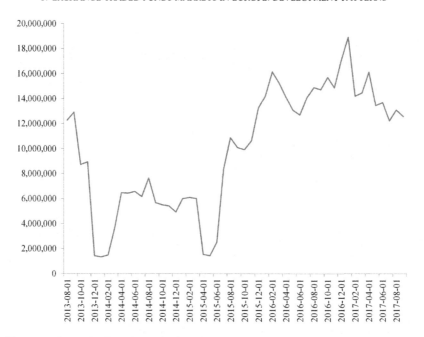

**FIGURE 3.24**    Assets of Lyxor WIG 20 UCITS ETF-C—EUR (WIG) in August 2013–September 2017 (USD). Source: *Own elaboration based on the Lipper database.*

According to the information on the fund's attributes available both in the provider's obligatory legal statements (Lyxor ETF, 2017) and the Lipper's database, its total expense ratio as of 2017 was reported to be 0.45% (per year). A comparison of this value with the mean costs noted on the European ETFs market (see Fig. 3.10) shows that the presented fund is much more expensive for its users than the average equity fund in the region. It may be attributed to its small size and inability to gather considerable assets and, thus, yield benefits from economies of scale. TER of ETFW20L may also be compared to the ratios for the biggest ETFs primary listed in Europe (see Table 3.2) which further underlines the relative advantage of the large funds. From the investor's perspective, the relatively high cost of the fund may be one of the factors discouraging potential users of this product and, consequently, limiting the development of the entire Polish ETFs market.

ETFW20L uses synthetic replication, therefore, the assets it actually holds does not need to be directly linked to the underlying benchmark. Closer analysis of the fund's portfolio proves that they differ significantly from the ones comprising WIG20. As of end of September 2017, assets from advanced economies comprised most of the fund's portfolio (nearly 99% out of which 70% included highly liquid shares of German, Spanish, and Japanese companies, mostly from the financial, industrial, health-care, and similar sectors). Interestingly, it held no Polish assets, e.g., stocks of the Polish companies (which is not necessary in the utilized tracking method).

To supplement the analysis of ETFW20L, it is necessary to mention that for a few years another ETF, very strongly related to ETFW20L, was available. This "twin" fund, formally labeled as Lyxor WIG 20 UCITS ETF-C—EUR (it was actually a part of the same fund that offered two share classes, but due to a few distinctive features we treat them as separate entities). Its shares were listed at Euronext Paris, thus, the fund's currency was EUR (which was a source of the currency risk as the tracked index is denominated in PLN); the ticker used at the French exchange was WIG (Lyxor ETF, 2017). The "French" fund had been launched 3 years later than its "Polish" counterpart, on August 19, 2013. Its assets have remained considerably lower (see Fig. 3.24), with an average value of c. 10 mln USD; and were closest to the Polish fund on the verge of 2016 and 2017. On March 9, 2018 it was delisted from the Euronext exchange due to the decision made by Lyxor to merge the share class of the Lyxor WIG 20 UCITS ETF-C—EUR into the main fund, ETFW20L (Multi Units Luxembourg, 2018); this meant, among others, that all assets of the French fund were transferred to the Polish one. The reason for this decision was to increase the liquidity of the fund's shares by "rationalizing" their classes. Shares of the fund tracking WIG20 are still listed on the Euronext Paris exchange, but currently it is merely the cross-listing of the ETFW20L rather than of a separate fund which ceased to exist.

ETFW20L is not the only innovative fund whose shares are listed and traded on the Polish stock exchange. Two other funds had been introduced on the WSE in May 2011, and they are also managed by Lyxor. They are, however, accessible through cross-listing and Poland is not their primary listing location. Both funds are listed

**TABLE 3.12**  Exchange-Traded Funds (ETFs) Traded on the Warsaw Stock Exchange Primary Listed outside Poland. End of August 2017

| Fund | Assets (bln USD) | Benchmark | Primary listing exchange | Domicile | Total expense ratio (%) | Replication method |
|---|---|---|---|---|---|---|
| Lyxor DAX (DR) UCITS ETF EUR | 1.22 | DAX 30 | Xetra (Germany) | Luxembourg | 0.15 | Physical |
| Lyxor S&P 500 UCITS ETF D-EUR | 1.98 | S&P 500 | Xetra (Germany) | Luxembourg | 0.15 | Synthetic |

*Own elaboration.*

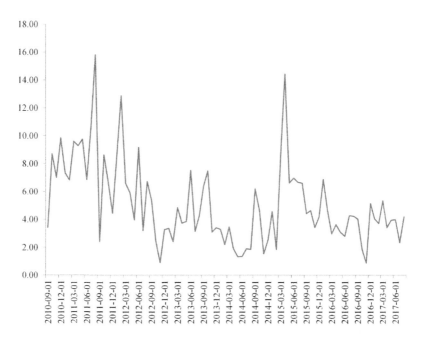

**FIGURE 3.25**  Turnover of the shares of ETFs on the Warsaw Stock Exchange. September 2010—August 2017, monthly data (million USD). Source: *Own elaboration based on monthly reports of WFE.*

on multiple European exchanges and their base currency is EUR. Their key features are presented in Table 3.12. If they are compared with the corresponding attributes of ETFW20L, it can be noticed that they are much bigger (in both cases assets exceed 1 billion USD) and less expensive (i.e., with considerably lower TERs). This may be explained, however, by referring to the tracked benchmarks whose constituents are much more liquid, in particular in case of S&P 500. Furthermore, they are much more intensively traded, with significantly higher turnover of their shares (when all listing locations are considered). The apparent relative advantages of these two funds may be regarded as one of the factors which hinder the increase in demand for the only fund primary listed in Poland in favor of the other ETFs available on the WSE.

After extensive presentation of the Polish ETFs market based on the data on assets, now we focus briefly on the turnover statistics. Analysis of the turnover of the shares of ETFs on the only Polish stock exchange, WSE, confirms the underdevelopment of the local market for innovative funds. The average monthly turnover has been slightly above $5 million; among the 12 analyzed countries lower values have been observed only on the Greek and Hungarian stock exchanges (two other economies with scarce signs of broader adoption of ETFs). Peak monthly values of turnover were noticed in the mid-2011, February 2012, and April 2015 (see Fig. 3.25 for details) and only in those months did it exceed $10 million. Bearing in mind the overall low value of turnover, even single transactions of relatively high value (e.g., a few million PLN) can strongly influence the total number for a certain month. Evaluation of the trends in time provides no signs of the development; in 2016 or 2017 either average monthly or cumulated annual turnover was lower than in the first years of the Polish ETFs market. It should be added that transactions on the WSE are conducted in shares of three ETFs (see Table 3.12). The structure of the turnover in terms of the shares of particular funds has been changing over time, but over the period

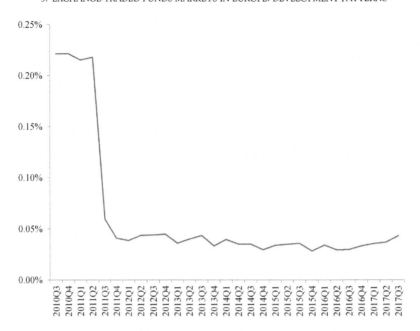

FIGURE 3.26   Share of ETFs in the assets of the Polish investment funds. Quarterly data, Q3 2010–Q3 2017. *ETF*, Exchange-traded fund.
Source: *Own elaboration based on EFAMA's reports and Lipper's database.*

2015–17 ETFW20L has been traded most actively, followed by Lyxor DAX (DR) UCITS ETF EUR and Lyxor S&P 500 UCITS ETF D-EUR.

The position of ETFs in the Polish financial system may be analyzed by referring to their share in the aggregate market for investment funds (i.e., including mutual funds, ETFs, and the other categories; see Fig. 3.26). The general trend in the market share has closely resembled the one observed for ETFW20L assets in absolute terms (compare Fig. 3.22) due to the lack of other ETFs primary listed in Poland as well as similarity of its rate of growth to the increase rate of the entire investment funds market. The only Polish ETF has not, therefore, strengthened its position versus conventional funds. Excluding the first few quarters (period of introduction and the sudden drop in the assets of ETFW20L), the average share of ETFs for the period Q3 2011, Q3 2017 was at c. 0.04% which is a negligible value without noticeable upward tendency. If only UCITS-compliant investment funds are considered, the position of ETFs was slightly stronger, that is, the share of ETFs in the total market was higher with an average value at c. 0.08%, reaching 0.11% at the end of this period, the highest observed level, yet still extremely low. It may, thus, be concluded that ETFs primary listed in Poland have not become a significant part of either Polish investment funds market or the entire financial system. Moreover, it may be reasonably stated that it is highly improbable that they could have affected (positively or negatively) any part of the financial sector or economy at large—we verify this statement in Chapter 5, Exchange-Traded Funds and Financial Systems of European Countries: A Growth Factor or Threat to Stability?

Estimates of the diffusion models for the Polish ETFs market clearly imply that it is one of the least developed in Europe, with no convincing evidence for the diffusion of ETFs. Moreover, the projections prepared using the diffusion models show that the future diffusion of the innovative funds in Poland may not be reliably predicted, in particular taking into consideration the fact there remains the only fund primary listed in this country. There are a number of potential barriers that could be identified as hindering the development of the Polish ETFs market, unfortunately most of them are difficult or impossible to evaluate objectively and/or to quantify. In this section we discuss two possible barriers drawing considerably from Miziołek (2013). The issue of factors that influence the development of the Polish ETFs market is further addressed in Chapter 4, Determinants of the European Exchange-Traded Funds Markets Development.

The first barrier to the widespread adoption of ETFs in Poland is, paradoxically, their distribution channel which in Chapter 2, Exchange-Traded Funds: Concepts and Contexts, was presented as one of their main benefits in relation to conventional funds. However, in the case of Poland (and obviously many other countries) the popularity of capital market investments and, consequently, usage of brokerage accounts is severely limited which restricts the potential group of ETFs market participants. Units of mutual funds or other financial products which may be regarded as substitutes for ETFs are, on the contrary, distributed through a widespread network of bank offices and, to a lesser extent, financial advisory companies. ETFs could, obviously, also be promoted and sold through such channels. However, the incentives of the financial companies to offer ETFs are limited by the fact that most mutual funds are managed by financial institutions associated with banks and by different compensation systems employed by the innovative funds which are less favorable for intermediaries.

The second, and maybe the most fundamental, reason for the insubstantial adoption of ETFs in Poland lies in the investors' awareness. Some financial corporations have marketed their ETFs among Polish investors, but these actions have not been followed by the introduction of the innovative funds on the Polish exchange. Probably the most notable example is the Deutsche Bank whose campaign promoting ETFs focused on encouraging Polish investors to buy the funds provided by this financial group yet it was implicitly assumed that investors would have to buy funds listed outside Poland (the Deutsche Bank's ETFs have never been listed in Poland). Even though the awareness of the attributes of ETFs among more sophisticated Polish investors can be expected to be growing (some signs could already observed as indicated by publications in business press or websites; one of the most vivid promoters of ETFs is the website www.etf.com.pl), due to the very limited range of funds listed in Poland such investors will most probably enter foreign markets through their brokerage accounts, allowing for accessing a very broad and diversified group of, for example, US- or UK-listed ETFs. The deep underdevelopment of the Polish ETFs market in comparison to its counterparts in some other European countries may mean that it will be difficult to catch up with these markets, even after the possible launch of new funds many investors may still prefer to use the foreign-listed ones as it is rather improbable that suddenly a few hundred funds will be listed, or even cross-listed, on the Polish exchange.

Another potential barrier is the underdevelopment of the Polish robo-advising industry. Despite its rapid growth in the European region, in Poland the availability of such financial services is very low as of early 2018 the only European robo-advising platform available for the Polish customers is the UK-based ETFmatic; there are no Poland-based platforms. It may be perceived as a kind of negative feedback loop for the Polish ETFs market due to the prevalence of the shares of ETFs in the portfolios offered by robo-advisors (Kaya, 2017; Phoon & Koh, 2017).

One of the key aspects of the ETFs market is the legal environment of the local investment funds industry which may be either a barrier or accelerator of its development. In the case of Poland, there are two main types of legal acts that determine legal requirements of the ETFs market: local and EU. To large extent, local acts are transpositions of the EU regulations, we will, therefore, focus on their implementation in Poland (we omit various regulations which are self-imposed, for instance, by the local associations of investment funds).

Both EU directives which regulate the way ETFs may be incepted and managed, UCITS (its newest editions is UCITS V) and AIFMD (for more details see Section 3.1.4) were implemented in the Polish legal system together as an amendment to the Polish act on investment funds. It was enacted by the Polish parliament in March 2016 (Funds Axis, 2016) and entered into force in June 2016 (Olechowski, Iwański, & Blocher, 2017), with a 6-month or 1-year transitory period depending on the fund's type (the shorter period applies for most entities). However, the changes were introduced with delays in relation to the deadlines assumed by both directives; in the case of AIFMD (less important in the Polish context) the delay was substantial, that is, almost 3 years. For the much more relevant UCITS it was a few months. It may be stated, however, that these two basic EU investment funds acts have been included in the Polish legal system and Poland does not stray from the other countries of the EU, including the ones with highly developed ETFs markets.

In Section 3.1.4 we emphasized the potential importance of the MiFID II and MiFIR directives for the development of ETFs markets in Europe. As both directives came into force as of early 2018 and some of the implementation legal acts are still under preparations, their exact effects on the Polish market for innovative funds are difficult to assess. As in other European countries, the more extensive disclosures of the fees paid to the managing companies may boost the demand for low-cost investment products such as ETFs. This effect may be particularly significant due to the dominance of the active mutual funds in the Polish investment funds industry which are in the vast majority of cases considerably more expensive than passive funds. MiFID II may also affect the incentives within the most common distribution channels, making ETFs more favorable. There are, however, some potential drawbacks of the new regulations. For example, some banks may withdraw from distribution of investment products managed by the unrelated providers (Fryc, 2017); as no Polish banks or their investment arms manage ETFs this could indefinitely close this distribution channel for innovative funds.

Finally, after discussing ETFs that are primary or cross-listed in Poland, we briefly address the issue of Polish assets in the portfolios of the other ETFs, some of them listed in locations very distant from Poland. We use data extracted from the Lipper's database, based on two criteria: country allocation to Poland (mostly in case of equity funds) or currency allocation to PLN that applies mostly to bond funds, for which country allocation information is not available. The data is as of end August 2017 in order to ensure consistency of the analysis which means that funds that were closed before that date (or launched more recently) are excluded. For obvious reasons we do not include funds for which data are not available in the Lipper's database. Another approach to the issue of ETFs with some links to the Polish economy yet listed abroad would include analysis of the funds that offer exposure to the Polish assets; however, such analysis is hindered by difficulties in obtaining relevant data. It may also be added that it would mostly cover the same funds as evaluated in our sample. It remains an issue rarely addressed in the research literature, with the notable exceptions of Płókarz (2010) and Marszk (2016), which we improve by using the more up-to-date and comprehensive database.

We identify 39 ETFs with Polish assets in their portfolio (some of them are technically various class shares of one fund yet they are included separately due to different locations of the primary listing; it must be underlined that this list is by no means exhaustive). Their aggregated assets reached, as of end of August 2017, c. $21.4 billion, out of which approximately 10% were Polish assets. This means that they were substantially higher than the assets of ETFW20L. The three largest of these funds are bond ETFs that offer exposure to bonds issued in emerging markets: iShares JP Morgan EM Local Gov Bond UCITS ETF ($7.1 billion of assets), VanEck Vectors JP Morgan EM Local Currency Bd ETF ($4.3 billion), and SPDR Barclays Emerging Mkts Loc Bd UCITS ETF ($3.4 billion). They are also the funds with the biggest values of the Polish assets in their portfolios (the highest value was $713 million in the first of these ETFs); another fund with considerable Polish assets is iShares MSCI Poland Capped ETF ($356 million) and, as its name suggests, it is an equity ETF that focuses on the Polish stock market. Looking at the listing locations, the key countries and exchanges of the primary listing of the Poland-linked ETFs are:

1. United States (c. 44% in terms of the Polish assets)—almost entirely listed on the New York Stock Exchange.
2. United Kingdom (c. 42%)—LSE.
3. Germany (c. 12%)—Xetra.

The remaining 2% are split among two funds primary listed in France, and one each in Italy, Lithuania, Latvia, and Switzerland.

In this group of 39 ETFs there are a few funds that require a bit more thorough presentation due to the prevalence of the Polish assets in their holdings. For brevity, we consider exclusively the funds with at least 70% of their portfolios composed by the Polish assets (using data as of August 2017). As a result, we distinguish five funds, listed in Table 3.13 in decreasing order. As it may be noted, only two of the presented funds managed assets exceeding $100 million, both of them operating under the BlackRock's iShares label. However, the explicit leader is the iShares "Polish" ETF listed in the United States; due to the very high share of the Polish assets and overall value of its holdings it may be considered the largest ETF with Polish exposure globally (there are a few funds with higher values of Polish assets in their portfolios, e.g., iShares JP Morgan EM Local Gov Bond UCITS ETF, but they account for a small share of their total holdings). It was launched in 2010 and its benchmark is the index of the Polish equity market, that is, the MSCI Poland IMI 25/50 Index (broader than WIG20, with c. 40 constituents), and the biggest single assets in the portfolio are stocks of the large Polish banks and national oil company (BlackRock, 2018). Its name was changed by the end of 2017 to "iShares MSCI Poland ETF" (i.e., "Capped"

**TABLE 3.13** Exchange-Traded Funds (ETFs) with the Highest Contributions of the Polish Assets in Their Total Portfolios. End of August 2017

| Fund | Share of Polish assets (%) | Total assets (mln USD) | Fund type | Primary listing exchange | Domicile | Base currency |
|---|---|---|---|---|---|---|
| iShares MSCI Poland Capped ETF | 99.97 | 356.1 | Equity ETF | NYSE (USA) | USA | USD |
| iShares MSCI Poland UCITS ETF USD (Acc) | 99.72 | 109.4 | Equity ETF | London Stock Exchange (UK) | Ireland | GBP |
| VanEck Vectors Poland ETF | 88.65 | 21.2 | Equity ETF | NYSE (USA) | USA | USD |
| Amundi ETF MSCI East Europe ExRussia UCITS ETF EUR | 72.14 | 41.4 | Equity ETF | Euronext Paris (France) | France | EUR |
| Amundi ETF MSCI East Europe ExRussia UCITS ETF USD | 72.14 | 9.59 | Equity ETF | Euronext Paris (France) | France | USD |

*Own elaboration.*

was dropped). It should be added that two final ETFs in Table 3.13 are, in fact, two class shares of the same fund managed by Amundi, yet with different base currencies.

Apart from these ETFs, one more fund needs to be mentioned. It was not included in the core analysis due to its later launch date. Expat Poland WIG20 UCITS ETF started issuing shares in December 2017 and it is primary listed in Bulgaria on the Bulgarian Stock Exchange in Sofia (Bulgaria is also its domicile), while its secondary listing location is the XETRA exchange in Germany. It tracks the WIG20 index, similarly to ETFW20L, yet it applies the physical replication method which means that it holds the stocks of companies covered by that index. Its assets remain insignificant; according to the data published by its provider, Expat Asset Management, as of mid-April 2018 they have not exceeded $200,000.

# References

Abner, D. (2016). *The ETF handbook. How to value and trade exchange-traded funds* (2nd ed.). John Wiley & Sons.

Alshaleel, M. K. (2016). Undertakings for the collective investment in transferable securities directive V: Increased protection for investors. *European Company Law*, 13(1), 14–22.

Amenc, N., Ducoulombier, F., Goltz, F., & Le Sourd, V. (2015). *The EDHEC European ETF Survey 2014*. Nice: EDHEC-Risk Institute.

Amenc, N., Goltz, F., & Le Sourd, V. (2017). *The EDHEC European ETF and Smart Beta Survey*. EDHEC-Risk Institute.

Andagulova, Z. *Euroclear Bank (ICSD). Presentation on: International ETF structure*. (2015). <http://aecsd.org/upload/iblock/a90/02_andagulova_euroclear.pdf> Accessed 18.02.18.

Association of the Luxembourg Fund Industry (2013). *Luxembourg: The global fund centre*.

BlackRock (2010). *The rise of UCITS III*.

BlackRock (2011). *Alternative Investment Fund Managers Directive ("AIFMD"): An overview and analysis*.

BlackRock (2015). *Re: Notice Seeking Comment on Asset Management Products and Activities (FSOC 2014-0001). Note for Financial Stability Oversight Council*.

BlackRock (2018). *iShares MSCI Poland ETF*.

BMD (2011). *The first Islamic ETF: Turkey's experience*.

Bodellini, M. (2016). Does it still make sense, from the EU perspective, to distinguish between UCITS and non-UCITS schemes? *Capital Markets Law Journal*, 11(4), 528–539.

Busch, D. (2017). MiFID II and MiFIR: Stricter rules for the EU financial markets. *Law and Financial Markets Review*, 11(2-3), 126–142.

Bush, P., Lee, M., Ferguson, M., & Forstenhausler, M. (2015). *European mutual funds. An introduction to UCITS for US asset managers*. Ernst & Young LLP.

Chance, C. (2016). EU regulatory developments. *Law and Financial Markets Review*, 10(1), 56–63.

Chodnicka, P., & Jaworski, P. (2012). Śledząc parkiet—analiza jakości odwzorowania indeksu WIG20 przez pierwszy na polskim rynku fundusz Exchange Traded Fund [Analyzing the Market—Mapping Quality Analysis of WIG20 by the Exchange Traded Fund, the First Fun on the Polish Market]. *Problemy Zarządzania*, 39(4), 198–205. (in Polish).

De Winne, R., Gresse, C., & Platten, I. (2014). Liquidity and risk sharing benefits from opening an ETF market with liquidity providers: Evidence from the CAC 40 index. *International Review of Financial Analysis*, 34, 31–43.

Deutsche Bank (2017a). *ETF monthly Asia November 2017*.

Deutsche Bank (2017b). *ETF monthly Europe December 2017*.

Deutsche Bank (2017c). *Europe ETF + quarterly directory*.

Donovan-Smith, S., & Gibson, T. (2014). *Global management of regulated funds—A comparison of UCITS and U.S. mutual funds*. K&L Gates.

E&Y. (2014). MiFID II: Time to take action. Wealth & asset management. EY's Global Wealth & Asset Management Center.

Edde, J., & Vaghela, V. *MiFID Seen Sending European ETFs over trillion dollar mark*. (2017). <https://www.bloomberg.com/news/articles/2017-08-10/mifid-seen-sending-european-etfs-over-the-trillion-dollar-mark> Accessed 18.02.18.

ETFGI (2016). *ETFGI monthly newsletter June 2016*.

ETFGI (2017). *ETFGI global ETF and ETP industry highlights—December 2016*.

Euronext. *Listings—Exchange traded funds (ETF)*. (2018). <https://www.euronext.com/fr/node/14318> Accessed 20.03.18.

European Fund and Asset Management Association (EFAMA). (2015). Trends in the European Investment Fund Industry in the first quarter of 2015. *EFAMA Quarterly Statistical Release*, 61, 1–11.

Financial Conduct Authority. *AIFMD*. (2018). <https://www.fca.org.uk/firms/aifmd> Accessed 12.05.18.

Financial Times (2018). ETF providers hope Mifid II will spur European growth. Financial Times Series Launch of Mifid II. *Financial Times*. <https://www.ft.com/content/35ef8194-e578-11e7-8b99-0191e45377ec> Accessed 03.04.18.

Fitzpatrick, N. (2017). Europe's newest ETF providers select Euroclear platform. *Funds Europe*. <http://www.funds-europe.com/news/europe-s-newest-etf-providers-select-euroclear-platform> Accessed 10.02.18.

Forsal. *ETF na WIG20 już nie będzie wypłacał dywidendy [WIG20 ETF will no longer pay out dividends]*. (2012). <https://forsal.pl/artykuly/649696,etf-na-wig20-juz-nie-bedzie-wyplacal-dywidendy.html> Accessed 20.11.17.

Fryc, J. *Jedna unijna dyrektywa wywoła rewolucję w Polsce. Niektórzy już trzęsą się ze strachu [One EU directive will causa a revolution in Poland. Some are already trembling in fear]*. (2017). <https://businessinsider.com.pl/finanse/fundusze/mifid-ii-dyrektywa-unijna-co-to-jest-konsekwencje-wprowadzenia/kds5djc> Accessed 12.12.18 (in Polish).

Fuhr, D. *Deborah Fuhr: the murky world of non-Ucits ETFs*. (2011). <http://citywire.co.uk/wealth-manager/news/deborah-fuhr-the-murky-world-of-non-ucits-etfs/a582675> Accessed 08.01.18.

Fuhr, D. (2015). Appendix A. The global footprint of ETFs and ETPs. In J. M. Hill, D. Nadig, & M. Hougan (Eds.), *A comprehensive guide to exchange-traded funds (ETFs)* (pp. 160–181). Charlottesville, VA: CFA Institute Research Foundation.

Funds Axis. *Poland: Amendments made to the Act on Investment Funds.* (2016). <https://www.funds-axis.com/news-articles/poland-amendments-made-to-the-act-on-investment-funds/> Accessed 14.11.17.

Gastineau, G. L. (2010). *The exchange-traded funds manual (2nd ed).* John Wiley & Sons.

Gierałtowska, U. M. (2015). ETF w warunkach polskich [ETF in Poland]. *Annales Universitatis Mariae Curie-Skłodowska, sectio H—Oeconomia, 49* (4), 129—143. (in Polish).

Golub, B., Novick, B., Madhavan, A., Shapiro, I., Walters, K., & Ferconi, M. (2013). *Exchange-traded products: Overview, benefits and myths.* BlackRock Viewpoint.

Gomber, P., Clapham, B., Lausen, J., & Panz, S. (2018). The impact of MiFID II/MiFIR on European market structure: A survey among market experts. *The Journal of Trading, 13*(2), 35—46.

Gozbasi, O., & Erdem, E. (2010). Are exchange-traded funds effective instruments to invest in Islamic markets? Early evidence from Dow Jones DJIM Turkey ETF. *American Journal of Finance and Accounting, 2*(2), 119—142.

Haentjens, M., & de Gioia Carabellese, P. (2018). *European banking and financial law statutes.* Routledge.

Hull, I. (2016). The development and spread of financial innovations. *Quantitative Economics, 7*(2), 613—636.

Investment Company Institute (2017). *Investment Company Fact Book 2017.*

Jackson, O. (2018). Mifid II prompts shift from traditional funds to ETFs. *International Financial Law Review.* Available from http://www.iflr.com/Article/3790630/Mifid-II-prompts-shift-from-traditional-funds-to-ETFs.html.

Jesch, T., Renz, H., Culhane, S., Firth, S., Sausen, D., Schneider, W., et al. (2014). Fortress Europe? UCITS V and the US Fund Manager. *Journal of Investment Compliance, 15*(2), 36—38.

Kamerling, J. (2018). *The future of EU supervision.* Warsaw: CFA Institute, 2.02.2018.

Kaya, O. (2017). Robo-advice—A true innovation in asset management. *Deutsche Bank Research EU Monitor.*

Lachowski, S. (2012). *Disruptive innovation in banking—A business case in low-cost finance. How to win against the leaders by creating strategic competitive advantage and real value for customers.* Studio EMKA Publishing House.

Lannoo, K. (2018). MiFID II will profoundly affect the portfolio management business. *European Capital Markets Institute Commentary, 47,* 1—4.

Laven Partners (2011). *UCITS: The definitive guidebook to UCITS IV funds.*

Letkowski, D. (2017). Fundusze ETF na Giełdzie Papierów Wartościowych w Warszawie [ETF funds on the Warsaw Stock Exchange]. In S. Wieteska, & D. Burzyńska (Eds.), *Granice finansów XXI wieku. Finanse publiczne, rynek finansowy, finanse przedsiębiorstw [Frontiers of XXI century finance. Public finance, financial market, corporate finance].* Lodz University Press. (in Polish).

Lettau, M., & Madhavan, A. (2018). Exchange-traded funds 101 for economists. *Journal of Economic Perspectives, 32*(1), 135—154.

Lyxor E.T.F. (2017). *Lyxor ETF monthly report Lyxor UCITS ETF Wig 20.*

Marszk, A. (2016). Impact of innovative financial products on financial systems: Exchange traded products and the Polish financial system. *Ekonomia Międzynarodowa, 14,* 114—132.

Micheler, E. (2016). Building a capital markets union: Improving the market infrastructure. *European Business Organization Law Review, 17*(4), 481—495.

Mitrenga, D. (2014). Oszacowanie błędu naśladowania indeksu WIG20 przez dostępny na polskim rynku fundusz ETF wraz z określeniem jego przyczyn [Estimation of the tracking error of the WIG20 index by the ETF available on the Polish market and its reasons]. *Studia Ekonomiczne, 177,* 7—20. (in Polish).

Miziołek, T. (2013). *Pasywne zarządzanie portfelem inwestycyjnym—indeksowe fundusze inwestycyjne i fundusze ETF. Ocena efektywności zarządzania na przykładzie akcyjnych funduszy ETF rynków wschodzących [Passive management of investment port folio—index funds and ETFs. Evaluation of the management effectiveness using the example of equity emerging markets ETFs].* University of Łódź Publishing House (in Polish).

Miziołek, T. *5 lat funduszu Lyxor WIG20 UCITS ETF na GPW w Warszawie [5 years of the Lyxor WIG20 UCITS on the WSE].* (2015). <http://www.etf.com.pl/Analizy-i-komentarze/5-lat-funduszu-Lyxor-WIG20-UCITS-ETF-na-GPW-w-Warszawie-tytuly-uczestnictwa-aktywa-i-naplyw-netto-kapitalu> Accessed 12.10.17.

Miziołek, T. (2016). Europejski rynek indeksowych funduszy inwestycyjnych i determinanty jego rozwoju [European market for index investment funds and determinants of its development]. *Annales Universitatis Mariae Curie-Skłodowska, sectio H—Oeconomia, 50*(4), 325—338. (in Polish).

Miziołek, T. *20 lat funduszy indeksowych w Polsce [20 years of index funds in Poland].* (2017). <http://www.etf.com.pl/Analizy-i-komentarze/20-lat-funduszy-indeksowych-w-Polsce> Accessed 12.10.17 (in Polish).

Miziołek, T. *Echa załamania na amerykańskich giełdach na rynku funduszy ETF i instrumentów typu ETP [Echoes of the crash on the US stock exchanges on the ETFs and ETPs markets].* (2018). <http://www.etf.com.pl/Aktualnosci-Swiat/Echa-zalamania-na-amerykanskich-gieldach-na-rynku-funduszy-ETF-i-instrumentow-typu-ETP> Accessed 02.09.18.

Morningstar (2017). *A guided tour of the European ETF marketplace.*

Muller, C., & Braunstein, C. (2014). UCITS VI: In practice. *Journal of Securities Operations & Custody, 6*(3), 220—227.

Multi Units Luxembourg. *Lyxor WIG 20 UCITS ETF.* (2017). <http://www.lyxoretf.pl/pl/instit/etffinder/lyxor-wig-20-ucits-etf-capi/pln#> Accessed 12.01.18.

Multi Units Luxembourg. *Notice to the shareholders of the share classes C-EUR and PLN of the sub-fund "Multi Units Luxembourg—Lyxor WIG20 UCITS ETF" (the "Sub-Fund").* (2018). <http://www.lyxoretf.fi/pdfDocuments/uk---mul--notice-amalgamation-of-classes---lyxor-wig-20-ucits-etf-c3ae9386f8ec935803301152ec3f93b68d051e46.pdf> Accessed 12.01.18.

O'Sullivan, C., Cunniff, S., Harrington, D., & Murphy, K. (2011). *Ireland: UCITS and non-UCITS funds in Ireland.* Mondaq. <http://www.mondaq.com/ireland/x/136878/Fund + Management + Hedge + Mutual + Investment/UCITS + And + NonUCITS + Funds + In + Ireland> Accessed 10.02.18.

Olechowski, M., Iwański, W., & Blocher, M. (2017). Poland—Fundraising. In S. L. Ritchie (Ed.), *The private equity review (6th ed.)* (pp. 150—159). The Law Reviews.

Phoon, K., & Koh, F. (2017). Robo-advisors and wealth management. *The Journal of Alternative Investments, 20*(3), 79—94.

Płókarz, R. (2010). Fundusze inwestycyjne typu ETF a polski rynek akcji [Investment funds in the category of ETFs and the Polish stock market. In M. Kalinowski, & M. Pronobis (Eds.), *Innowacje na rynkach finansowych [Innovations on the financial markets* (pp. 51−68). CeDeWu. (in Polish).

Preece, R. (2017). *MiFID II: A new paradigm for investment research. Investor perspectives on research costs and procurement.* CFA Institute.

Riedl, D. *Legal structure of ETFs: UCITS.* (2017). <https://www.justetf.com/uk/news/etf/legal-structure-of-etfs-ucits.html> Accessed 10.02.18.

Schumacher, D. *MiFID II making markets fair.* (2018). <https://www.bloomberg.com/quicktake/mifid-making-markets-fair> Accessed 10.02.18.

SEB Bank. *Information about MiFID, i.e. the markets in financial instruments directive.* (2018). <https://www.seb.ee/eng/investor-protection/information-about-mifid-ie-markets-financial-instruments-directive> Accessed 10.02.18.

Stanton, K. (2017). Financial services and regulation. In P. Giliker (Ed.), *Research handbook on EU tort law* (pp. 273−292). Edward Elgar Publishing.

Tarassov, E. B. (2017). The Russian ETF puzzle and its possible reasons. *Algorithmic Finance, 6*(3-4), 93−102.

Watts, T. *European Union: MiFID II: What is it and what does it mean for the world of finance?* (2018). <http://www.mondaq.com/uk/x/664554/Financial + Services/MiFID + II + What + is + it + and + what + does + it + mean + for + the + world + of + finance> Accessed 07.04.18.

Weber, A. *EU's MiFID deal on swiss exchanges sends signal for Brexit.* (2017). <https://www.bloomberg.com/news/articles/2017-12-21/eu-s-mifid-deal-on-swiss-exchanges-sends-signal-for-brexit-talks> Accessed 04.01.18.

World Bank (2017). *World development indicators.*

Xact. *About Xact.* (2018). <http://en.xact.se/About-Xact/> Accessed 23.03.18.

Yiannaki, S. M. (2015). ETFs performance Europe-a good start or not? *Procedia Economics and Finance, 30*, 955−966.

# 4

# Determinants of the European Exchange-Traded Funds Markets Development

## 4.1 IDENTIFYING DETERMINANTS OF THE EUROPEAN EXCHANGE-TRADED FUNDS MARKETS DEVELOPMENT

In this section we present the results of the panel data analysis of the factors that could potentially influence the diffusion of ETFs (used henceforth as a synonymous term for the development of ETFs markets, in line with our fundamental research approach) in the examined European countries. Section 4.2 will discuss country-specific results. We start by presenting the selected variables as well as their sources and additional information, necessary for a full understanding of the analysis that follows in this chapter and partially in Chapter 5, Exchange-Traded Funds and Financial Systems of European Countries: A Growth Factor or Threat to Stability?. Then we discuss in brief the distribution of the variables (except for our base indicator of the development of the ETFs markets, i.e., value of the assets of ETFs, which was presented in detail in the chapter 3). A major part of this Section 4.1 comprises the interpretation of the estimated panel models that we use to analyze the potential determinants of the diffusion of ETFs, starting with the models with a single explanatory variable, then we present models with multiple independent variables (both static and dynamic models are shown).

We focus on the identification of the determinants and more in-depth discussion of the obtained results as well as comparisons are presented in Section 4.3 after the results of the country-level analysis. It should be stressed that we focus exclusively on the macroeconomic and similar determinants (see Section 2.3) and do not consider directly the microeconomic factors due to the extensive previous research in this area; see the discussion

*Exchange-Traded Funds in Europe.*
DOI: https://doi.org/10.1016/B978-0-12-813639-3.00004-3

concerning the attributes of ETFs in Sections 2.1 and 2.2. However, we take them into account indirectly through variables such as stock market return (most European ETFs have exposure to equities) or the related variables of stock market turnover and capitalization.

## 4.1.1 Introductory Remarks

All variables that are used in the estimations are presented in Table 4.1. We select a number of variables showing various aspects of the financial and economic systems. Due to the possible theoretical linkages outlined in Section 2.3 we focus on the indicators from the following groups: capital markets (in particular stock markets), other parts of the financial system, economic growth and related variables (that may be used to decompose the rate of economic growth, i.e., growth of the labor quality and quantity, growth of capital services (further divided into services provided by ICT and non-ICT assets), and growth of total factor productivity). We consider growth rates of the economic growth and related variables. We also take into account the other economic indicators that represent various determinants regarded as influencing the investment funds industry in general (such as interest rates or savings rate). More

**TABLE 4.1** List of Variables Used in the Analysis of the Determinants of the Diffusion of ETFs (i.e., ETFs Market Development)

| Acronym | Full name of the variable | Units | Sources of data | Additional remarks | F/NF |
|---|---|---|---|---|---|
| ETF | Assets of ETFs primary listed in certain country | % of GDP | Lipper | — | — |
| BM | Broad money growth | % | World Development Indicators and own estimates based on data extracted from OECD.Stat https://stats.oecd.org/ | Year-on-year | F |
| BT | Bond turnover | % of GDP | World Federation of Exchanges and country-specific sources | Aggregated annual turnover on the local stock exchanges | F |
| CPI | CPI growth | % | World Development Indicators | Year-on-year | NF |
| CSICT | Growth of capital services provided by ICT assets | % | Total Economy Database May 2017 by The Conference Board | — | NF |
| CSNonICT | Growth of capital services provided by non-ICT assets | % | Total Economy Database May 2017 by The Conference Board | — | NF |
| DC | Domestic credit to private sector | % of GDP | Global Financial Development Database | — | F |
| EMPL | Employment to population ratio | % | World Development Indicators | 15 +, total modeled ILO estimate | NF |
| FBS | Fixed broadband subscriptions | Per 100 inhabitants | World Telecommunication/ICT Indicators | — | NF |
| FD | Financial development index | *Index* | IMF Financial Development Index Database | Normalized between 0 and 1; methodology discussed in Sahay et al. (2015) and Svirydzenka (2016), also in Section 5.1 | F |
| FI | Financial institutions index | *Index* | IMF Financial Development Index Database | See above | F |
| FM | Financial markets index | *Index* | IMF Financial Development Index Database | See above | F |
| FSD | Financial system deposits | % of GDP | Global Financial Development Database | — | F |
| GDP | GDP growth | % | Total Economy Database May 2017 by The Conference Board | — | NF |

*(Continued)*

**TABLE 4.1** (*Continued*)

| Acronym | Full name of the variable | Units | Sources of data | Additional remarks | F/NF |
|---------|---------------------------|-------|-----------------|--------------------|------|
| IFT | Investment funds turnover | % of GDP | World Federation of Exchanges and country-specific sources | Aggregated annual turnover on the local stock exchanges; values do not include turnover of shares of ETFs (or other types of ETPs) | F |
| IU | Internet users | Per 100 inhabitants | World Telecommunication/ICT Indicators | – | NF |
| LQL | Growth of labor quality | % | Total Economy Database May 2017 by The Conference Board | – | NF |
| LQT | Growth of labor quantity | % | Total Economy Database May 2017 by The Conference Board | – | NF |
| MFA | Assets of mutual funds | % of GDP | Global Financial Development Database | Some values were modified in order to ensure that they do not include assets of ETFs | F |
| ODDS | Outstanding domestic private debt securities | % of GDP | Global Financial Development Database | – | F |
| ODI | Official deposit or similar interest rate | % | Various country-specific sources and international databases | For the Eurozone interest rates of the European Central Bank are used | NF |
| PC | Private credit by deposit money banks and other financial institutions | % of GDP | Global Financial Development Database | – | NF |
| S | Gross savings rate | % of GDP | World Development Indicators | – | NF |
| SFT | Stock index futures turnover | % of GDP | World Federation of Exchanges and country-specific sources | Aggregated annual notional turnover on the local stock exchanges | F |
| SMC | Stock market capitalization | % of GDP | Global Financial Development Database and World Federation of Exchanges | – | F |
| SMR | Stock market return | % | Global Financial Development Database and World Federation of Exchanges | Year-on-year; growth rate of the average stock index (in the Global Financial Development Database) or broad stock market index (for data extracted from the reports of the World Federation of Exchanges)—both yield comparable data | F |
| SMT | Stock market turnover ratio | % | Global Financial Development Database and World Federation of Exchanges | Value of the aggregated turnover divided by the average stock market capitalization | F |
| SMTT | Stock market total turnover | % of GDP | Global Financial Development Database and World Federation of Exchanges | Aggregated annual turnover on the local stock exchanges | F |
| SOT | Stock index options turnover | % of GDP | World Federation of Exchanges and country-specific sources | Aggregated annual notional turnover on the local stock exchanges | F |
| SPV | Stock price volatility | *Index* | Global Financial Development Database (calculated by Bloomberg) | Mean of the 360-day volatility of the stock index | F |
| TCS | Growth of total capital services | % | Total Economy Database May 2017 by The Conference Board | – | NF |
| TFP | Growth of total factor productivity | % | Total Economy Database May 2017 by The Conference Board | – | NF |

*Note*: For information concerning detailed sources (i.e., original source of data in the databases) and methods of calculation see the documentation of the particular database. Financial versus nonfinancial distinction is mostly technical and was introduced in order to facilitate further analysis. *F*, Financial; *NF*, nonfinancial.
*Own elaboration.*

broadly, all supposed determinants are included in one of the two groups: financial (F in Table 4.1) or nonfinancial (NF). It should be stressed that the division between financial and nonfinancial variables was made mostly for technical reasons in order to facilitate the presentation of results.

Financial determinants include all variables that demonstrate various attributes of the capital markets. Due to the structure of the European ETFs markets we concentrate on the stock market, therefore, a number of equity market indicators are utilized in our study; there are also some variables of the bond and derivatives markets, and, to lesser extent, of the banking sector. Furthermore, we include some scarce available consistent data on the investment funds in the European countries: assets of mutual funds (MFA; data excludes assets of ETFs as in some databases ETFs are classified as a subcategory of mutual funds) and turnover of investment funds listed on the stock exchanges (IFT; it does not include ETFs or mutual funds, but rather consists of the transactions in the units of closed-end funds and REITs, etc.). We also use three indicators of the financial development (FD) provided by the International Monetary Fund: overall FD, divided into categories: development of the financial institutions (FI) and financial markets (FM). However, all three indexes play a secondary role, i.e., the values of FD are fundamental data used in the analysis of the diffusion of ETFs' impact on the development of the financial systems in the further part of our analysis, in Chapter 5, Exchange-Traded Funds and Financial Systems of European Countries: A Growth Factor or Threat to Stability?. The second broad category, nonfinancial determinants, includes the variables concerning economic growth and other general determinants of the development of the investment funds.

In the joint tables and graphs we present information concerning the variables examined as determinants in the following order: firstly, two ICT variables from the nonfinancial group (which are of substantial significance for the diffusion of ETFs and therefore shown earlier and separately from the other nonfinancial factors), secondly, financial variables (starting with the ones retrieved mostly from reports of the World Federation of Exchanges, through to the ones from the Global Financial Development Database and ending with the indexes of the FD), and, finally, remaining nonfinancial variables (first, the ones showing various aspects of the economic growth and, second, others related to the markets for investment funds. It should be emphasized again that this classification is mostly technical (e.g., interest rate is obviously also a financial-type variable yet we present it separately as our "financial" determinants include mainly indicators of various aspects of the FD). This presentation facilitates better understanding of the examined relationships than applying alphabetical order.

As a supplement, we provide a few more technical comments. If necessary, in order to facilitate the analysis based on data referring to countries with substantially different sizes of the local economies, data extracted from the databases was expressed as the share of the particular country's GDP (such translations were not essential in the case of growth rates, interest rates, and indexes). We minimized the number of utilized sources in order to ensure the maximum possible consistency of data. However, in some cases it was necessary to use country-specific sources. We took all necessary actions to guarantee their comparability to the international data; if reaching a sufficient level of certainty in this aspect resulted to be impossible then the final effect were missing observations in our dataset. Most missing observations were marked for the financial determinants (usually due to impossibility to include data calculated according to the consistent methodology). For some countries no data for a particular variable was obtainable. This applies above all to IFT, SFT and SOT, usually due to lack of such financial instruments on the local stock exchanges. A similar in-kind problem refers to lack of data on the FD indexes. Finally, it should be added that in the case of France, data retrieved from the reports of the World Federation of Exchanges includes data for the entire Euronext stock exchange; as discussed in Section 3.1, this approach is expected not to lead to any significant biases due to the prevalence of the French segment of the Euronext. In another similar case, Sweden, such an assumption would be too far-reaching due to multiple exchanges within Nasdaq Nordic (located in highly heterogeneous countries in terms of financial and economic development); dividing the published values across the members of Nasdaq Nordic would have been possible yet it would have yielded no substantial improvement in terms of the robustness of our analysis.

In our analysis presented throughout in this chapter and Chapter 5, Exchange-Traded Funds and Financial Systems of European Countries: A Growth Factor or Threat to Stability?, we use, above all, annual data as no data with higher frequency is available for most of the considered variables (we switch to monthly observations in Section 5.2 that includes analysis for which such dataset can be constructed). The period of our analysis is 2004−16, subject to data availability at the time our study was conducted.

## 4.1.2 Distribution of the Variables

After the introductory (above all methodological) remarks concerning the selected variables we now consider their distributions using histograms (see Fig. 4.1); for brevity and their relative irrelevance in the context of the

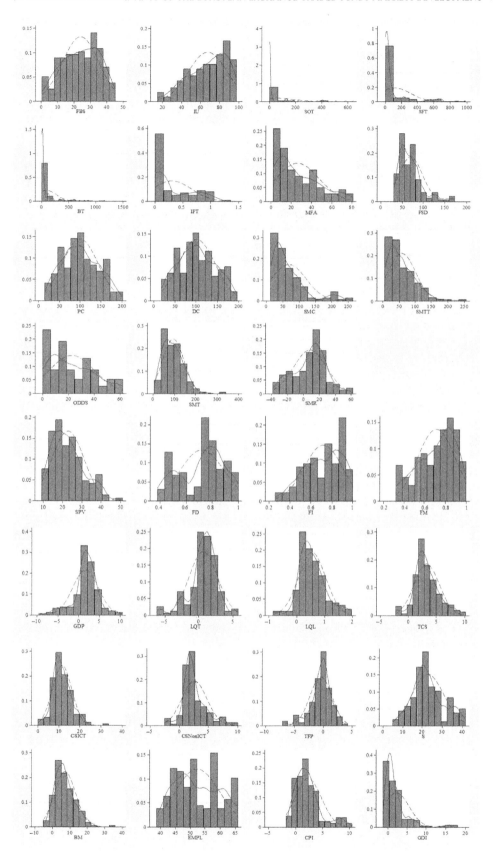

**FIGURE 4.1** Histograms of the selected variables. 2004—16, annual data.
*Note*: On the *Y*-axis—fraction; *dash line*—normal density plot; *solid line*—kernel density plot (kernel = epanechnikov). Raw data used. For an explanation of the variables see Table 4.1. *Source: Authors' elaboration.*

further analysis we omit a detailed examination with the other methods of the descriptive statistics (such as means). If necessary, we state whether the variability referred to the differences between countries or in-time.

Graphical representation of the distribution of the two analyzed ICT variables (FBS and IU) proves the discrepancies between the access to the new technologies measured using these two indicators. For FBS (i.e., rapid type of Internet connections) in the examined countries over 2004–16 values were spread rather evenly (with the mean of approximately 25). However, in the case of IU (access to the Internet in general) more in-depth penetration (in some cases close to 100% in terms of users in relation to the inhabitants) was more frequent in this time period in our sample (yet at its beginning in some countries it was low or very low).

The distribution of the two stock index derivatives turnover variables, SOT and SFT, is very similar as the vast majority of observations were very low. Aggregated annual turnover was mostly below 100% of the local GDP (it applies in particular to the turnover of options), only in some rare cases, on the largest stock exchanges such as the ones in Germany or France, it exceeded 100, sometimes even substantially; in Germany the mean value of SFT for 2004–16 has been at c. 617%. Very similar conclusions may be formulated for BT.

The next two variables presented in Fig. 4.1 are the two indicators of the development of the other types of investment funds (i.e., other than ETFs). As the graph for IFT implies, the typical aggregated annual turnover of the non-ETFs on the stock exchanges was very low in relation to the country's GDP (it has very rarely been higher than 1%). Assets of mutual funds (also in the relative dimension), MFA, differed considerably between countries—for a given country the in-time changes were less substantial. There were a number of countries in which they remained low (in relatively less economically developed countries but also in, for instance, Norway) yet there were also a few countries for which in some years the values of the mutual funds' assets exceeded 50% of the local GDP (e.g., France, Germany, and Switzerland).

The next three variables may be associated with the development of the banking sector in terms of deposits (FSD) and credits (PC and DC). Values of most observations of FSD ranged between 40 and 90 (% of GDP), higher ones were rarely noticed—one of the most notable examples is Switzerland due to the role of its banking sector. Distribution of PC and DC is almost identical as both variables cover a very similar category of entities involved in the credit operations. It is rather symmetrical; values of both variables correspond to a large extent to the level of particular country's economic development.[1]

Subsequently, in Fig. 4.1, there are five stock market variables and one representing in part the bond market (similar to BT), i.e., ODDS. Starting with the latter, its graph proves high variability of the observations, but in most cases the values were rather low. The first two stock market indicators, SMC and SMT, have very similar distributions, even though they represent two different aspects of the stock market's development. In the analyzed time period, in most considered countries they were below or slightly above 50 (% of GDP). The two countries in which both variables reached the values markedly above average were the United Kingdom and Switzerland. The curve shown for SMR implies that 2004–16 was generally the period of negative or very low positive rates of returns on the broad stock market (in some cases the rates were even as low close to −40%, for instance, in Greece). As far as the volatility measure (SPV) is concerned, most observations were rather similar, between 10 and 30, but in some years of financial turmoil the volatility increased to high levels—the most variability was observed in-time rather than between countries). SMT is not discussed as it is an indicator derived from slightly modified SMC and SMTT (we do not use SMT in most of the further analysis, except for the single explanatory variable model).

Distribution curves of the three IMF indexes of FD prove that evaluated countries were heterogeneous with regard to these complex measures. These differences are particularly noticeable in case of the most general index, FD, as there were countries at high or even very high levels (with the values of FD of over 0.7) and some less advanced in this aspect (the in-time variability was low).

Distribution of the seven economic growth variables (GDP to TFP) is rather similar (with some differences that will not be discussed due to their relative irrelevance for the further analysis). As the graph for the variable GDP shows, over the 2004–16 time period, the annual GDP growth rate in the sample countries was usually between 0% and 5%. At some rather rare moments it reached higher values, e.g., in Turkey in 2011 it exceeded 10%, or negative ones, i.e., slightly below 0% (particularly in the aftermath of the 2008 global financial crisis or Eurozone debt crisis) or even lower (below −5%) as in Greece between 2010 and 2012. However, in the largest studied countries, the rate of economic growth was rather stable (slightly positive).

---

[1]For this reason (confirmed by their high correlation), we do not use them together with economic growth variables as independent variable in the estimated models (see Tables 4.4 and 4.5).

As the last group, we discuss the five remaining nonfinancial variables. Gross savings rates ranged in most cases between 10% and 30%. In Norway and Switzerland values of S exceeded 30%, but in most cases was close to 20%, showing that variability of this variable was insubstantial (mostly noticeable between countries). Values of BM were positive in almost all cases, implying the annual rate of growth of broad money of less than 20%, usually at about 5%. Again, as observed in case of S, the dispersion of BM was not considerable, in particular between countries. There were some changes in time in particular countries, usually linked to the decisions concerning monetary policy during or in the aftermath of the financial or economic crises. Quite similar conclusions may be formulated for the CPI (inflation rate) variable; the values of most observations were comparable, between 0% and 5%, with a few positive (e.g., Turkey) and negative outliers (marking deflation in some Eurozone countries). It means that 2004—16 in the examined countries was a period of low inflation or even deflation. The next variable, EMPL, was included in our analysis in order to account for at least some aspects of the situation on the labor markets in the sample economies. As could be expected, almost all variation can be observed between countries as the in-time changes in particular economy were minor. Analysis of the graph for the last variable, ODI, needs to account for the fact that five of the considered countries are member states of the Eurozone, thus, their values of ODI were identical (and close to 0; at the end of the analyzed time period they were slightly negative). This explains the shape of the distribution curve. In the other countries values of this variable were also prevalently below 5% (higher ones were observed at the beginning of this time period, in the less-developed economies). This apparent lack of variability of the discussed variable could make its use in further analysis questionable yet we decided to include it due to its assumed importance for the development of the investment funds market.

## 4.1.3 Panel Data Analysis

This primary analysis was performed with the application of the panel data models (see Methodological annex, Method 4). Firstly, we adopted a rather simple approach and estimated models with only one explanatory variable in order to examine the potential relationship between particular assumed factor and the diffusion of ETFs. Tables 4.2 and 4.3 demonstrate the obtained results; in order to ensure sufficient clarity, explanatory variables were divided into two groups. It should be added that the correlation matrix was also prepared and used for the correct specification of the estimated models, yet it was not included due to its size (resulting from the number of variables) which would make it illegible. Other research methods were also tested, but they yielded similar results and, therefore, we decided to apply the relatively least complicated approach that facilitates a more clear-cut interpretation.

Table 4.2 presents the results of the analysis for the 18 financial variables considered to be linked to the diffusion of ETFs. Estimates of the coefficients of the independent variable were identified as statistically significant in slightly less than half (i.e., seven) specifications, with considerably varying values of $R^2$. First such specification

**TABLE 4.2** Diffusion of ETFs—Financial Determinants. Random Effects Models With a Single Explanatory Variable. 2004—16, Annual Data

| ETF | RE(1) | RE(2) | RE(3) | RE(4) | RE(5) | RE(6) | RE(7) | RE(8) | RE(9) | RE(10) | RE(11) | RE(12) | RE(14) | RE(15) | RE(16) | RE(17) | RE(18) |
|---|---|---|---|---|---|---|---|---|---|---|---|---|---|---|---|---|---|
| SOT | 0.14 | | | | | | | | | | | | | | | | |
| | [0.08] | | | | | | | | | | | | | | | | |
| SFT | | **0.26** | | | | | | | | | | | | | | | |
| | | **[0.09]** | | | | | | | | | | | | | | | |
| BT | | | − 0.04 | | | | | | | | | | | | | | |
| | | | [0.06] | | | | | | | | | | | | | | |
| IFT | | | | 0.11 | | | | | | | | | | | | | |
| | | | | [0.11] | | | | | | | | | | | | | |
| MFA | | | | | **1.5** | | | | | | | | | | | | |
| | | | | | **[0.20]** | | | | | | | | | | | | |

*(Continued)*

**TABLE 4.2**    *(Continued)*

| ETF | RE(1) | RE(2) | RE(3) | RE(4) | RE(5) | RE(6) | RE(7) | RE(8) | RE(9) | RE(10) | RE(11) | RE(12) | RE(14) | RE(15) | RE(16) | RE(17) | RE(18) |
|---|---|---|---|---|---|---|---|---|---|---|---|---|---|---|---|---|---|
| FSD | | | | | | **3.08** | | | | | | | | | | | |
| | | | | | | **[0.51]** | | | | | | | | | | | |
| PC | | | | | | | 0.55 | | | | | | | | | | |
| | | | | | | | [0.37] | | | | | | | | | | |
| DC | | | | | | | | 0.18 | | | | | | | | | |
| | | | | | | | | [0.38] | | | | | | | | | |
| SMC | | | | | | | | | 0.35 | | | | | | | | |
| | | | | | | | | | [0.31] | | | | | | | | |
| SMTT | | | | | | | | | | **0.28** | | | | | | | |
| | | | | | | | | | | **[0.11]** | | | | | | | |
| ODDS | | | | | | | | | | | 0.02 | | | | | | |
| | | | | | | | | | | | [0.13] | | | | | | |
| SMT | | | | | | | | | | | | 0.04 | | | | | |
| | | | | | | | | | | | | [0.18] | | | | | |
| SMR | | | | | | | | | | | | | **− 0.23** | | | | |
| | | | | | | | | | | | | | **[0.09]** | | | | |
| SPV | | | | | | | | | | | | | | **0.58** | | | |
| | | | | | | | | | | | | | | **[0.21]** | | | |
| FD | | | | | | | | | | | | | | | 1.8 | | |
| | | | | | | | | | | | | | | | [1.2] | | |
| FI | | | | | | | | | | | | | | | | **1.9** | |
| | | | | | | | | | | | | | | | | **[0.8]** | |
| FM | | | | | | | | | | | | | | | | | − 0.006 |
| | | | | | | | | | | | | | | | | | [0.83] |
| Breuch−Pagan test (prob > $\chi^2$) | 88.02 | 178.9 | 537.1 | 229.9 | 334.9 | 415.1 | 395.8 | 391.1 | 338.7 | 323.2 | 302.9 | 418.6 | 187.6 | 289.9 | 265.1 | 238.7 | 322.4 |
| | [0.00] | [0.00] | [0.00] | [0.00] | [0.00] | [0.00] | [0.00] | [0.00] | [0.00] | [0.00] | [0.00] | [0.00] | [0.00] | [0.00] | [0.00] | [0.00] | [0.00] |
| $R^2$ (overall) | 0.67 | 0.59 | 0.06 | 0.89 | 0.68 | 0.33 | 0.32 | 0.30 | 0.51 | 0.37 | 0.11 | 0.00 | 0.03 | 0.13 | 0.53 | 0.49 | 0.36 |
| Rho | 0.83 | 0.86 | 0.91 | 0.55 | 0.82 | 0.92 | 0.88 | 0.88 | 0.83 | 0.84 | 0.89 | 0.93 | 0.91 | 0.86 | 0.81 | 0.85 | 0.86 |
| # of observations | 79 | 88 | 119 | 83 | 123 | 112 | 124 | 124 | 117 | 118 | 93 | 114 | 84 | 124 | 112 | 112 | 112 |

*Note*: All values are logged; SE below coefficients; results account for random-effects GLS regressions (both fixed and random panel models were tested. Results of Hausman tests suggested application of random effects models); extreme observations excluded; panel—balanced; constant included—not reported; in bold—results statistically significant at 5% level of significance. For explanation of the variables see Table 4.1.
*Authors' estimates.*

includes SFT, i.e., the value of respective coefficient is positive; taking into account the value of $R^2$ for this model (one of the highest among all estimated) it may be stated that the statistical association between ETFs and stock index futures (more accurately, their turnover on the local stock exchanges) was positive, statistically significant, and robust. It is the only determinant among the capital market ones that we examine (with the exception of the stock market indicators) for which the conclusion of statistical significance was reached. The estimated value of the coefficient may be interpreted as an average effect of 1% change in the turnover of stock index futures (expressed as % of the country's GDP) over the assets of ETFs (again, as % of the country's GDP). In this case it is 0.26%. For the consecutive coefficients interpretation is parallel and is skipped due to its relative insignificance at the current stage of the analysis—we refer again to this issue at the beginning of Section 4.3.

**TABLE 4.3** Diffusion of ETFs—Nonfinancial Determinants. Random Effects Models With a Single Explanatory Variable. 2004—16, Annual Data

| ETF | RE(1) | RE(2) | RE(3) | RE(4) | RE(5) | RE(6) | RE(7) | RE(8) | RE(9) | RE(10) | RE(11) | RE(12) | RE(13) | RE(14) |
|---|---|---|---|---|---|---|---|---|---|---|---|---|---|---|
| FBS | 1.17 | | | | | | | | | | | | | |
| | [0.16] | | | | | | | | | | | | | |
| IU | | 1.4 | | | | | | | | | | | | |
| | | [0.36] | | | | | | | | | | | | |
| GDP | | | − 0.31 | | | | | | | | | | | |
| | | | [0.11] | | | | | | | | | | | |
| LQT | | | | − 0.09 | | | | | | | | | | |
| | | | | [0.08] | | | | | | | | | | |
| LQL | | | | | − 0.12 | | | | | | | | | |
| | | | | | [0.10] | | | | | | | | | |
| TCS | | | | | | − 0.63 | | | | | | | | |
| | | | | | | [0.15] | | | | | | | | |
| CSICT | | | | | | | − 0.13 | | | | | | | |
| | | | | | | | [0.18] | | | | | | | |
| CSNonICT | | | | | | | | − 0.68 | | | | | | |
| | | | | | | | | [0.16] | | | | | | |
| TFP | | | | | | | | | − 0.28 | | | | | |
| | | | | | | | | | [0.14] | | | | | |
| S | | | | | | | | | | − 1.4 | | | | |
| | | | | | | | | | | [0.54] | | | | |
| BM | | | | | | | | | | | − 0.30 | | | |
| | | | | | | | | | | | [0.09 | | | |
| EMPL | | | | | | | | | | | | 1.38 | | |
| | | | | | | | | | | | | [1.4] | | |
| CPI | | | | | | | | | | | | | − 0.29 | |
| | | | | | | | | | | | | | [0.11] | |
| ODI | | | | | | | | | | | | | | − 0.34 |
| | | | | | | | | | | | | | | [0.06] |
| Breuch−Pagan test (prob > $\chi^2$) | 510.6 | 498.4 | 382.2 | 252.6 | 466.5 | 505.7 | 567.9 | 331.8 | 82.5 | 583.6 | 407.3 | 485.8 | 264.9 | 250.2 |
| | [0.00] | [0.00] | [0.00] | [0.00] | [0.00] | [0.00] | [0.00] | [0.00] | [0.00] | [0.00] | [0.00] | [0.00] | [0.00] | [0.00] |
| $R^2$ (overall) | 0.26 | 0.22 | 0.03 | 0.05 | 0.01 | 0.06 | 0.00 | 0.31 | 0.07 | 0.03 | 0.06 | 0.31 | 0.25 | 0.31 |
| Rho | 0.92 | 0.91 | 0.92 | 0.90 | 0.93 | 0.93 | 0.92 | 0.91 | 0.90 | 0.93 | 0.92 | 0.89 | 0.86 | 0.92 |
| # of observations | 136 | 135 | 107 | 94 | 121 | 128 | 135 | 124 | 53 | 136 | 120 | 136 | 108 | 102 |

*Note*: All values are logged; SE below coefficients; results account for random-effects GLS regressions (both fixed and random panel models were tested. Results of Hausman tests suggested application of random effects models); extreme observations excluded; panel—balanced; constant included—not reported; in bold—results statistically significant at 5% level of significance. For explanation of the variables see Table A.
*Authors' estimates.*

The next specification that includes a statistically significant coefficient is the one estimated for MFA. Again, the value of the coefficient is positive and $R^2$ for this model is the highest among all presented in Table 4.2 which leads to the conclusion that the statistical relationship between ETFs and the largest category of the other investment funds (both expressed in terms of assets) was, like in case of SFT, positive, statistically significant, and robust.

The next two considered equations, with FSD and SMTT as independent variables (i.e., the former referring above all to the banking sector and the latter to the equity market), indicate their statistically significant positive impact and the values of $R^2$ of these models are similar and much lower than for the two variables discussed in the preceding paragraphs, making these results less robust and more dubious.

Specifications with the two further stock market indicators, SMR and SPV, include statistically significant coefficients (negative for the first and positive for the second) but the values of $R^2$ in both cases are very low which means that their interpretation as having some links to the diffusion of ETFs would be highly questionable.

Finally, the last model with statistically significant explanatory variable was estimated for one of the used IMF indexes, i.e., FI. The value of the coefficient implies the positive relationship with the dependent ETFs variable and the $R^2$ value of c. 0.5 means that this result may be considered to be less robust than in case of MFA or SFT, but still less dubious than for the remaining potential determinants.

The estimates of the second group of the models with single explanatory variable are presented in Table 4.3, each covering one of the examined 14 nonfinancial variables. In the case of 10 out of 14 specifications coefficients of the independent variable are statistically significant at 5% level of significance. The first two specifications with such variables are the ones including the ICT variables, i.e., FBS and IU. As the values of the coefficients are positive, it could be stated that the statistical relationship between the diffusion of ETFs and adoption of new technologies is positive. However, $R^2$ of both FBS and IU models are rather low, much lower than in case of, for instance, models with the SFT or MFA variable—the values are 0.26 and 0.22 for the two ICT variables respectively. This means that the robustness of these models is quite dubious.

The second group of nonfinancial determinants are the economic growth rate (GDP) and various linked variables. With one exception (CSNonICT), either coefficients of the explanatory variables are statistically insignificant or $R^2$ of the models are extremely low (see, for example, results for GDP). As a result, interpreting the returned estimates as the evidence for the linkages between the rate of economic growth (and related variables) would be an overstatement.

In the last considered group we included variables indicated as the factors that may affect the development of the investment funds markets. In four estimated specifications the independent variables resulted to be statistically significant (except for EMPL). $R^2$ of the models with S and BM included are very low and, thus, these specifications are omitted. The two remaining variables are CPI and ODI. Analogously to the specifications with the ICT variables, their robustness is questionable. For both CPA and ODI the estimated coefficients are negative.

We now proceed to discuss the estimates of models with multiple explanatory variables. The selection of the variables that were used as independent in particular specifications was based with regard to their pair-wise correlations returned (in order to avoid emerging multicollinearity) and their statistically significant relationship with the diffusion of ETFs identified with the application of the single explanatory variable models.[2] Two groups of models were estimated: firstly with static specifications (see Table 4.4); and secondly with dynamic specifications in order to capture potential impact of the lagged dependent variable (see Table 4.5). In both cases the presentation of the obtained results follows our outline; it starts with a discussion concerning specifications exclusively with the financial independent variables, followed by specifications exclusively with the nonfinancial independent variables and, finally, specifications merging these two groups.

Two variables are included in almost all financial specifications—i.e., RE(1)–RE(6)—and their coefficients are proven to be statistically significant: SFT (not included in RE(3)) and MFA, see Table 4.4. Moreover, the values of their coefficients are positive and similar regardless of the model, except for the much lower coefficient of MFA in RE(1). Two other variables that resulted to be statistically significant in all specifications in which they were included are FSD and SPV. Values of the estimated coefficients of these four variables are positive. For SMTT and FI the results are mixed yet in most specifications these variables are insignificant. Due to its correlation with the other variables, SMR could be included in only one model, in RE(3), in which it is insignificant.

---

[2]Other approaches to the selection of explanatory variables were checked yet the one finally adopted yielded the best results (with most statistically significant parameters and the highest $R^2$ in case of static models). The only variable excluded in our approach was TFP due to the low number of observations in the case of the lagged values.

**TABLE 4.4** Diffusion of ETFs: Selected Financial and Nonfinancial Determinants. Random Effects Models With Multiple Explanatory Variables. 2004−16, Annual Data

| ETF | RE(1) | RE(2) | RE(3) | RE(4) | RE(5) | RE(6) | RE(7) | RE(8) | RE(9) | RE(10) | RE(11) | RE(12) | RE(13) | RE(14) |
|---|---|---|---|---|---|---|---|---|---|---|---|---|---|---|
| SFT | **0.40** | **0.45** | | **0.51** | **0.53** | **0.51** | | | | | | | **0.32** | **1.6** |
| | **[0.11]** | **[0.08]** | | **[0.10]** | **[0.11]** | **[0.09]** | | | | | | | **[0.08]** | **[0.23]** |
| MFA | **0.87** | **1.4** | **1.5** | **1.4** | **1.4** | **1.6** | | | | | | | **1.2** | |
| | **[0.19]** | **[0.18]** | **[0.23]** | **[0.20]** | **[0.21]** | **[0.19]** | | | | | | | **[0.21]** | |
| FSD | **4.18** | **5.5** | **2.2** | | | **4.3** | | | | | | | | |
| | **[0.70]** | **[0.70]** | **[0.54]** | | | **[0.76]** | | | | | | | | |
| SMTT | − 0.32 | | | − 0.68 | **− 0.57** | − 0.27 | | | | | | | | |
| | [0.19] | | | [0.18] | **[0.18]** | [0.16] | | | | | | | | |
| SMR | | | − 0.03 | | | | | | | | | | | − 0.05 |
| | | | [0.07] | | | | | | | | | | | [0.08] |
| SPV | | | 1.01 | 1.0 | 1.0 | 0.64 | | | | | | | 0.75 | |
| | | | [0.25] | [0.18] | [0.20] | [0.17] | | | | | | | [0.19] | |
| FI | | − 5.6 | | | − 1.2 | − 4.9 | | | | | | | | |
| | | [1.3] | | | [1.2] | [1.3] | | | | | | | | |
| FBS | | | | | | | 1.1 | 0.99 | 0.67 | | | | 1.06 | 0.83 |
| | | | | | | | [0.18] | [0.21] | [0.27] | | | | [0.19] | [0.19] |
| IU | | | | | | | | | | 1.07 | 1.6 | − 0.11 | | |
| | | | | | | | | | | [0.47] | [0.41] | [0.58] | | |
| GDP | | | | | | | − 0.10 | − 0.13 | − 0.18 | − 0.16 | **− 0.22** | | | − 0.24 |
| | | | | | | | [0.10] | [0.11] | [0.14] | [0.12] | **[0.10]** | | | [0.12] |
| TCS | | | | | | | − 0.38 | 0.36 | | | | | | |
| | | | | | | | [0.21] | [0.39] | | | | | | |
| S | | | | | | | **− 2.3** | | | **− 2.5** | | | | − 1.02 |
| | | | | | | | **[0.76]** | | | **[0.90]** | | | | [0.75] |
| BM | | | | | | | 0.005 | | | | | − 0.16 | | − 0.12 |
| | | | | | | | [0.11] | | | | | [0.13] | | [0.11] |
| CSNonICT | | | | | | | | − 0.42 | | | | 0.03 | | |
| | | | | | | | | [0.27] | | | | [0.32] | | |
| CPI | | | | | | | | − 0.10 | − 0.01 | − 0.26 | | | − 0.06 | |
| | | | | | | | | [0.12] | **[0.15]** | **[0.90]** | | | [0.09] | |
| ODI | | | | | | | | | − 0.40 | | | **− 0.33** | | |
| | | | | | | | | | [0.12] | | | **[0.11]** | | |
| Breuch−Pagan test (prob > $\chi^2$) | 71.5 | 30.29 | 144.6 | 66.3 | 45.8 | 33.7 | 272.2 | 129.9 | 105.8 | 135.2 | 371.9 | 117.4 | 47.4 | 76.6 |
| | [0.00] | [0.00] | [0.00] | [0.00] | [0.00] | [0.00] | [0.00] | [0.00] | [0.00] | [0.00] | [0.00] | [0.00] | [0.00] | [0.00] |
| $R^2$ (overall) | 0.77 | 0.90 | 0.76 | 0.86 | 0.86 | 0.92 | 0.15 | 0.35 | 0.32 | 0.18 | 0.18 | 0.32 | 0.87 | 0.63 |
| Rho | 0.84 | 0.64 | 0.81 | 0.77 | 0.61 | 0.71 | 0.93 | 0.91 | 0.88 | 0.91 | 0.92 | 0.85 | 0.78 | 0.84 |
| Mean VIF | 1.70 | 1.35 | 1.35 | 1.64 | 2.21 | 3.1 | 1.7 | 1.7 | 1.6 | 1.3 | 1.08 | 1.6 | 1.72 | 1.89 |
| # of observations | 77 | 70 | 74 | 77 | 70 | 70 | 98 | 75 | 73 | 85 | 106 | 85 | 66 | 71 |

*Note*: All values are logged; SE below coefficients; results account for random-effects GLS regressions (both fixed and random panel models were tested; results of Hausman tests suggested application of random effects models); extreme observations excluded; panel—balanced; constant included—not reported; in bold—results statistically significant at 5% level of significance. For explanation of the variables see Table 4.1.
*Authors' estimates.*

**TABLE 4.5**  Diffusion of ETFs: Selected Financial and Nonfinancial Determinants. Dynamic Panel Models With Multiple Explanatory Variables. 2004–16, Annual DataAuthors' estimates.

| ETF | DPD (1) | DPD (2) | DPD (3) | DPD (4) | DPD (5) | DPD (6) | DPD (7) | DPD (8) | DPD (9) | DPD (10) | DPD (11) | DPD (12) | DPD (13) | DPD(14) |
|---|---|---|---|---|---|---|---|---|---|---|---|---|---|---|
| ETF L1 | **0.32** | **0.29** | **0.28** | **0.39** | **0.39** | **0.33** | 0.22 | 0.29 | 0.26 | **0.34** | 0.36 | **0.38** | **0.31** | Not applicable—number of instruments for level equation exceeds number of observations |
|  | **[0.07]** | **[0.05]** | **[0.11]** | **[0.06]** | **[0.06]** | **[0.05]** | [0.19] | [0.18] | [0.19] | **[0.15]** | [0.18] | **[0.12]** | **[0.06]** | |
| SFT | 0.13 | 0.17 |  | 0.13 | 0.16 | 0.17 |  |  |  |  |  |  | 0.04 | |
|  | [0.08] | [0.12] |  | [0.08] | [0.11] | [0.11] |  |  |  |  |  |  | [0.06] | |
| MFA | **0.83** | **0.96** | **0.65** | **1.3** | **1.4** | **1.3** |  |  |  |  |  |  | **1.7** | |
|  | **[0.33]** | **[0.31]** | **[0.19]** | **[0.33]** | **[0.27]** | **[0.27]** |  |  |  |  |  |  | **[0.31]** | |
| FSD | **2.9** | **3.6** | − 1.3 |  |  | 1.4 |  |  |  |  |  |  |  | |
|  | **[0.70]** | **[0.74]** | [1.2] |  |  | [0.80] |  |  |  |  |  |  |  | |
| SMTT | − 0.02 |  |  | **− 0.20** | − 0.17 | − 0.13 |  |  |  |  |  |  |  | |
|  | [0.07] |  |  | **[0.09]** | [0.09] | [0.09] |  |  |  |  |  |  |  | |
| SMR |  |  | − 0.05 |  |  |  |  |  |  |  |  |  |  | |
|  |  |  | [0.0] |  |  |  |  |  |  |  |  |  |  | |
| SPV |  |  | 0.26 | **0.71** | **0.73** | **0.59** |  |  |  |  |  |  | **0.71** | |
|  |  |  | [0.17] | **[0.16]** | **[0.17]** | **[0.20]** |  |  |  |  |  |  | **[0.17]** | |
| FI |  | − 0.45 |  |  | 1.3 | − 1.4 |  |  |  |  |  |  |  | |
|  |  | [1.2] |  |  | [1.4] | [1.5] |  |  |  |  |  |  |  | |
| FBS |  |  |  |  |  |  | 0.48 | 0.24 | 0.23 |  |  |  | **0.62** | |
|  |  |  |  |  |  |  | [0.39] | [0.42] | [0.37] |  |  |  | **[0.27]** | |
| IU |  |  |  |  |  |  |  |  |  | − 0.27 | 0.06 | − 0.66 |  | |
|  |  |  |  |  |  |  |  |  |  | [0.29] | [0.55] | [0.47] |  | |
| GDP |  |  |  |  |  |  | 0.02 | − 0.04 | − 0.007 | − 0.05 | − 0.12 |  |  | |
|  |  |  |  |  |  |  | [0.08] | [0.06] | [0.11] | [0.07] | [0.04] |  |  | |
| TCS |  |  |  |  |  |  | − 0.22 |  | 0.41 |  |  |  |  | |
|  |  |  |  |  |  |  | [0.21] |  | [0.48] |  |  |  |  | |
| S |  |  |  |  |  |  | − 0.89 |  |  | 0.95 |  |  |  | |
|  |  |  |  |  |  |  | [1.1] |  |  | [0.88] |  |  |  | |
| BM |  |  |  |  |  |  | − 0.02 |  |  |  |  | − 0.26 |  | |
|  |  |  |  |  |  |  | [0.10] |  |  |  |  | **[0.13]** |  | |
| CSNonICT |  |  |  |  |  |  |  | 0.06 |  |  |  | **0.28** |  | |
|  |  |  |  |  |  |  |  | [0.31] |  |  |  | **[0.10]** |  | |
| CPI |  |  |  |  |  |  |  | **− 0.13** | − 0.08 | **− 0.13** |  |  | 0.06 | |
|  |  |  |  |  |  |  |  | **[0.05]** | [0.07] | **[0.04]** |  |  | [0.05] | |
| ODI |  |  |  |  |  |  |  |  | − 0.09 |  |  | **− 0.13** |  | |
|  |  |  |  |  |  |  |  |  | [0.08] |  |  | **[0.06]** |  | |
| Wald $\chi^2$ (Prob $> \chi^2$) | 280.6 | 306.0 | 26.7 | 319.3 | 1512.3 | 4597.9 | 34.7 | 30.4 | 25.5 | 47.7 | 6.73 | 52.0 | 1067.1 | |
|  | [0.00] | [0.00] | [0.00] | [0.00] | [0.00] | [0.00] | [0.00] | [0.00] | [0.00] | [0.00] | [0.08] | [0.00] | [0.00] | |

*(Continued)*

TABLE 4.5 (Continued)

| ETF | DPD (1) | DPD (2) | DPD (3) | DPD (4) | DPD (5) | DPD (6) | DPD (7) | DPD (8) | DPD (9) | DPD (10) | DPD (11) | DPD (12) | DPD (13) | DPD(14) |
|---|---|---|---|---|---|---|---|---|---|---|---|---|---|---|
| # of instruments | 57 | 50 | 36 | 57 | 21 | 52 | 54 | 40 | 33 | 40 | 59 | 46 | 47 | |
| Arellano−Bond test for 3rd order (Prob > z) | 1.40 [0.16] | 1.26 [0.21] | 0.61 [0.54] | 0.62 [0.53] | 0.47 [0.36] | 0.32 [0.74] | 0.28 [0.78] | − 1.1 [0.26] | − 1.08 [0.28] | − 1.2 [0.22] | 0.18 [0.085] | 0.66 [0.50] | 1.10 [0.27] | |
| # of observations | 61 | 57 | 38 | 61 | 54 | 54 | 60 | 50 | 40 | 50 | 72 | 55 | 48 | |

Note: All values are logged; SE below coefficients; one-step GMM estimator applied; extreme observations excluded; panel—balanced; constant included—not reported; in bold—results statistically significant at 5% level of significance. For an explanation of the variables see Table 4.1. "ETF L1" stands for the 1-year lagged value of ETF.

It must be emphasized that $R^2$ of the panel models with the multiple financial explanatory variables are unambiguously the highest among all analyzed specifications; they range from 0.76 to 0.92. For comparison, the $R^2$ of the models with multiple nonfinancial variables are between 0.15 and 0.35, proving their relatively lower robustness, analogously to the conclusions based on the single independent variable models.

One of the ICT variables, i.e., either FBS or IU, was used in every nonfinancial specification: RE(7)−RE(12). Estimations of the models' coefficient show that FBS is statistically significant regardless of the other incorporated variables, whereas for IU there is one specification for which other results were returned, i.e., RE(12). All values of the ICT coefficients are positive. For the remaining potential nonfinancial determinants of the diffusion of ETFs results are mixed. Apart from FBS and IU, the only nonfinancial variable that is statistically significant in all models is S (with negative coefficients). In the case of GDP, TCS, BM, and CSNonICT coefficients are almost entirely insignificant; for CPI and ODI the results are inconclusive (coefficients are always negative regardless of the significance).

As a third group in Table 4.4, RE(13)−RE(14), we present the estimates for the models with both financial and nonfinancial explanatory variables; the choice of the examined determinants was made using identical criteria as in the case of the models applied for the financial and nonfinancial determinants separately. In the first, more robust specification ($R^2$ of 0.87; one of the highest in our study) there are three financial independent variables, all of which resulted to be statistically significant with positive coefficients, as well as two nonfinancial, one statistically significant as in the discussed models (FBS; again the implied impact of ICT adoption is positive), and one was insignificant (CPI). In the second specification (substantially less robust, yet still with much higher $R^2$ than in the case of the nonfinancial determinants-only models), again six explanatory variables are included, but in this case, two of them are financial and the remaining are from the nonfinancial category. As in all previous models, coefficients of both SFT and FBS resulted to be statistically significant and positive which may be perceived as further evidence of their importance. None of the remaining determinants are statistically significant at 5% level of significance; even S for which a negative influence was observed in the models that excluded financial factors.

The final part of our analysis of the ETFs' diffusion determinants is based on the dynamic panel models in which we added the 1-year lagged value of the assets of ETFs (ETF L1) as the explanatory variable (the other ones are again considered in three groups, starting from financial; in order to ensure at least some degree of comparability with the previous specifications we adopted a rather simple approach and added the lagged variable to those models, with no other changes in their composition). For the results see Table 4.5. Estimated results provide some interesting insights yet the conclusions that can be formulated overlap, to some extent, with the ones from the static models, therefore, our discussion is concise.

The first and the most crucial conclusion that may be drawn from the specifications presented in Table 4.5 is that in the majority of them the ETF L1 variable is statistically significant (more specifically, in 9 out of 13 cases); moreover, its coefficient is always positive and ranges from 0.28 [in DPD(3)] to 0.39 [DPD(4) and DPD(5)], regardless of the other included independent variables. The only exception is 4 out of 6 models with the nonfinancial variables. A second conclusion can be formulated with reference to the potential financial determinants of the diffusion of ETFs in Europe. Estimates of the dynamic models confirm the statistical significance of MFA (and, consequently, its positive impact) and in most cases the same applies to SPV. Nonetheless, for FSD the results are mixed (split in half) and coefficients of the most of the remaining financial variables are insignificant in almost all specifications; it applies even to SFT (this is probably the biggest difference in relation to the static models). Finally, with the exception of CPI (in two models) and a bunch of variables in one single specification [DPD(12)], no role of the nonfinancial factors was identified when ETF L1 was included—in contrast with the static models. The estimates of the only combined dynamic model [DPD(13)] provide no other information, except for FBS being statistically significant.

## 4.2 COUNTRY-SPECIFIC STUDY OF THE DETERMINANTS OF THE EUROPEAN EXCHANGE-TRADED FUNDS MARKETS DEVELOPMENT

In Section 4.1 we discussed the results of the panel data analysis of the relationships between the diffusion of ETFs and determinants of this process. In this section we continue that study by examining the evidence on the country level, i.e., using country-specific data for the considered European economies. We do not evaluate all potential determinants listed at the beginning of the Section 4.1, but rather only those variables that were recognized (based on the theoretical overview discussed in Chapter 2: Exchange-Traded Funds: Concepts and Contexts) as potentially exerting an impact on the diffusion of ETFs; in some cases these relationships were identified in the preceding evaluation based on panel data models, in others the results were, at best, mixed. Among the selected seven variables (we limit their number to seven in order to make the analysis as concise as possible; SFT is not analyzed due to the substantial number of missing observations for some countries) there are two indicating the development of the other types of investment funds that may be perceived as competing with ETFs (IFT and MFA), one that can be used to measure the development of the most closely linked part of the capital markets; stock market (SMTT), two ICT indicators (FBS and IU) that we use to evaluate the role of new technologies, and, finally, two other identified in the literature as potentially applicable for the explanation of the development of the investment funds market (ODI, S). In the presentation of the results determinants are outlined in alphabetical order or in the above-mentioned groups. The detailed design of the research methods is presented in the annex.

The structure of this section is: We start with an analysis of the country level correlation coefficients between the examined variables and the applied measure of the diffusion of ETFs (development of the ETFs markets) in order to shed some light on the discussed linkages. In the second part, we interpret the results of the nonparametric analysis showed individually for each particular explanatory variable for a given country, searching for any additional insights (in particular any deviations from the conclusions that can be reached using panel data models or correlation coefficients). In the second part, we draw conclusions on the emerging relationships basing on the descriptive and graphical evidence.

### 4.2.1 Correlation Analysis

Table 4.6 and Fig. 4.2 show the calculated correlation coefficients between the ETFs variables and the seven selected potential determinants for each country in our sample. In the case of a complete lack of data, the relevant information is provided in Table 4.6 (this applies exclusively to IFT as such funds are either not traded on exchanges in some countries or no data on their turnover could be acquired).

Country-specific results obtained for the two ICT indicators are almost identical (with the exception of Greece and the United Kingdom, although in those countries they are quite close), analogically to the estimated single explanatory variable panel models (see Table 4.3 in Section 4.1) which means they can be analyzed jointly. In almost all countries both ICT variables are strongly positively correlated with the development of the ETFs market (see Fig. 4.2); calculated values of the correlation coefficients are in most countries the highest among all evaluated variables. It could imply that, analogously as in the majority of the discussed panel models, FBS and IU impacted the diffusion of ETFs; we verify this preliminary presumption in the next parts of this section. The only exception with regard to the high and positive correlation of ETFs versus FBS and IU is Turkey (for which it is close to 0) and, to a lesser extent, Greece and Poland, with values that are positive yet below 0.5. It could, thus, be stated that, based on the correlation analysis, the relationship between adoption of ICT and diffusion of ETFs is, on average, weaker in the less economically developed countries.

The next examined variable is IFT. As can be clearly noticed in Fig. 4.2, the dispersion of the calculated correlation coefficients is the highest among the seven considered variables. It is also the variable with a lack of data for some countries, meaning that there are, in fact, only eight calculated coefficients. It should also be

**TABLE 4.6**  ETFs versus FBS, IFT, IU, MFA, ODI, S, SMTT. Country-Level Correlation Matrix. Period 2004−16, Annual Data

|  | France | Germany | Greece | Hungary | Italy | Norway | Poland | Spain | Sweden | Switzerland | Turkey | United Kingdom |
|---|---|---|---|---|---|---|---|---|---|---|---|---|
| FBS | 0.87 | 0.94 | 0.41 | 0.49 | 0.96 | 0.63 | 0.41 | 0.77 | 0.58 | 0.89 | 0.06 | 0.68 |
| IFT | − 0.62 | − 0.88 | − 0.65 | 0.79 | − 0.49 | N.A. | − 0.37 | N.A. | N.A. | 0.91 | − 0.13 | N.A. |
| IU | 0.82 | 0.96 | 0.29 | 0.51 | 0.91 | 0.65 | 0.46 | 0.75 | 0.56 | 0.92 | − 0.05 | 0.91 |
| MFA | 0.02 | 0.82 | − 0.68 | 0.48 | 0.17 | 0.43 | − 0.13 | − 0.32 | 0.65 | 0.76 | − 0.23 | 0.94 |
| ODI | − 0.63 | − 0.81 | − 0.39 | − 0.22 | − 0.83 | − 0.31 | − 0.35 | − 0.37 | − 0.41 | − 0.04 | − 0.11 | − 0.76 |
| S | − 0.58 | 0.61 | − 0.75 | 0.18 | − 0.06 | − 0.29 | − 0.13 | − 0.23 | − 0.52 | − 0.64 | 0.02 | − 0.74 |
| SMTT | − 0.43 | − 0.37 | − 0.09 | 0.33 | − 0.51 | − 0.03 | 0.18 | 0.02 | − 0.27 | 0.21 | 0.32 | − 0.03 |

*Note*: Pairwise correlations, raw data used. For an explanation of the variables see Table 4.1 and Section 4.1.
*Authors' calculations.*

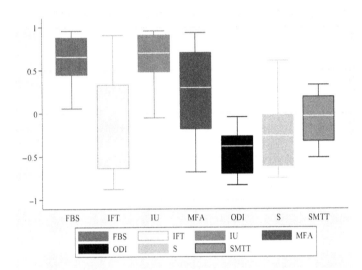

**FIGURE 4.2**  ETFs versus FBS, IFT, IU, MFA, ODI, S, and SMTT. Country-level pairwise correlations ranges. 2004−16, annual data.
*Note*: For pairwise correlations, raw data was used. For an explanation of the variables see Table 4.1 in Section 4.1. *Source: Authors' calculations.*

remembered that values of this variable are very low in most countries (particularly in relation to the turnover or assets of ETFs) due to the scarcity of such funds on the local stock exchanges; its variability is high due to year-to-year fluctuations caused, in some cases, by single large transactions. Regardless of these stipulations, some interpretations are possible. In two out of the four largest European ETFs markets correlation coefficients between IFT and diffusion of ETFs are substantially negative: −0.62 for France and −0.88 for Germany. On the contrary, for Switzerland its value is positive and very high, comparable to the one observed for the ICT indicators (for the United Kingdom no data could be acquired). In the only country from the group of mid-developed ETFs markets, i.e., Italy, the value is negative, close to −0.5. For the least-developed ETFs markets the results are mixed. It seems, therefore, that the analyzed relationship does not depend on either the level of diffusion of ETFs or of the country's economic development. Additional examination shows that the average value of IFT in a particular country is also irrelevant as, for instance, in France and Switzerland they are comparable.

In Section 4.1 MFA was identified in all estimated panel models in which it was included, as the variable with a potentially strong influence on the diffusion of ETFs. On the country level the results of the correlation analysis are, however, mixed (their dispersion is close to IFT, see Fig. 4.2) and less convincing concerning the strength and (to lower degree) direction of the links between these variables. Starting again with the most developed ETFs markets, for three of them the correlation is high and positive, yet for France it is close to 0 (interestingly, it is the country with the highest average value of MFA over 2004−16 among all considered). Discrepancies in the mid-group of European ETFs markets are even more striking as correlation coefficients range from $-0.32$ for Spain to $0.65$ for Sweden. In the least-developed ETFs markets they are negative, except for Hungary. The overall impact of MFA was assessed as positive, yet on the country-specific level it is impossible to formulate some convincing conclusions concerning the explanation of the observed differences. With some stipulations it may be stated that correlation is predominantly positive in the more-developed economies and negative in the less-developed ones.

In case of the next variable, ODI, dispersion of the country-level pairwise correlations is the lowest among all determinants examined here which means that the calculated values are similar in most countries. Moreover, in all countries the coefficients are negative, ranging from $-0.04$ in Switzerland to $-0.83$ in Italy; in most countries they are, however, moderately negative at c. $-0.5$. With the exception of Switzerland, correlation between ODI and diffusion of ETFs is very low in the largest European markets for the innovative funds: France, Germany, and the United Kingdom. For the countries with less developed ETFs markets (and also mostly at a lower level of economic development) it is generally closer to 0; see, for instance, Hungary or Turkey. It may be, thus, stated that ODI and the diffusion of ETFs are linked negatively and those links strengthen with the increasing adoption of the innovative funds.

The correlation between the S variable and diffusion of ETFs is more dispersed than in the case of the discussed interest rate yet most of the coefficients are rather similar in value; they are moderately negative. Such results are consistent with the ones reached based on the regional-level analysis; see the estimates of the panel models in Section 4.1 in which the savings variable coefficient was always negative if statistically significant. There are, however, two exceptions to this apparent rule: Germany (positive correlation coefficient of more than $0.6$) and Hungary; for Turkey as well as Italy it is close to 0. It is impossible to explain the observed differences in the correlation between S and ETFs by referring to the level of local economic development, the degree of diffusion of ETFs or other factors such as the value of the S in the given country (they are the highest in Switzerland and Norway); the apparent conclusion is that it is highly idiosyncratic and shaped by country-specific factors other than the ones considered in our study. Generally it is, however, negative.

Finally, the last string of correlation coefficients in Table 4.6 was calculated for the variable that can be perceived as one of the crucial significance with regard to the diffusion of ETFs; SMTT (at least taking into account the theoretical outlook as the estimates of the panel models provide a slightly different picture). Their dispersion is comparable to the one observed for the ODI variable which means that the values for particular countries are rather similar. Their average value is close to 0 (c. $-0.06$), the only case among the variables we consider in this section. Similarly to the correlation between the savings rate and diffusion of ETFs, it seems rather unfeasible to mark any patterns in the distribution of the coefficients concerning SMTT as they are apparently not related to any of the factors that we mentioned in our interpretations. Still, the relationship between SMTT and ETFs seems to be negative or neutral (i.e., characterized by null coefficient) in most of the largest or mid-European ETFs markets and positive or neutral in the remaining.

## 4.2.2 Country-Specific Models

Country-specific regression results for France confirm some intuitions that were formulated using the correlation coefficients. The relationship between the ICT adoption (regardless of the considered ICT diffusion indicator) and diffusion of ETFs was unambiguously positive, with a clear upward tick for the highest values of these variables (observed in the final years of 2004–16 time period); for the lower values, i.e., in the earlier years, evidence is slightly less convincing and the upward slope less positive. In contrast, for IFT and ODI it was clearly negative as suggested by the correlation coefficients. The same applies to SMTT, yet for the highest values of the stock turnover the linkages seem to become more complicated (mostly due to single-year outlier) which makes the earlier conclusion concerning the negative relationship slightly less robust (it is rather weakly negative). In case of the two remaining variables, MFA and S, some new information is revealed by the estimates of the regression. The correlation coefficient for MFA showed that when the entire 2004–16 time period is taken into account its relationship with the diffusion of ETFs was null. However, it appears that it was in fact reverse U-shaped: positive up to some peak point and subsequently negative. For the S variable the results are even more complicated as the direction of possible impact switches from positive to negative and back (correlation was simply implied to be rather strongly negative).

Estimates of the regressions for Germany are almost entirely consistent with the conclusions drawn from the analysis of the correlation coefficients as the relationships are to large extent linear (see second part of the

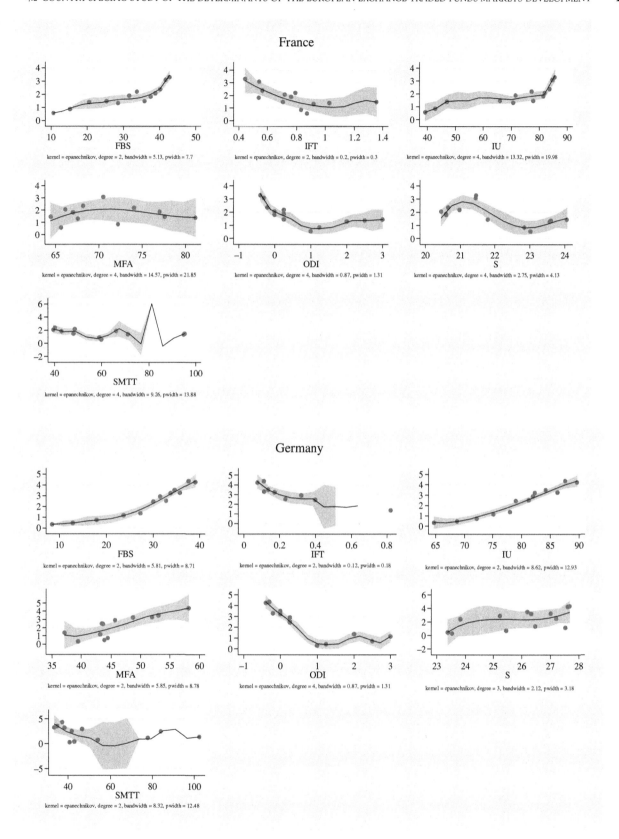

**FIGURE 4.3** ETFs versus FBS, IFT, IU, MFA, ODI, S, and SMTT. 2004−16, monthly data.
*Note*: On *Y*-axis ETFs Raw data used. Kernel weighted local polynomial smoothing applied (kernel = epanechnikov). Plot confidence bands applied for 95% confidence level. For explanation of the variables see Table 4.1. *Source: Authors' elaboration.*

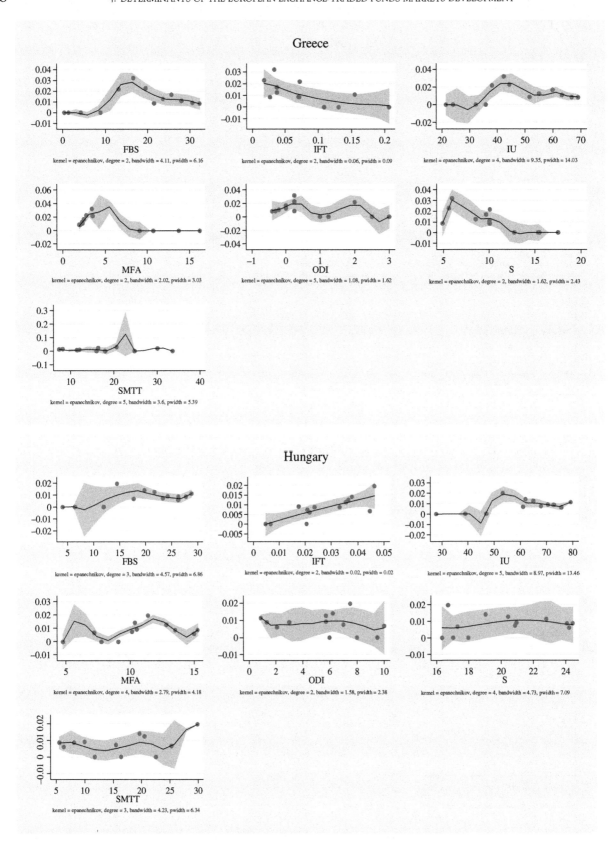

**FIGURE 4.3** (Continued).

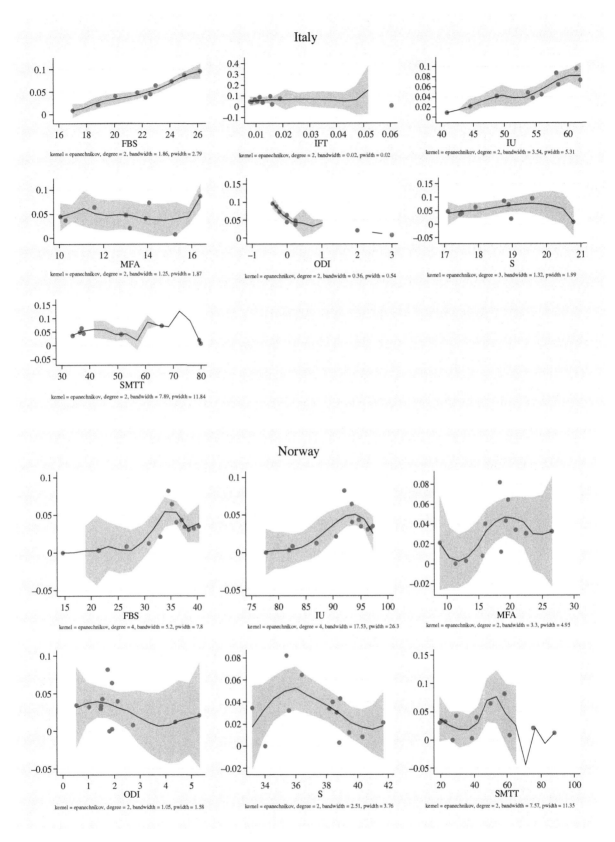

**FIGURE 4.3**    (Continued).

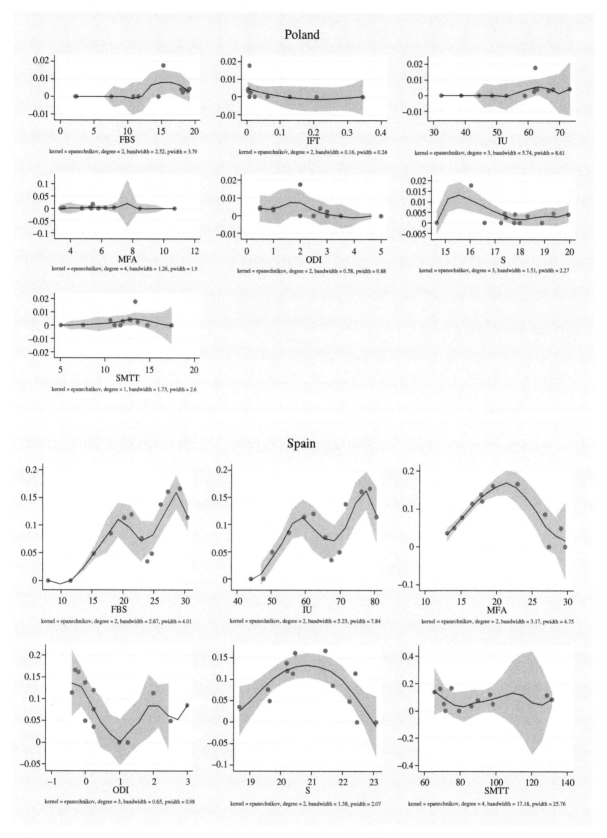

**FIGURE 4.3**    (Continued).

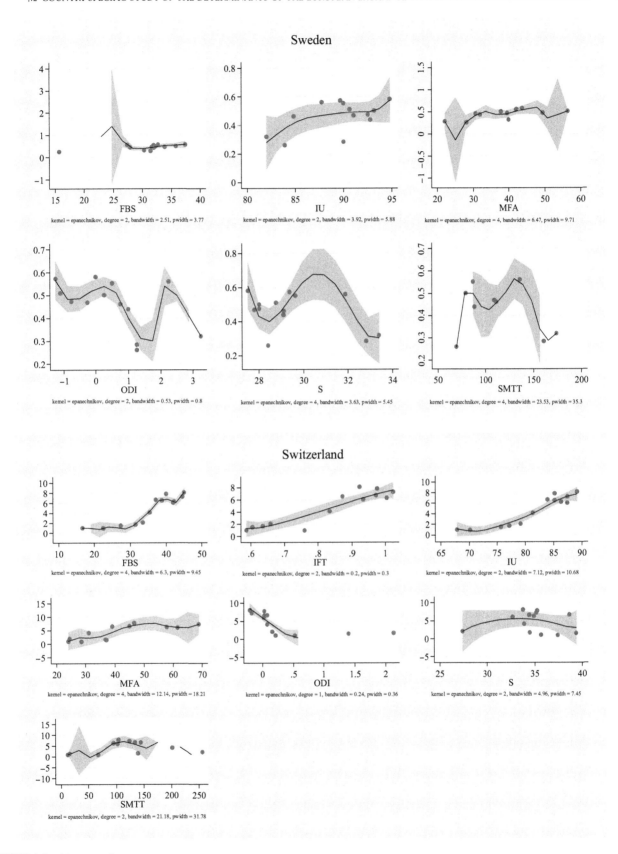

**FIGURE 4.3** (Continued).

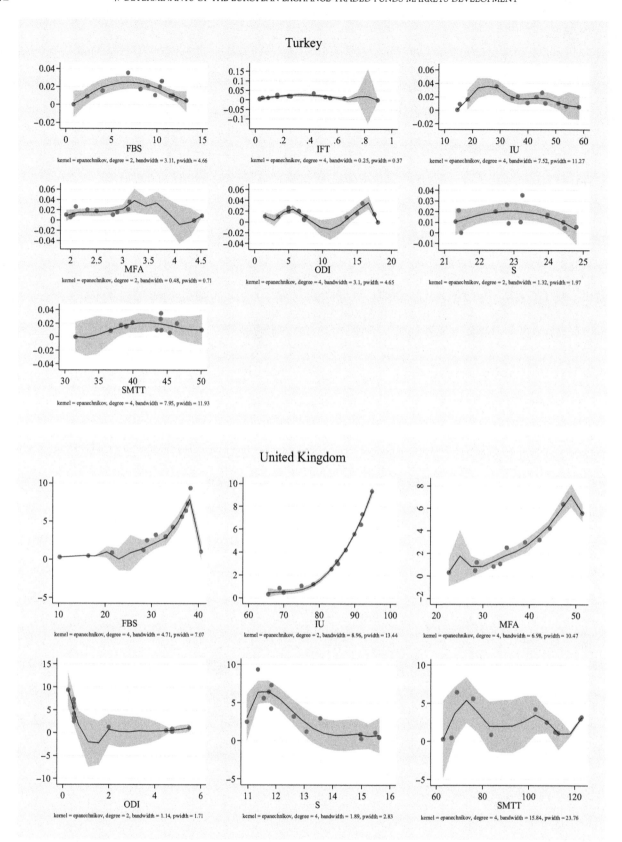

**FIGURE 4.3**    (Continued).

Fig. 4.3), particularly in the case of FBS, IU, and MFA (for all three variables the implied influence is positive). The same can be noted with regard to the linear relationship in the case of IFT yet in this case the impact on the development of the local ETFs market was negative (exact results are distorted by an outlier which proves our initial stipulation that interpretation of the estimated parameters would lead to unnecessary confusion). For the ODI and S variables, the negative and positive impact, respectively, was confirmed (in the former case it appears to be considerably less substantial for the higher values of this variable). Even though the correlation coefficient for SMTT is clearly negative ($-0.37$) graphical evidence shows that its association with the diffusion of ETFs is more complicated: negative for the low values of SMTT and null or even weakly positive for the higher values (in the graphical shape of very flat U).

After two of the countries with the most developed ETFs markets in Europe, we focus now on a few much less-advanced countries, starting with Greece. Estimations of regressions for this country lead to a number of interesting conclusions, in some ways not entirely consistent or conflicting with the ones formulated based on the correlation coefficients. Firstly, the relationship between the adoption of ICT and diffusion of ETFs is reverse U-shaped rather than moderately positive; in the case of MFA it is also shaped this way despite the considerably negative correlation. Secondly, the impact of IFT seems clearly negative (as indicated by its correlation); the same applies to S (overall result is distorted by apparently positive impact for the low values of this variable). Thirdly, despite the distinctively negative correlation coefficient for MFA, the actual relationship seems much more complicated; positive for the low values of MFA and flat for the remainder. Finally, for ODI determination of the direction of impact seems impossible. The results for Greece become more logical when we consider the trajectory of the diffusion of ETFs in this economy; the assets of the innovative funds (both regarded absolutely and in relation to the local GDP) declined sharply in the first years of the analyzed time period, then increased slightly, yet this growth was followed by further decline. At the end of the analyzed time period, the Greek ETFs market was among the least developed in Europe. This means that the results of the regression analysis for this country should be regarded with caution as the noted relationship is mostly the effect of the high variability of the assets of ETFs (linked strongly to the events in the local economy and financial system) rather than evidence for the role of the examined determinants. The other important stipulation refers to the "flat" segments on the graphs for Greece; they are explained by the null values of assets of ETFs over 2004−07 and should not be included in the interpretations (for Greece and for the remaining countries, they were, however, included in the estimations as they may provide some insights into the reasons why ETFs markets started their development relatively later in some countries).

For Hungary, the latter of the mentioned comments also applies; the value of the assets was, though, more stable than in Greece and in the final years did not vary substantially. As indicated by the correlation coefficients, the influence of the adoption of ICT and turnover of the other investment funds was positive (less obvious for the higher values of both ICT indicators due to the signaled insignificant changes in the assets of ETFs in the years close to 2016). For MFA the impact was also prevalently positive. However, in the case of the two macroeconomic variables, ODI and S, there seems to be almost no link to the development of the Hungarian ETFs market, analogously for the last one, i.e., SMTT.

Similarly to France and Germany, the analysis conducted for Italy proves the positive role of FBS and IU (i.e., adoption of the new technologies) in the context of the local ETFs market development; the relationship for the ODI variable appears to be mostly negative. Despite the varying correlation coefficients for the remaining variables (IFT, MFA, S, and SMTT) their impact on the diffusion of ETFs was ambiguous, in the case of IFT and SMTT in sharp contrast with the negative relationship indicated by the correlation coefficients.

Due to the complicated, nonlinear development path of the Norwegian ETFs market, characterized by the shape of reverse U (see Section 3.2), the analysis of determinants of this process seems particularly important with regard to the possible explanation of the rise and subsequent decrease in the diffusion of local ETFs. Taking into account the results of regression for the two ICT indicators, it appears that the relationship is reverse U-shaped, yet with an overall noticeable positive trend (as suggested by the correlation); for the S variable this shape is even more evident. This means that these factors could have contributed to the unusual trajectory of the diffusion of ETFs in Norway. For the next three potential determinants the impact seems to be positive in some intervals and negative in the other, thus, hindering any explicit implications concerning the direction of the impact (for ODI it is, overall, rather weak).

Results obtained for Poland are discussed very briefly due to the substantial underdevelopment of the local ETFs market; lack of ETFs prior to 2010, and in the following years very low assets of the innovative funds with the exception of 2010. For most of the examined factors almost no impact on the diffusion of ETFs may be identified; the only exception is the weak positive influence of the spread of ICT as well as negative influence of ODI.

Spain is a country with much more advanced ETFs market than its economy. Positive correlation coefficients of both FBS and IU with the assets of ETFs are confirmed by the results of the country-specific regression (with some slight deviations from the positive relationship for certain values of the variables that may be linked to the rather complicated trajectory of the development of the local ETFs market). Even though negative correlation coefficients of both MFA and S indicated a possible negative relationship, it appears to be clearly reverse U-shaped—positive for the values of explanatory variables up to some peak point and negative for the subsequent values. In contrast, even though the relationship between the diffusion of ETFs and ODI seems to be negative for most observations (as implied by the correlation coefficient), it is overall rather U-shaped. No significant impact of SMTT can be identified, similarly to some of the already-presented countries.

Analysis of the diffusion of ETFs in Sweden proved the rather stable spread of innovative funds in the local financial system. This may be related to the positive impact of ICT diffusion yet, interestingly, such conclusions are feasible exclusively for the IU indicator as in case of the FBS variable the overall results are much less clear-cut (partially due to an outlier; observation for 2004 that diverges from the remaining in terms of the value of FBS), but also predominantly show positive impact. With distinction to the moderately positive correlation coefficient of c. 0.65 the estimates of the regression imply almost no impact of the MFA variable. Even though the correlation coefficients for the three remaining potential determinants were clearly negative (above all in case of S), the influence implied by the country-specific regression is more problematical; approximately U-shaped for ODI and reverse U-shaped for S and SMTT (with some variability).

Switzerland was presented as an example of country with prominent diffusion of the innovative funds over 2004–16. Analysis of the values of the correlation coefficients (see Table 4.6) signaled that there were five factors that could have supported this process (labeled as): FBS, IFT, IU, MFA, and, to a lesser extent, SMTT. In the case of ODI no influence was evidenced whereas for S a negative role could be preliminarily indicated. These intuitions were verified using country-level regression analysis that backed some of the preliminary findings. Both ICT indicators were confirmed to exert a positive impact on the diffusion of ETFs, in particular striking for the broader IU variable. The relationship between IFT and assets of ETFs resulted to be almost linearly positive, as expected. For the other variable concerning the further competing category of mutual funds, i.e., MFA, the initial statement of positive impact was also supported yet, the results are considerably less convincing. However, the impact of the stock market variable, SMTT, is difficult to determine and it is apparently not positive as indicated by the correlation coefficient. Estimates of the regression for the ODI and S variables provide ground for conclusions inconsistent with the ones suggested by their correlation with the diffusion of ETFs; negative in the case of the former and null (or weakly reverse U-shaped) for the latter.

Results of the regression analysis for Turkey suffer from the same problems as outlined in case of Norway (above all concerning the shape of the local ETFs market development path) and, to lower degree, of Poland (due to low level of the market's development). Almost the entire string of correlation coefficients calculated for Turkey were values close to 0 (weakly negative for the MFA variable). Estimates of the regression confirm that the impact of most of the considered variables on the diffusion of ETFs in Turkey was negligible, with no clear positive or negative influence feasible to identify.

In contrast with the previous country, results returned for the United Kingdom allow for some rather reliable conclusions. The relationship between adoption of the new technologies and spread of the innovative funds seems to be clearly positive on this largest ETFs market in Europe (results for the FBS variable are slightly less persuasive yet the key attribute, i.e., the fact that the influence is generally positive, is difficult to reject). Furthermore, in the case of the subsequent variable the positive links are also explicit at all values of MFA. However, for the next three variables the picture becomes more complex and possible conclusions are less robust. Generally, the relationship between both ODI and S and the diffusion of ETFs is negative, with some questionable results for the higher values of both variables (for such levels it seems to "flatten" graphically, thus, indicating unchanged values of the assets of ETFs in spite of changes in the levels of ODI and S). Finally, similarly with many previous countries, results for the SMTT variable are inconclusive and can be regarded, overall, as lack of convincing evidence for any relationship with the changes in the assets of innovative funds.

# 4.3 DISCUSSION: KEY FACTORS OF THE EUROPEAN EXCHANGE-TRADED FUNDS MARKETS DEVELOPMENT AND CROSS-COUNTRY DIFFERENCES

The previous two sections were dedicated firstly to panel data models and, secondly, to country-specific analysis of the determinants of the diffusion of ETFs. The studied indicator of the diffusion of ETFs was assets of the primary listed ETFs in relation to the local GDP, in order to ensure consistency with the other variables; due to data availability time series consisting of annual observations were used. The main aim of this section is to present and compare the results obtained in Section 4.1 (panel data analysis) and, to lesser extent, in Section 4.2 (results obtained for particular countries, using country-wise regressions), focusing on the identification of the most important factors that influence the diffusion of ETFs. We also discuss briefly the identified differences between the examined countries, attempting to explain their occurrence with regard to country-specific factors that could have been their cause. However, our main focus is on the region-broad implications as country-level analysis would require an in-depth study of each analyzed economy. In addition, we cover more elaborately some issues that were generally described earlier in this chapter such as the empirical role of ICT for the diffusion ETFs in Europe. In the final part we analyze the region-broad decomposition of the changes in the assets of ETFs in Europe.

## 4.3.1 Panel Regression Analysis: Major Conclusions

### 4.3.1.1 Single Explanatory Variable Models

In the course of the panel data analysis, with the application of the single independent variable panel models, we identified the following significant determinants of the diffusion of ETFs in Europe (see Table 4.2):

1. *Financial variables:* Stock index futures turnover, assets of mutual funds, stock market (total) turnover, financial system deposits (all divided by the local GDP), stock market return, stock price volatility, and FI index.
2. *Nonfinancial variables:* Fixed broadband subscriptions, Internet users, GDP growth (and some of its components, although we do not discuss them separately), gross savings rate, broad money growth, CPI growth, and official deposit interest rate (or the closest similar rate).

Comparison of the role of the particular determinant based on the estimates of the single explanatory variable regressions is, for the rather apparent reasons, highly simplified. Nevertheless, it may be stated that for six out of the seven financial variables identified using this method their impact on the diffusion of ETFs was assessed as positive (due to positive values of the regression coefficients). The only exception was stock market return, for which it was negative, yet $R^2$ of that model was extremely low, close to 0, meaning that any relationship with ETFs may be regarded as highly doubtful. Moreover, as the further analysis showed, it was statistically significant in none of the panel multiple explanatory variable models. As a result, this variable is not considered in the further discussion.

Some comparison may be made for the two turnover variables as they are constructed in a similar manner (juxtaposing turnover variables with the asset-based ones would be more questionable, not to mention the others listed above): stock index futures turnover and stock market total turnover. Values of their coefficients are highly similar (see models RE(2) and RE(10) in Table 4.2): 0.26 and 0.28, respectively, meaning that the expected impact of the change in the turnover of either stock index futures or equities on the diffusion of ETFs is alike when other determinants are not considered ($R^2$ for the stock market's model is, though, much lower).

While the positive relationship between equity turnover and diffusion of ETFs should not be perceived as surprising due to the potentially strong links between the stock markets and innovative funds (the majority of which offer exposure to equities, usually stock market indexes), similar linkages between stock index futures and ETFs may regarded as weak proof that, in spite of the outlined theoretical framework within which stock index futures are competitive financial instruments in relation to ETFs (Amenc, Goltz, & Grigoriu, 2010; Gastineau, 2010; Arnold & Lesné, 2015), the actual relationships observed on regional level Europe are different; above all, they seem to be positive. The same applies to the mutual funds. Our estimates indicate a positive relationship in spite of the competition between these two categories assumed (and to some extent proven) broadly in the academic and professional literature. This important issue requires further scrutiny.

In our analysis the we considered stock market turnover as the indicator of the market's liquidity, but to enrich this research we add a few other equity market variables yet exclusively for the stock price volatility statistical significance was identified albeit with very low $R^2$ of the model (as already noted, for similar reason we omit the stock market return). It may be considered the weak evidence for the positive relationship between this aspect of stock market's instability and diffusion of ETFs; however, particularly in this case, the direction of the impact is important as it may as well be evidence for the negative impact of ETFs on the stock markets. We address this issue in Chapter 5, Exchange-Traded Funds and Financial Systems of European Countries: A Growth Factor or Threat to Stability?.

Two remaining statistically significant financial variables in the single independent variables models can be discussed jointly as both refer above all to the banking sector: financial system deposits and FI index. For both the positive influence on the diffusion of ETFs was noticed (with lower robustness than in case of the stock index futures or mutual funds). This could confirm the links between the development of the banking segment of the financial system and spread of the innovative funds in the European economies, in line with the theoretical framework—proven in case of mutual funds by Klapper, Sulla, and Vittas (2004) and Khorana, Servaes, and Tufano (2005).

Lastly, a brief comment is necessary with regard to the insignificant financial variables. Estimates of the single explanatory variable models prove no relationship between the diffusion of ETFs and turnover of stock index options, investment funds (those that are traded on exchanges yet other than ETFs or other ETPs, e.g., closed-end funds) and bonds, showing that spread of ETFs is more strongly linked to equities or stock index futures as well as lack of direct relationship with the closed-end funds. Furthermore, the important aspect of the stock markets is their liquidity rather than size as proven by the insignificance of the capitalization variable. Finally, it seems that the development of the ETFs markets is Europe is not dependent on the credit activity (as noted above, there are some links to the value of deposits) and general level of financial development as well as the development of the financial markets (determined using the IMF methodology), with the few mentioned exceptions.

### 4.3.1.2 Multiple Explanatory Variable Models

As the single explanatory models may be perceived an insufficient basis for the formulated conclusions, we discuss the issue of relationships between the financial determinants and diffusion of ETFs in more detail in the context of more convincing evidence obtained with the models with the multiple variables. It may, however, be stated that the two main potential determinants that were identified using the single independent variables models are stock index futures turnover and mutual funds' assets (due to their statistical significance and the highest $R^2$ of the models in which they were included). The secondary, relatively less relevant group includes stock market turnover, financial system deposits, and FI index. The third and least robust group covers the remaining variables.

In case of the group of the nonfinancial potential determinants of the diffusion of ETFs, it may be noticed that more of the considered variables resulted to be statistically significant (10 out of 14; the only four insignificant ones were three from the economic growth decomposition and the labor market indicator). Nevertheless, this apparent advantage of the noneconomic category in terms of quantity does not necessarily mean that factors from this group are more relevant for the explanation of the diffusion of ETFs in the analyzed region and countries.

Another important difference between the results obtained for the financial versus nonfinancial explanatory variables is much lower $R^2$ of the models in the latter category. Apart from the two specifications with ICT variables as well as growth of capital services provided by non-ICT assets, CPI growth, and official deposit interest rate, for the remaining models in the nonfinancial category $R^2$ are close to 0 (for none it exceeds 0.10). However, even for these five variables the values are rather low, in particular in comparison to the six discussed financial determinants. This means that these results should be interpreted with caution.

Again, the comparison of the impact of the particular nonfinancial determinant based on the single explanatory variable models can be made only on a basic level, with some general conclusions. Values of the coefficients obtained for both ICT determinants are positive and similar, but slightly higher for the more general variable: 1.17 for FBS and 1.4 for IU (see models RE(1) and RE(2) in Table 4.3). These results have two implications. First and foremost, they may be regarded as the proof (yet rather weak due to the low explanatory power of the estimated models) of the positive impact of the ICT adoption on the diffusion of ETFs. Second, they could indicate that the role of the mere access to the Internet is more important than the quality of the connection (as in fixed broadband connection) or, in a different perspective, accessing the Internet through mobile connections (not included in the values of FBS indicators) is also of some significance for the spread of the innovative funds. Nevertheless, such interpretations may be too far-reaching and more accurate verification is hindered by insufficient data. We discuss the role of ICT in more detail in Section 4.3.3.

Estimated coefficients for the rate of economic growth and linked variables are in all cases negative, but, more importantly, $R^2$ of the models are extremely low which hinders any reliable interpretations based on the single explanatory variable specifications. It may be observed, though, that negative values of the coefficients could imply that the relationship between the processes of economic growth and diffusion of ETFs is negative. One possible explanation that may be formulated can refer to the rate of economic growth in the countries in our sample; the economies which have grown most rapidly (e.g., Turkey and Poland) are the ones in which ETFs markets have remained underdeveloped. Conversely, ETFs markets have developed (diffusion of ETFs has been most widespread) in the most advanced countries, with the most developed FI (FI index was proven to be statistically significant in the single explanatory variable models; this does not necessarily apply to the development of the FM as for FM index no such conclusions was reached). It does not necessarily prove the causal relationship; on contrary, based on the theoretical links and general financial intuition it could be rather stated that ETFs markets should have been developing more rapidly in line with the accelerated economic growth that leads to higher level of economic development (Khorana et al. 2005; Borowski, 2011; Perez, 2012; Stańczak-Strumiłło, 2013). It needs to be emphasized again that our interpretation is based on very weak evidence and could be overstated. In conclusion, we do not devote more attention to the discussion of the links between economic growth and ETFs as subsequent estimates (with multiple independent variables) provide no further evidence.

In case of the remaining nonfinancial variables, i.e. the determinants that may influence the development of the investment funds markets in general (according to previous studies), statistical significance was identified for four out of five considered variables. However, for two of them, i.e., gross savings rate and broad money growth, $R^2$ of the models are very low, similarly to the economic growth variables. Consequently, formulating robust conclusions based on these estimations could lead to too far-reaching statements. It may be only noticed that the coefficients of both variables were negative, thus, implying a negative relationship between gross savings rate as well as the broad money aggregate and diffusion of ETFs in the European countries. For CPI growth and official deposit interest rate $R^2$ of the models are much higher yet still low. In the case of both the values of the respective coefficients are negative. It may be considered a (rather) weak proof that both high inflation and high interest rates discourage investments in the innovative funds due to, for example, the prevalence of the equity funds that become less attractive for investors with the possible higher rates of return of other investment opportunities. Nonetheless, it may also be linked to the structure of the European ETFs market in terms of division of assets between countries; they are the highest in the most developed economies that are also on average the ones with the relatively lower inflation or interest rates. Another reason mentioned in the country-specific discussion is monetary policy and counterrecession measures undertaken since 2008 onwards. Again, these potential impacts are further verified using the subsequent panel and country-specific models.

Estimates of the panel models with multiple independent variables confirm many of the conclusions reached based on the models with single explanatory variables. We provide their interpretation in the same order they were presented previously, i.e., starting with static models with exclusively financial variables, followed by static models with nonfinancial variables and mixed specifications, and, finally, equivalent dynamic models.

We begin our discussion of the static financial variables models with the estimates obtained for the two determinants that were identified as the most crucial ones in the preceding analysis: stock index futures turnover and mutual funds' assets. In case of both of them, their positive and statistically significant influence on the diffusion of ETFs identified with the application of the single explanatory variables was supported by the models with multiple determinants.

Positive impact of the stock index futures may be regarded, as already noted, as surprising in the light of the theoretical discussions, according to which this category of derivatives should be substitute for ETFs rather than complimentary financial products. Results of the country-specific analysis show that the discussed relationship is also prevalently positive on the country level in Europe; however, for approximately one-third of the examined countries it cannot be evaluated due to insufficient data. This could mean that turnover of the stock index futures reinforces the development of the European ETFs markets, possibly due to the varying applications of these products (Madhavan, Marchioni, Li, & Du, 2014; Arnold & Lesné, 2015; CME Group, 2016) and the scale of switching between the two categories of the financial products is rather limited. Positive influence could also be explained by referring to the structure of the European ETFs market in terms of the replication method, with the noticeable (yet gradually declining as discussed in Section 5.3) share of the synthetic funds whose tracking mechanisms are inextricably linked to derivatives and thus may to some degree benefit from the growing turnover of the stock index futures; these links are, however, to be verified more robustly in future research as usually other types of derivatives are utilized by the synthetic funds.

Interpretation of the links between mutual funds and ETFs indicated by the panel models is even more ambiguous than in case of the derivates. Theoretical outlines and results of the previous studies clearly indicate that traditional investment funds (mutual funds) and innovative ones (ETFs) should be treated as substitutes (see the in-depth discussion in Section 2.2). In spite of this expected negative relationship, we obtained results that unequivocally imply the positive impact of the mutual funds (considered, like ETFs, in terms of assets) on the diffusion of ETFs. These results can be used to formulate the conclusion that the development of the mutual funds markets in Europe supports the spread of the innovative funds. This conclusion refers, however, to the panel data analysis as estimates of country-specific models provide a different, somewhat more complicated picture. Consequently, we present our analysis of the possible linkages between mutual funds and ETFs in Europe within the country-specific discussion.

In the second, apparently relatively less important group of determinants (in terms of their robustness), we included the basic stock market indicator (turnover) as well as two measures associated mostly with the banking sector.

In case of the former variable the estimates of the extended panel specifications deliver a substantially different picture than in the case of models with a single explanatory variable. Firstly, this variable was statistically significant in only one out of four models in which it was included, thus, making any relationship between the activity on the stock markets and diffusion of ETFs more dubious. Secondly, and probably more importantly, the value of the coefficient of the stock turnover variable was negative, suggesting a surprising negative impact of the stock market's liquidity on the development of the ETFs markets, despite considerably different implications of the theoretical linkages, confirmed in some empirical studies, e.g., Ferreira, Keswani, Miguel, and Ramos (2013). This could suggest that when the determinants of the diffusion of ETFs other than liquidity of the equity markets are taken into account, its role becomes negligible or even negative which means that the development of the market for stock index futures, other categories of investment funds or banking sector (see the next paragraph) is more important. Nonetheless, it should be emphasized that there was only one specification from which robust conclusions may be drawn.

For the two banking sector's development indicators we obtained inconclusive and conflicting results. The impact of the financial system's deposits was recognized as statistically significant and positive in all relevant specifications; it may be, thus, regarded as evidence for the positive influence of the development of the banking sector on the spread of the innovative funds, at least if the former process is considered in the perspective of the deposits (i.e., their value); the other approach could involve focusing on the credits provided to the economic entities outside the financial sector (i.e., assessed using data on credits provided). In this perspective no impact was identified (our empirical results confirm, thus, the initial intuitions based on the literature review). To complicate this picture even further, the second variable (FI index) was insignificant in most specifications and in only one it was significant; its relationship to ETFs was determined to be negative whereas in the preceding one explanatory variable model it was positive. This result may be explained jointly by referring to the index methodology and by considering the role of the other determinants. While the deposits variable seems to capture the positive role of the banking sector, the negative coefficient of the FI index variable suggests depressing role of some of its other components in terms of entities, such as pension funds; the other explanation could focus on their efficiency (for the detailed methodology see Sahay et al., 2015). It should, however, be remembered that this conclusion was formulated based on one specification and could be too far-reaching.

Two more determinants were examined in this part of the analysis, both of them representing attributes of the stock markets. In line with previous observations, no significance of the stock market's returns was noticed, thus, implying that development of the ETFs markets in Europe was unrelated to the gains that could be gained on equities, despite the prevalence of the funds with equity exposure. Even though this result may be regarded as unanticipated, it should be linked to the fact that diffusion of ETFs is simply shaped to higher degree by the other factors. The next explanation is the time lag between the observed returns and investment decisions as well as, even more importantly investment horizon—usually multiannual in case of the investment funds; see the overview of the evidence for the US market presented in ICI (2001); surveys of the European ETFs market conducted by the EDHEC-Risk Institute show that most investors tend to have long-term holding horizon (Amenc, Ducoulombier, Goltz, & Le Sourd, 2015; Amenc, Goltz, & Le Sourd, 2017).

The last financial variable discussed with regard to this part of the study is stock price volatility. While the robustness of the single variable model was very low, it appears nonetheless that it is an important determinant of the diffusion of ETFs. In all specifications it resulted to be statistically significant with a positive coefficient, thus, suggesting that the development of innovative funds is positively connected to the volatility of the equity markets; this attribute appears to be more important than their size, liquidity, or returns on stocks. However, the issue of causality is here of crucial significance, due to a number of possible complicated interactions (we elaborate on this topic in Chapter 5: Exchange-Traded Funds and Financial Systems of European Countries: A Growth Factor or Threat to Stability?).

Application of the models with multiple nonfinancial variables confirmed the statistically significant positive impact of the ICT adoption on the development of the European ETFs markets even when other economic determinants are accounted for in the specification. For the remaining determinants almost no additional insights were obtained. In case of the economic growth variables the estimates of the models provided no evidence for their importance in the discussed context.

The only two nonfinancial variables for which statistical significance was determined are, apart from the two ICT indicators, gross savings rate and CPI growth (at least in most of the relevant specifications). Their coefficients are negative, identically as in the single explanatory variable estimations. Potential links between the inflation rate and diffusion of ETFs have already been addressed. However, the negative relationship between gross savings rate and the assets of the innovative funds may be perceived as somewhat unanticipated and inconsistent with the results of the previous studies concerning the factors of the investment funds markets development. It appears that, in the regional perspective, penetration of ETFs is lower in the countries with higher percentage of gross savings as GDP (the reverse would thus also be implied) which seems counterintuitive as it implies that in the economies with larger supply of accessible funds the investments in the shares of ETFs are lower (it could also mean that they are less preferred than other investment choices, e.g., bank deposits, real estate or mutual funds). Likewise, the role of mutual funds, the further country-specific analysis sheds some light on these results.

The third and final group of the estimated static models was specifications with both financial and nonfinancial explanatory variables. In the case of the financial determinants, the obtained results confirmed the positive impact of the three factors already indicated as being among the key ones: turnover of the stock index futures, assets of mutual funds and volatility of the stock markets; the negligence of the returns of the local equities was also implied. For the nonfinancial determinants in these specifications the positive influence was observed exclusively for the ICT variable and for the remaining no impact can be stated which further underlines the conclusions from the preceding paragraphs.

As far as the robustness of the panel analysis is addressed, it should be stated that the values of the $R^2$ of the static models differ substantially yet it may be noticed that the specifications exclusively with the financial variables are generally characterized by much higher values than the specifications with nonfinancial variables or jointly for both categories. Therefore, the explanatory power of the financial variables can be evaluated as relatively the highest, denoting their crucial role for understanding the factors behind the diffusion of ETFs.

For the next group of models estimated in the course of our study, dynamic panel models, such direct comparisons of the specifications are not possible. The main conclusion from the analysis using dynamic panel models refers to their key extension in relation to the static specifications; inclusion of the 1-year lagged values of the dependent variable. Statistical significance of the lagged assets of ETFs to GDP variable in most of the dynamic specifications and its positive coefficients prove that the diffusion of ETFs in the analyzed European countries is clearly a strongly endogenous and self-perpetuating process. Such results should not be perceived as surprising bearing in mind the analysis presented in Section 3.2 in which the trajectory of the diffusion processes was evaluated and, even more importantly, taking into account the fact that we analyze the assets indicator whose values usually do not change rapidly, in particular in the month-to-month or even year-to-year perspective. Strictly technically, the month-end or year-end values of the assets of ETFs may change in each time period for two reasons: (1) changes in the market values of the managed assets resulting from the changes in their prices (i.e., due to the valuation of the assets of the fund); or (2) the creation or redemption of the shares of the funds inflicted by the changes in the investor's interest in particular funds or, in the associated reactive process, by the launch or liquidation of the funds by providers. Yet, in each case the starting value is the one from the previous period's end which changes due to these two reasons (we present the analysis of the European ETFs market in this dimension in Section 4.3.4). Obviously, the other source of variability is the changes in the GDP or exchange rates between USD and the fund's base currency.

Referring to the distinction introduced in Section 3.3, the endogeneity may be perceived from both the demand and supply side of the ETFs markets. On the former side, the demand for the shares of these funds may change due to their perceived attractiveness for investors in relation to the other financial products with exposure to the same asset classes because of the (innovative or other distinctive) features of ETFs. Such awareness among investors can be anticipated to change with the number and diversity of the ETFs available in the particular financial system.[3] On the latter, supply side, linked processes can be expected to take place, i.e., providers of ETFs may make the decisions to offer or terminate such products (or simply enter or leave the ETFs market) based on the demand observed in the previous periods or in the attempt to increase their competitiveness in relation to the rival FI.

Interestingly, statistical significance of the lagged ETFs variable disappears in most dynamic specifications that apart from it include exclusively the nonfinancial determinants. The interpretation of these results is difficult as it cannot be linked to the impact of the other explanatory variables; their coefficients are also insignificant, with one exception—see DPD(8) in Table 4.5. It could imply, as stated with regard to the static models, that the robustness of the models covering only economic determinants of the diffusion of ETFs is highly problematic in relation to the ones focusing on the financial sector.

For the remaining dynamic specifications, the inclusion of the lagged ETF variable overshadows the remaining determinants and hinders evaluation of their role. Still, the positive influence of the mutual funds, banking sector as well as stock market's volatility was generally confirmed. However, in sharp contrast with the static specifications, the stock index futures variable resulted to be insignificant in all models in which it was used. One likely explanation is that the lagged variable of the assets of ETFs covers all variability inputted previously by the one linked to the derivatives market.

The results of our regional analysis of the determinants of diffusion of ETFs in Europe may be compared to the analysis presented in the similar study by Marszk and Lechman (2018) who analyzed analogous relationships yet with the examination of the only partially overlapping group of countries (all ETFs markets in the world, including the European ones) and applying a different indicator of the ETFs market development (turnover in relation to the GDP). They identified the significance of the following factors: adoption of ICT, stock market turnover, FD, and development of FM. It may, thus, be stated that on the global level the number of factors that affect the diffusion of ETFs is generally lower than unveiled for the European region.

## 4.3.2 Country-Specific Analysis: Major Conclusions

After the panel data analysis, we studied the selected determinants of the diffusion of ETFs in the analyzed countries by examining the correlation coefficients and results of nonparametric analysis. We discuss these results next and they may be regarded as an extension of the region-broad study.

Firstly, we considered the two ICT indicators. Country-specific results are quite unambiguous and prove that the positive impact of the adoption of the new technologies identified with the application of the panel models can also be identified in particular analyzed European countries. There are, though, a few exceptions such as Greece and Norway for which this relationship seems more complicated it may be explained by the atypical development paths of the local ETFs markets and, thus, should not be considered as evidence contrary to the overall positive linkages.

In contrast with the almost clear-cut results for the ICT variables, both values of the correlation coefficients and estimates of country-level regressions provide a much more complicated outlook in case of the turnover of investment funds (other than ETPs). As already noted, this determinant was proven to be statistically insignificant in the panel data analysis. Nevertheless, we decided to include it in the country-specific study in order to examine whether on the country level some relationship between these categories of investment funds may be identified (at least in certain economies; this applies exclusively to the funds whose units are listed on the stock exchanges—mutual funds are discussed subsequently). The results are highly inconclusive and it is impossible to explain the between-country differences by referring to the level of development of the local ETFs market or even the value of turnover of the other investment funds. It can, thus, be concluded that no robust generalization is possible concerning the role of these investment funds in the diffusion of ETFs. However, with the exception of Italy it is prevalently negative, thus, being weak evidence for the possible switching (substitution) between the innovative and traditional investment funds, as expected based on the theoretical outline.

The results of the country-level analysis obtained for one of the variables perceived as the key determinant of the diffusion of ETFs based on the panel models, i.e., assets of mutual funds, are highly mixed and inconclusive, particularly when correlation coefficients are considered; more insights are provided by the country-specific regressions on which we focus. Generally, however, with some exceptions the relationship between the two

---

[3]Of course, it may also be caused by the trends on, for instance, equity markets that shape the demand for various products with the identical or similar exposure (e.g., following this example, equity ETFs and equity mutual funds) and, thus, influence the selection between varying investment choices.

categories of investment funds in Europe seems to be positive in the economies that are more advanced (which usually means that their ETFs markets are more developed) in comparison to the other (see results for Germany, Switzerland, and the United Kingdom). France is probably the most noticeable exception in this top group (with a reverse U-shaped relationship) which could be linked to the fact that assets of mutual funds in this country are the largest in our sample (as % of French GDP). There are also some countries for which no impact was observed (or it is impossible to determine its attributes). Generally, the relationship seems be explicitly positive for the most developed ETFs markets (for France up to some peak point) and weakly positive or neutral in case of the remaining.

Apart from the country-specific factors, the general observation that can be made with regard to the country-level role of the mutual funds for the diffusion of ETFs is that in the initial stages of the diffusion of the innovative funds, i.e., on the less-developed ETFs markets they seem not to either substantially compete or be supported (i.e., they are mostly unaffected) by the more established type of investment companies. It may be explained by the initially typically undiversified array of ETFs; usually it consists of passive equity funds (in some cases accompanied by bond ETFs) with exposure to the major indexes that could compete with only the particular group of the already functioning mutual funds. The other cause is the group of early users that consists above all of the most sophisticated entities in the investment industry whereas the general investing public has little or no awareness of ETFs. Furthermore, generally ETFs have a weaker position in the distribution networks which favor selling units of mutual funds that, for example, generate higher distribution fees.

When the local ETFs markets becomes more mature, these barriers may be overcome and the relationship between mutual funds and innovative funds evolves into a positive relationship; the two categories seem to reinforce each other's growth of assets, becoming complimentary financial products, with varying applications (e.g., utilized for active vs passive investing). Reaching that stage is most probable in the advanced economies as in the less developed ETFs markets have stayed nascent. However, in some cases, after some point, the relationship may switch its direction and become negative, meaning that ETFs and mutual funds become substitutes; it can occur in countries with ETFs markets at various development levels; in our study we identified such change for both France and Spain which differ substantially in terms of the development of the local ETFs market.

Results of the correlation analysis for the official deposit interest rate imply, analogously to the conclusions based on the panel models, that this relationship is negative in all examined countries. Estimates of the country-level regressions mostly confirm this conclusion. There is, however, one important necessary clarification to add. For most of the countries considered, in case of the higher values of the interest rates the graphs showing the relationship seem to abruptly flatten in relation to the lower (or in particular negative in some countries) interest rates. Explanation of this phenomenon is rather straightforward—monetary authorities of the analyzed countries lowered the interest rates after the 2008 global financial crisis. Overall, it needs to be emphasized that in most of the discussed countries development of the local ETFs markets has taken place in the period during which interest rates have been lowered; it seems that diffusion of ETFs has been shaped predominantly by other factors and concluding that there is significant relationship, meaning that there was impact of interest rates, would be an overstatement. Still, some influence was probably exerted—for an explanation see our comment with regard to the panel models.

Results for the gross savings rate variable are probably most intriguing. Estimates of the panel model indicated negative linkages between the gross savings rate and diffusion of ETFs. Most correlation coefficients support this conclusion as they are also negative; estimates of the country-specific models provide a more complicated picture. For one country, Germany, the relationship is positive, albeit for the remaining it seems neutral or, in most cases, reverse U-shaped: positive for the lower values of the rate and negative for the higher ones. Taking into consideration the changes in the gross savings rate in Germany, with gradual increase over the 2004—16 period and the fact that it has been the period of convincing development of the local ETFs market, their positive relationship is easy to understand yet establishment of the causal link and detailed explanation requires further study. The same applies to the counterintuitive lack of relationship or its changing nature in the remaining countries. It seems, though, that the gross savings rate is not robustly linked to the development of the European ETFs markets and the spread of the innovative funds is to large extent unaffected by the changes in the supply of available financial resources to be used for investments into the shares of ETFs. This result is more understandable if the size of the local ETFs markets (of maximum several percent of the local GDP) is considered; insufficient financial resources may not, thus, be considered a barrier to the development of the European ETFs market. The reverse U-shaped relationship was inflicted mostly by the increase in the gross savings rates in the examined countries (mostly prior to 2008 global financial crisis), followed by their decline (discussion of this phenomenon and its reasons are outside the scope of this book), while at the same time most analyzed ETFs markets have been developing (usually with some variability).

For the sole equity market variable examined in the country-specific analysis, stock market (total) turnover, the results are mixed as indicated by the average correlation coefficient of approximately 0. Outcomes of the regression analysis also provide weak evidence for the robust relationship between the activity on the local stock markets and assets of ETFs the examined countries. These results are contrary to the evident importance of the stock markets implied by the theoretical outline and in the previous studies (e.g., Ferreira et al., 2013) yet in line with the insignificance of this variable in most panel specifications. Taking into account the importance of the other determinants discussed in this section, it seems that the significance of the stock market's liquidity for the diffusion of ETFs has been overemphasized, even in spite of the prevalence of the funds with exposure to equities. From the other perspective, it means that the value of transactions that must be conducted in order to assert correct functioning of the equity ETFs is relatively small in comparison to the overall transactions on the European stock markets. Furthermore, it could mean that the liquidity of the linked stock market is not highly substantial for the users of ETFs as it does not significantly affect the demand for the shares of innovative funds; we consider the assets indicator (of market development) yet any changes in the assets must be a direct or indirect result of the demand. In Europe it is evidenced on a regional scale by the inflows to funds as their main source of growth (see the decomposition in Section 4.3.4).

### 4.3.3 Adoption of ICT and Diffusion of ETFs in Europe: Discussion

As the results of our analysis prove the importance of the adoption of ICT and its positive relationship with the diffusion of ETFs (with a few minor exceptions), we cover in more detail some contemporary aspects of the applications of the new technologies in the European financial sector. It should be emphasized that adoption of ICT was the only determinant that was almost unambiguously identified as important for the diffusion of ETFs.

The role of ICT for the development of the European ETFs markets may be observed in some particular areas. One of the most notable examples is the rise of robo-advising, i.e., online platforms that offer automated portfolio management services, affordable also for investors with low assets, in contrast with the traditional services (the concept of robo-advising is presented in Section 2.3). In Europe, the most popular robo-advising platforms (e.g., Moneyfarm or Nutmeg in the United Kingdom, Vaamo in Germany, and TrueWealth in Switzerland) use ETFs as their basic investment instruments in the strategies they provide for users, mostly due to their low costs (Morningstar, 2017). Potential of robo-advising companies has been also noted by the commercial banks or providers of ETFs. For example, in 2017, the largest European provider of ETFs, BlackRock, became minority shareholder of robo-advising company Scalable Capital (Tearn, 2017). The issue of robo-advising in Europe requires close analysis due to its strong linkages to the ETFs market, mostly on its demand side.

Despite the possibilities for this new type of investment industry to influence many segments of the financial system, the role of automated online investment management services in Europe seems to be limited due to the reluctance of the European retail customers. According to the study conducted by Ipsos for ING in May 2017 (ING, 2017) that covered almost 15,000 respondents in 15 countries (mostly European, including all largest ETFs markets with the exception of Switzerland), more than one-third of the people surveyed expressed no interest in robo-advising services (we refer to data on the European respondents only). Some 55% of the respondents accepted some support from the robo advisor (29% advice only, 26% also decisions but with the requirement of final approval by the user). Only 3% would accept fully automated services. In a slightly broader perspective, merely 4% chose online computer program as the primary source of advice regarding investment. The most often selected answer was "a financial or bank adviser"—40% of respondents declared it to be the preferable source of such recommendation which proves the significant prevalence of the conventional solutions. Authors of the cited report attribute the unwillingness to employ robo-advisory application to the psychological mechanism; "control premium," i.e., reluctance to lose (real or perceived) control over decisions, regardless of the possibility to achieve a better outcome (ING, 2017, p. 8).

Readiness of European customers to use robo-advisory varies between countries which may to some extent be used to explain the noted differences in the impact of ICT on the development of local ETFs markets; such impact is obviously limited by the very narrow role of automated services. We refer again to the study published by ING (2017) which presents the preferences of respondents in selected countries. The level of aversion to delegate the investment management duties fully to the computer programs is similar in all analyzed countries. It should be stressed that US respondents are more willing to make such decision than in any other considered country which in some way explains why robo-advising is more popular in the United States; however, the reverse explanation may also be true. It has been offered for more years than in Europe so customers are more aware of its basics and familiar with the potential advantages. However, when the percentage of clients who are ready to accept at least some advice (i.e., partial readiness) from automated services is taken into account (see Table 4.7) some significant conclusions may be drawn.

Among the countries analyzed in the ING report, the highest partial acceptance (as already stated, level of full readiness is very low in all countries) of the robo-advisory services was observed in the two relatively less advanced economies under scope: Turkey and Poland. In both countries more than one-third of the respondents is ready to let the automated software prepare the investment decisions, not only consider its advice, which may be regarded as a more advanced form of using robo-advising. Furthermore, when responses to the other yet related question, are taken into account, Turkey and Poland are the countries with the highest share of customers who selected online software as the primary source of investment advice (7% and 6%, respectively). Both countries are also the leaders of the mobile banking adoption which may be perceived as strongly connected to the acceptance of robo-advising (customers are already familiar with one form of online financial services). More formally, it means that in accordance with the "leapfrogging" concept (Soete, 1985; Kee & Lim, 2001; Schilling, 2003) clients of FI in these countries have passed directly to technologically advanced services in the absence of developed traditional brick and mortar institutions. However, as of early 2018 access to robo-advising based on ETFs in both countries is severely restricted: only one platform, European robo-advisory company (ETFmatic) offers its services to Polish clients; no platform for Turkish clients could be identified. Consequently it can be stated that robo-advising has played no role in the development of either Polish or Turkish ETFs markets. It might be concluded, however, that the lack of such services (despite apparent readiness of customers) can be identified as one of the barriers that hinder the broader adoption of innovative investment funds.

In Italy, the total level of partial readiness to use robo-advising is close to the one noted for Poland, yet most customers in this group are interested only in obtaining investment advice. Results of the survey for Italy cannot be explained by referring to the frequent usage of mobile banking as in this aspect it substantially lags behind. Italian customers seem also to be rather satisfied with the services offered by the traditional FI (45% selected them as the primary source of investment advice, the highest level among all analyzed countries). Reasons for the relatively high interest in robo-advising seem, thus, to be explained by factors outside the ones covered by the analyzed survey; for more details about the Italian ETFs market see Section 4.4. More generally, the estimated country-specific models also prove the positive impact of the ICT adoption on the development of the local ETFs market.

In the next three countries outlined in Table 4.7 (Germany, the United Kingdom, and Spain) the readiness of the surveyed customers to use automated investment services is relatively similar (in Spain it is slightly higher because the share of customers willing to consider decisions of such software is comparable to the one noted for Italy). In the case of Germany, it may be explained in a rather straightforward manner: among all countries in scope it is the economy with the lowest declared usage of mobile banking and one of the highest preferences of personalized professional investment advice (accordingly low acceptance of online suggestions). British customers seem to distrust advice received from "real," personal sources in the financial companies (significantly

TABLE 4.7    Partial Readiness to Use Robo-Advising Investment Services in Selected European Countries

| Country | Advice only (% of respondents) | Advice and decisions requiring final approval by the user (% of respondents) | Total partial readiness (% of respondents) |
|---|---|---|---|
| France | 23 | 17 | 40 |
| Germany | 31 | 16 | 47 |
| United Kingdom | 28 | 21 | 49 |
| Spain | 23 | 26 | 49 |
| Italy | 35 | 26 | 61 |
| Poland | 29 | 33 | 62 |
| Turkey | 29 | 40 | 69 |

*Own elaboration based on ING. (2017).* Mobile banking — the next generation. How should ways to bank and pay evolve in future?.

lower share of respondents chose this option in comparison to the European average), but they also are reluctant to use automated online services (probably as they are associated with the FI at large); however, the share of British respondents who declared Internet websites as the main source of their investment advice was the highest in all analyzed countries (27% vs the European average of 16%). It may mean that the reason for reluctance to use robo-advising is simply insufficient education. Results of surveys for Spain place this country in the middle of the analyzed group in most aspects, with average acceptance of the online financial services. For all three countries, the contribution of the increasing ICT penetration to the diffusion of ETFs was confirmed by the estimates of the country-specific models discussed in Section 4.2.

Finally, the lack of acceptance of robo-advising by French customers may be attributed to a strong preference for not virtual (physical) sources of investment advice; only 40% could consider receiving some support from automated software and, more importantly, only 9% of French respondents prefer advice from any type of online source (including websites; the lowest level in the whole group). Interestingly, when mobile banking services are considered, their declared usage in France is close to the European average which means that the mentioned distrust towards online finance does not apply to all types of services (as in Germany). What is more, estimates of the country-specific regression for France also prove that, while the relationship between adoption of ICT and diffusion of ETFs is generally positive as in the other countries, it appears to be weaker (particularly in the case of the IU indicator)—compare the respective results for France, Germany, and the United Kingdom in Section 4.2.

## 4.3.4 Decomposition of the Changes in the Assets of ETFs in Europe

As a final point and as a supplement to the preceding discussion, we adopt a slightly different approach to the analysis of the reasons behind the development of the European ETFs markets, based on the decomposition of the changes in the assets of the innovative funds into their two sources: (1) changes in the prices of the securities (or other assets) held in their portfolios; and (2) net flows to the funds (i.e., positive contribution in case of inflows higher than outflows and negative in the opposite scenario; with regard to the mechanisms of the ETFs markets it may be viewed also within the creation or redemption of the shares of the funds).[4] Due to data availability our analysis is conducted for the region-broad values of assets, using the monthly data provided by the Deutsche Bank in line with its methodology (for details concerning its approach and differences in relation to our baseline method of analysis see Section 3.1). The time period of the analysis is January 2013–August 2017.

As presented in Chapter 3, Exchange-Traded Funds Markets in Europe: Development Patterns, the assets of the European ETFs have increased in the analyzed time period. It is also proven by the positive average monthly changes in the assets of c. 1.58% (and median value of 1.60%). Fig. 4.4 shows that monthly increases were much more common than decreases. Most variability was observed in 2015, with some monthly changes exceeding 5% or even 10%. What is important in the context of the analysis of the ETFs market is the fact that the key reason behind its development were inflows of capital rather than appreciation of the assets in the portfolios of the innovative funds. Average change in their price accounted for 0.53% out of 1.58% average total growth while the flows accounted for the remaining 1.05%. What is more, between 2013 and 2017 there were only 2 months in which outflows from the funds exceeded inflows (i.e., the balance of the flows was negative), both in 2013; in the remaining the balance was positive or at least null. Fluctuations of the price change's contribution were much larger, for rather obvious reasons (such as changes in the prices of equities, the most common asset class). To sum up, it denotes that growth of the European ETFs was caused by the actual interest of the investors and not merely an effect of updates in the values of assets.

The analysis presented leads to at least three important conclusions concerning the examination of the factors that affected the development of the European ETFs markets (considering the 2013–17 time period). First and foremost it may be stated that even though we formally evaluated the development measured in terms of assets of ETFs, in fact our analysis referred also to the net flows to these investment funds as they were the main contribution to the changes in assets. Furthermore, it means that our implications are above all linked to the changes in the actual activity on the analyzed ETFs markets (resulting from the interaction of demand and supply) and are not explanations of the changes in the prices of the assets held in their portfolios which would make them erroneous or at least not sufficiently backed by the theoretical underpinnings and the previous studies. Finally, the rather stable proportion of the division between price changes and flows (c. 1:2) indicates that these conclusions

---

[4]In the source reports no detailed calculation methodology is provided, yet examination of the provided data could imply that it takes into account the impact of the launches and closures of funds—most probably it is included in the values of flows.

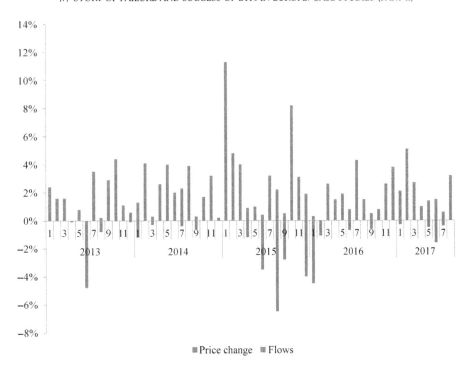

**FIGURE 4.4**  Decomposition of the changes in the assets of European ETFs. 2013–17, monthly data. *Source: Own elaboration.*

are valid on average for the entire time period of, at least, 2013–17. Lack of data for the months prior to January 2013 limits making assured statements that these conclusions can be applied to the entire time period of the study. Still, it may be reasonably assumed that the structure of the assets' growth had been rather similar in the earlier years.

## 4.4 STORY OF FAILURE AND SUCCESS OF ETFs IN EUROPE: CASE STUDIES (PART II)

The second presented case study of the European ETFs market is the one for which the analysis of the diffusion of the innovative funds is hindered by the structure of its stock exchange, i.e., part of the London Stock Exchange (LSE) Group. As shown in Section 4.3, the value of the assets of ETFs primary listed in Italy is not very substantial, in particular in relation the size of the local economy (for example, assets of Swedish ETFs are much higher, both in absolute and relative terms, i.e., as % of local GDP). However, when value of the turnover of the shares of ETFs is considered, a radically different picture of the Italian ETFs market is unveiled. Consequently, in this section we make an exception to our main approach to the examination of the development of the ETFs market (based on the data on assets) by employing turnover indicators. Another distinctive feature of the Italian ETFs market—yet not unique as discussed in the third case study, concerning Germany (see Section 5.4)—is the availability of the ETNs and ETCs. For these and other reasons outlined throughout this section, we analyze the ETFs market in Italy separately by presenting some aspects that can contribute to better understanding of its development and, to some extent, facilitating a response to the implicit question formulated in the section's heading. In this section, analogically to the previous one, we use the term "Italian ETFs" to designate exclusively ETFs with the Italian stock exchange as its primary listing location. However, when we discuss turnover of the shares of ETFs in Italy, transactions in all shares of ETFs that can be traded on the local stock exchange are considered (both primary and cross listed; transactions in the units of ETNs and ETCs are also included due to their significant role; we analyze, therefore, in fact the turnover of ETPs). Using data exclusively on the primary listed funds would show only partially the actual trading activity. All data on the turnover were extracted from the reports of the World Federation of Exchanges and statistics of Borsa Italiana (data given in EUR were translated into USD using month-end exchange rates for particular month or mean monthly rate in case of annual data). It needs to be added that values of assets of Italian ETFs that we used in our study differ noticeably from the values provided in, for example, the reports of the Italian stock exchange; the discrepancies are caused by the fact that we used exclusively data on the primary-listed funds in order to avoid double counting while analyzing and comparing the European markets whereas in most other reports assets of all listed funds are included. The Italian ETFs market did not attract substantial attention of researches, as proven by a scarce number of studies devoted to this issue.

Even though the Lipper's database includes no data on the Italian ETFs for the period preceding March 2007 (therefore, we considered this month as an approximate establishment of the Italian ETFs market in the primary listing approach), its beginnings may be traced back to 2002 when first innovative funds had been cross listed on the Milan Stock Exchange (known also as Borsa Italiana; we use both names). It took place in the final days of September 2002 when first three innovative funds became listed; however, the necessary infrastructure was ready a few months earlier when Borsa Italiana had launched multilateral trading facility in July 2002 as electronic exchange that could be used for trading in the shares of closed-end funds or ETFs (Zanotti & Russo, 2005; Borsa Italiana − London Stock Exchange Group, 2009; Bianchi, Loddo, & Miele, 2011). Over the next few years the range of available ETFs broadened rapidly both in terms of their number and their exposure as, among other, bond funds were listed. However, none of these funds could be classified as primary listed in Italy. According to Deville (2008) listing policy of the Italian stock exchange was initially very restrictive (as only funds with exposure to specific indexes were allowed).

One of the most important events in the history of the Italian ETFs market (and, more broadly, of the Italian financial system) took place in 2007 (with some effects taking place in the following years). It was the merger of the LSE and Borsa Italiana. Terms of the transaction which may be regarded as the acquisition of Borsa Italiana by the much larger UK stock exchange were agreed in June 2007; its value was estimated at c. $2 billion and was conducted as exchange of 4.9 ordinary shares of the LSE for each respective share of Borsa Italiana; board of the directors of the merged company comprised in majority of members appointed by the LSE (Borsa Italiana & London Stock Exchange, 2007a; Willey, 2007). Completion of the merger was announced on October 1, 2007—in the announcement, the expected positive effects included: creation of the leading European diversified exchange group, platform for additional accelerated growth, as well as operating the most advanced trading platform and post-trade services in Europe (Borsa Italiana & London Stock Exchange, 2007a, 2007b).

A description of the both markets' situation preceding the merger's decision and its basic consequences may be found in Lee (2017) from which we derive our presentation. After the 2008 global financial crisis shareholders of Borsa Italiana (such as banks) wished to sell their shares due to the problems with cash flows. There were a number of reasons of the attractiveness of this purchase for LSE; at least two of them require some scrutiny. Firstly, LSE wished to acquire MTS (full name: *Società per il Mercato dei Titoli di Stato*), government bond-trading platform co-owned by Borsa Italiana which could contribute to the range of services provided by the UK stock exchange. The second cause was the clearinghouse of Borsa Italiana (CC&G; *Cassa di Compensazione e Garanzia*) as LSE had not established such entity and acquisition of the already-functioning Italian organization had been aimed at creation of the trading venue comprising all necessary systems for its users (i.e., the whole trading cycle). Furthermore, LSE wanted to acquire the strong derivatives trading platform of Borsa Italiana (Jordan, 2016). From a different perspective (Lees, 2012), the decision of the LSE could have been motivated by the attempt of the UK stock exchange to defend itself from the takeover by the US NASDAQ; Lee (2017) states that it had wished to prevent such move by its largest European counterpart, i.e., the Deutsche Börse.

According to Lee (2017), despite various declared benefits of the merger, as of 2017 most synergies have been reached at the organizational level through the restructuring of the company which seems to have affected mostly the Italian division (due to, among others, employment redundancies). In terms of the processes that could most significantly affect the turnover of securities, i.e., trading, clearing and settlement, the Italian and UK segments have remained separate, with weak linkages. In particular (in the context of the topic of ETFs) no common trading platform has been created, mostly due to the opposition from the Italian entities.

In a few years after the merger became effective, its results in the context of the assumed benefits were evaluated in a few studies. Floreani and Polato (2010) concluded that the benefits of the merger were overestimated, for example in the derivatives segment. A similar conclusion was reached in another paper by these authors (Polato & Floreani, 2010). According to the statement of G. Vegas from 2012, the head of the Italian capital market authority, the expected positive results of the merger were not reached at that time as cross-market opportunities (such as capital flows between the two markets) did not materialize, in particular with regard to the Italian market for the smaller companies (Sanderson, Masters, & Grant, 2012). Dorodnykh (2014) assessed the effects of the merger more positively by stating that it led to increased liquidity pool for the listed companies and decreased their cost of capital as well as diversification of the product and customer bases. Abukari and Otchere (2016) stated that the merger resulted in the increased market share of the merging stock exchanges (understood as share in the total value of stock trading on all exchanges) and decreasing shares of their rivals.

Decision of LSE and Borsa Italiana may be also viewed in the context of other similar activities and examination of their effects in the academic literature. The effects of the merger of stock exchanges evidenced by the research are mixed yet some of the potential results include—the first two are the assumed aim of the mergers, the rest are effects observed on the linked financial markets (Nielsson, 2009; Cantillon & Yin, 2011; Khan & Vieito, 2012; Kokkoris, 2013; Yepes-Rios, Gonzalez-Tapia, & Gonzalez-Perez, 2015; Charles, Darné, Kim, & Redor, 2016; Teplova & Rodina, 2016; Valdes, Cramon-Taubadel, & Engler, 2016; Yang & Pangastuti, 2016; Lee, 2017; Andreu & Padilla, 2018):

- Exploiting economies of scale by stock exchanges that combine different geographic markets.
- Broadening the range of provided services by stock exchanges that combine different areas of expertise.
- Increased stock market efficiency, dependent on a number of factors such as size, diversification (geographical or industrial), and the development of the merging entities.
- Increased liquidity of the traded securities (at least in some segments of the combined market such as large companies).
- Transformation of the brokerage sector through, inter alia, mergers and acquisitions on both local and international level.
- Mixed effect concerning the impact on attracting new listings.

Mergers of stock exchanges lead also to a number of side-effects such as challenges for the financial authorities (Kokkoris & Olivares-Caminal, 2008).

An important question in the context of our analysis is whether the merger of the two stock exchanges influenced positively the development of the ETFs markets in Italy and the United Kingdom. Examination of this event's impact is rather difficult due to the vast array of other determinants that impacted the discussed processes. Still, some conclusions may be reached based on, for instance, the graphical evidence. Firstly, in terms of assets, no extensive comparison of the Italian market before and after the merger is feasible due to lack of data for 2006 and earlier years. However, even when data for the 7 months (March 2007–September 2007) preceding the merger are compared to the next (from October 2007 onwards) a substantial increase may be noticed. Before the merger, the assets of ETFs primary listed in Italy had been minimal, afterwards they reached quickly the level of a few hundred USD millions. In the case of the UK market, the rate of growth of the ETFs' assets was similar before and after the merger which could indicate that in this dimension Italian market benefitted more from the establishment of the joint group of exchanges. In the second approach, based on the turnover data, the results are less straightforward. The value of the turnover of the ETFs' shares on the Italian stock exchange declined markedly in 2008 (see Fig. 4.5), followed by the rebound since 2009 and over the next years it had grown rather

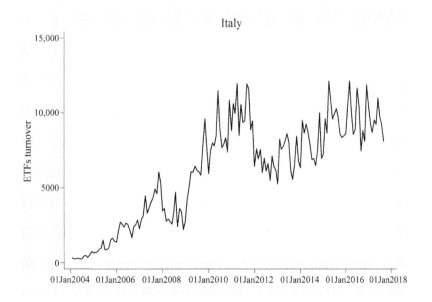

**FIGURE 4.5** Turnover of ETPs in Italy. 2004–17, monthly data.
*Note*: Data covers transactions in all types of exchange-traded products (ETPs) available on Borsa Italiana, i.e., ETFs, ETNs, and ETCs. *Source: Authors' elaboration.*

quickly. It is impossible to assess whether the decline in 2008 was in any substantial way linked to the merger or if it was rather the effect of the overall situation in the global financial system and economy. For the UK market the development path in terms of turnover has been highly similar to the one previously analyzed based on the value of assets. As noted, the reasons for the apparent lack of impact of the merger on the turnover of the analyzed securities could be lack of common trading platform and lower than expected transnational capital flows.

Apart from the merger of LSE and Borsa Italiana, another important event was the launch of ETFplus which had taken place a few months earlier, in April 2007 (Borsa Italiana, 2013). ETFplus is a segment of Borsa Italiana dedicated for the transactions in the shares (units) of ETFs (of all categories) as well as ETNs and ETCs. It is divided into four subsegments (Borsa Italiana, 2009, 2013):

1 Basic ETFs (i.e., without modified returns):
   a. equity ETFs
   b. bond ETFs
2 Geared ETFs:
   a. inverse and other ETFs (e.g., with embedded options)
   b. leveraged ETFs
3 Active ETFs
4 ETNs and ETCs:
   a. without leverage
   b. with leverage multiplier of 2
   c. with leverage multiplier higher than 2

As far as the technical aspects of ETFplus are concerned, it is an order-driven market and requires at least one market maker and specialist to support the liquidity of each listed instrument; the latter is arranged by the issuer—it is mandatory for the shares (or units) to be admitted to listing (London Stock Exchange Group, 2017). Trading is continuous, with the closing auction at the end of the trading day. Both physical and synthetic ETFs are listed on ETFplus; some of them with exposure to foreign markets, e.g., Asian (Elia, 2010).

Before we present the results of the analysis with the application of the turnover indicators, we summarize the key conclusions that may be drawn based on the assets' indicator. Overall, when the entire period 2004–17 is analyzed, the mean assets of the Italian ETFs has been c. $935 million. The maximum level was reached in the final analyzed month, i.e., in August 2017, after the subperiod of rapid growth (see Figure 3.18). This increase in assets was driven mostly by the inflows to the funds rather than growth in the value of the managed securities. There was a number of reasons responsible for this trend (interestingly, turnover remained stable, see Fig. 4.5, which proves that high inflows are not accompanied by the substantial activity on the stock exchanges in the shares of ETFs). One of the key causes was growing demand from the investment intermediaries and FI like, for instance, pension funds (Villegas, 2017) which invested in the bond or enhanced indexing funds. An important factor that has influenced the trend on the Italian ETFs market were various political events, e.g., elections or referendum of 2016 (Vlastelica, 2016). Dynamic of the Italian ETFs market development (in terms of assets) has been very high over the entire time period; the average monthly dynamic has been the highest among all the examined countries (when extreme month-to-month changes are excluded).

In January 2004, the monthly turnover of the shares of ETFs on the Italian stock exchange (Borsa Italiana has been over 2004–17 the only stock exchange in Italy) was at c. $310 million USD. For comparison, at this time in Germany it exceeded $4 billion USD, on Euronext it was slightly below $2 billion USD and in Switzerland at c. $900 million; there is no comparable data for the United Kingdom. At the end of the analyzed time period, in August 2017, position of the Italian stock exchange strengthened substantially in relation to the other mentioned countries: in Italy monthly turnover exceeded $8 billion, while in Germany it was at c. $12 billion, on Euronext at approximately $10 billion, in Switzerland below $10 billion.[5] This means that Italian exchange has, in this aspect, approached the previously distinctively leading countries. For example, in relation to the German market, turnover on the Italian market has increased from below 8% to approximately two-thirds of the corresponding value for Germany. To some extent this improvement may be associated with the merger. It should be emphasized that for Italy we use data on the turnover of all ETPs (not only ETFs); in order to ensure consistency of our results we use analogical indicators for the other examined countries as well.

---

[5]We discuss data for one single month yet they are comparable to the values observed in the surrounding time period and, thus, may be regarded as at least partially representative.

Fig. 4.5 shows how the turnover of ETFs on Borsa Italiana has evolved over time between 2004 and 2017. Since January 2004 it increased steadily until 2008 when substantial decline could be noticed. After a few months of stabilization at relatively low levels of turnover, it started to grow, exceeding for the first time $10 billion in May 2010 during one of the peak points of the Eurozone crisis; very high values of turnover (not only in the shares of ETFs) were reached also in most other major European economies. However, intensive trading in ETFs observed in 2010 and 2011 may be perceived as transitory due to sharp decrease in 2012 and 2013. Over the next years it was growing, stabilizing since 2016 on the levels of c. $10 billion per month. Overall this may mean that in terms of turnover the Italian ETFs market has reached a period of stabilization at a high level of development, demonstrating no clear-cut signs of further growth in this dimension. Additionally, important in the context of the further analysis, the trajectory of the changes in the turnover of ETFs in Italy may be regarded to a high degree as S-shaped as required by the logistic growth model which signals the possibility to use it to evaluate the observed and predicted ETFs market development.

Tables 4.8 and 4.9 include the estimates of the diffusion models for Italy, yet with the application of different conceptualization of the diffusion indicator than in Sections 3.2 and 3.3. We measure here this process using the value of turnover rather than assets (for the already presented reasons). The outline of the analysis is identical as we assume that ETFs may be regarded as financial innovations (see Methodological appendix); instead of $i$ we use $Itat$ to denote turnover of ETFs in Italy and to distinguish it from $Ita$, i.e., estimates for Italy based on the values of assets.

Firstly, we analyze results for the 2004–17 time period (see Table 4.8). Results can be interpreted due to the lack of obvious misspecifications. The value of the $\kappa_{Itat}^{ETF}$ parameter (ceiling and growth limit of the diffusion process) was estimated at c. $9 billion and is similar to the actual average value in the final years of the examined time period. It may, therefore, be regarded as the level at which the Italian ETFs market has stabilized (increases to the monthly values of $10 billion and above were unsustainable). Further results support this conclusion as $Tm_{Itat}^{ETF}$ was estimated as 51 months (i.e., March 2008) and $\Delta t_{Itat}^{ETF}$ as merely 73 months (c. 6 years); both could imply that the diffusion of ETFs in Italy was in the last analyzed years in the final, third stage assumed in the diffusion framework. $R^2$ of the model is relatively high. Nonetheless, the period of 2010–11 distorts the results as it leads to (when analyzed graphically) significant deviation of the empirical path from the theoretical logistic growth curve. To conclude, results of the conducted analysis confirm that in the turnover's dimension, ETFs have evaded the Italian capital markets.

TABLE 4.8   Estimate of the Diffusion Model of Turnover of ETFs in Italy. 2004–17, Monthly Data

| | |
|---|---|
| $\kappa_{Itat}^{ETF}$ (ceiling/upper asymptote) | 8960.2 |
| $Tm_{Itat}^{ETF}(\beta_{Itat}^{ETF})$ (midpoint) | 51 (III 2008) |
| $\alpha_{Itat}^{ETF}$ (rate of diffusion) | 0.06 |
| $\Delta t_{Itat}^{ETF}$ (specific duration) | 73 |
| $R^2$ of the model | 0.80 |
| # of obs. | 164 |

*Authors' estimates.*

TABLE 4.9   Estimated Parameters of the ETFs Diffusion in Italy in Terms of Turnover for the Selected (predicted) Values of the Upper Limits

| Upper limit ($\kappa_{Itat,n}^{ETF}$)—*fixed* (value of assets of ETFs; mln USD) | $Tm_{Itat,n}^{ETF}(\beta_{Itat,n}^{ETF})$ (midpoint)—*predicted* | $\alpha_{Itat,n}^{ETF}$ (rate of diffusion)—*predicted* | $\Delta t_{Itat,n}^{ETF}$ (specific duration)—*predicted* | $R^2$ of the model |
|---|---|---|---|---|
| 8930 | Already achieved | | | |
| 11,163 | Already achieved | | | |
| 16,744 | 119 (XI 2013) | 0.016 | 280 | 0.68 |
| 29,302 | 203 (XI 2020) | 0.011 | 383 | 0.65 |
| 58,604 | 309 (IX 2029) | 0.01 | 451 | 0.63 |

*Authors' estimates.*

Results obtained for the diffusion in terms of the turnover may be compared to the ones returned for the analysis in terms of the ETFs' assets (see Table 3.7). Apart from the lower $R^2$ (0.71 vs 0.80), other estimates imply that the diffusion in the assets approach has taken place at a lower rate (shown by lower rate of diffusion and, consequently, higher specific duration). Moreover, higher estimated value of the midpoint parameter in case of assets (c. 4 years later, in March 2012) indicate that in that perspective diffusion has been relatively delayed in comparison to turnover.

Table 4.9 presents the estimates concerning the predicted future diffusion of ETFs in Italy. Imposed levels of $\kappa_{\text{Itat},n}^{\text{ETF}}$ were calculated using the methodology presented at the beginning of Section 3.3. No estimates were returned for the first two levels ($\kappa_{\text{Itat},1}^{\text{ETF}}$ and $\kappa_{\text{Itat},2}^{\text{ETF}}$) as these values of turnover were reached multiple times over 2004−17 and are regarded as already achieved within the diffusion framework (yet, as already discussed above, they were reached only temporarily). For the third level, $\kappa_{\text{Itat},3}^{\text{ETF}}$ (c. \$16.7 billion) estimations are feasible. Midpoint for this level is at c. 119 months—November 2013 which means that it could have already been reached. However, approaching the turnover close to the assumed upper limit is projected to take substantial amount of time as implied by $\Delta t_{\text{Itat},3}^{\text{ETF}}$ of more than 23 years, making this projection rather uncertain. It may, though, be interpreted as indicating that value of monthly turnover of ETFs exceeding \$15 billion are predicted to be reached in the second half of the 2020s. For the subsequent levels, $\kappa_{\text{Itat},4}^{\text{ETF}}$ and $\kappa_{\text{Itat},5}^{\text{ETF}}$, all parameters refer to a less or more distant future which makes them highly unreliable. Decreasing values of $\alpha_{\text{Itat},n}^{\text{ETF}}$ imply a slowing down in the diffusion's pace. $R^2$ of all three models are noticeably lower than in the case of the model presented in Table 4.8, implying that the diffusion framework is relatively less suitable in the case of the selected values of upper limits. This conclusion is supported by the observation made in the context of the shape of the development path for 2004−17 and results that refer strictly to that time period. They both show that, at least as of August 2017, the Italian ETFs market has gone through all three stages characteristic for the diffusion of innovation and the phase of the rapid expansion ended as the value of turnover reached (at least temporarily) saturation with regard to the local capital markets.

In Tables 4.10 and 4.11 we present seven ETPs listed on Borsa Italiana with the highest annual turnover in 2015 and 2016, respectively. It may be clearly noticed that both in 2015 and 2016 majority of the most actively traded products were the ones primary listed outside Italy, i.e., with Borsa Italiana as the place of their cross-listing. Another conclusion is the lack of direct relationship between the value of turnover and the value of the assets managed by the particular ETP. For example, in 2015 the most traded ETP was Lyxor UCITS ETF FTSE MIB Daily Leveraged (with geared (leveraged) exposure to the Italian stock market index) with annual turnover of c. \$7.2 billion, i.e. many times (c. 22) higher than its year-end assets. In 2016 it was the fourth most-traded instrument listed on ETFPlus. A similar example is yet another fund with geared (inverse-leveraged) exposure, Lyxor FTSE MIB Daily Double Short Xbear UCITS ETF, whose assets were relatively low yet turnover was among the highest; the same can be observed for ETCs. Overall, three groups of the most actively traded ETPs in Italy

**TABLE 4.10** ETFs, ETNs, and ETCs with the Highest Values of Turnover in Italy in 2015

| ETP | Type of ETP (ETF, ETN or ETC) | Country of primary listing | Value of the annual turnover (mln USD) | Share in the total turnover (%) | 2015 year-end value of the assets (mln USD) |
|---|---|---|---|---|---|
| Lyxor UCITS ETF FTSE MIB Daily Leveraged | ETF | Italy | 7244.86 | 7.6 | 329.87 |
| Lyxor UCITS ETF FTSE MIB | ETF | France | 5569.40 | 5.9 | 1259.33 |
| Lyxor FTSE MIB Daily Double Short Xbear UCITS ETF | ETF | Italy | 3717.48 | 3.9 | 99.02 |
| iShares EURO STOXX 50 UCITS ETF EUR (Dist) | ETF | UK | 3175.37 | 3.3 | 6872.82 |
| Boost Wti Oil 3X Leverage Daily ETC | ETC | UK | 2740.59 | 2.9 | 141.63 |
| Lyxor Euro Stoxx 50 (DR) UCITS ETF D-EUR | ETF | France | 1798.25 | 1.9 | 8171.10 |
| ETFS WTI Crude Oil ETC | ETC | UK | 1730.03 | 1.8 | 646.08 |

*Note*: Names and countries of primary listing as provided in the Lipper's database.
*Authors' elaboration.*

**TABLE 4.11**  ETFs, ETNs and ETCs With the Highest Values of Turnover in Italy in 2016

| ETP | Type of ETP (ETF, ETN or ETC) | Country of primary listing | Value of the annual turnover (mln USD) | Share in the total turnover (%) | 2016 year-end value of the assets (mln USD) |
|---|---|---|---|---|---|
| Boost Wti Oil 3X Leverage Daily ETC | ETC | UK | 4220.59 | 4.3 | 156.94 |
| Lyxor UCITS ETF FTSE MIB | ETF | France | 4008.52 | 4.1 | 861.99 |
| Lyxor FTSE MIB Daily Double Short Xbear UCITS ETF | ETF | Italy | 3350.55 | 3.4 | 145.85 |
| Lyxor UCITS ETF FTSE MIB Daily Leveraged | ETF | Italy | 3342.40 | 3.4 | 320.21 |
| Lyxor Euro Stoxx 50 (DR) UCITS ETF D-EUR | ETF | France | 2368.14 | 2.4 | 7414.49 |
| iShares EURO STOXX 50 UCITS ETF EUR (Dist) | ETF | UK | 2013.78 | 2.1 | 5747.06 |
| Boost Wti Oil 3X Short Daily ETC | ETC | UK | 1758.20 | 1.8 | 19.88 |

*Note*: Names and countries of primary listing as provided in the Lipper's database.
*Authors' elaboration.*

can be distinguished: ETFs with either simple or geared exposure to the Italian stock market [usually tracking the FTSE MIB index (Smith, 2012)], ETCs with exposure to the oil market (usually geared) and, in the third group, some of the Europe's largest ETFs that are cross-listed on many stock exchanges (for example, Lyxor Euro Stoxx 50 (DR) UCITS ETF D-EUR, was in 2017 listed on at least seven stock exchanges). Other types of ETFs than equity funds, such as bond or commodity ETFs, are outside this list. What is also worth noticing is the lack of the largest Italian primary listed fund, Lyxor FTSE Italia Mid Cap PIR (DR) UCITS ETF D-EUR, among the most traded which further confirms the lack of a straight relationship between the turnover and assets on the Italian ETPs market.

One of the characteristic attributes of the Italian ETFs market (or, more generally, Italian capital markets) is the relatively higher share of the retail investors than in other European countries (Sieber, 2015). Their role can be noticed, for instance, when the detailed statistics concerning the transactions in the shares of ETFs on various European stock exchanges are compared. The Italian ETFs market has been over most of the analyzed time period (since 2005) the European leader in terms of the number of trades, even though in terms of their total value its position has been lower (Borsa Italiana — London Stock Exchange Group, 2017); this means that the average value of the conducted transactions has been relatively low as typical in case of retail participants (Borsa Italiana, 2007). It may be noticed even more markedly with respect to the turnover of ETNs and ETCs. Using annual data for 2016 for the Italian market, value of transactions in the units of these financial products was about two-thirds lower than in case of shares of ETFs, but the number of trades was slightly higher—at the same time, their assets were at merely c. 10% of the respective value for ETFs according to the Borsa Italiana statistics (Borsa Italiana — London Stock Exchange Group, 2017).

Regardless of the comparatively stronger role of the individual users, the main participants of the Italian ETFs market who have driven its development in the analyzed time period are institutional investors (Deloitte Audit, 2017). The main reasons for this may be considered from two perspectives: (1) the relative lack of demand from the individual users; or (2) the increasing demand from the institutional users. In the first, underdevelopment of the retail segment have resulted from the narrow offer of ETFs in the traditional channels of distribution because of their lower profitability which means that they are used mostly by sophisticated investors familiar with the online platforms (Deloitte Audit, 2017). In the second perspective, institutional investors use ETFs for a number of applications, ranging from inexpensive asset allocation solutions, through short-term tactic exposures and risk management, to liquidity management (Deloitte Audit, 2017; Villegas, 2017).

In order to supplement our overview of the Italian ETFs market, we extend briefly the presentation of the other ETPs listed in Italy. Firstly, ETNs and ETCs were launched in Italy after the start of the ETFplus segment and within a few years they became a noticeable (but not dominant) segment of the Italian ETPs market (i.e., combined market for ETFs, ETNs, and ETCs). Their role differs slightly depending on whether assets or turnover indicators are taken into account. In terms of assets, the combined share of ETNs and ETCs has increased gradually, reaching c. 28.8% of the assets of all ETPs as of end of August 2017; in 2016 their average share was even higher at c. 32.2% (in 2015 at c. 24.2%). Most of these assets are managed by ETNs rather than ETCs.[6] Three largest ETNs primary-listed in Italy as of end of August 2017 were BOOST BUND 10Y 3X SHORT DAILY ETN (c. $86 million of assets), Boost FTSE MIB 3x Short Daily ETN (c. $66 million) and ETFs 3X Short USD Long EUR ETN (c. $50 million); notes with bond, equity and currency exposure, respectively. In the ETCs segment, three largest products were ETFS EUR Daily Hedged Industrial Metals (c. $73 million), ETFS EUR Daily Hedged WTI Crude Oil ETC (c. $49 million) and ETFS EUR Daily Hedged Wheat ETC (c. $25 million). To some extent the strong position of ETNs and ETCs in this aspect may be explained by the low number of ETFs that are primary listed in Italy; if data on all ETFs listed on Borsa Italiana are considered (including cross-listed funds), the share of ETNs and ETCs declines to c. 10% (August 2017).

When turnover of ETNs and ETCs is considered, in the final examined month their share in the total turnover on ETFplus was at c. 19%. Using the aggregate turnover for 2016 it was at c. 25% and in 2015 at c. 21%. It may be, thus, concluded that the position of ETPs other than ETFs on the Italian stock exchange has been, in this perspective, relatively weaker despite the few very intensively traded ETCs (see Tables 4.10 and 4.11).

# References

Abukari, K., & Otchere, I. K. (2016). Merging corporatized financial markets. *Journal of Financial Studies, 24*(3), 1−44.
Amenc, N., Ducoulombier, F., Goltz, F., & Le Sourd, V. (2015). *The EDHEC European ETF survey 2014*. Nice: EDHEC-Risk Institute.
Amenc, N., Goltz, F., & Grigoriu, A. (2010). Risk control through dynamic core-satellite portfolios of ETFs: Applications to absolute return funds and tactical asset allocation. *Journal of Alternative Investments, 13*(2), 47−57.
Amenc, N., Goltz, F., & Le Sourd, V. (2017). *The EDHEC European ETF and smart beta survey*. EDHEC-Risk Institute.
Andreu, E., & Padilla, J. (2018). *Quantifying horizontal merger efficiencies in multi-sided markets: An application to stock exchange mergers. Rethinking Antitrust Tools for Multi-Sided Platforms* (pp. 151−188). OECD.
Arnold, M., & Lesné, A. (2015). *The changing landscape for beta replication − Comparing futures and ETFs for equity index exposure*. State Street Global Advisors.
Bianchi, M. L., Loddo, M., & Miele, M. G. (2011). The exchange traded funds in Italy. *Bancaria Editrice, 1*, 90−102.
Borowski, G. (2011). *Rynek funduszy inwestycyjnych w Unii Europejskiej* [Investment funds market in the European Union]. CeDeWu (in Polish).
Borsa Italiana − London Stock Exchange Group. (2009). *ETF—Exchange traded funds: Simple products, sophisticated strategies.*
Borsa Italiana − London Stock Exchange Group. (2017). *ETFplus MonitorQ4 2016 October−December.*
Borsa Italiana. (2007). *Borsa Italiana achieves the goal of 100 ETFs listed − Press Release.*
Borsa Italiana. (2009). *ETC − Exchange traded commodities: A new way of investing in commodities.*
Borsa Italiana. (2013). *ETFplus: The ETF and ETC/ETN market: Transparency and liquidity.*
Borsa Italiana. (2018). *What is an ETN?*
Borsa Italiana, & London Stock Exchange. (2007a). *Borsa Italiana − London Stock Exchange media presentation.*
Borsa Italiana, & London Stock Exchange. (2007b). *Borsa Italiana and London Stock Exchange combine. Shares in enlarged group begin trading.* <https://www.lseg.com/sites/default/files/content/documents/borsa-italiana-merger-circular-merger-completed-1oct2007.pdf> Accessed 08.08.18.
Cantillon, E., & Yin, P.-L. (2011). Competition between exchanges: A research agenda. *International Journal of Industrial Organization, 29*(3), 329−336.
Charles, A., Darné, O., Kim, J. H., & Redor, E. (2016). Stock exchange mergers and market efficiency. *Applied Economics, 48*(7), 576−589.
CME Group. (2016). *The big picture: A cost comparison of futures and ETFs.*
Deloitte Audit. (2017). *Asset management in Italy: a snapshot in an evolutive context.*
Deville, L. (2008). Exchange traded funds: History, trading and research. In M. Doumpos, P. Pardalos, & C. Zopounidis (Eds.), *Handbook of financial engineering* (pp. 67−98). Springer.
Dorodnykh, E. (2014). *Stock market integration: An international perspective*. Palgrave Macmillan.
Elia, M. (2010). Premiums and arbitrage of Asian Exchange Traded Funds. *Bancaria Editrice, 12*, 23−42.
Ferreira, M. A., Keswani, A., Miguel, A. F., & Ramos, S. B. (2013). The determinants of mutual fund performance: A cross-country study. *Review of Finance, 17*(2), 483−525.
Floreani, J., & Polato, M. (2010). Measuring value in Stock Exchanges' merger. In R. Bottiglia, E. Gualandri, & G. N. Mazzocco (Eds.), *Consolidation in the European Financial Industry* (pp. 182−206). Palgrave Macmillan.
Gastineau, G. L. (2010). *The exchange-traded funds manual.* (2nd ed.). John Wiley & Sons.
ICI. (2001). Redemption activity of mutual fund owners. *Fundamentals − Investment Company Institute Research in Brief, 10*(1), 1−8.
ING. (2017). *Mobile banking − The next generation. How should ways to bank and pay evolve in future?*
Jordan, C. (2016). *The London Stock Exchange − Prey and predator.* <https://ssrn.com/abstract=2814208 or https://doi.org/10.2139/ssrn.2814208> Accessed 22.08.18.

[6]However, the only difference in the classification used on Borsa Italiana for distinguishing between ETNs and ETCs is their exposure: ETCs track returns on various commodities whereas ETNs all other assets (Borsa Italiana, 2018). Both are defined as "financial instruments issued against a direct investment by the issuer in the underlying…or underlying derivative contracts" (Borsa Italiana, 2018). For an explicit definition of ETCs see Borsa Italiana, 2009, p. 3.

Khan, W., & Vieito, J. P. (2012). Stock exchange mergers and weak form of market efficiency: The case of Euronext Lisbon. *International Review of Economics & Finance, 22*(1), 173–189.

Khorana, A., Servaes, H., & Tufano, P. (2005). Explaining the size of the mutual fund industry around the world. *Journal of Financial Economics, 78*(1), 145–185.

Klapper, L., Sulla, V., & Vittas, D. (2004). The development of mutual funds around the world. *Emerging Markets Review, 5*(1), 1–38.

Kokkoris, I. (2013). A new episode in the stock exchange mergers saga: Intercontinental Exchange (ICE)/New York Stock Exchange (NYSE). *Competition Policy International*. Available from https://www.competitionpolicyinternational.com/a-new-episode-in-the-stock-exchange-mergers-saga-intercontinental-exchange-ice-new-york-stock-exchange-nyse/.

Kokkoris, I., & Olivares-Caminal, R. (2008). Lessons from the recent stock exchange merger activity. *Journal of Competition Law & Economics, 4*(3), 837–869.

Lee, J. (2017). Synergies, risks and the regulation of stock exchange interconnection. *Masaryk University Journal of Law and Technology, 11*(2), 291–321.

Lee, K., & Lim, C. (2001). Technological regimes, catching-up and leapfrogging: Findings from the Korean industries. *Research Policy, 30*(3), 459–483.

Lees, F. A. (2012). *Financial exchanges: A comparative approach.* New York: Routledge.

London Stock Exchange Group. (2017). *A guide for market makers on ETFplus.*

Madhavan, A. N., Marchioni, U., Li, W., & Du, D. Y. (2014). Equity ETFs versus IndexFutures: A comparison for fully funded investors. *The Journal of Index Investing, 5*(2), 66–75.

Marszk, A., & Lechman, E. (2018). New technologies and diffusion of innovative financial products: Evidence on exchange-traded funds in selected emerging and developed economies*Journal of Macroeconomics*, in press. Available from https://doi.org/10.1016/j.jmacro.2018.10.001.

Morningstar. (2017). *A guided tour of the European ETF marketplace.*

Nielsson, U. (2009). Stock exchange merger and liquidity: The case of Euronext. *Journal of Financial Markets, 12*(2), 229–267.

Perez, K. (2012). *Fundusze inwestycyjne. Rodzaje, zasady funkcjonowania, efektywność.* [Investment funds. Categories, rules of operations, effectiveness]. Wolters Kluwer Business Publishing House (in Polish).

Polato, M., & Floreani, J. (2010). Value and governance in the exchange industry: The case of diversified conglomerate exchanges. In F. Fiordelisi, & P. Molyneux (Eds.), *New issues in financial institutions management* (pp. 274–290). Palgrave Macmillan.

Sahay, R., Cihak, M., N'Diaye, P., Barajas, A., Bi, R., Ayala, D., et al. (2015). Rethinking financial deepening: Stability and growth in emerging markets. IMF staff discussion note (p. 15). https://www.ft.com/content/492f84aa-5e26-11e1-8c87-00144feabdc0.

Sanderson, R., Masters, B., & Grant, J. (2012). LSE draws fire over Borsa synergies. *Financial Times.*

Schilling, M. A. (2003). Technological leapfrogging: Lessons from the US video game console industry. *California Management Review, 45*(3), 6–32.

Sieber, T. (2015). ETFs – A global perspective. A review of why ETFs are becoming an increasingly important part of investor portfolios – including US, Germany and Italy. *The stock market show conference.* 12 September 2015, London.

Smith, S. (2012). Italian equity ETFs are the "best-looking in the European ugly parade". *ETF Strategy,* June 11, 2012.

Soete, L. (1985). International diffusion of technology, industrial development and technological leapfrogging. *World Development, 13*(3), 409–422.

Stańczak-Strumiłło, K. (2013). *Uwarunkowania rozwoju funduszy inwestycyjnych w Polsce.* [Determinants of the investment funds development in Poland]. Difin (in Polish).

Svirydzenka, K. (2016). Introducing a new broad-based index of financial development. *IMF working paper, 16/5.*

Tearn, T. *BlackRock looks to Europe robo-advising market with minority stake in scalable capital.* (2017). <https://www.forbes.com/sites/greatspeculations/2017/06/22/blackrock-looks-to-europe-robo-advising-market-with-minority-stake-in-scalable-capital/#16c6859a70a6> Accessed 14.06.18.

Teplova, T. V., & Rodina, V. A. (2016). Does stock exchange consolidation improve market liquidity? A study of stock exchange acquisition in Russia. *Research in International Business and Finance, 37,* 375–390.

Valdes, R., Cramon-Taubadel, S., & Engler, A. (2016). What drives stock market integration? An analysis using agribusiness stocks. *Agricultural Economics, 47,* 571–580.

Villegas, A. (2017). Italian investors salute ETFs. *Investment Europe.*

Vlastelica, R. (2016). Investors are piling into Italy ETFs ahead of referendum. *Market Watch.*

Willey, D. (2007). *London Stock Exchange buys Borsa.* <http://news.bbc.co.uk/2/hi/business/6233196.stm> Accessed 28.07.18.

Yang, A. S., & Pangastuti, A. (2016). Stock market efficiency and liquidity: The Indonesia Stock Exchange merger. *Research in International Business and Finance, 36,* 28–40.

Yepes-Rios, B., Gonzalez-Tapia, K., & Gonzalez-Perez, M. A. (2015). The integration of stock exchanges: The case of the Latin American Integrated Market (MILA) and its impact on ownership and internationalization status in Colombian brokerage firms. *Journal of Economics, Finance and Administrative Science, 20*(39), 84–93.

Zanotti, G., & Russo, C. (2005). *Exchange traded funds versus traditional mutual funds: A comparative analysis on the Italian market.* <https://papers.ssrn.com/sol3/papers.cfm?abstract_id = 2819646> Accessed 03.08.18.

# 5

# Exchange-Traded Funds and Financial Systems of European Countries: A Growth Factor or Threat to Stability?

This chapter traces the links between the diffusion of the European exchange-traded funds (ETFs) and the development of financial systems. It is, therefore, in some way a continuation of the discussion from Chapter 4, Determinants of the European Exchange-Traded Funds Markets Development, in which we analyzed the potential impact of the financial development (FD) at large and its specific elements on the development of the European ETFs markets. However, in this chapter we examine the reverse relationship, that is, the possible influence of ETFs on the various aspects of financial systems development.

The core body of this chapter is divided into three sections. Section 5.1 is devoted to a general analysis as we analyze the FD understood most comprehensively while trying to identify the role of ETFs. In Section 5.2 we examine the mutual relationships between the selected parts of the financial system: ETFs, other investment funds traded through exchanges, as well as stock and bond markets. In Section 5.3 we deal with the issue of the possible impact of the spread of innovative funds on the stability of the financial systems in the European countries by trying to identify whether diffusion of ETFs could be a destabilizing factor.

Due to the rather short history of the European ETFs markets in the majority of the studied countries (in particular in comparison to the other parts of the financial systems such as equity markets), in our analysis we focus on the relationships that may be observed taking into account the entire group of the examined countries by checking whether ETFs markets, that are in most cases negligible in comparison to the size of the local economies or financial systems, influenced significantly broadly understood FD or some of its aspects. Country-level examination would be very difficult or impossible to perform due to the low number of annual observations (see Section 5.1) or could result in unnecessary complexity of the analysis (see Section 5.2). The exception is several parts of Section 5.3 in which we demonstrate country-level evidence.

In contrast with the previous studies that addressed the impact of ETFs on the financial system (in particular on financial markets; see Section 2.4), in this chapter we do not analyze issues such as the influence of ETFs on

Exchange-Traded Funds in Europe.
DOI: https://doi.org/10.1016/B978-0-12-813639-3.00005-5

the liquidity or other attributes of the individual stocks. Rather, we adopt a broader approach as we are interested in the examination of the links with the entire financial system (in Section 5.1) or its specific parts (in Section 5.2), analogously to the analysis in Chapter 4, Determinants of the European Exchange-Traded Funds Markets Development. Analysis on the level of individual funds and associated assets would substantially extend our study. Moreover, the literature on this topic, as already noted in the theoretical overview, has been burgeoning in recent years whereas almost no studies have focused on the higher-level effects.

# 5.1 EXCHANGE-TRADED FUNDS AND THE DEVELOPMENT OF FINANCIAL SYSTEMS IN EUROPE

In the first part of this section we focus on the changes in the FD's levels in the 12 examined European countries between 2004 and 2015. Next, in the second part of this section we examine potential determinants of these processes by focusing on the role of ETFs and including comparisons to the other factors. With these aims we use nonparametric analysis and panel regression models. It should be stressed that we do not attempt to repeat the analysis of the factors that contribute to or, conversely, hinder the process of FD which may be traced in a vast number of such studies (among some of the most recent see, for instance, Abubakar & Kassim, 2018; Allen et al., 2014; Ashraf, 2018; Asongu & De Moor, 2017; Asongu, 2014; Ayadi, Arbak, Naceur, & De Groen, 2015; Bhattacharyya & Hodler, 2014; Elkhuizen, Hermes, Jacobs, & Meesters, 2018; Hamdi, 2015; Hasan & Murshed, 2017; Horvath, Horvatova, & Siranova, 2017; Lee, Jung, & Lee, 2018; Raza, Shahzadi, & Akram, 2014; Sahay et al., 2015; Tang & Tan, 2014). Determinants of FD that were found to be significant in previous studies include: rule of law (more generally, the strength of legal institutions), level of economic development, trade openness, foreign direct investments, financial globalization, inflation rate, exchange rate, energy consumption, financial reforms, regulatory environment of the financial sector, and innovations in financial services, among others.

## 5.1.1 Introductory Remarks

The aim of our analysis is to identify existing links between the diffusion of ETFs and FD (i.e., the other side of the relationship examined in Chapter 4: Determinants of the European Exchange-Traded Funds Markets Development). The development of ETFs markets (i.e., diffusion of ETFs) may, however, be regarded as one of the components of the process of FD; see, for example, the definitions given by Čihák, Demirgüç-Kunt, Feyen, and Levine (2012). The same applies to the other financial variables considered in our analysis of the FD (such as turnover of stock index derivatives). Moreover, even though ETFs are not accounted for in the International Monetary Fund (IMF) FD index, it includes a similar variable for the mutual funds, that is, their assets in relation to GDP (inclusion of ETFs would not be feasible due to the globally relatively low number of countries with ETFs markets). This means that in our study we examine how certain elements of FD affect the overall process; analyzed potential financial determinants were chosen carefully in order to exclude the variables that are used to construct the index. Therefore, to be more precise, we investigate the impact of the diffusion of ETFs (and some additional parts of the financial sector) on the development of its other key aspects such as banking sector, equity markets etc., that is, the ones that are covered by the IMF index. Additional nonfinancial variables are included exclusively to account for the spread of new technologies (one of the themes discussed throughout the book) and the general condition of economy. Factors identified in the other studies are not included in order not to change the main angle of the analysis; additionally, some of them had to be excluded for reasons linked with the estimation methods (such as the high correlation with the remaining variables). Despite these stipulations, the results of our estimations are rather robust as proven by, for example, the $R^2$ of the panel models (see Table 5.1).

Some technical remarks are necessary prior to further discussion. The study of the FD for which the results are presented in this section was conducted using the FD index retrieved from the IMF Financial Development Index Database. Consequently, in order to gain a more comprehensive insight into the presented results, it is first necessary to outline the basic methodology of its construction and calculation—for a detailed discussion see Sahay et al. (2015) and Svirydzenka (2016); methodology of the index is based on the benchmarking concepts of Čihák et al. (2012), Čihák, Demirgüç-Kunt, Feyen, & Levine (2013).

FD covers both financial institutions and financial markets and it is constructed from two sub-indexes: the financial institutions index and financial markets index. They correspond to the financial institutions (FI) and financial markets (FM) variables that were analyzed in previous chapters. The former sub-index includes the

**TABLE 5.1** Financial Development (FD) versus Selected Determinants. Random Effects Models. 2004—15, Annual Data

| FD | RE(1) | RE(2) | RE(3) | RE(4) | RE(5) | RE(6) | RE(7) | RE(8) | RE(9) | RE(10) |
|---|---|---|---|---|---|---|---|---|---|---|
| FBS | 0.021 | | | | | | | | | **0.04** |
| | [0.01] | | | | | | | | | **[0.00]** |
| IU | | **−0.37** | | | | | | | | |
| | | **[0.07]** | | | | | | | | |
| ETF | 0.014 | **0.07** | | **0.02** | **0.02** | **0.02** | **0.04** | **0.02** | **0.02** | |
| | [0.02] | **[0.01]** | | **[0.00]** | **[0.00]** | **[0.00]** | **[0.01]** | **[0.00]** | **[0.00]** | |
| SOT | **0.03** | | | | | | | | | |
| | **[0.00]** | | | | | | | | | |
| SFT | | **0.02** | | | | | | | | **0.06** |
| | | **[0.00]** | | | | | | | | **[0.00]** |
| IFT | **0.02** | −0.02 | | | | | | | | |
| | **[0.00]** | [0.01] | | | | | | | | |
| GDP | | | **−0.01** | −0.003 | | −0.005 | | | −0.004 | 0.00 |
| | | | **[0.00]** | [0.00] | | [0.00] | | | [0.00] | [0.00] |
| LQT | | | | | 0.003 | | −0.001 | | | |
| | | | | | [0.00] | | [0.01] | | | |
| LQL | | | **−0.01** | −0.007 | | −0.008 | | | | |
| | | | **[0.00]** | [0.10] | | [0.01] | | | | |
| TCS | | | | | −0.03 | | −0.04 | | | |
| | | | | | [0.03] | | [0.05] | | | |
| CSICT | | | 0.01 | **0.08** | **0.09** | | **0.2** | | | |
| | | | [0.02] | **[0.03]** | **[0.04]** | | **[0.06]** | | | |
| CSNonICT | | | | | | | | **0.03** | **0.04** | |
| | | | | | | | | **[0.01]** | **[0.02]** | |
| TFP | | | | | | | 0.01 | | | |
| | | | | | | | [0.01] | | | |
| EMPL | | | **0.72** | 0.31 | **0.44** | **0.49** | | | | −0.03 |
| | | | **[0.17]** | [0.19] | **[0.21]** | **[0.18]** | | | | [0.11] |
| Breuch−Pagan test (prob > chi$^2$) | 109.9 | 41.6 | 255.9 | 37.04 | 29.49 | 37.04 | 7.04 | 218.3 | 99.9 | 232.9 |
| | [0.00] | [0.00] | [0.00] | [0.00] | [0.00] | [0.00] | [0.00] | [0.00] | [0.00] | [0.00] |
| $R^2$ (overall) | 0.57 | 0.75 | 0.38 | 0.63 | 0.64 | 0.61 | 0.79 | 0.42 | 0.42 | 0.36 |
| Rho | 0.97 | 0.01 | 0.89 | 0.77 | 0.85 | 0.75 | 0.88 | 0.85 | 0.85 | 0.94 |
| Mean VIF | 4.59 | 4.44 | 1.13 | 1.44 | 1.71 | 1.22 | 1.78 | 1.29 | 1.46 | 1.21 |
| # of observations | 47 | 55 | 108 | 90 | 82 | 90 | 40 | 116 | 95 | 76 |

*Note*: All values are logged; SE below coefficients; results account for random-effects GLS regressions; extreme observations excluded; panel—balanced; constant included—not reported; in bold—results statistically significant at 5% level of significance. For an explanation of the variables see Table 4.1 in Section 4.1. *Authors' estimates*.

following categories of institutions: banks, pension funds, mutual funds, and insurance companies. The latter accommodates equity and bond markets. What is important is that the two sub-indexes (FI and FM) can be decomposed even further, and in each case their three dimensions are considered: depth, access, and efficiency. It means that there are de facto six sub-indexes of the lower level that can be denoted as financial institutions depth (FID), financial institutions access (FIA), financial institutions efficiency (FIE), financial markets depth (FMD), financial markets access (FMA), and financial markets efficiency (FME). Below we list the exact indicators that are aggregated within each sub-index (Sahay et al., 2015, p. 34):[1]

- FID: Private-sector credit (% of GDP), pension funds' assets (% of GDP), mutual funds' assets (% of GDP), life and nonlife insurance premiums (% of GDP).
- FIA: Branches of commercial banks per 100 thousand adults, ATMs per 100 thousand adults.
- FIE: (all indicators apply exclusively to banks) Net interest margin, lending-deposits spread, noninterest income to total income, overhead costs to total assets, return on assets, return on equity.
- FMD: Stock market capitalization (% of GDP), stock turnover (% of GDP), international debt securities of governments (% of GDP), total debt securities of nonfinancial corporations (% of GDP), and total debt securities of financial corporations (% of GDP).
- FMA: Percent of market capitalization outside the top 10 largest companies, total number of issuers of debt (domestic and external, nonfinancial corporations, and financial corporations).
- FME: Stock market turnover ratio (stock turnover/capitalization).

These variables are aggregated into the upper level sub-indexes using the principal component analysis; as Svirydzenka (2016, p. 19) explains by using this method individual indicators which are collinear are grouped into a composite indicator that "captures as much as possible of the information common to individual indicators" while the aim of the procedure is to "account for the highest possible variation in the indicator set using the smallest possible number of factors." The same method is applied to develop the higher level sub-indexes from the lower level ones (ending at FD). In each case, the higher value of the given index denotes a higher level of the certain aspect of FD. Finally, it should be added that, in the preceding analysis of the factors influencing the diffusion of ETFs in Europe, FI was the only index of these discussed that resulted to be statistically significant (albeit with mixed results); however, for FD and FM no significance was identified, thus, proving that the development of the financial sector in these broad dimensions seems not to influence substantially the spread of innovative funds. A more detailed investigation showed, however, that some of their elements such as mutual funds (measured in terms of assets using the MFA variable) were linked to the diffusion of ETFs.

Before we proceed to discuss the results of our analysis performed with the application of the index, it must be stressed that it is not the only approach to quantify the level of FD. On the contrary, their number is very high and both theoretical and empirical literature regarding this topic is vast. FD was measured conventionally with single indicators by using, inter alia: credit to private sector in relation to the GDP—the most common measure utilized in numerous publications (see, e.g., Arcand, Berkes, & Panizza, 2015; Cavallo & Scartascini, 2012; Raza et al., 2014); or M2 money supply in relation to GDP (Hasan & Murshed, 2017). A number of different approaches that take into account various (more than one) indicators were suggested over the past several years (for a more detailed discussion see, *inter alia*, Čihák et al., 2012; Eryigit & Dulgeroglu, 2015; Huang, 2010).

A further complication refers to the terminology. The term "FD" is not the only one used to denote the process that very generally (without referring to too constrictive terms) may most basically be explained, according to Čihák et al. (2012, p. 4), as taking place when "financial instruments, markets, and intermediaries mitigate...the effects of imperfect information, limited enforcement, and transaction costs"; in the broader perspective (adopted in the cited authors' approach to the measurement of FD), it is an improvement in the quality of the key financial functions, provided by financial institutions and markets. The other (used as synonyms or in a closely related context) designations of this process that can be found in the academic publications are: financial depth (Demetriades & Rousseau, 2016; Panizza, 2018), or similarly, financial deepening (Rousseau & Wachtel, 2011, 2017); financial growth is used much less frequently (Grjebine & Tripier, 2016); another similar term is financial inclusion which is used in, for example, the database provided by the World Bank (Demirgüç-Kunt, Klapper, Singer, & Van Oudheusden, 2014).

---

[1]All values of indicators that are included in the calculations are normalized by applying the usual min—max procedure so that they range between 0 and 1 (the same applies to the obtained indexes). Other technical details such as the treatment of missing data, exclusion of extreme values, etc., are presented in Svirydzenka (2016).

In order to make our analysis as concise as possible we do not extend the discussion of various approaches to the conceptualization and measurement of FD as they lie outside the scope of this book. We decided to use the indicator presented in the IMF publications and available in the FD Index Database [it follows the ideas introduced by Čihák et al. (2012)] for two key reasons. Firstly, it is in our opinion the broadest available measure of the FD that encompasses various aspects of this process, not only in terms of the coverage of the financial sector's segments (e.g., not limited to the banking sector or stock market as in the other approaches), but also with regard to their dimensions (e.g., not only their size but also other attributes). The second reason is the broad coverage of the IMF Financial Development Index Database with regard to both the length of the time period and country sample; potentially the widest among all similar databases. It should also be added that due to its construction, FD takes into account the other indicators of the FD listed above such as credit to private-sector or capitalization of the stock markets. As far as the drawbacks of FD are concerned, there are two key stipulations that limit its applicability in our study. The first concerns one of its key advantages, that is, comprehensibility, as it takes into account various aspects and selection of the potential determinants must be very made very carefully in order to avoid obvious mistakes (we discuss this issue in more detail later on). The second constraint is more technical: exclusively time series with annual observations can be acquired, therefore, in this section analogously to Chapter 4, Determinants of the European Exchange-Traded Funds Markets Development, the analysis is conducted with the annual frequency and covers the 2004−15 time period.

## 5.1.2 Financial Development in European Countries

Fig. 5.1 shows how the values of FD have changed in the 12 countries in our sample. As it may be clearly noticed, in most cases the values of FD correspond closely to the levels of economic development—in the advanced economies they tend to be higher than in the emerging ones. The lowest values of FD were calculated for Greece, Hungary, Poland, and Turkey. With the exception of Greece, in the three other economies the average and median values of FD have been at about 0.5, that is, below the value provided by Sahay et al. (2015) as the mean and median calculated for the group of the advanced economies (yet much higher for the category of emerging markets). In Greece and Hungary, the level of FD declined after the 2008 global financial crisis whereas

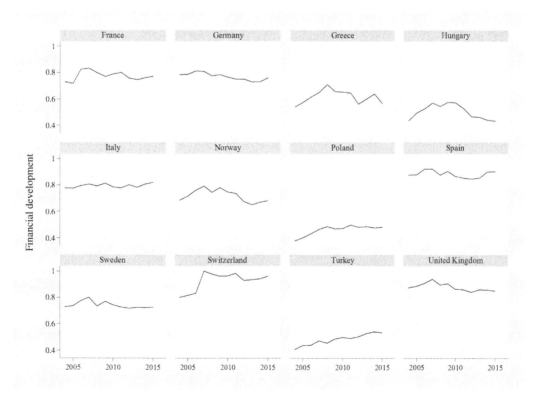

**FIGURE 5.1**    FD index time lines. 2004−15, annual data. *FD*, Financial development. *Source: Authors' elaboration.*

in both Poland and Turkey it has been increasing, thus, showing resilience to the turmoil in the global financial system. These results (in particular the ones observed for Greece) should not be surprising taking into account their economic and financial situation after 2008.

The hypothesized existence of a positive link between financial and economic development becomes less evident if the values of FD for Norway are considered; despite the very high levels of GDP per capita in this country, its FD measured using the IMF indicators has been close to that of the Greek economy and since the global financial crisis it has gradually been declining. Closer examination of the FD's components in the case of the Norwegian financial system unveils that its biggest weaknesses have been the issues of the financial institutions' depth and access (i.e., FID and FIA), in particular the latter aspect (measured using the relative number of bank branches and ATMs) has contributed to the relatively weak and still worsening results of the FD's evaluation in the case of Norway.

For all the remaining economies it can be stated that their financial systems have been highly developed and changes that have taken place between 2004 and 2015 have been rather insignificant. Probably the most striking exception is the country for which the highest level of FD was identified, that is, Switzerland. Its value of FD has grown over 2006—07 from c. 0.83 to 1 (indicating the position of the global leader); the underlying reason was a sharp increase in the sub-indexes of FM, inflicted by a strong increase of the stock turnover (as % of GDP) and, consequently, also the growth of the stock market turnover ratio, both which were upheld in the subsequent years. In the remaining countries no such dramatic changes can be noticed, even in the aftermath of the financial turmoil of 2008 or the eurozone debt crisis.

Taking into consideration the discussed differences in the values of FD it may be preliminarily stated, even without more advanced quantitative analysis, that they do not only match the levels of economic development of the countries in our sample, but also the diffusion of ETFs. For instance, all four countries that we denoted as the group of most advanced ETFs markets (France, Germany, Switzerland, and the United Kingdom) have also been among the regional leaders in terms of the FD. However, the results of the analysis of the ETFs diffusion determinants indicated no role of the FD variable, showing that the general level of FD has been neither a stimulant nor barrier to the spread of the innovative funds. The links between ETFs and FD (the other side of this relationship) are further verified with the regression analysis.

### 5.1.3 Exchange-Traded Funds and Financial Development

After the preliminary examination of the FD in the countries in our sample, we discuss the results of nonparametric analysis and panel regressions analysis. Prior to the presentation of the obtained results, it must be emphasized again that we do not evaluate all the variables analyzed in Chapter 4, Determinants of the European Exchange-Traded Funds Markets Development (or other possible determinants of the FD suggested in the literature). Most generally, we are interested in the examination of the linkages between various aspects of broadly understood FD (in particular the role of ETFs); other (partially related) crucial reason is that potential explanatory variables of FD needed to be selected carefully due to the methodology of the index calculation, in order to avoid the evident mistake of using the components of FD as its factors. Following the approach adopted in our research, we include some additional variables. As a result, we consider: ETF, SOT, SFT, IFT (four financial variables), FBS, IU (two ICT variables), GDP, LQT, LQL, TCS, CSICT, CSNonICT, TFP, and EMPL (eight general macroeconomic variables).

Firstly, we present the results of the nonparametric analysis of the single explanatory determinant of FD, conducted for the four financial variables. As in Section 4.3 we formulate the basic conclusions by referring to the graphical evidence (see Fig. 5.2). Taking into account the entire datasets for each variable, among the four examined potential factors of the general FD, a positive relationship may be noticed in two cases: assets of ETFs (the ETF variable) and turnover of other investment funds (IFT); for the remaining two (SOT and SFT) the direction of impact or its strength is impossible to determine. Analysis of the relationships for various levels of the explanatory variables shows that they are highly heterogeneous and differ substantially.

What is striking in the case of ETF, SOT, and SFT is the clustering of observations. This is caused by the prevalence of relatively low or very low values of the explanatory variables, regardless of the value of the FD. For instance, turnover of stock index options was very low in most of the countries in our sample (it should be emphasized that only on-exchange transactions are considered due to lack of sufficient data on the OTC turnover). Due to this low variability of the independent variables, it is difficult to identify their relationship with the dependent variable in case of values of ETF, SOT, or SFT that are close to 0 (% of GDP). It may be, however,

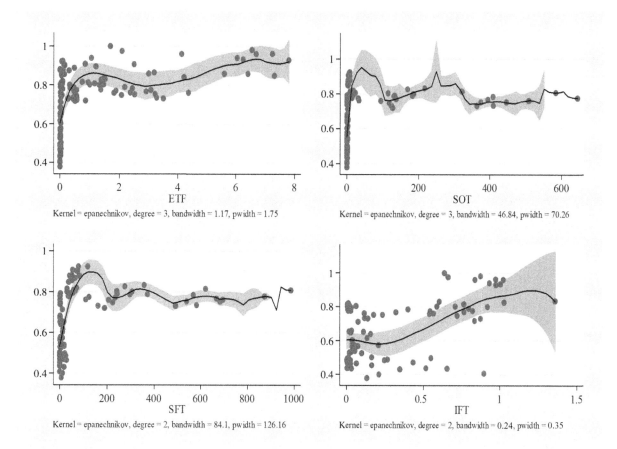

**FIGURE 5.2** FD index versus selected financial determinants. 2004–16, annual data.
*Note*: On the *Y*-axis—FD; raw data used; Kernel-weighed local polynomial smoothing applied; Kernel = epanechnikov; plot confidence bands applied for 95% confidence level. For an explanation of the variables see Table 4.1 in Section 4.1. *FD*, Financial development. *Source: Authors' elaboration.*

noticed that initially their higher levels are accompanied by rapidly growing levels of FD which could imply a positive relationship. Nonetheless, in all three cases after reaching a certain peak level the relationships become negative, yet for the highest values of explanatory variables no impact can be observed (in case of SOT and SFT) or it is slightly positive (for ETFs). It could be interpreted as the evidence for the evolving role of the turnover of stock index derivatives which, up to some point, influence positively the country's FD yet after reaching a maximum level their role may become detrimental or unimportant in this context. In the case of ETFs it appears that most of the positive contribution of the innovative funds to the process of FD occurs with their initial expansion and afterwards other factors appear to overshadow the impact of ETFs. A more detailed analysis of the potential channels through which ETFs may influence FD is presented in Section 5.2.

Formulating conclusions for the fourth variable (IFT) is less problematic as its impact seems evidently positive. It may, thus, be stated that, at least based on the single explanatory variable model, increasing turnover of the investment funds (other than ETPs) contributes positively to the FD; due to their low value in most analyzed countries and lack of such funds in many other, their role should not be overemphasized.

We now discuss the models approximating the impact of single nonfinancial determinants on the FD (two ICT and eight macroeconomic variables, with one exception all in the latter category are economic growth variables; indicators such as interest rates or gross savings rates that were considered in Chapter 4, Determinants of the European Exchange-Traded Funds Markets Development, could not be used due to the methodology of the FD index). Graphical evidence is shown in Fig. 5.3.

Starting with the two indicators of the ICT adoption, the relationship between the spread of the new technologies and FD appears to be unequivocally positive, except for the highest values of IU for which it becomes

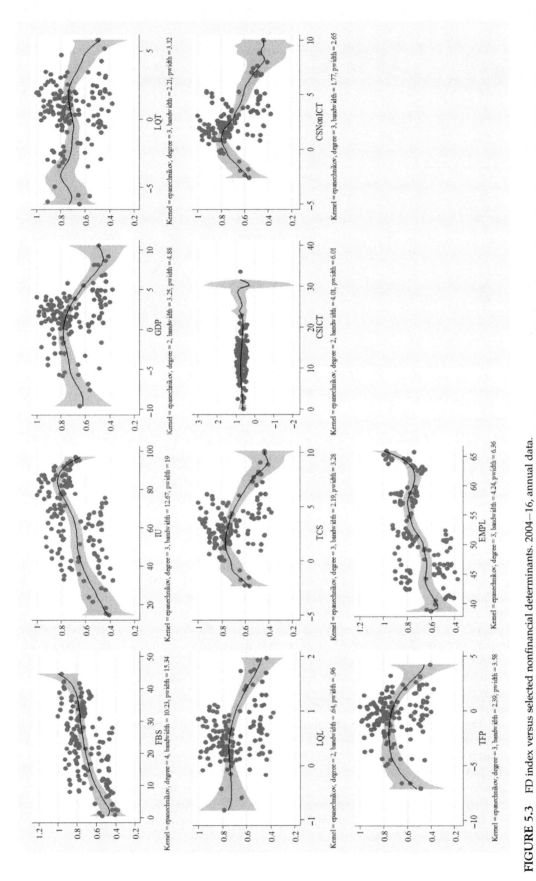

**FIGURE 5.3** FD index versus selected nonfinancial determinants. 2004–16, annual data.

*Note:* On the *Y*-axis—FD; raw values used; Kernel-weighed local polynomial smoothing applied; Kernel = epanechnikov; plot confidence bands applied for 95% confidence level. For explanation of the variables see Table 4.1 in Section 4.1. *FD,* Financial development. *Source: Authors' elaboration.*

negative (yet they constitute a minority of the observations). These results should not be considered surprising as this type of impact was verified and in most cases confirmed as positive in a number of previous studies on the role of ICT for FD; see, for instance, Asongu and Moulin (2016), Asongu, Anyanwu, and Tchamyou (2017), Drummer, Feuerriegel, and Neumann (2017), Salahuddin and Gow (2016), Sassi and Goaied (2013), Sepehrdoust (2018), Yartey (2008). What is also important in the context of our study is that new technologies were concluded to affect various segments of the financial system, including financial markets, that is, one of the key segments linked to ETFs as proven by, inter alia, Bhunia (2011), Okwu (2015), and Gardner, Lee, Alford, and Cresson (2017).

The relationship between the macroeconomic variables and FD (the remaining variables in Fig. 5.3) is much more complicated than in the case of ICT indicators. In the case of the economic growth variables for almost all the relationship with FD seems to be reverse U-shaped. Interestingly, the only exception is CSICT, that is, growth of capital services provided by ICT assets for which no clear link can be observed, which could imply that adoption of ICT affects FD in other ways than through the direct contribution of the associated assets. We address the issue of the linkages between economic growth and FD within the interpretation of the panel models. Finally, the positive relationship between the sole labor market variable (EMPL) and FD is evident; however, a more in-depth analysis of these linkages is not a part of our study. The issue of interdependencies between the labor market and FD was rarely undertaken in the literature; some examples of research in this field are Dromel, Kolakez, and Lehmann (2010), Çiftçioğlu and Bein (2017), and Kim, Chen, and Lin (2018).

To enrich the analysis, the examined relationships are next verified using the panel regression models.

We have estimated 10 different panel models (see Table 5.1), with the specific explanatory variables selected with regard to the aims of our study (we attempted to estimate as many models with the ETF variable as feasible). Some comments are necessary concerning the technical aspects of this part of the analysis. As shown in Table 5.1, the number of observations used for estimations of the models differs significantly between the examined specifications, ranging from 40 (in RE(7)) to 116 (in RE(8)). This is a consequence of using logged variables in order to facilitate the interpretations and lack of data on some indicators, above all IFT (which are not traded in all countries in scope) and SOT. Analogously to panel models that were estimated to identify the factors affecting diffusion of ETFs (see Chapter 4: Determinants of the European Exchange-Traded Funds Markets Development), based on the results of Hausman tests random effects models were used (for more information see the Methodological annex, Method 4). The robustness of these 10 panel regressions is mixed as indicated by the varying $R^2$ of the models. The most robust results were obtained for, firstly, the model with the majority of the considered financial variables (RE(2)) and, secondly, the model with the ETF variable and majority of potential economic determinants; in the latter case, $R^2$ is the highest in the entire group (albeit that only two explanatory variables are statistically significant in this specification: ETFs and CSICT).

Focusing on the interpretations of the models presented in Table 5.1, it needs to be noted that they unveil a somewhat different picture than in Figs. 5.2 and 5.3. However, the relationships that are the main focus of this study (i.e., between diffusion of ETFs and FD) are confirmed.

Despite the evidently arising positive influence of the ICT adoption on the FD that may be concluded from the nonparametric analysis, in line with the prevailing results of previous studies, inclusion of the other determinants in the examined specifications seems to lead to different conclusions. In order to obtain correctly formulated and robust models, ICT variables could be included exclusively in three specifications: RE(1), RE(2), and RE(10). In the first of these models FBS resulted to be statistically insignificant, in the second IU was significant albeit that the value of its parameter was negative (thus suggesting negative impact in contrast with the earlier conclusions), and, finally, in the third FBS was both statistically significant and characterized by the positive impact on the FD. These results show that relationship between the new technologies and FD becomes less straightforward when the other possible factors of this process are considered; in some scenarios it becomes immaterial or even negative. However, this evidence is by no means conclusive as more in-depth study should be performed.

The second group of potential determinants was the chosen financial variables, including the key one examined in our analysis, that is, the diffusion of ETFs (for that purpose it was included in 8 out of 10 estimated models and checked in conjunction with all remaining variables in variously formulated specifications). In the case of the ETF variable the results imply an unequivocally positive impact on the FD regardless of other included factors. Furthermore, the returned values of parameters of ETFs are rather similar (except for RE(2)), with the most common value of 0.02. It may be interpreted as indicating that an average effect of 1% change in the values of the assets of ETFs (expressed as % of the country's GDP) over the value of the FD indicator is 0.02%. Consequently, it may be stated that based on the evidence for the 12 countries, diffusion of ETFs was proven to increase the FD of European financial systems. Similar conclusions can be reached for the next two types of financial products, that is, stock index options and futures. For the investment funds other than ETPs the results are inconclusive as in the specification RE(2) that includes all financial variables except for SOT, IFT resulted to be insignificant, meaning that the other determinants capture more of the variability of FD, that is, the linkages between development of these parts of the financial sector seem to be stronger. However, the problem with making a correct examination of the IFT's role is insufficient data and, in some cases, simply lack of such financial products. To sum up, apart from ETF, the estimates of the panel models with financial variables lead to slightly different implications than resulted from the nonparametric analysis, that is, increasing turnover of both types of stock index derivatives is shown to contribute positively to the process of FD whereas such a clear-cut conclusion cannot be reached in the case of non-ETPs investment funds.

It should be emphasized that the statistical significance of the ETF variable was established also in models in which most of the other independent variables were potential economic determinants. Obviously, it is not our intention to state that diffusion of ETFs is the sole (or even one of the major) factor of the FD as such a conclusion would be too far-reaching, in particular when the size of the ETFs markets is taken into consideration. Still, it may be concluded that the development of ETFs markets boosts the FD rather than hindering it. Exact determination of the channels of the influence of ETFs is an issue that remains to be studied; we attempt to provide some possible explanations in the next section in which we examine the links between ETFs and their most closely related parts of the financial system. However, estimates presented here show that European financial systems at large (not only financial markets) seem to benefit from the spread of this category of investment funds.

The final issue that should be briefly addressed is the interpretation of the results obtained with regard to the macroeconomic variables; as it lies outside the scope of our study, the complex relationships between the economic growth variables and FD will not be discussed in detail. It must be stressed that there is vast literature on this topic, known as finance-growth nexus (Demetriades & Rousseau, 2016); there are also many theoretical and empirical studies that address various aspects of the links between these two fundamental processes and their conclusions are frequently radically different or even contradictory. Some of the seminal works include Shaw (1973), Bencivenga and Smith (1991), Greenwood and Jovanovic (1990), King and Levine (1993), de Gregorio and Guidotti (1995), Demetriades and Hussein (1996), Greenwood and Smith (1997), Levine (1997), Levine and Zervos (1998), Levine, Loayza, and Beck (2000), Beck and Levine (2004), and Rousseau and Wachtel (2011); for a recent overview of the research in the this field conducted in the period after the global financial crisis see Carré and L'œillet (2018). One of the key elements of the conducted studies is not only the strength of the impact, but also to the direction of the relationship. There are obviously crucial cause-and-effect issues that must be taken into account in the analysis of the finance-growth nexus; the inconclusive results of the research formulated over the years for various countries, with the application of various indicators, led to formulation of a few groups of hypotheses whose main categories may be broadly divided into: demand-leading (with the initiating role of economic growth), supply-leading (with the starting role of the FD) and two-way relationships. Due to the structure of our analysis we investigated the demand-leading hypothesis (as we assessed the impact of economic growth variables on the FD) that is well represented by the statement from Robinson (1952, p. 86): "where enterprise leads, finance follows." However, our estimates imply that the relationship is not straightforward. As implied by Fig. 5.3, the relationship is not simply linear. Our results seem, thus, in some way to support the findings of Sahay et al. (2015); even though these authors analyzed the other side of the finance-growth relationship (the effect of the FD on the economic growth), they also stated that it is reverse U-shaped, i.e., "bell-shaped," see Sahay et al. (2015, p. 15-21). Lastly, estimates of the panel models confirm the positive impact of the EMPL variable.

## 5.2 EXCHANGE-TRADED FUNDS AND DEVELOPMENT OF THE SELECTED PARTS OF EUROPEAN FINANCIAL SYSTEMS

The previous section was devoted to the analysis of the role of ETFs in the context of FD in Europe on the most aggregate level. In this section we move our study to a more specific focus as we scrutinize the relationships between the selected segments of the financial sector. We investigate exclusively the segments of the financial system that can be expected to be influenced by the diffusion of ETFs based on the review of both theoretical and empirical literature in this field as well as the preceding examination of the structure of European ETFs markets in terms of, e.g., the exposure of the funds. Consequently, we consider the following parts of the financial system: markets for investment funds other than ETFs (exclusively the ones listed on stock exchanges), stock markets, and bond markets. First we focus on the standalone impact of ETFs and we present the results of nonparametric analysis. However, due to possible high interdependencies between these markets, their mutual relationships are also taken into account in assessing the influence of ETFs; we estimate panel data models in which all potential linkages between ETFs, stock markets, bond markets and markets for the other investment funds listed on exchanges are considered.

In order to ensure high robustness of the analysis we use the monthly time series for the analogous period as considered in the examination of the diffusion of ETFs, that is, January 2004−August 2017. The drawback of this approach is the lack of its applicability for the examination of the influence of ETFs on the markets for mutual funds (as in the latter case only annual or quarterly data are acquirable). However, we decided to utilize exclusively monthly data in all parts of the analysis in order to ensure its consistency (it should be added that all data, except values of assets of ETFs, were acquired from the same database). For the same reason we do not analyze the IMF FD sub-indices: FI and FM (only annual data are published). Furthermore, the links with the largest part of financial systems in most economies, that is, the banking sector, are not explored as it appears highly unlikely that diffusion of ETFs could play any significant role in its development (no previous publications indicate such a relationship).

Variables used in this part of the study of the analysis are listed in Table 5.2. All values are expressed in USD millions rather than as a share of local GDP due to lack of GDP data with the required monthly frequency. As it may be noticed, we consider two dimensions of the equity markets: their size (by analyzing the capitalization of domestic companies) and liquidity (by including the stock turnover variable) in order to account for these two basic dimensions of its development. As in the entire study we use the values of assets of ETFs; it may appear as inconsistency as most of the other indicators refer to the turnover. However, it should be remembered that assets and turnover of ETFs are generally strongly related; supplementary analysis with ETFs turnover indicators was also conducted (its results are not presented), yielding highly similar results.

The upper left graph in Fig. 5.4 shows the results obtained for the two categories of investment funds traded on the stock exchanges: ETFs and other types (such as closed-end funds, REITs, or other unit trusts, depending on the particular country's regulations; it must be strongly underlined that the biggest category, that is, mutual funds, are not considered). The results are unambiguous; the relationship between ETF and SIFT was positive. It may thus be stated that development of the ETFs markets in Europe can be hypothesized to reinforce the turn-over of the other types of investment funds that are listed and traded on similar trading venues; it must be emphasized that in this part of the analysis we ignore any other potential factors. This conclusion may appear to be somewhat surprising taking into account the results presented in the previous chapter. Analysis of the factors underlying the spread of innovative funds was inconclusive: estimated, by the use of panel data models, para-meters indicated no impact of the other investment funds traded on the stock exchanges whereas country-level evidence was mixed (in the case of some countries, however, a positive impact was identified). Consequently, it

**TABLE 5.2** List of the Variables Used in the Analysis of the Relationships Between the Selected Segments of the Financial Sector

| Acronym | Full name of the variable | Units | Sources of data | Additional remarks |
|---------|---------------------------|-------|-----------------|--------------------|
| ETF | Assets of ETFs primary listed in certain country | mln USD | Lipper | – |
| BT | Bond turnover | mln USD | World Federation of Exchanges and country-specific sources | Aggregated annual turnover on the local stock exchanges |
| DMC | Domestic (stock) market capitalization | mln USD | World Federation of Exchanges and country-specific sources | – |
| SIFT | Investment funds turnover on the stock exchanges | mln USD | World Federation of Exchanges and country-specific sources | Aggregated annual turnover on the local stock exchanges; values do not include turnover of shares of ETFs (or other ETPs) |
| ST | Stock turnover | mln USD | World Federation of Exchanges and country-specific sources | Aggregated annual turnover on the local stock exchanges |

*Note*: For additional information concerning detailed sources and methods of calculation see the documentation of the particular database.
*Own elaboration.*

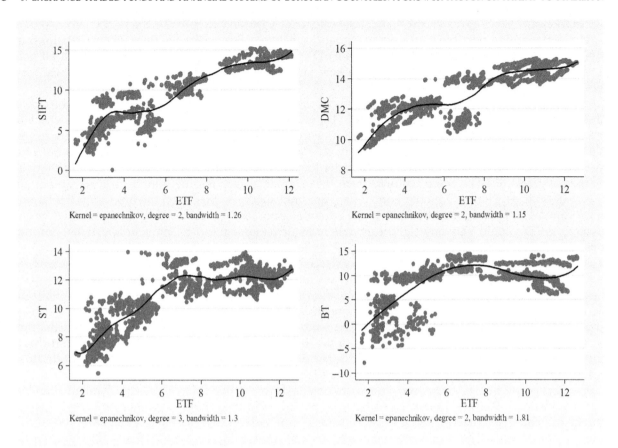

**FIGURE 5.4**   SIFT, DMC, ST, and BT versus ETF. 2004–17, monthly data.
*Note*: all values are logged. *Source: Authors' elaboration.*

may be stated that the role of the other investment funds for the diffusion of ETFs in Europe is on a regional scale insignificant (albeit in some countries it can be identified), they are neither a barrier nor accelerator of this process; in the case of the other side of the relationship some influence may be noticed and as it is positive it appears that they are complimentary financial products rather than substitutes. Nevertheless, due to insignificance of the exchange-listed investment funds other than ETFs (or other ETPs) in most countries in our scope (their turnover is usually very low in relation to the local GDP) or even lack of such financial products, these results should be interpreted with caution and not as a conclusive evidence for the attributes of these linkages. Moreover, it means that they should not be regarded as one of the key channels through which ETFs affect the general FD.

The upper right and lower left graphs show the results of the analysis for the two examined stock market variables. Stock markets may be perceived as the key segment of the financial markets if the structure of the European ETFs is considered; the vast majority of the European ETFs are funds with the equity exposure, usually tracking stock market indexes (it is the dominant category in terms of assets). Relationship between diffusion of ETFs and the size of the certain country's equity market (approximated by the capitalization of the domestic listed companies) resulted to be positive, similarly to the results for the other types of investment funds. More precisely, it appears to be most strongly positive in the case of the lower values of both DMC and ETF, whereas for the higher ones it flattens. As a consequence, the most significant relationship between ETFs and DMC, in other words the impact of the innovative funds on the capitalization of the listed companies, can be noted in the initial stages of the diffusion of ETFs; later on the contribution of ETFs becomes much less substantial. Results obtained for the next stock market variable, ST, are very similar to the ones for DMC. The two stages of the impact of ETFs (first, substantially positive and second, neutral) are even more evident. Consequently, it can be claimed that the impact of ETFs on both dimensions of the equity market (size and liquidity, approximated by ST and DMC) is comparable according to the evidence provided by the single independent variable models. Nevertheless, due to the mechanisms of ETFs, it is more likely that they affect the turnover of equities rather than their capitalization (possibly through the effects on the prices of securities rather than decisions of public companies to conduct public offering of equities); the positive relationship between ETFs and DMC may be a "byproduct" of the positive link between DMC and ST (see Table 5.3).

Taking into account the estimates for both DMC and ST it may be concluded that in the case of the high values of the assets of ETFs the role of innovative funds with regard to the development of the equity markets becomes neutral. This interesting conclusion is rather unexpected as it could imply that even in the initial phase of the development of the ETFs market they can contribute positively to attributes of the local equity market such as its size or liquidity (obviously, their role is limited by the much lower size of the ETFs markets in relation to their equity counterparts). After reaching some peak point their impact does not become, however, negative but simply unimportant—all possible reinforcement effects are achieved earlier. Moreover, this conclusion could not have been reached using panel models that do not allow considering the changing parameters of the relationship. Finally, taking into account the results of the analysis of the determinants of the diffusion of ETFs (shown in Chapter 4: Determinants of the European Exchange-Traded Funds Markets Development) makes this picture even more complicated: the impact of the equity markets on the development of the ETFs markets was difficult to establish; in the case of the variable parallel to DMC it resulted to be statistically insignificant and for the equivalent of ST the results were inconclusive even with regard to whether it was positive or negative (country-level results were also highly mixed as proven by, e.g., the average correlation for the entire sample was close to 0). Therefore, analogously to IFT, it may be claimed that the side of ETFs-equity markets relationship analyzed in this section is relatively more relevant.

The final (lower right) graph presents the bond markets' variable (BT) and it unveils a similar image to the two discussed for the equity market variables. There appear to be two types of the impact of ETFs on BT: positive for the lower values of both ETF and BT, and mostly neutral (to some extent even weakly negative) in case of the higher ones. One stipulation that could be made to this part of the study concerns the selected bond market's development indicator, that is, turnover of bonds on the exchanges. In most cases it is much lower in comparison to the equity turnover or, even more importantly, to the value of the outstanding debt securities

**TABLE 5.3** SIFT, DMC, ST, and BT versus ETF. Random Effects Models. 2004–17, Monthly Data

| | SIFT | | DMC | | ST | | BT | |
|---|---|---|---|---|---|---|---|---|
| | **RE(1)** | **RE(2)** | **RE(3)** | **RE(4)** | **RE(5)** | **RE(6)** | **RE(7)** | **RE(8)** |
| ETF | **0.37** | **0.25** | **0.15** | **0.12** | − 0.001 | **− 0.16** | **− 0.08** | **− 0.60** |
| | **[0.03]** | **[0.02]** | **[0.008]** | **[0.01]** | [0.01] | **[0.01]** | **[0.04]** | **[0.06]** |
| SIFT | − | − | − | **0.05** | − | **0.44** | − | **1.32** |
| | | | | **[0.02]** | | **[0.02]** | | **[0.09]** |
| DMC | − | **0.18** | − | − | − | **0.59** | − | **− 0.46** |
| | | **[0.06]** | | | | **[0.03]** | | **[0.19]** |
| ST | − | **0.87** | − | **0.32** | − | − | − | − 0.20 |
| | | **[0.03]** | | **[0.02]** | | | | [0.14] |
| BT | − | **0.11** | − | **− 0.01** | − | **− 0.01** | − | − |
| | | **[0.00]** | | **[0.00]** | | **[0.00]** | | |
| Breuch−Pagan test (prob > chi$^2$) | 24,439 | 44,372 | 54,868 | 41,429 | 46,843 | 23,934 | 57,277 | 20,677 |
| | [0.00] | [0.00] | [0.00] | [0.00] | [0.00] | [0.00] | [0.00] | [0.00] |
| $R^2$ (overall) | 0.81 | 0.74 | 0.77 | 0.63 | 0.62 | 0.56 | 0.23 | 0.08 |
| Rho | 0.83 | 0.95 | 0.91 | 0.94 | 0.87 | 0.88 | 0.89 | 0.78 |
| Mean VIF | − | 4.6 | − | 5.01 | − | 4.37 | − | 5.28 |
| # of observations | 1097 | 1058 | 1531 | 1058 | 1530 | 1058 | 1491 | 1058 |

*Note:* All values are logged; SE below coefficients; results account for random-effects GLS regressions; extreme observations excluded; panel—balanced; constant included—not reported; in bold—results statistically significant at 5% level of significance.
*Authors' estimates.*

(due to various trading venues and low liquidity of some bonds). However, due to the fundamental attributes of ETFs and their mechanisms it can be expected that they should affect above all the turnover of bonds (by, for instance, transactions related to the creation/redemption mechanism of the shares of funds) rather than activities on the primary bond markets. Another reason is simply lack of sufficient data on the bond markets' size indicator (at least with the monthly frequency). No role of the bond markets for the diffusion of ETFs in Europe, considered either in the size or turnover dimension, was identified in the analysis presented in Chapter 4, Determinants of the European Exchange-Traded Funds Markets Development, thus, again implying that this relationship seems to be one-sided.

In the second part of our analysis we comment briefly on the estimates of the panel data models with single or multiple independent variables estimated separately for each examined variable of the financial sector (see Table 5.3). We investigate both equity market variables in order to account for both size and liquidity of the stock market—formal tests prove that it does not affect negatively the robustness of the results. If available, we also refer to the results of previous studies in this field.

The first two models, RE(1) and RE(2) were used to investigate the impact of ETFs, equity, and bond markets on the turnover of the investment funds on the stock exchanges. The positive role of innovative funds was confirmed in both specifications; see positive coefficients of the statistically significant variable. The same applies to both stock market indicators and bond turnover. Comparison of the exact values of the estimated parameters in RE(2) specification indicates that stock turnover is the key determinant of the SIFT while the remaining factors influence it relatively less strongly. What is important is that $R^2$ of the two models for SIFT are among the highest of all estimated, thus, implying their robustness; in particular the model with only the ETF variable included appears to be important evidence for the role of ETFs (the highest $R^2$ in the whole group); it should be stressed that $R^2$ of each single and multiple explanatory variable models are not directly comparable due to different numbers of observations. The topic of the determinants of the turnover of investment funds (closed-end funds are among the leading subcategories) was not covered in the previous research as most studies focused on the issues such as differences between the prices of their shares and net asset values (for an overview see Anderson, Born, & Schnusenberg, 2010); initial public offerings by closed-end funds were analyzed by, for example, Cherkes, Sagi, and Stanton (2009).

Determinants of the stock market's development were studied with the models RE(3)−RE(6). In case of the specifications for DMC, all explanatory variables are statistically significant. In both RE(3) and RE(4) the estimated parameters of ETF are positive which confirms the conclusions reached. Moreover, as also could be expected, the stock turnover is positively linked to the stock market's capitalization; estimates of RE(6) show that this relationship is mutual as DMC also positively affects ST. Even though the estimated parameters for both SIFT and BT are statistically significant, they are close to 0 (in particular in case of BT it is at merely −0.01) thus showing their lesser importance. Specifications for ST (RE(5) and RE(6)) provide a much more complicated picture than in case of DMC. ETF variable is insignificant in the RE(5) model; in contrast with the observations made based on nonparametric analysis, panel model suggests no contribution of ETFs to the changes in the turnover of the stocks of listed companies. However, it appears that the results of the panel model estimations are distorted by the two-staged relationship that can be noticed on the relevant graph in Fig. 5.4. This is even more evident in the case of RE(6) in which the coefficient of (statistically significant) ETF variable is negative. BT and ST variables seem unrelated according to the estimated models (see RE(6) and RE(8)). There is a vast number of studies on the factors that affect the development of the stock markets; in the past few years it has been intensively studied and discussed in both theoretical and empirical literature (their review lies outside the scope of this book). According to Ho and Lyke (2017) factors of stock market development may be divided into two broad categories: macroeconomic and institutional. The former includes real income (and its growth rate), banking sector, interest rate, private capital flows, inflation, and exchange rates. The latter includes legal origins, stock market integration, corporate governance, financial market liberalization, and trade openness. Other recent studies are, for example, Naceur, Ghazouani, and Omran (2007), Rahman, Sidek, and Tafri (2009), Yartey (2010), Kurt-Gumuş, Evrim-Mandaci, Tvaronavičienė, and Aktan (2013), Rudzkis and Valkavičienė (2014), Ng, Dewandaru, and Ibrahim (2015), Jordaan, Dima, and Gole (2016), Ng, Ibrahim, and Mirakhor (2016), Shahbaz, Rehman, and Afza (2016), Bayar (2017), Newton (2017), Aluko and Azeez (2018), and Ho and Odhiambo (2018). Despite the large number of publications, the role of ETFs was not examined, most probably due to their relatively short history.

Results obtained for the last examined segment of the financial system, that is, bond market, are relatively least robust; see the very low $R^2$ of RE(7) and RE(8), meaning that the included explanatory variables are not among the most crucial determinants of the bond market's development (it appears to be shaped by the other factors).

However, some interpretations are possible. All variables, except for ST, are statistically significant. Implicated role of ETFs and stock markets (considered in the capitalization dimension) is negative and the impact of investment funds is positive. The results obtained for ETF variable are in contradiction to the ones examined with the application of nonparametric analysis. However, estimated parameter of ETF in RE(7) is close to 0, thus, implying that the overall impact of ETFs on the bond turnover is almost neutral. Fig. 5.4, that can be regarded here as more reliable evidence, shows that the actual relationship is more complicated. Still, ETFs can be expected to affect more strongly the equity market rather than the bond market due to, above all, their prevalent equity exposure. Development of bond markets was studied using various indicators with regard to various regions and even though the results are far from inconclusive, some of the determinants identified in the previous research include, inter alia, the size of the economy, trade openness, fiscal balance, GDP per capita, interest rate volatility, size of the banking system, and stronger institutions (Bhattacharyay, 2013; Burger & Warnock, 2006; Eichengreen & Luengnaruemitchai, 2004; Mu, Phelps, & Stotsky, 2013; Schinasi & Todd Smith, 1998; Smaoui, Grandes, & Akindele, 2017). Claessens, Schmukler, and Klingebiel (2007) claimed that stock market capitalization is related positively to the size of domestic currency bond market (we used a different indicator so it is impossible to compare these results to our estimates that suggest the negative role of equity markets). The impact of ETFs was not previously considered.

Finally, it should be added that two out of the four variables discussed in this section are constituents of the FD index: DMC and ST. Even though the third variable, BT, is not directly included in our index, it is obviously linked to the bond market indicators used in the calculation of the FMD and FMA sub-indexes (see Section 5.1). Only the IFT variable was not taken into account in the assessment of the FD, either directly or by using some proxy variable. As a result, we analyzed also some of the potential channels of impact of ETFs on the general FD process (approximated by, for instance, the FD index). It can be concluded that in the examined European countries diffusion of ETFs contributed positively to the FD through its influence on both stock and bond markets. However, it seems that ETFs markets that reached high levels of development (in terms of assets) were no longer impacting the other segments of the financial system (or could even have had a slightly negative effect as suggested by the estimates of some panel models). Generally, though, the role of ETFs in terms of FD has been positive.

## 5.3 EXCHANGE-TRADED FUNDS AND STABILITY OF THE EUROPEAN FINANCIAL SYSTEMS

In this section we present the final part of our analysis concerning the impact of ETFs on the European financial system as we investigate their potential contribution to the financial (in)stability. We start by clarifying some key concepts. Next, we present the results of our study, conducted by applying the selected composite index of the financial stress. Some additional issues are covered after the core analysis. In the final part of this section we discuss briefly one of the potential sources of instability triggered by the diffusion of ETFs: synthetic ETFs. Theoretical aspects of the discussed relationships were outlined in Section 2.4, therefore they are not recalled unless necessary.

### 5.3.1 Key Concepts

In our analysis of the impact of ETFs on the stability on the European financial system we use a financial stress index. As Vermeulen et al. (2015, p. 384) stated, financial stress indexes are one of the tools that "are widely used by policymakers as an instrument for monitoring financial stability." As they noticed, similar conclusions can be found in Oet, Bianco, Gramlich, and Ong (2012). There are various financial stress indexes employed in the academic research or for policy purposes. For a detailed overview of the approaches to the construction of the financial stress indexes (based on the US example) see Kliesen, Owyang, and Vermann (2012); more recent discussions can be found in, for instance, Ernst, Semmler, and Haider (2017), Vašíček et al. (2017), Adam, Benecká, and Matějů (2018), and Apostolakis and Papadopoulos (2018).

The financial stress index that we use to assess the financial stability in the analyzed countries is provided by the European Central Bank (ECB), and labeled as Country-Level Index of Financial Stress (CLIFS). Methodology of CLIFS was presented in Duprey, Klaus, and Peltonen (2015) and Duprey, Klaus, and Peltonen (2017) and its applications were shown in Duprey and Klaus (2017). It is composed of the three sub-indexes capturing financial stress in the three segments of the financial system that cover these variables (Duprey et al., 2015, p. 7—11; in our presentation names of the variables are slightly modified and some technical details are omitted):

1. *Equity market sub-index:* Monthly realized stock volatility (monthly average of absolute daily log-returns of the index of real stock prices) and cumulative maximum loss (maximum loss compared to the highest level of the index of real stock prices over 2 years).
2. *Bond market sub-index:* Monthly realized bond volatility (monthly average of absolute daily changes in the real 10-year yields of government bonds) and cumulative difference (maximum increase in the real government bond spread in comparison to Germany over a 2-year rolling window).
3. *Foreign exchange (FX) market sub-index:* Realized FX volatility (monthly growth rate of the real effective exchange rate) and cumulative change (change of the real effective exchange rate over 6 months).

Each sub-index is calculated as the average of the two variables and the final index (CLIFS) is obtained using a portfolio theory approach; the weights of sub-indexes are based on their cross-correlation with the others (for more details see Duprey et al., 2015). As a result, CLIFS does not take into account each type of risk to the financial stability separately, but rather their correlation. Higher values of CLIFs indicate higher levels of financial stress (in other words, higher financial instability).

There are two basic limitations of the CLIFS index in the context of our study. Firstly, we cannot apply it to analyze the entire sample of the 12 European countries with ETFs markets. In the core analysis we consider nine countries discussed in the previous sections as ECB does not provide data for the three countries that are not member states of the EU: Norway, Switzerland, and Turkey (we discuss them separately). Secondly, it was prepared with different research purposes than in the case of our study, that is, to investigate the financial cycle and identify the episodes of financial stress. Consequently, some of its aspects (such as the aggregation method or its targeted forward-looking application) do not correspond fully to the main focus of our analysis.

However, despite these limitations utilizing the CLIFS indicator offers certain benefits in comparison to other possible approaches. For obvious reasons, using some type of financial stress index is a more plausible solution than focusing on one selected indicator. Yet the choice of such index is also problematic. Above all, in the vast majority of cases the indexes of financial stress take into account both financial markets (including money markets) and the banking sector (Cardarelli, Elekdag, & Lall, 2011; Holló, Kremer, & Lo Duca, 2012; Kliesen et al., 2012; Oet et al., 2012). Using such indexes in our study could lead to some problematic conclusions as it would be too far-reaching to assume that diffusion of ETFs could affect the stability of the banking sector or money markets (consequently, we omitted them in the previous sections). Due to their fundamental attributes and the most frequent exposure of the available funds it may, however, be presumed that they may to some extent influence the stability of the equity or bond markets as well as FX markets (in the last case the possible linkages are more complicated and vaguer, yet they may be connected to the funds with foreign exposure). Therefore CLIFS, with its three sub-indexes, seems to be the optimal solution in this context. Its further advantage is the monthly frequency of data [for this reason we decided not to apply other measures of financial stability, e.g., the ones suggested in Sahay et al. (2015) or indicators built on data from the Global Financial Development Database].

In addition to data on ETFs and CLIFS, in order to formulate some general conclusions concerning the stability of the analyzed financial systems, we also use the database with the list of financial crises in Europe in the period 1970—2016 provided as of 2017 by the ECB and European Systemic Risk Board. It covers all EU countries and Norway. What is important is that it includes data on the attributes of the crisis (most basically, what were its sources or which segments of the financial system were most affected) that enables a more accurate evaluation of the potential impact of ETFs. The methodology of the database's construction, above all the adopted approach to the identification and classification of the financial crises, is presented in Lo Duca et al. (2017). Two types of crises are covered: systemic crises and residual events (episodes of elevated financial stress that do not fulfill the criteria listed below). Episodes of financial stress are classified as systemic financial crises if they fulfill at least these criteria (Lo Duca et al., 2017, p. 10):

1. Financial system contributed to originating or amplifying of the shocks.
2. Financial system was distressed.
3. Policies were adopted in order to preserve either financial or bank stability.

## 5.3.2 Empirical Evidence

Before we proceed to the formal analysis of the possible relationships between the diffusion of ETFs and financial stability, it is first necessary to show the general position of ETFs in the European countries; the assumption that potential threats posed by ETFs increase along with the growing size of the ETFs markets is mostly accepted in the literature or at least implicitly assumed in similar analyses (see, for example, Aggarawal & Schofield, 2014; Naumenko & Chystiakova, 2015). Table 5.4 presents data on the assets and turnover of ETFs in the examined countries in relation to their GDP. As clearly noticed, in both dimensions ETFs markets have been a rather insignificant part of the local economies and, consequently, of financial systems. It may, thus, be preliminary hypothesized that it is highly unlikely that they could have affected the stability of the entire financial system. In the further discussion we focus on the economies in which the size of the ETFs markets exceeded in at least one of the dimensions in Table 5.4 (assets or turnover) an arbitrary threshold of 2% of GDP. We assume, therefore, that in the remaining economies local primary listed ETFs have simply been too small to play any significant role. Five countries fulfill the 2% criterion: France, Germany, Italy, Switzerland, and the United Kingdom.

Fig. 5.5 shows the evolution of the two key variables examined in this section over 2004–17, that is, ETFs and CLIFS. In the analysis, data on the assets of ETFs in the absolute dimension, that is, values in the millions of USD were used rather than in the relation to GDP (in the relative perspective) due to the lack of consistent monthly data on GDP. We can, therefore, increase the number of observations in our study with the aim of the higher robustness of its results.

Trends in the assets of ETFs were presented in Chapter 3, Exchange-Traded Funds Markets in Europe: Development Patterns, therefore, we skip their analysis here. In the case of the CLIFS index, it is evident that the period of its highest values in most countries was in the second half of 2008 and first half of 2009; it may, thus, be stated that it was the time of the relatively highest instability of most European financial systems. It is particularly noticeable in the case of countries in which the overall level of the CLIFS index has been low, indicating that that their financial systems have been stable, such as Sweden: the only "spike" in the level of financial stress as implied by CLIFS can be noticed for 2008–09 (extending to 2010, yet for different reasons). It was an element of the global financial crisis (labeled also as subprime crisis in order to underline one of the categories of financial instruments that came into spotlight of the broad audience), with the collapse of the Lehman Brothers banks as one of the turning points; it expanded from the US market to the European market due to the interconnectedness of the financial systems and cross-border spillovers.

**TABLE 5.4**  Average Assets and Turnover of ETFs in the 12 European Countries Over 2004–16

| Country | Average end-of-year assets of ETFs (% of GDP) | Average annual turnover of the shares of ETFs (% of GDP) |
| --- | --- | --- |
| France | 1.83 | 4.30 |
| Germany | 2.36 | 4.94 |
| Greece | 0.01 | <0.01 |
| Hungary | <0.01 | <0.01 |
| Italy | 0.05 | 3.45 |
| Norway | 0.03 | 1.61 |
| Poland | <0.01 | <0.01 |
| Spain | 0.09 | 0.44 |
| Sweden | 0.46 | n.a. |
| Switzerland | 4.62 | 9.52 |
| Turkey | 0.01 | 0.68 |
| United Kingdom | 3.50 | 7.04 |

*Authors' calculations.*

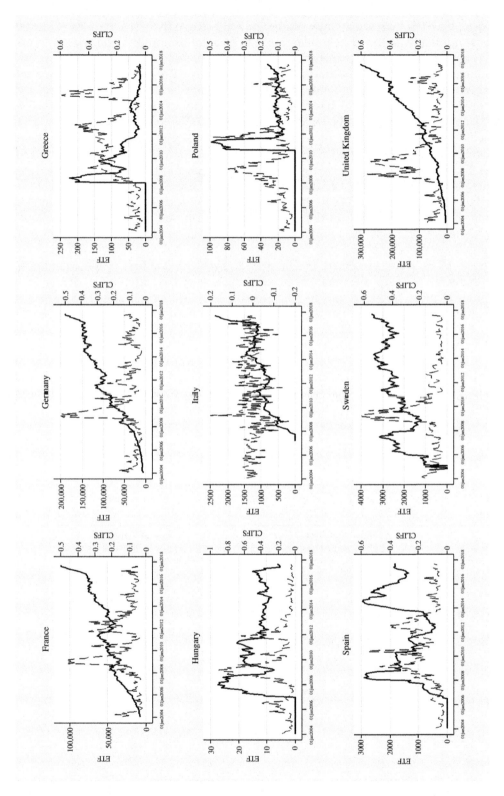

**FIGURE 5.5** ETFs versus CLIFS. 2004–17, monthly data.
*Note*: Raw data used. Assets of ETFs—*solid line* (left scale). CLIFS—*dashed line* (right scale) *Source: Authors' elaboration.*

Another period of increased financial stress begins from the Spring 2010 and may be broadly explained as the eurozone debt crisis. However, this event was much less severe in most evaluated countries (compare the levels of CLIFS for 2008/09 and the subsequent years), with countries in Southern Europe being the noteworthy exception (in particular Greece in which the debt crisis had several stages in the years after 2010, see the peak levels of CLIFS in 2015; for Italy this problem was relatively least substantial). In the financial crises database (Lo Duca et al., 2017) the events in 2008 were classified as systemic financial crises in seven out of nine EU countries (plus Norway; Switzerland, and Turkey which are not included yet at least in the former country systemic crisis was identified in the database by Laeven and Valencia [2012]; Turkey was more robust). The only exceptions were Greece and Poland (the resilience of Poland may, however, not be in any way explained by the positive impact of ETFs as the first fund was launched in 2010). In comparison, the second period of increased financial stress was explicitly classified as systemic for Greece, Italy, and Spain (in the first country as separate event, in the next two as a continuation of the previous crisis); in some other countries it slightly (yet much less significantly) overlapped with the final part of the previous crisis; for obvious reasons in the case of the non-EU countries it may not be regarded as systemic (or even a residual event). Even though in most cases of the increased financial stress one of its aspects was, as noted in the database of Lo Duca et al. (2017), significant correction of asset prices, it resulted from the global-scale or regional-scale events and possible role of ETFs in the transmission of shocks can be assessed as insignificant (as of 2008 or 2010 their assets or turnover were in most countries still very small so it is highly improbable that they contributed to the crisis on systemic level).

In order to verify more accurately the links between diffusion of ETFs and financial stability we employ a basic albeit sufficiently informative method in this context, that is, analysis of their correlation (see Table 5.5). It should be stressed that we do not attempt to establish the direction of causality between the diffusion of ETFs and financial stability as it would require using more advanced research methods; the results of the subsequent analysis show that in this context it would be an unnecessary extension of the study. The results presented in Table 5.5 should not be perceived as unexpected as they generally support the initial conclusion of the weak influence of ETFs on the levels of financial stress due to the relatively low size of the markets for innovative funds in the European countries.

The highest positive values of correlation coefficients were calculated for Greece and Italy. However, in the former country both assets and turnover of ETFs have been extremely low (below 0.01% of GDP, see Table 5.4), therefore, it may be stated that the positive correlation in this case is a result of, to some extent, coinciding movements of the values of assets of ETFs and CLIFS (i.e., financial instability) or, in other words, evidence for the fact that Greek ETFs markets suffered during the time of the financial crisis similarly to the other parts of the financial system and economy. The reverse relationship is exceptionally unlikely. In the case of Italy the correlation coefficient was calculated at 0.18, that is, at a higher level than in any other country except for Greece yet it is very low and seems insufficient evidence for any possible relationship between ETFs and financial stability,

**TABLE 5.5**  ETFs versus CLIFS: Country-Level Pairwise Correlations. 2004—17, Monthly Data

| | |
|---|---|
| France | −0.07 |
| Germany | −0.08 |
| Greece | 0.27 |
| Hungary | 0.08 |
| Italy | 0.18 |
| Norway | n.a. |
| Poland | −0.19 |
| Spain | 0.10 |
| Sweden | −0.37 |
| Switzerland | n.a. |
| Turkey | n.a. |
| United Kingdom | −0.27 |

*Authors' calculations.*

particularly when we take into account the causes of the financial crises in this country and their course. According to the financial crises database (Lo Duca et al., 2017), over 2004–2017 two periods of increased financial stress occurred in Italy. Firstly, since January 2008 (no definite end dates are provided in case of neither of the two events), is labeled as residual event and associated with the global financial crisis; its consequences in Italy were rather modest due to the structure of the Italian banking system. Secondly, since August 2011, inflicted by the tensions on the sovereign bond markets of the eurozone crisis. Even though in both cases they were accompanied by substantial declines on the stock markets, it is not possible to establish any possible role of ETFs. Over the entire 2004–17 time period the turnover of ETFs in relation to GDP has been much lower than that of any other financial instruments analyzed in the preceding sections: stocks, bonds, stock index futures, or stock index options (the assets indicators cannot be compared due to lack of corresponding values).

For France, Germany, Hungary, and Spain correlation coefficients are close to 0 (relatively high for the last of these countries, yet it is the one with very small ETFs markets in comparison to the size of the local economy). The same remark, concerning the small relative size of the ETFs markets, applies to the two remaining countries, Poland and Sweden. The second case is somewhat interesting as the correlation coefficient has the highest value in absolute terms and, what is even more striking, it is negative. Due to the marginal size of the Swedish market, this case of the apparent negative relationship is not analyzed; we consider similar results for this much larger ETFs market.

Finally, the last EU country in the sample is the United Kingdom for which the correlation coefficient was calculated as −0.27 (the lowest apart from Sweden) which is an interesting result that allows for some quite surprising (yet far from evident) conclusions. It implies that development of the UK ETFs market (which has been most stable in the entire sample, see Chapter 3: Exchange-Traded Funds Markets in Europe: Development Patterns) has been negatively linked to the level financial stress; in other words, it could suggest that it has mitigated the occurrence of financial crises rather than contributed to their outbreak. As in most other countries in 2008 and 2009 United Kingdom experienced the highest levels of the financial stress over 2004–17 (see the values of CLIFS in Fig. 5.5; they were also one of the highest in the region). However, ETFs continued their expansion even during this period, with only short-lived declines of assets and turnovers. Since 2010 onwards, in the time when ETFs started to become a relatively important (in comparison to other countries) part of the local financial system, no substantial episodes of elevated financial stress can be identified. It should be stressed that concluding that diffusion of ETFs was one of the important factors that contributed to the decrease of the level of stress in the UK financial stress would be too far-reaching (in particular we do not claim the direction of the relationship) albeit it may be stated that our analysis provides some (highly preliminary and inconclusive) evidence for the possible positive role of innovative funds in this context. One of the requirements of such a relationship seems to be, as in case of the UK ETFs markets, its relatively high level of development and substantial diversification in various aspects (United Kingdom is the European leader in both dimensions).

The ECB database does include data for the non-EU member states: Norway, Switzerland, and Turkey. Both for Norway and Switzerland the average size of ETFs markets exceeded 1% which means that innovative funds could be presupposed to have exerted some impact on the financial stability. However, for Norway, only the average turnover was slightly above 1% (1.61%), therefore we decided not to consider this country (assets were below the cut-off level set at 2%) as one with the possible relationship between ETFs and financial stability. Moreover, according to the financial crises database, the duration of the systemic crisis linked to the 2008 global turmoil was among the shortest in the entire sample and no other similar period of elevated financial stress occurred in the analyzed time period. In the case of Switzerland, the episode of systemic financial crisis was identified to have taken in place in 2008 according to the database of Laeven and Valencia (2012); over the next few years no episodes of substantially increased financial stress can be identified for this country. Taking into account the fact that in 2008 or 2009 Swiss ETFs market was still in the early stage of its development that accelerated over the next years (see diffusion paths in Section 3.2) establishing links between the propagation of the shock in the financial system to Switzerland and the diffusion of ETFs is impossible. Furthermore, despite lack of exact data on the levels of financial stress, the basic analysis of the diffusion of ETFs in Switzerland and stability of its financial system leads to a conclusion similar to the one formulated for the UK market concerning the positive association between ETFs and financial stability (of course, we do not state the attributes of these linkages). In the case of the third evaluated non-EU country, Turkey, hypothesizing the possible influence of ETFs on the financial stability would be too far-reaching due to their extremely low mean assets and turnover in relation to the GDP (see Table 5.4).

To sum up, our analysis did not uncover convincing evidence for the possible negative impact of ETFs on the emergence or mounting of the financial instability in the European countries; we focused on the periods of the most important financial crises in the recent years, that is, the 2008 global financial crisis and eurozone debt crisis. In fact, ETFs markets have generally developed in the subsequent years, in the period of the decreased financial stress in most examined economies. The relationship between diffusion of ETFs and increased possibility or intensity of the financial crises appears to be very vague; it does not seem to become more evident for the more developed ETFs markets. In contrast, as indicated by the correlation coefficients, in case of the largest ETFs markets in Europe, ETFs were positively related to the financial stability (i.e., negatively to the level of financial stress) whereas in the case of smaller ones it was generally reversed. Our findings are in line with the results discussed by Amenc, Ducoulombier, Goltz, and Tang (2012) who compared the size of the ETFs markets to the stock market capitalization or the notional value of equity futures and swaps, also stating that assets of ETFs were too negligible to create any systemic risks to the financial system.

Apart from these potential threats to the financial stability, caused by the diffusion of ETFs, that can be broadly associated with the increased risk of contagion (or indirectly negative impact on liquidity or other attributes of the linked assets) if we refer to the mechanisms discussed in Section 2.4, there are also some other similar possible effects such as the impact of ETFs on the volatility of the commodity markets. However, they may be dismissed as negligible in the context of the European financial systems (e.g., the possible threats to the commodity markets are highly limited due to very low assets of commodity ETFs (or ETCs)) in relation to the respective markets for the underlying assets. The same applies to the almost nonexistent volatility ETFs. Synthetic ETFs are discussed next.

### 5.3.3 Role of Synthetic ETFs in Europe

One of the final issues that we address is the potential impact on the financial stability linked to the structure of the European ETFs markets in terms of the replication method used by the managing companies. Synthetic ETFs (including geared ETFs) are mentioned in many publications as potential source of the financial instability; see the discussion in Section 2.4 where we outlined the main possible transmission mechanisms. These worries seem to be of particular significance in case of the European ETFs markets in which synthetic funds are much more frequent than in any other region (in fact in most other regions there are no such funds or their role is negligible). However, it may be stated that these reservations are substantially exaggerated. In order to conduct the essential analysis, we use data provided in the reports of the Deutsche Bank that include division between physical and synthetic funds in terms of, for example, assets or cash flows.

Fig. 5.6 shows the structure of the aggregated European ETFs market in terms of the exposure of the funds. As it may clearly noticed, up to 2010 synthetic funds had been increasing their market share; in 2010 they reached the maximum share of c. 43% which may be regarded as the peak point in the development of this segment. Decisions of European ETF providers to employ synthetic replication were (and usually still are) motivated by the possible limitation of the tracking error and costs in the case of passive ETFs (see outline of the synthetic funds in Chapter 2: Exchange-Traded Funds: Concepts and Contexts). More generally, according to Morningstar (2017), two main motivations of the sponsors of the innovative funds to use synthetic structure are the possibility to track indexes of less accessible markets (due to, for instance, barriers for flows of foreign capital, e.g., in emerging countries) or less liquid markets (e.g., bond markets). However, since 2011 onwards synthetic ETFs have been becoming relatively less popular as evidenced by their decreasing market share. Even though their assets have grown, the increase in the assets of their physical counterparts has been much more significant and as a result as of end of 2016 the market share of funds that use derivatives declined in Europe to c. 20%. The retreat from the synthetic funds is also evident when we consider data on net cash flows to both categories; in the case of synthetic ETFs they have become negative (indicating withdrawal of investors) as in 2013 or stayed positive yet much lower than in case of physical ETFs (throughout 2016 and 2017 (see Fig. 5.7)).

Among the reasons that contributed to the decreasing popularity of the synthetic funds one reason seems to be of particular importance—the intensive debate on their risks that took place particularly in 2011 and 2012, during which many more or less substantiated allegations concerning the threats of the synthetic funds in comparison to the physical ones had been formulated, leading to the negative sentiment towards synthetic products; for more of these publications see Section 2.4. As a result, change in the replication method used in the newly launched funds and switching to the physical structures in the ones already operating have been observed for most European providers, even in the companies recognized previously as the main proponents of ETFs based on derivatives such as Lyxor. For marketing reasons, some European providers of the synthetic funds decided to modify their promotional materials of the offered ETFs by replacing the term "synthetic" with "indirect." As the

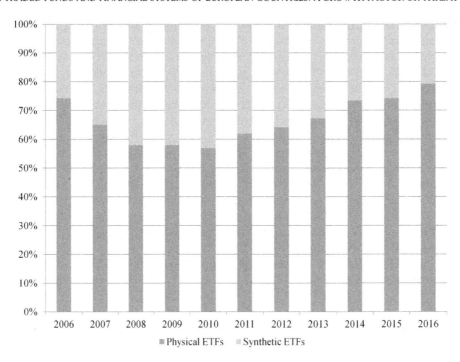

**FIGURE 5.6**   Assets of physical and synthetic ETFs in Europe. 2006–16, year-end data. *Source: Authors' elaboration based on the Deutsche Bank's monthly reports.*

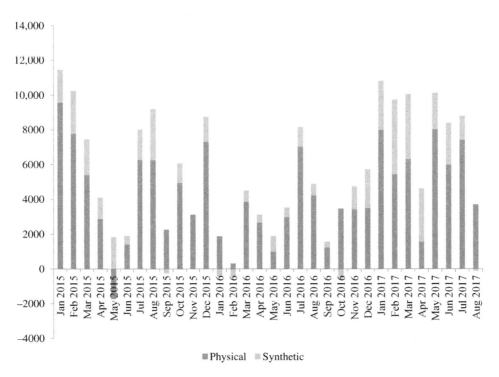

**FIGURE 5.7**   Net cash flows to physical and synthetic ETFs in Europe (mln EUR). January 2015–August 2017, monthly data. *Source: Authors' elaboration based on the Deutsche Bank's monthly reports.*

report by Morningstar (2017, p. 5) stated, synthetic funds in Europe are increasingly regarded by the providers as "secondary options."

Despite the decreasing position of the synthetic ETFs on the European market for innovative funds, the question that remains to be answered concerns their possible contribution to the financial instability (one of the factors in the discussion that led to the weakening of their popularity). We may refer here to some of the key publications that addressed the issue of the both micro- and macro-level risks posed by the European ETFs: Amenc et al. (2012), Amenc, Ducoulombier, Goltz, and Le Sourd (2015), and Amenc, Goltz, and Le Sourd (2017) with the special discussion devoted to the synthetic ETFs. The authors dismissed the possible threats related to this subcategory of innovative funds. They stated that synthetic ETFs are highly regulated in similar extent to the other types of these funds (e.g., under UCITS and MiFID regulation). Specific types of risks attributed to synthetic ETFs such as counterparty risk are mitigated by regulations concerning the maximum exposure to specific counterparty or collateralization and other provisions. They also emphasized that physical ETFs may also be exposed to the counterparty risk through security lending, thus, it should not be perceived as a type of risk specific to synthetic funds. For the geared ETFs, which were accused of contributing to the volatility of the markets for the underlying assets, they underlined lack of any empirical evidence; they also emphasized that despite the claims concerning their complexity and opacity, ETF providers actually disclose sufficient information to investors. Moreover, they stated that the possible impact of synthetic (or also the other types of) ETFs on the financial stability should not be considered separately, but rather in connection with the other segments of the financial system.

To conclude the analysis of the impact of innovative funds on the financial sector one additional comment seems necessary. Even though we deal in this section exclusively with the topic of financial stability (in the previous section we considered FD), another crucial and interesting topic could be the examination of the potential impact of the diffusion of ETFs on the economic growth or, more generally, on the real sector of the economy; as we prove in the two preceding sections, the influence of ETFs on the development of financial system can be established (with some cautionary remarks). Such discussion could be conducted within the finance-growth nexus framework (see key references in Section 5.1) or by separate study of the role of ETFs. Nonetheless, it seems that it is still too early to even hypothesize any potential positive or detrimental effects of ETFs, mostly due to their negligible assets in relation to the size of European economies (see Table 5.4). If the development of at least some European ETFs markets continues, then such a study may robustly be performed within several years. Still, it is already worth mentioning that as Andrianova and Demetriades (2018) claimed, the positive impact of the FD (we can assume that it covers also the diffusion of ETFs) on the economic growth can occur if the following are minimized: financial regulation and supervision, and the influence of ruling elites on the rule of law.

## 5.4 STORY OF FAILURE AND SUCCESS OF ETFs IN EUROPE: CASE STUDIES (PART III)

The third and the final case study of the European ETFs market is the case of Germany. In contrast with the two previously presented countries—Poland (a clear example of lack of development of the innovative financial products, with the exception of funds listed outside this country yet tracking Polish assets) and Italy where the ETFs market development has been ambiguous (in terms of assets of ETFs it was one of the mid-developed markets; its growth has been much more apparent in terms of turnover), for Germany in absolute terms it may be stated firmly that the local ETFs market has undergone substantial development. However, comparing the assets of German ETFs to the size of the local economy may raise some doubts. Broadly understood structure of the German market is particularly interesting; apart from ETFs, German investors have access to ETNs and ETCs (like in, for example, Italy). German market for exchange-traded products is thus one of the most diversified in the world, comparably to its US or UK counterparts. Moreover, Germany is among the oldest ETFs markets in Europe and in the world. In this section we present first some general supplementary information about the German market, complementary in relation to the discussion in Section 3.2. Then we concentrate on the German market for the exchange-traded products other than ETFs, that is, ETNs and ETCs, by discussing their size in terms of the number of the available products, their assets, turnover, exposure, and other selected aspects, analogically to the examination of the ETFs market.

Our presentation of the German ETFs market is limited to the selected key aspects. Due to their significance (both on a regional and global scale) various attributes of the German ETFs, extending beyond the scope of our study, were examined in a number of publications, including Schmidhammer, Lobe, and Röder (2010), Cuthbertson and Nitzsche (2012), Rompotis (2012), Czauderna, Riedel, and Wagner (2015), Milonas and Rompotis (2015), Miquel-Flores (2015), Osterhoff and Kaserer (2016), Bhattacharya, Loos, Meyer, and Hackethal (2017), and Marszk (2017a).

The history of the German ETFs market started with the launch of the trading venue that could be used for the transactions in the shares of the innovative funds. The Deutsche Börse's segment for ETFs (labeled XTF) was launched in April 2000 at approximately the same time as the similar trading venue of the London Stock Exchange; both were among the first such trading venues in the entire region (Deutsche Börse, 2016b; Deville, 2008). XTF is available through the Xetra electronic trading system (shares of ETFs are continuously traded); in the further discussion we use this name. Xetra is the leading listing location for ETFs in Germany—in terms of primary listing it accounts of almost 99% of all ETFs in Germany; in terms of turnover in 2016 and 2017 it was c. 90% (Deutsche Börse, 2016b; Xetra, 2018a). We also discuss briefly selected statistics for the second-largest Stuttgart Stock Exchange. The other German stock exchanges (e.g., Munich Stock Exchange) are omitted.

Between January 2004 and August 2017 the assets of ETFs primary listed in Germany have increased from c. $5.7 billion to above $188 billion (second place in the region). Development of the German ETFs market has been steady over the examined time period (see the diffusion pattern in Figs. 3.16. and 3.18), with seldom and short-lived subperiods of declining values of assets. The total growth rate has been among the highest in the group of the largest markets in Europe. German market has become also much more diversified in terms of the range of available funds; it began with the most traditional equity ETFs yet over the years it has broadened to include equity ETFs with non-European exposure, bond ETFs and many types of alternative ETFs—such as currency funds or funds with exposure to the hedge funds market (Deutsche Börse, 2016b). Some of the key dates in the history of the German ETFs market are listed in Table 5.6. The success of ETFs in Germany is proven by, for instance, the fact that their shares have become more intensively traded than the blue-chip equities listed on the Deutsche Börse. Nevertheless, it has raised some doubts regarding the potential impact of ETFs on the entire German stock market (Dohle, 2016). Fast development of the German ETFs market has been spurred by, inter alia, relatively lax procedures concerning the listing of new funds (Deville, 2008); however, a few years earlier, Brunner-Reumann (2005) presented opposite view by stating that the legislation concerning ETFs in Germany is complex, with rare exemptions or eased listing procedures.

We do not discuss the most recent structure of the German ETFs market categorized according to the exposure or the largest funds as these issues were already addressed in Section 3.2. However, Xetra provides a number of other indicators concerning XTF segment that can be used to evaluate the German market in more detail (it should be remembered, though, that they refer to all listed ETFs, not only the primary listed ones, we use these data until the end of the German market's analysis in this section). We analyze three aspects of the Xetra-listed ETFs: employed replication method, turnover and liquidity.

In Section 2.1 we distinguished between physical and synthetic ETFs in terms of the applied tracking mechanism; in Section 5.3.3 we examined the regional level data showing the utilization of the two methods in Europe. It should be remembered that Germany is globally one of the main locations where derivatives-based ETFs are listed. According to Xetra's data as of end of August 2017 (Xetra, 2017), majority of assets held by ETFs listed on Xetra were held in the physical funds (c. 80.9%); the rest (c. 19.1%) were managed by the synthetic funds. Three largest synthetic funds traded on Xetra (in terms of assets) were Amundi ETF Floating Rate USD Corporate UCITS ETF; Hedged EUR, Amundi ETF MSCI Emerging Markets UCITS ETF − EUR and Source S&P 500 UCITS

**TABLE 5.6** Selected Most Important Events in the History of the German ETFs Market

| Year | Short description of the new categories of funds or other event |
| --- | --- |
| 2000 | ETFs available through Xetra |
| 2003 | Bond ETFs (with exposure to German government bonds and European corporate bonds) |
| 2005 | Commodity ETF with exposure to global commodity markets |
| 2006 | Leveraged ETF tracking DAX index (with the multiple of 2) |
| 2007 | Inverse ETFs |
| 2012 | Listing of 1000th ETF on Xetra |
| 2014 | ETF with direct exposure to Chinese stock market |
| 2015 | Bond ETFs with exposure to Chinese and Indian government bonds |
| 2016 | Various new categories of ETFs (e.g., with exposure to Israeli equities) |

*Own elaboration based on Deutsche Börse Cash Market. 15 years of ETF trading in Europe & on Xetra. Facts & Figures. (2015); Xetra. ETF trading on Xetra. Facts & figures for the year 2017. (2018a).*

ETF (Xetra, 2017). Two former primary were listed in France, the latter in Germany. They were, though, not among the most actively traded synthetic ETFs (in this dimension there were many geared ETFs in the leading group). In both perspectives (assets and turnover) synthetic ETFs were not within the leaders of the entire German market as there were many larger and more actively traded physical ETFs. It may, thus, be concluded that even though in comparison to the other countries the category of synthetic funds in Germany seems to be developed, when their position on the local market is taken into account it seems rather clear that it is dominated by the funds that use the physical replication method, either with full or optimized replication.

The value of the turnover of ETFs in Germany has increased substantially between 2004 and 2017; using data exclusively for Xetra, it has grown from c. $4.4 billion per month in January 2004 to c. $12.3 billion in August 2017.[2] Overall trail of changes has been rather different than the one observed for assets (discussed in the context of diffusion of ETFs) as it reached the peak levels in 2011, followed by significant decline and stabilization at about $15 billion per month since 2012 onwards. Using data on order book turnover for August 2017 (Xetra, 2017; OTC turnover statistics are similar), three ETFs with the highest turnover were (in the ascending order): iShares Core DAX UCITS ETF (DE), iShares EURO STOXX 50 UCITS (DE) ETF, and iShares STOXX Europe 600 UCITS (DE) ETF; in Section 3.2 we listed the same three funds as the ones with the highest assets among the primary listed in Germany (the largest cross-listed funds are relatively less traded). Turnover of the equity funds has been much higher than that of the other categories, including bond funds (similarly to the differences in terms of assets).

This analysis proves that, while in the study based on the assets indicators the development of the German ETFs market is clear-cut, in terms of turnover the results are less positive. As noticed in the report by Xetra (2018a) turnover of ETFs in Germany is strongly positively correlated with the stock market's volatility. The role of the individual investors in terms of turnover has been negligible as they have accounted for c. 5% of the trading volume and approximately one third of the number of transactions (Deutsche Börse Cash Market, 2015; Xetra, 2018a,b).[3]

The third aspect of the German ETFs that can be analyzed using data provided by Xetra is the liquidity of their shares. For each listed ETF (as well as ETN and ETC) Xetra publishes the value of Xetra liquidity measure (XLM) that shows the liquidity of the electronic book trading in the dimension of the implicit transaction costs that is stated as basis points for a selected value of the transaction in euro; in the case of ETFs it is usually provided for the roundtrip transaction of €100,000 (Xetra, 2018b).[4] As of August 2017, there were almost 25 ETFs with XLM lower than 5 b.p. and more than 160 with XLM lower than 10 b.p. (out of 1156 listed (Xetra, 2017)). Lyxor Euro Cash UCITS ETF was the fund with the highest liquidity as its XLM was at just 0.97. Excluding some extreme values of XLM, its arithmetic mean for ETFs was calculated as c. 45 b.p. and weighted mean (weighted using the shares in total assets) was much lower, at c. 17 b.p.; for most of the largest ETFs liquidity is very high (as usual on most markets). For synthetic funds the weighted mean XLM was above the average for the entire market (c. 20.7 b.p.). Again it may be explained by the prevalence of the relatively smaller (in comparison to physical) funds in this category. We address the issue of liquidity again at the end of this section.

One of the most distinguishing innovations on the German ETFs market, yet still of minimal significance, are active ETFs. According to some sources (Meziani, 2016; Wiandt, 2000) first such funds in Germany had been launched as early as 2000. However, due to scarce data it is difficult to assess whether they had in fact could have been categorized as ETFs or if they had been another type of investment fund yet labeled in a similar way (reports of XTF from 2001 include the category of "actively managed funds" which was later dropped; it could suggest the second explanation). According to the list of the active funds provided in the XTF report for August 2017 (Xetra, 2017), the oldest ETF in this group still listed at the time report was prepared was launched in January 2011. Their role in the subperiod for which detailed statistics are acquirable (i.e., since 2014) has remained negligible: their assets constituted merely c. 0.7% of the combined market for all types of ETFs available through Xetra and even less (c. 0.2%) of the aggregate turnover. Approximately 60% of all active ETFs' assets and turnover were in the shares of one single fund, that is, PIMCO Euro Short Maturity Source UCITS ETF.

---

[2]According to the monthly reports of the World Federation of Exchanges.

[3]All orders of the value not exceeding €25,000 are classified as placed by "private" rather than institutional investors.

[4]Detailed methodology is described in Gomber and Schweickert (2002). Values of XLM may be interpreted in terms of the market impact costs (consisting of liquidity premium and adverse price movement), e.g. XLM of 10.0 means that in case of order of €100,000, the market impact costs of buying and selling shares of certain ETF were at €100. Consequently, the higher the value of XLM, the lower the liquidity of the fund's shares.

Stuttgart Stock Exchange (*Börse Stuttgart*) is the second largest trading venue for the shares of ETFs in Germany in terms of value of turnover (there are only a few funds classified as primary listed on this exchange according to the Lipper's database). It is the biggest exchange in Germany in terms of the number of listed ETFs, with approximately one third more than on XTF. One of its parts is ETFs' trading segment, ETF Bestx that is aimed at providing services for the retail investors, in contrast with the Xetra ETFs' segment dominated by institutional users; it covers, though, about 400 out of more than 1500 listed funds (Börse Stuttgart, 2018). ETNs and ETCs are also traded on the Stuttgart Stock Exchange. Statistics of the Federation of European Securities Exchanges (FESE) show that in 2015 Stuttgart Stock Exchange was on the sixth place in Europe in terms of the value of ETFs' turnover and in 2016 on even higher fourth place (Federation of European Securities Exchanges, 2018). However, they do not include Borsa Italiana and London Stock Exchange, therefore actual place of this exchange was two places lower as on both the turnover was markedly higher. In comparison to its main German counterpart, XTF of the Deutsche Börse, position of the Stuttgart Stock Exchange is very weak. In 2015 it accounted for only c. 6% of the total turnover in the shares of ETFs on these two German stock exchanges (turnover on the remaining exchanges is much lower) and in 2016 for c. 7% (Federation of European Securities Exchanges, 2018).

The future development of the German ETFs market will be affected by a number of determinants, some of them common for most European countries, including the legal changes such as the ones linked to MiFID II. One of the directive's requirements concerns the necessary disclosures with regard to the OTC transactions in the shares of ETFs; trade reporting services provided by the Deutsche Börse (2016a) were declared by the controlling company to meet these requirements which may further boost the development of the funds listed on this exchange. Other possible factors were discussed in Chapter 4, Determinants of the European Exchange-Traded Funds Markets Development.

After the discussion concerning German ETFs market, we now present the other, related segment of the capital markets in this country, that is, markets for ETNs and ETCs (in order to ensure better flow of the analysis, we label ETFs, ETNs, and ETCs together as ETPs). Analysis of ETNs and ETCs in terms of their assets is hindered by insufficient data in the Lipper's database that we applied for the analysis of the corresponding parameter in case of ETFs (there are many breaks in the time series and for some products no information is provided). As a result, in the remainder of this section we use mostly data from the reports on the XTF segment of the Deutsche Börse published by Xetra[5] (we omit other German exchanges), publications of the Deutsche Bank and, as supplement, data extracted from the Lipper's database and other sources. We examine all ETNs and ETCs listed on Xetra (regardless of their primary listing location) and focus, as in the previous sections, on the assets indicators.

The first ETCs were launched in Germany in 2006 and ETNs in 2009 (Marszk, 2017a). According to the Xetra's reports, the oldest ETCs and ETNs still listed in August 2017 had listing dates in October 2006 and March 2010 respectively; in both cases the first such products were launched by the provider ETF Securities. In spite of some historical discrepancies (Deutsche Bank, 2010), German ETNs and ETCs have become highly similar, with the two enduring important differences:

1. *Exposure:* ETCs track the returns of commodities (indexes of commodity markets or particular commodities) whereas ETNs track non-commodity indexes.[6]
2. *Replication method:* ETCs employ both physical and synthetic structure (the former usually in case of metals) whereas ETNs exclusively synthetic.

Most importantly, both have the form of bonds traded on the stock exchange. Basic attributes of ETCs and ETNs were presented in Section 2.2. A more detailed overview can be found in, inter alia, the publications of Bienkowski (2007), Deutsche Bank (2010), Wright, Diavatopoulos, and Felton (2010), Fassas (2011), Commerzbank (2016), Marszk (2017a, 2017b), Rakowski, Shirley, and Stark (2017), Dorfleitner, Gerl, and Gerer (2018), and Lettau and Madhavan (2018).

ETCs play much more significant role in the German ETPs market than ETNs in all dimensions possible to analyze. As of August 2017, their number was at 246 while there were 132 listed ETNs. Differences between the two categories become even more significant when their assets are considered. Figs. 5.8 and 5.9 show the changes in the assets of ETCs and ETNs listed on Xetra in the period 2010–2016. As it may be clearly noticed, the assets of ETCs as well as their shares in the total assets of ETPs have been much higher than those of ETNs; however,

---

[5]Acquired from http://www.deutsche-boerse-cash-market.com/dbcm-en/instruments-statistics/statistics/etf-etp-statistics/.

[6]There are some rare ETNs with partial commodity exposure such as ETFS Bearish USD versus Commodity Currency Basket Securities ETN or ETFS Bearish EUR versus G10 Currency Basket ETN.

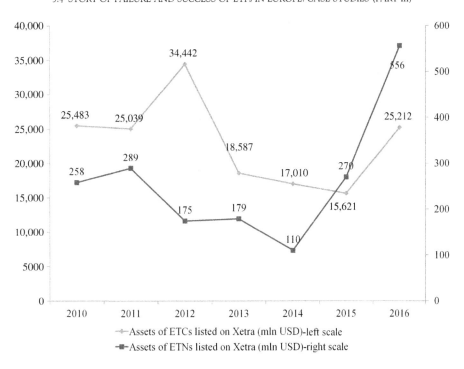

**FIGURE 5.8**    Values of assets of ETCs and ETNs listed on Xetra. 2010–16, year-end data. *Source: Authors' elaboration.*

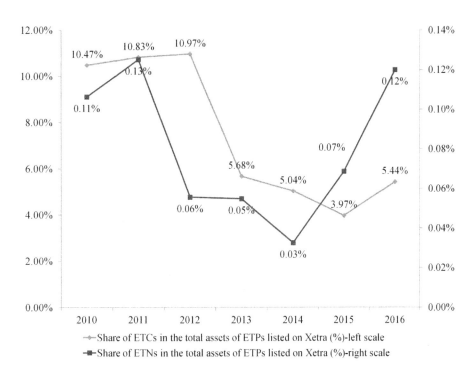

**FIGURE 5.9**    Shares of ETCs and ETNs in the total market for ETPs on Xetra. 2010–16, year-end data. *Source: Authors' elaboration.*

in both dimensions German ETPs market has been dominated over the entire period by ETFs. Maximum value of the assets of ETCs reached c. $34 billion at the end of 2012; peak assets of ETNs (at c. $556 million) were observed at the end of 2016. However, for comparison, at the end of 2016 total assets of ETFs listed on Xetra were at the record-high level of $406 billion (the assets of ETFs primary listed in Germany were considerably lower, at $149 billion yet still much higher than in case of the other products). With the exception of some subperiods (e.g., 2010–12 in case of ETCs, or 2014–16 in case of ETNs) their market share was not increasing (see Fig. 5.9) which proves that assets of ETFs have generally been increasing more rapidly (in other words, we may state that the diffusion of ETFs has been more rapid and their expansion on the local capital markets more prevalent). Three categories of ETPs may also be compared based on turnover's statistics. Similarly to the data on assets, turnover of ETCs and ETNs has been below 10% of the total turnover of ETPs over the entire considered time period (relatively the highest at about 2013). Turnover of ETCs has been many times higher than that of ETNs (in August 2017 the difference was over 40 times).

In line with their most fundamental attribute, German ETCs provide exposure to the commodity markets. Most assets in this category are managed by ETCs tracking the returns of precious metals, above all gold. Other significant categories are products with exposure to the oil market, industrial metals and agriculture yet with much smaller assets. Most ETCs track returns of single commodities, funds with exposure to baskets of commodities are less popular. Main categories of ETNs (in terms of managed assets) include products with exposure to the indexes of the stock market (usually geared) and currencies (it is the oldest group), less important groups are ETNs linked to the volatility indexes, or bond market (Johnston, 2011), among others. The main provider of the ETCs listed on Xetra is ETF Securities (c. 45% of the total assets), other significant issuers are the Deutsche Börse Commodities and Deutsche AM. ETF Securities is also the biggest provider of ETNs, with even bigger market share of over 60%. Most of the remaining market share belongs to Boost ETP, the subsidiary of WisdomTree Investments. Structure of the German ETC and ETN market in terms of turnover is comparable.[7]

Tables 5.7 and 5.8 include key information about the ten largest ETCs and ETNs traded on Xetra, sorted according to their size. Table 5.7 confirms that the key group of Xetra-listed ETCs were products with the exposure to gold; 7 out of 10 ETCs presented in Table 5.7. were such products. The biggest one was Xetra-Gold, with over 22% of the total market's assets (and more than 43% in terms of turnover). It was also one of the most liquid ETCs available, with XLM of 4.75 b.p. (there were only three ETCs with the lower XLM, among them ETFS Physical Gold, the second-largest product in this category). Interestingly, it was the only ETP provided by the Deutsche Börse Commodities, a joint venture of the German leading stock exchange and several banks (as well as operator of the gold refineries); it employed physical replication method which means that gold is bought and stored—each unit of Xetra-Gold was covered by one gram of gold (Xetra-Gold, 2018). Other gold ETCs listed in Table 5.7 were products provided by ETF Securities and Deutsche AM (one by Source); their liquidity was also very high and, as their names indicate, they also physically held gold. Apart from gold ETCs, among the 10 largest ETCs in Germany there was one product with the exposure to another precious metal, silver, and two tracking the returns on various types of crude oil; all three were managed by ETF Securities and were much less liquid than their gold counterparts. Another conclusion that may be drawn from Table 5.7 is that ETCs listed on Xetra were rarely domiciled in Germany and more frequently in Jersey (for legal reasons).

In the case of the largest ETNs (see Table 5.8) there is no category of products they may be classified as distinctive leader of this group. The biggest ETN was Boost Bund 10Y 3× Short Daily ETP aimed at tracking BNP Paribas Bund Future Index, with assets of about $60 million and over 13% share in the total assets of ETNs. However, in terms of turnover its share was much lower, below 2%. All remaining ETNs listed in Table 5.8 are products with the exposure to either equity or currency market (with substantially different tracked indexes). The biggest equity ETN listed on Xetra in the examined time was Boost S&P 500 3× Short Daily ETP that provided investors with the inverse daily returns on the S&P 500 index (total return) multiplied by three. Even though it gathered substantial assets, its units were rather illiquid as proven by very high XLM (the highest in the group of the largest products) and low value of turnover (below 0.5% share in the total turnover of ETNs on Xetra).[8] Other largest equity ETNs offered exposure to, among other, the indexes: EURO STOXX 50, NASDAQ 100, and DAX 30 (prevalently geared). ETFS Long USD Short EUR was the biggest currency ETN (again, its turnover was rather low). All three currency ETNs listed in Table 5.8 were linked in various ways to the exchange rate of the US dollar. Analogically to ETCs, almost all largest ETNs were domiciled outside Germany and were managed by Boost ETP or ETF Securities (Ireland was used as domicile by the former and Jersey by the latter); the only exception is ETN provided by Commerzbank within its Coba product line.

---

[7]All turnover data presented in the remainder of this section are monthly order book turnover values in August 2017 (Xetra, 2017). Both ETCs and ETNs are also traded OTC; for ETCs the value of OTC turnover (data on OTC transactions provided by Clearstream, also part of the Deutsche Börse group) was approximately three times higher than in the case of the order book transactions, for ETNs it was considerably lower.

[8]Over the next few months (after the analyzed time period) the assets of this ETN have decreased significantly in favor of the "twin" ETN, Boost S&P 500 3x Leverage Daily ETP, due to the increases of S&P since September 2017 onwards. The same applies to most other short equity ETN (and other ETPs).

**TABLE 5.7** The Biggest ETCs Primary-Listed in Germany According to the Values of Assets as of End of August 2017

| ETC | Assets (mln USD) | Share in the total assets of ETCs in Germany (%) | Exposure class | Provider | Domicile | XLM (b.p.) |
|---|---|---|---|---|---|---|
| Xetra-Gold | 7190.04 | 22.50 | Gold | Deutsche Börse Commodities | Germany | 4.75 |
| ETFS Physical Gold | 6092.68 | 19.06 | Gold | ETF Securities | Jersey | 4.15 |
| Source Physical Gold ETC (P-ETC) | 4795.70 | 13.22 | Gold | Source | Ireland | 7.84 |
| Gold Bullion Securities | 4225.37 | 15.00 | Gold | ETF Securities | UK | 4.82 |
| db Physical Gold Euro Hedged ETC | 1729.35 | 5.41 | Gold | Deutsche AM | Germany | 6.77 |
| ETFS Physical Silver | 960.78 | 3.01 | Silver | ETF Securities | Jersey | 12.96 |
| ETFS WTI Crude Oil | 792.82 | 2.48 | Crude oil | ETF Securities | Jersey | 14.28 |
| db Physical Gold ETC (EUR) | 555.39 | 1.74 | Gold | Deutsche AM | Jersey | 5.70 |
| ETFS Physical Swiss Gold | 544.79 | 1.70 | Gold | ETF Securities | Jersey | 11.02 |
| ETFS Brent 1mth | 386.63 | 1.21 | Crude oil | ETF Securities | Jersey | 19.26 |

*Note*: All data according to Deutsche Bank (2017) and monthly reports of Xetra. Domiciles determined based on the reports of the providers. *XLM*, Xetra liquidity measure.
*Authors' elaboration.*

**TABLE 5.8** The Biggest ETNs Primary-Listed in Germany According to the Values of Assets as of End of August 2017

| ETN | Assets (mln USD) | Share in the total assets of ETNs in Germany (%) | Exposure class | Provider | Domicile | XLM (b.p.) |
|---|---|---|---|---|---|---|
| Boost Bund 10Y 3× Short Daily ETP | 82.28 | 13.20 | Bond | Boost ETP | Ireland | 31.63 |
| Boost S&P 500 3× Short Daily ETP | 60.07 | 9.64 | Equity | Boost ETP | Ireland | 232.65 |
| ETFS Long USD Short EUR | 56.50 | 9.07 | Currency | ETF Securities | Jersey | 17.98 |
| Coba ETN 1× SPXF Daily Long | 45.51 | 7.30 | Equity | Commerzbank | Germany | 115.10 |
| Boost EURO STOXX 50 3× Short Daily ETP | 28.58 | 4.59 | Equity | Boost ETP | Ireland | 86.22 |
| ETFS Bullish USD vs Commodity Currency Basket Securities | 28.14 | 4.52 | Currency | ETF Securities | Jersey | 25.29 |
| Boost NASDAQ 100 3× Short Daily ETP | 26.97 | 4.33 | Equity | Boost ETP | Ireland | 122.65 |
| ETFS Short USD Long EUR | 25.34 | 4.07 | Currency | ETF Securities | Jersey | 19.73 |
| Boost EURO STOXX Banks 3× Leverage Daily ETP | 20.55 | 3.30 | Equity | Boost ETP | Ireland | 54.16 |
| ETFS 3× Daily Short DAX 30 | 19.07 | 3.06 | Equity | ETF Securities | Jersey | 25.29 |

*Note*: All data according to the Deutsche Bank (2017b) and monthly reports of Xetra. Domiciles determined based on the reports of the providers. *XLM*, Xetra liquidity measure.
*Authors' elaboration.*

Another aspect of ETCs and ETNs that should be considered is the tracking method utilized by their providers in order to gain the declared exposure. Due to the prevalence of ETCs with exposure to the prices of precious metals (above all gold; see Table 5.7), the most often applied structure of the Xetra-listed ETCs is physical, including the purchase and storage of the tracked type of precious metal. Such products accounted for over 90% of the total assets of ETCs. The rest is managed mostly by ETCs with synthetic structure, supported by the collaterals held in trusts. In the case of ETNs almost all products are built and managed using the latter method (with a few very minor exceptions backed by the third party rather than collateral).

**TABLE 5.9**   Xetra Liquidity Measure (XLM) for the Xetra-Listed ETFs, ETCs, and ETNs as of August 2017

| Category of ETPs | Arithmetic mean (b.p.) | Weighted mean (b.p.) | Lowest XLM in the category (b.p.) | Name of the product with the lowest XLM |
|---|---|---|---|---|
| ETFs | 45 | 17 | 0.97 | Lyxor Euro Cash UCITS ETF |
| ETCs | 102 | 14 | 4.15 | ETFS Physical Gold |
| ETNs | 98 | 84 | 17.16 | ETFS Long AUD Short EUR |

*Note*: Extremely high values of XLM were excluded. Weights applied are shares in total assets of the given category. Only products with assets of at least $1 million were considered in the determination of the products with the lowest XLM.
*Authors' elaboration.*

Finally, in order to complete our discussion of the German ETPs market, we shortly compare the values of XLM (base liquidity measure provided by Xetra) for the three types of ETPs: ETFs, ETCs, and ETNs (see Table 5.9). Despite substantial differences between arithmetic means for ETFs and ETCs, caused by the composition of the ETCs market (with a large number of small illiquid products), weighted means are highly similar; the difference is only 3 b.p. It shows that, in terms of liquidity, Xetra-listed ETFs and ETCs are comparable, in particular when the largest products in both categories are considered (their XLM are usually at about 10, rarely exceeding this value). The fund with the lowest XLM (i.e., the most liquid) was one of the money-market synthetic ETFs (provided by Lyxor) and in case of ETCs it was one of the physically backed gold ETFs. ETCs that provide exposure to asset classes other than precious metals are generally relatively less liquid.

The underdevelopment of the ETN segment (indicated earlier by, for instance, the assets and turnover measures) is proven also in this dimension. Average values of the XLM indicators of the Xetra-listed ETNs are much higher than in the case of the two other types of ETPs. Even in the case of the most liquid product in August 2017 (with exposure to the AUD and EUR exchange rate) it was well above 10 b.p. In contrast with ETFs and ETCs, the largest ETNs are not necessarily more liquid than the smaller product. It proves the illiquidity of ETNs which may be perceived as one of their underdevelopment's symptoms (however, from a different perspective, it may be regarded as a cause of this situation rather than its effect). Overall, ETNs remain a niche on the German ETPs market; the role of ETCs is more significant yet still much less substantial than the position of the dominating ETFs.

# References

Abubakar, A., & Kassim, S. (2018). Institutional and macroeconomic determinants of financial development in the OIC countries. *Global Business and Economics Review*, 20(4), 410–424.

Adam, T., Benecká, S., & Matějů, J. (2018). Financial stress and its non-linear impact on CEE exchange rates. *Journal of Financial Stability*, 36, 346–360.

Aggarwal, R., & Schofield, L. (2014). The growth of global ETFs and regulatory challenges. In J. Kose, A. K. Makhija, & S. P. Ferris (Eds.), *Advances in financial economics* (pp. 77–102). Emerald Group Publishing Limited.

Allen, F., Carletti, E., Cull, R., Qian, J., Senbet, L., & Valenzuela, P. (2014). The African financial development and financial inclusion gaps. *Journal of African Economies*, 23(5), 614–642.

Aluko, O. A., & Azeez, B. A. (2018). Effectiveness of legal institutions in stock market development in sub-Saharan Africa. *Economic Change and Restructuring*, 1–13. Available from https://link.springer.com/article/10.1007%2Fs10644-018-9233-x.

Amenc, N., Ducoulombier, F., Goltz, F., & Le Sourd, V. (2015). *The EDHEC European ETF survey 2014*. Nice: EDHEC-Risk Institute.

Amenc, N., Ducoulombier, F., Goltz, F., & Tang, L. (2012). *What are the risks of European ETFs?* EDHEC-Risk Institute.

Amenc, N., Goltz, F., & Le Sourd, V. (2017). *The EDHEC European ETF and smart beta survey*. EDHEC-Risk Institute.

Anderson, S., Born, J., & Schnusenberg, O. (2010). *Closed-end funds, exchange-traded funds, and hedge funds*. US: Springer.

Andrianova, S., & Demetriades, P. O. (2018). Financial development and financial fragility: Two sides of the same coin? *Comparative Economic Studies*, 60(1), 54–68.

Apostolakis, G., & Papadopoulos, A. P. (2018). Financial stability, monetary stability and growth: A PVAR analysis. *Open Economies Review*, in press.

Arcand, J. L., Berkes, E., & Panizza, U. (2015). Too much finance? *Journal of Economic Growth*, 20(2), 105–148.

Ashraf, B. N. (2018). Do trade and financial openness matter for financial development? Bank-level evidence from emerging market economies. *Research in International Business and Finance*, 44, 434–458.

Asongu, S. A. (2014). Financial development dynamic thresholds of financial globalisation: Evidence from Africa. *Journal of Economics Studies*, 41(2), 166–195.

Asongu, S. A., Anyanwu, J. C., & Tchamyou, V. S. (2017). Technology-driven information sharing and conditional financial development in Africa. *Information Technology for Development*, in press.

Asongu, S. A., & De Moor, L. (2017). Financial globalisation dynamic thresholds for financial development: Evidence from Africa. *The European Journal of Development Research*, 29(1), 192–212.

Asongu, S. A., & Moulin, B. (2016). The role of ICT in reducing information asymmetry for financial access. *Research in International Business and Finance, 38*, 202–213.

Ayadi, R., Arbak, E., Naceur, S. B., & De Groen, W. P. (2015). Determinants of financial development across the Mediterranean. In R. Ayadi, M. Dabrowski, & L. De Wulf (Eds.), *Economic and social development of the Southern and Eastern Mediterranean countries*. Cham: Springer.

Bayar, Y. (2017). *Foreign capital inflows and stock market development in Turkey. New Trends in finance and accounting* (pp. 71–81). Springer.

Beck, T., & Levine, R. (2004). Stock markets, banks and growth: Panel evidence. *Journal of Banking and Finance, 28*(3), 423–442.

Bencivenga, V. R., & Smith, B. D. (1991). Financial intermediation and endogenous growth. *The Review of Economic Studies, 58*(2), 95–209.

Bhattacharya, U., Loos, B., Meyer, S., & Hackethal, A. (2017). Abusing ETFs. *Review of Finance, 21*(3), 1217–1250.

Bhattacharyay, B. N. (2013). Determinants of bond market development in Asia. *Journal of Asian Economics, 24*, 124–137.

Bhattacharyya, S., & Hodler, R. (2014). Do natural resource revenues hinder financial development? The role of political institutions. *World Development, 57*, 101–113.

Bhunia, A. (2011). An impact of ICT on the growth of capital market – Empirical evidence from Indian stock market exchange. *Information and Knowledge Management, 1*(2), 7–14.

Bienkowski, N. (2007). Exchange traded commodities. Led by gold, ETCs opened world of commodities to investors. *Alchemist, 48*, 6–8.

Börse Stuttgart. *About ETF Bestx.* (2018).

Brunner-Reumann, U. (2005). Exchange traded funds from a lawyer's perspective – The case of Germany. In E. Hehn (Ed.), *Exchange traded funds: Structure, regulation and application of a new fund class* (pp. 95–117). Springer.

Burger, J., & Warnock, F. (2006). Local currency bond markets. *NBER working paper, 12552*.

Cardarelli, R., Elekdag, S., & Lall, S. (2011). Financial stress and economic contractions. *Journal of Financial Stability, 7*(2), 78–97.

Carré, E., & L'œillet, G. (2018). The literature on the finance–growth nexus in the aftermath of the financial crisis: A review. *Comparative Economic Studies, 60*(1), 161–180.

Cavallo, E., & Scartascini, C. *Interest groups and government capabilities matter for financial development.* (2012). <https://voxeu.org/article/what-matters-financial-development?quicktabs_tabbed_recent_articles_block = 1> Accessed 02.09.18.

Cherkes, M., Sagi, J., & Stanton, R. (2009). A liquidity-based theory of closed-end funds. *The Review of Financial Studies, 22*(1), 257–297.

Çiftçioğlu, S., & Bein, M. A. (2017). The relationship between financial development and unemployment in selected countries of the European Union. *European Review, 25*(2), 307–319.

Čihák, M., Demirgüç-Kunt, A., Feyen, E., & Levine, R. (2012). *Benchmarking financial development around the world. World Bank policy research working paper, 6175*. Washington, DC: World Bank.

Čihák, M., Demirgüç-Kunt, A., Feyen, E., & Levine, R. (2013). Financial development in 205 economies, 1960 to 2010. *Journal of Financial Perspectives, 1*(2), 17–36.

Claessens, S., Schmukler, S., & Klingebiel, D. (2007). Government bonds in domestic and foreign currency: The role of institutional and macroeconomic factors. *Review of International Economics, 15*(2), 370–413.

Commerzbank. (2016). ETCs & ETNs. Gesichert ist einfach besser *[ETCs and ETNs. Safe is simply better]*. Frankfurt/Main: Commerzbank AG. (in German).

Cuthbertson, K., & Nitzsche, D. (2012). Winners and losers: German equity mutual funds. *The European Journal of Finance, 19*(10), 951–963.

Czauderna, K., Riedel, C., & Wagner, N. (2015). Liquidity and conditional market returns: Evidence from German exchange traded funds. *Economic Modelling, 51*, 454–459.

de Gregorio, J., & Guidotti, P. (1995). Financial development and economic growth. *World Development, 23*(3), 433–448.

Demetriades, P. O., & Hussein, K. A. (1996). Does financial development cause economic growth? Time-series evidence from 16 countries. *Journal of Development Economics, 51*, 387–415.

Demetriades, P. O., & Rousseau, P. L. (2016). The changing face of financial development. *Economics Letters, 141*, 87–90.

Demirgüç-Kunt, A., Klapper, L., Singer, D., & Van Oudheusden, P. (2014). The Global Findex database 2014: Measuring financial inclusion around the world. *World Bank policy research working paper, 7255*.

Deutsche Bank. (2010). *The race for assets in the European commodity exchange-traded products space*. London.

Deutsche Bank. *Europe ETF + quarterly directory.* (2017).

Deutsche Börse. *ETF lifecycle solutions: Listing & trading.* (2016a).

Deutsche Börse. *Xetra: Europe's largest trading platform for ETFs.* (2016b).

Deutsche Börse Cash Market. *15 years of ETF trading in Europe & on Xetra. Facts & Figures.* (2015)

Deville, L. (2008). Exchange traded funds: History, trading and research. In M. Doumpos, P. Pardalos, & C. Zopounidis (Eds.), *Handbook of financial engineering* (pp. 67–98). Springer.

Dohle, M. (2016). Dax ETFs: Tracking or shaping the market? *Investment Europe, February 22, 2016*.

Dorfleitner, G., Gerl, A., & Gerer, J. (2018). The pricing efficiency of exchange-traded commodities. *Review of Managerial Science, 12*, 255–284.

Dromel, N. L., Kolakez, E., & Lehmann, E. (2010). Credit constraints and the persistence of unemployment. *Labour Economics, 17*(5), 823–834.

Drummer, D., Feuerriegel, S., & Neumann, D. (2017). Crossing the next frontier: The role of ICT in driving the financialization of credit. *Journal of Information Technology, 32*(3), 218–233.

Duprey, T., & Klaus, B. (2017). How to predict financial stress? An assessment of Markov switching models. *European Central Bank working paper series, 2027*.

Duprey, T., Klaus, B., & Peltonen, T. (2015). Dating systemic financial stress episodes in the EU countries. *European Central Bank working paper series, 1873*.

Duprey, T., Klaus, B., & Peltonen, T. (2017). Dating systemic financial stress episodes in the EU countries. *Journal of Financial Stability, 32*, 30–56.

Eichengreen, B., & Luengnaruemitchai, P. (2004). Why doesn't Asia have bigger bond markets? *NBER working paper, 10576*.

Elkhuizen, L., Hermes, N., Jacobs, J., & Meesters, A. (2018). Financial development, financial liberalization and social capital. *Applied Economics, 50*(11), 1268–1288.

Ernst, E., Semmler, W., & Haider, A. (2017). Debt-deflation, financial market stress and regime change – Evidence from Europe using MRVAR. *Journal of Economic Dynamics and Control, 81*, 115–139.

Eryigit, S. B., & Dulgeroglu, E. (2015). How to measure the level of financial development. In Ö. Olgu, H. Dinçer, & Ü. Hacıoğlu (Eds.), *Handbook of research on strategic developments and regulatory practice in global finance* (pp. 260–286). Hershey, PA: IGI Global.

Fassas, A. P. (2011). Exchange-traded products investing and precious metal prices. *Journal of Derivatives & Hedge Funds, 18*(2), 127–140.

Federation of European Securities Exchanges. *Historical data. Monthly factsheets.* (2018).

Gardner, L., Lee, S., Alford, M., & Cresson, J. (2017). The effects of information communication technology on stock market capitalization: A panel data analysis. *Business and Economic Research, 7*(1), 261–272.

Gomber, P., & Schweickert, U. (2002). Der Market Impact: Liquiditätsmaß im Elektronischen Wertpapierhandel [The market impact – Liquidity measure in electronic securities trading]. *Die Bank, 7*, 485–489. (in German).

Greenwood, J., & Jovanovic, B. (1990). Financial development, growth, and the distribution of income. *Journal of Political Economy, 98*(5), 1076–1107.

Greenwood, J., & Smith, B. (1997). Financial markets in development, and the development of financial markets. *Journal of Economic Dynamics and Control, 21*, 145–182.

Grjebine, T., & Tripier, F. (2016). Finance and growth: From the business cycle to the long run. *Working papers 2016–28, CEPII Research Center.*

Hamdi, K. (2015). The determinants of financial development: Empirical evidence from developed and developing countries. *Applied Economics and Finance, 2*(4).

Hasan, M. R., & Murshed, S. M. (2017). Does civil war hamper financial development? *Defence and Peace Economics, 28*(2), 188–207.

Ho, S.-Y., & Lyke, B. N. (2017). Determinants of stock market development: A review of the literature. *Studies in Economics and Finance, 34*(1), 143–164.

Ho, S.-Y., & Odhiambo, N. M. (2018). Analysing the macroeconomic drivers of stock market development in the Philippines. *Cogent Economics & Finance, 6*(1), 1451265.

Holló, D., Kremer, M., & Lo Duca, M. (2012). CISS – A composite indicator of systemic stress in the financial system. *European Central Bank working paper series, 1426.*

Horvath, R., Horvatova, E., & Siranova, M. (2017). *Financial development, rule of law and wealth inequality: Bayesian model averaging evidence. BOFIT discussion papers, 12/2017.* Bank of Finland, Institute for Economies in Transition.

Hunag, Y. (2010). *Determinants of financial development.* Palgrave Macmillan.

Johnston, M. (2011). Country-specific bond ETNs debut. *ETF Database*, March 24, 2011.

Jordaan, J. A., Dima, B., & Gole , I. (2016). Do societal values influence financial development? New evidence on the effects of post materialism and institutions on stock markets. *Journal of Economic Behavior & Organization, 132*, 197–216.

Kim, D.-H., Chen, T.-C., & Lin, S.-C. (2018). Finance and unemployment: New panel evidence. *Journal of Economic Policy Reform*, in press.

King, R., & Levine, R. (1993). Finance and growth: Schumpeter might be right. *The Quarterly Journal of Economics, 108*(3), 717–737.

Kliesen, K. L., Owyang, M. T., & Vermann, E. K. (2012). Disentangling diverse measures: A survey of financial stress indexes. *Federal Reserve Bank of St. Louis Review, 94*(5), 369–397.

Kurt-Gumuş, G., Evrim-Mandaci, P., Tvaronavičienė, M., & Aktan, B. (2013). Determinants of stock market development: Evidence from advanced and emerging markets in a long span. *Business: Theory and Practice, 14*(1), 51–56.

Laeven, L., & Valencia, F. (2012). Systemic banking crises database: An update. *IMF working paper, 12/163.*

Lee, M., Jung, C., & Lee, T. (2018). Social order and financial development. *Economics Bulletin, 38*(2), 901–907.

Lettau, M., & Madhavan, A. (2018). Exchange-traded funds 101 for economists. *Journal of Economic Perspectives, 32*(1), 135–154.

Levine, R. (1997). Financial development and economic growth: Views and agenda. *Journal of Economic Literature, 35*(2), 688–726.

Levine, R., Loayza, N., & Beck, T. (2000). Finance and the sources of growth. *Journal of Financial Economics, 58*(1/2), 261–300.

Levine, R., & Zervos, S. (1998). Stock markets, banks and economic growth. *American Economic Review, 88*, 537–558.

Lo Duca, M., Koban, A., Basten, M., Bengtsson, E., Klaus, B., Kusmierczyk, P., et al. (2017). A new database for financial crises in European countries. *European Central Bank Occasional Paper Series, 194.*

Marszk, A. (2017a). Development of innovative financial products in Europe: Case of exchange-traded products in Germany. *Institute of Economic Research working papers, 153/2017.*

Marszk, A. (2017b). Exchange traded commodities as a category of innovative products on European financial markets. *e-Finanse, 13*(2), 14–21.

Meziani, A. S. (2016). *Exchange-traded funds: Investment practices and tactical approaches.* Palgrave Macmillan.

Milonas, N. T., & Rompotis, G. G. (2015). The performance of German fixed-income ETFs in the presence of the debt crisis. *Aestimatio: The IEB International Journal of Finance, 11*, 46–77.

Miquel-Flores, I. *Do leveraged ETFs induce volatility on their underlying indices? The German case.* (2015). <https://papers.ssrn.com/sol3/papers.cfm?abstract_id = 2928716> Accessed 30.08.18.

Morningstar. (2017). *A guided tour of the European ETF marketplace.*

Mu, Y., Phelps, P., & Stotsky, J. G. (2013). Bond markets in Africa. *Review of Development Finance, 3*, 121–135.

Naceur, S. B., Ghazouani, S., & Omran, M. (2007). The determinants of stock market development in the Middle-Eastern and North African region. *Managerial Finance, 33*(7), 477–489.

Naumenko, K., & Chystiakova, O. (2015). An empirical study on the differences between synthetic and physical ETFs. *International Journal of Economics and Finance, 7*(3), 24–35.

Newton, S. (2017). The determinants of stock market development in emerging economies: Examining the impact of corporate governance and regulatory reforms (I). In M. Ojo, & J. Van Akkeren (Eds.), *Value relevance of accounting information in capital markets* (pp. 114–125). Hershey, PA: IGI Global.

Ng, A., Dewandaru, G., & Ibrahim, M. H. (2015). Property rights and the stock market-growth nexus. *The North American Journal of Economics and Finance, 32*, 48–63.

Ng, A., Ibrahim, M. H., & Mirakhor, A. (2016). Does trust contribute to stock market development? *Economic Modelling, 52*, 239–250.

Oet, M.V., Bianco, T., Gramlich, D., & Ong, S. (2012). Financial stress index: A lens for supervising the financial system. *Federal Reserve Bank of Cleveland working paper, 12–37.*

Okwu, A. T. (2015). ICT adoption and financial markets: A study of the leading stock exchange markets in Africa. *Journal of Accounting and Management, V*(2), 53–76.

Osterhoff, F., & Kaserer, C. (2016). Determinants of tracking error in German ETFs − The role of market liquidity. *Managerial Finance, 42*(5), 417–437.

Panizza, U. (2018). Nonlinearities in the relationship between finance and growth. *Comparative Economic Studies, 60*(1), 44–53.

Rahman, A. A., Sidek, N. Z. M., & Tafri, F. H. (2009). Macroeconomic determinants of Malaysian stock market. *African Journal of Business Management, 3*(3), 95–106.

Rakowski, D., Shirley, S. E., & Stark, J. R. (2017). Tail-risk hedging, dividend chasing, and investment constraints: The use of exchange-traded notes by mutual funds. *Journal of Empirical Finance, 44,* 91–107.

Raza, S. H., Shahzadi, H., & Akram, M. (2014). Exploring the determinants of financial development (using panel data on developed and developing countries). *Journal of Finance and Economics, 2*(5), 166–172.

Robinson, J. (1952). *The rate of interest and other essays.* London: MacMillan.

Rompotis, G. G. (2012). The German exchange traded funds. *The IUP Journal of Applied Finance, 18*(4), 62–82.

Rousseau, P., & Wachtel, P. (2011). What is happening to the impact of financial deepening on economic growth? *Economic Inquiry, 49*(1), 276–288.

Rousseau, P., & Wachtel, P. (2017). Episodes of financial deepening: Credit booms or growth generators? In P. Rousseau, & P. Wachtel (Eds.), *Financial systems and economic growth* (pp. 52–75). Cambridge University Press.

Rudzkis, R., & Valkavičienė, R. (2014). Econometric models of the impact of macroeconomic processes on the stock market in the Baltic countries. *Technological and Economic Development of Economy, 20*(4), 783–800.

Sahay, R., Cihak, M., N'Diaye, P., Barajas, A., Bi, R., Ayala, D., et al. (2015). Rethinking financial deepening: Stability and growth in emerging markets. *IMF staff discussion note, 15.*

Salahuddin, M., & Gow, J. (2016). The effects of internet usage, financial development and trade openness on economic growth in South Africa: A time series analysis. *Telematics and Informatics, 33*(4), 1141–1154.

Sassi, S., & Goaied, M. (2013). Financial development, ICT diffusion and economic growth: Lessons from MENA region. *Telecommunications Policy, 37*(4), 252–261.

Schinasi, G.J., & Todd Smith, T. (1998). Fixed-income markets in the United States, Europe, and Japan-some lessons for emerging markets. *IMF working paper, 98/173.*

Schmidhammer, C., Lobe, S., & Röder, K. (2010). Intraday pricing of ETFs and certificates replicating the German DAX index. *Review of Managerial Science, 5,* 337–351.

Sepehrdoust, H. (2018). Impact of information and communication technology and financial development on economic growth of OPEC developing economies. *Kasetsart Journal of Social Sciences,* in press.

Shahbaz, M., Rehman, I. U., & Afza, T. (2016). Macroeconomic determinants of stock market capitalization in an emerging market: Fresh evidence from cointegration with unknown structural breaks. *Macroeconomics and Finance in Emerging Market Economies, 9*(1), 75–99.

Shaw, E. (1973). *Financial deepening in economic development.* New York: Oxford.

Smaoui, H., Grandes, M., & Akindele, A. (2017). The determinants of bond market development: Further evidence from emerging and developed countries. *Emerging Markets Review, 32,* 148–167.

Svirydzenka, K. (2016). Introducing a new broad-based index of financial development. *IMF working paper, 16/5.*

Tang, C. F., & Tan, B. W. (2014). The linkages among energy consumption, economic growth, relative price, foreign direct investment, and financial development in Malaysia. *Quality & Quantity, 48,* 781–797.

Vašíček, B., Žigraiová, D., Hoeberichts, M., Vermeulen, R., Šmídková, K., & de Haan, J. (2017). Leading indicators of financial stress: New evidence. *Journal of Financial Stability, 28,* 240–257.

Vermeulen, R., Hoeberichts, M., Vašíček, B., Žigraiová, D., Šmídková, K., & de Haan, J. (2015). Financial stress indices and financial crises. *Open Economies Review, 26,* 383–406.

Wiandt, J. (2000). *World's first active ETFs begin trading in Germany.* Index Fund Advisors. https://www.ifa.com/articles/ Worlds_First_Active_ETFs_Begin_Trading_in_Germany/. Accessed 31.08.18.

Wright, C., Diavatopoulos, D., & Felton, J. (2010). Exchange-traded notes: An introduction. *The Journal of Index Investing, 1*(1), 164–175.

Xetra. *XTF segment of Deutsche Börse Group. Turnover report: August 2017.* (2017).

Xetra. *ETF trading on Xetra. Facts & figures for the year 2017.* (2018a).

Xetra. *Xetra Liquidity Measure (XLM) for ETFs.* (2018b).

Xetra-Gold. *Deutsche Börse commodities. Established process chain − Well-known partners.* (2018).

Yartey, C. A. (2008). Financial development, the structure of capital markets, and the global digital divide. *Information Economics and Policy, 20* (2), 208–227.

Yartey, C. A. (2010). The institutional and macroeconomic determinants of stock market development in emerging economies. *Applied Financial Economics, 20*(21), 1615–1625.

## 6.1 INTRODUCTION

The global investment industry experiences continuous changes and may be regarded as one of the most dynamic segments of the financial system. Various deep changes are inflicted by the technological revolution, for example, the rising popularity of robo-advising or data science technologies (Madhavan, 2016). Other changes are the result of events that have profoundly impacted the global economic and financial system, such as the economic slowdown caused by the financial crisis that started on the mortgage market in the United States, for example, regulatory changes introduced in some of the world's leading economies that affected also the investment funds. Undeniably, the launch and expansion of exchange-traded funds (ETFs) may be perceived as one of the most important processes that have already to some extent shaped investment industries in many countries. Their global growth has not been hindered, even by the most serious events such as the 2008 financial crisis, despite significant turbulences in other parts of the financial system. However, it needs to be stressed that growth of the ETFs markets in various regions and countries has been highly unequal; for example, in Europe which, as an entire region is an example of rather substantial spread of innovative funds, there are massive and persisting differences between ETFs markets in particular countries despite the apparent similarity of many aspects of their economic and financial systems.

Since the launch of the first ETF—in 1990 in Canada (Foucher & Gray, 2014)—global ETFs market has been undergoing continuous evolution. It is evidenced by the introduction of new categories of funds, in some cases being a rather radical departure from the initial concept of ETFs as cheap and highly accessible passive investing tools with exposure to the equity markets. One of the most notable examples is the still marginal category of active ETFs or the funds that are midway between active and passive investment strategies, that is, enhanced indexing ETFs. Currently, on the most-developed ETFs markets (above all in the United States) there are funds that offer an array of investment strategies and exposure to asset classes as wide as in the case of the more established mutual funds or even broader. Moreover, ETFs continue to be a unique type of investment fund in terms of their mechanisms and give their users access to a number of distinctive features in relation to the leading type of these financial institutions, that is, mutual funds, or much less popular closed-end funds. This means that ETFs may still be categorized as an example of financial innovations and deemed to be innovative investment

*Exchange-Traded Funds in Europe.*
DOI: https://doi.org/10.1016/B978-0-12-813639-3.00006-7

funds. It is, thus, possible to treat the development of the ETFs market as synonymous to their diffusion, as in the case of the other types of innovations. This assumption makes it also possible to analyze ETFs with the application of the innovation framework and, in particular, to use the logistic growth model to study their past and projected diffusion.

The innovative attributes of ETFs that are considered by their users when making investment decisions may not be regarded as the only factor that influences the development of the ETFs markets. It would be too simplistic to focus exclusively on the demand-side determinants associated with the issues such as the return-risk profile of the shares of ETFs or their performance as tracking tools. Among the other factors that need to be considered, three crucial categories can be distinguished: (1) the development of financial markets; (2) the adoption of the new technologies; and (3) the impact of governmental actions. Moreover, despite their uniqueness in many aspects, ETFs are still a category of investment funds and part of the broadly considered market for investment funds. Therefore, it seems feasible to assume that their development depends, at least partially, on the factors common for the entire market for investment funds. In this empirical study we verified the significance of the possible determinants of the development of ETFs market, focusing on the factors identified as a result of our extensive literature review.

Increasing assets of ETFs worldwide have attracted attention of both academics and regulatory bodies that started to investigate the possible impact of innovative investment funds on the financial system; in the earlier years such analysis had been unfeasible because of the marginal significance of ETFs. Due to the structure of the global ETFs market in terms of the funds' exposure, most potential effects were indicated with regard to the equities (e.g., the influence of ETFs on the liquidity of tracked stocks). One of the key issues that emerged was the potential destabilizing effects of the specific categories of ETFs such as synthetic ETFs. Another intensively discussed area was the possible propagation of shocks between various markets. Discussion concerning this issue became particularly intensive in the aftermath of the 2010 Flash Crash in the United States. We examined some of these links in our empirical study.

In line with the key aim of the book, we explored the issues linked to the development of the European ETFs markets over the 2004−17 period. Our analysis covered 12 countries. The base indicator that was applied throughout the book was total net assets of ETFs that were primary listed on the stock exchanges in certain country. In our research we concentrated on three empirical perspectives that to the best of our knowledge were insufficiently addressed in the previous studies. Hence our study focused on:

- Explaining development patterns of the European ETFs markets (i.e., diffusion of ETFs) and providing predictions for their possible changes in the future.
- Identifying seminal factors that influenced the spread of this category of investment funds on regional and country levels.
- Examining potential consequences of the diffusion of these financial products for European financial systems, focusing on the impact on the capital markets and financial stability.

In this chapter we summarize our main findings with regard to these perspectives.

## 6.2 DEVELOPMENT PATTERNS OF THE EUROPEAN EXCHANGE-TRADED FUNDS MARKETS

Development of the ETFs markets in Europe was first studied on the regional level, that is, taking into account all countries. Data on the European ETFs on the regional level are rather straightforward and provide evidence of the undeniable expansion of innovative investment funds. Between 2004 and 2016 the assets of European ETFs increased from $33 billion to the record-high level value of $511 billion. The growth of the aggregate European ETFs market has also taken place in the other dimensions: number of the listed funds and the turnover of their shares. The vast majority of the European ETFs (in terms of assets and their number) are consistent with the basic concept of ETFs as they are equity funds tracking the indexes of the developed stock markets. One of the fundamental issues that was covered as the part of the discussion of the regional European ETFs market was the regulatory framework, above all the regulations introduced within the European Union. Among the key EU directives that have shaped the ETFs markets in Europe there are, above all, the ones concerning their legal structure and subsequent versions of the Undertakings for Collective Investment in Transferable Securities directives that have allowed their distribution in multiple countries, not only in the EU. Another important element of the legal environment is the second version of the Markets in Financial Instruments Directive; it may have profound effects for the European investment industry due to the higher transparency of trading in financial instruments and disclosure of costs for investors, both of which are among its key provisions. These consequences are usually evaluated as highly positive for ETFs (Edde & Vaghela, 2017; Jackson, 2018; Lannoo, 2018).

The indisputable development of the regional European market for innovative funds should not be associated with the similarly clear evidence on the country-level. On the contrary, even a cursory analysis of the basic indicators confirms significant cross-country disparities. Apart from the small group of countries in which the assets of ETFs reached a relatively high level (both in absolute terms and in relation to the local GDP), that is, the United Kingdom, Germany, France, and Switzerland (listed in decreasing order according to the values of assets as of end of 2016), there are several countries in which innovative funds are available, but have only managed to accumulate negligible assets which may not be attributed to their level of economic development (e.g., Norway and Sweden) or size of their economy (e.g., Poland and Spain). These striking differences in the development of the European ETFs markets were not addressed in previous studies (or no attempts of in-depth analysis were made). In our study we have intended to fill this gap and contribute to the better understanding of the processes of the development of the European ETFs markets. We examined country-specific trajectories of the diffusion of the innovative funds with the special focus on the country-level attributes of these processes; their determinants and consequences were also studied. In line with the well-grounded perception of ETFs as financial innovations that can be found in, for example, Amenc, Goltz, and Le Sourd (2017), Gastineau (2010), Madhavan (2016), and previous similar studies in this field, for example, Hull (2016), Marszk and Lechman (2018), we adopted the methodological framework based on the logistic growth model of the innovation diffusion by equating the process of the development of ETFs market with their diffusion.

Conclusions reached based on the estimates of the diffusion models and examination of each European ETFs market's attributes confirmed their considerable diversity. The most convincing evidence supporting the diffusion of ETFs was obtained in the case of all four most-developed ETFs markets as well as Italy and Sweden; for the remaining countries the results were, at best, mixed—the assets of ETFs remained very low and the periods of their growth were short and unsustainable. This means that in only half of the countries in our sample diffusion of ETFs could be established. What is more, the analysis of the inequality indicators showed that in the studied time period differences between the most and least-developed ETFs markets in Europe have been increasing, in particular prior to the global financial crisis. The small group of leading countries has experienced a very rapid expansion of the innovative funds whereas the rest has been increasingly lagging behind. Apart from the country-level study, we also analyzed jointly the assets of ETFs in the five largest countries of the EU in order to evaluate the diffusion patterns in this group of highly integrated economies that accounted for the vast majority of all the assets of European ETFs. Development of this joint ETFs market was characterized as following the logistic trajectory, yet it is still in the stage of rapid growth rather than saturation and shows potential for future increases. Comparison of the estimates of the speed of diffusion in the joint dimension to the pace estimated for specific countries in this group indicated that diffusion of ETFs in Germany and Spain has taken place at an above-average rate, in France at below-average, and in Italy and United Kingdom it has been neither considerably slower nor faster.

Analysis of the past data served as a starting point for the projections concerning the future diffusion of ETFs in Europe that further confirms the significant variations in these processes. The group of the most-developed markets can be predicted to grow even further, with the sustained position of the United Kingdom as the regional leader. In case of the mid-developed ETFs markets (Italy, Spain, and Sweden) some future diffusion can be projected yet is rather limited; approaching the levels of the leading markets is highly improbable. Finally, in case of the remaining, least-developed ETFs markets, no reliable predictions of their possible future development can be formulated based on the available data; only for Norway could the scenario of some (very limited) diffusion not be dismissed. To sum up, projections of diffusion indicate future divergence of the development levels (diffusion) of European ETFs markets and show that diffusion of innovation funds such as ETFs is definitely not uniform, even in the group of regionally leading countries.

The key limitation of the analysis conducted using the diffusion model involves its basic assumption, that is, S-shaped trajectory of the development of the ETFs market; it is assumed that the growth is logistic, with three explicit stages of diffusion. The graphical evidence uncovered that in the case of some countries the diffusion paths were radically different, thus, limiting the applicability of this approach. However, it does not limit severely the robustness of our analysis as for all except the least-developed ETFs markets the findings were not substantially distorted. The other reservation refers to the possible impacts of the economic or political events and shifts in the investment industry that are impossible to predict—one of the most recent examples is the possible consequences of Brexit.

## 6.3 FACTORS INFLUENCING DIFFUSION OF EXCHANGE-TRADED FUNDS IN EUROPE

After confirming the high dynamics of the changes in the development of the European ETFs markets and sustaining deep differences between particular countries, we have addressed the arising question that has received almost no attention in the empirical literature, that is, concerning the factors that are their determinants. To this aim, we have extended our database through the inclusion of a number of variables, classified as financial and nonfinancial mostly for technical reasons in order to facilitate the presentation of the results; the potential explanatory variables were chosen based on the literature review and were intended to represent the impact on the diffusion of ETFs of the potentially most important factors. The study was conducted using, firstly, panel models, and, secondly, with a local polynomial regression in order to examine country-level evidence. The time period of the analysis was 2004–16.

The picture arising from the analysis of the determinants of the diffusion of ETFs is quite complicated, with no clear-cut conclusions. To begin with, we discuss the results of the analysis conducted using the static and dynamic panel models with multiple explanatory variables; we omit the discussion of models with single explanatory variables as they were in fact mostly a starting point for the more complex analysis. Two among the most crucial potential determinants are assets of mutual funds and turnover of stock index futures. In light of the literature review and outlined comparison of various financial products, the relationships between them and ETFs were expected to be negative. However, in both cases we have identified their positive and statistically significant impact, thus, showing that development of both the markets for mutual funds and stock index futures reinforced the diffusion of ETFs in Europe. The results concerning mutual funds are discussed in the context of the country-specific evidence; in case of the stock index futures the positive relationship can be explained by, inter alia, different yet to some extent complimentary applications of such contracts and ETFs.

What is even more striking, in spite of the well-grounded and broadly recognized hypothesized influence of the stock markets on the diffusion of ETFs, the results obtained using panel models have uncovered a complicated picture. The convincing evidence was demonstrated for only one studied dimension of the equity markets (stock price volatility) and no influence of the hypothesized key factor, that is, stock market turnover, was identified thus showing that the other determinants of the diffusion of ETFs (e.g., assets of mutual funds or adoption of information and communication technologies (ICT)) are of higher significance. The results obtained for the other possible financial determinants (e.g., bond markets or financial institutions) were highly unconvincing and no robust conclusions could be reached. The most notable exception was the financial system's deposits variable for which the impact was documented as positive and statistically significant, thus, being evidence for the positive impact of the development of the banking sector.

Among the nonfinancial determinants, we have unambiguously confirmed the statistically significant and positive impact of ICT adoption, in line with our expectations and the results of previous empirical studies (e.g., Blitz & Huij, 2012; Calamia, Deville, & Riva, 2013; Lechman & Marszk, 2015; Madhavan, 2016). A positive role was revealed both for overall access to the Internet and to the fast (fixed broadband) connections. One of the factors that can explain the impact of the new technologies on the diffusion of ETFs in Europe is the increasing importance of robo-advising services albeit being limited by the reluctance of the European retail investors, as implied by the results of the survey of ING (2017). Apart from the ICT indicators, some (yet weaker) evidence was also uncovered for the negative impact of the gross savings rate and inflation rate, implying that, firstly, diffusion of ETFs does not depend on the supply of savings (due to the small size of most European ETFs markets), and, secondly, the higher inflation environment discourages investments into ETFs.

Estimates of the dynamic panel models, with the lagged values of the development of the ETFs markets among the explanatory variables, have mainly uncovered that the diffusion of ETFs in the analyzed European countries is evidently a strongly endogenous and self-perpetuating process.

Country-level analysis of the selected potential factors of the diffusion of ETFs provided some additional insights. In case of the ICT adoption, interest rates, and stock market turnover the conclusions reached using panel models were to a large extent confirmed with regard to the individual European ETFs markets. However, in the case of the other determinants some differences were demonstrated. For the assets of mutual funds, their impact on the diffusion of ETFs seemed to be unequivocally positive for the most-developed ETFs markets and weakly positive or neutral for the remaining markets. It can, thus, be stated that generally ETFs and mutual funds in Europe were proven to be complimentary categories of investment funds regardless of the level of the diffusion of the innovative funds. Nonetheless, examination of the influence of mutual funds at various stages of the development of the European ETFs markets showed that in the initial stages of the diffusion of the innovative funds, it appeared to be neutral. It may be explained by the usually very narrow initial range of available ETFs, mostly passive equity funds that compete with only a small group of mutual funds. Apart from that, early users of ETFs are mostly sophisticated investors and the general investing audience has little knowledge of such financial products. This means that little competition or support can be expected between these two types of investment funds. When the ETFs market matures, these barriers can diminish and the relationship between mutual funds and innovative funds can become positive; they reinforce each other's growth of assets due to, for instance, various applications—for example, in active versus passive investing—or attracting overall more clients to the investment industry. Nevertheless, in some cases ETFs and mutual funds may become substitutes—we identified two such countries, France and Spain—yet explanation of this relationship remains to be identified. To sum up, our study yielded some seminal conclusions concerning the fundamental relationship between ETFs and mutual funds that seems more complicated than usually assumed.

In case of gross savings rate and turnover of investment funds—funds listed on the stock exchanges other than ETFs and other exchange-traded products or mutual funds—the results were even more complicated; the gross savings rate was demonstrated not to be robustly linked to the development of the European ETFs markets in contrast with the negative impact implied by the panel models and, for the latter variable, the relationships were mostly country-specific.

Additionally, we studied the sources of the changes in the assets of European ETFs with their decomposition into two exhaustive sources: changes in the prices of assets and net flows to the funds; analysis was conducted for the time period 2013–17 subject to data availability. It demonstrated that our analysis throughout the book—at least with regard to the 2013–17 time period, that is, the time of the most rapid expansion of the innovative funds—can, in fact, be referred not only to the assets (the base indicator that we have applied) but also to the net flows that were the main contribution to the changes in assets. Moreover, it can be stated that our study addressed the actual activity on the examined ETFs markets and not merely the diffusion resulting from the changes in the prices of the assets.

## 6.4 DIFFUSION OF EXCHANGE-TRADED FUNDS IN EUROPE: POSITIVE OR NEGATIVE FOR FINANCIAL SYSTEMS?

Our study has demonstrated that the diffusion of ETFs has taken place at least in some of the European countries and they have become a part of the financial system that can no longer be disregarded as negligible; the most convincing proof are the assets of ETFs that have reached hundreds of billions of US dollars in the leading markets. Therefore, we addressed the issue of the impact of ETFs on the financial systems in Europe and intended to fill a significant gap in the previous research in this field. We have verified firstly, the influence of ETFs on the financial development (FD), secondly, their impact on the development of the most closely linked parts of the financial system (above all, capital markets), and, thirdly, their diffusion in the context of financial stability. The research methods were parallel to the ones applied for the study of the factors that affect the development of the ETFs markets. Even though we have taken into account a number of variables that could affect broadly or narrowly understood FD, we discuss here exclusively the conclusions concerning the role of ETFs. With the exception of the influence on the financial stability, we focused on the relationships that may be observed taking into account the entire group of the examined countries as analysis of country-specific evidence would be problematic in the case of the European ETFs markets that are small in relation to the local financial systems.

The impact of the diffusion of ETFs on the FD of European countries was examined using the FD indicators published by IMF, above all the most comprehensive indicator, the FD index. Nonparametric analysis has demonstrated that most of the positive contribution of the innovative funds to the process of FD occurred during their initial expansion and afterwards other factors appear to overshadow the impact of ETFs. Furthermore, estimates of the panel models showed that the impact of the diffusion of ETFs on the FD was unequivocally positive, regardless of the other included factors, such as adoption of ICT or GDP growth. Accordingly, we have confirmed that, based on the evidence for the 12 European countries in our sample, the development of the ETFs markets was a substantial factor of the development of the European financial systems.

In the second part of the analysis we evaluated the relationships between the selected segments of the financial sector. Apart from ETFs markets, we considered markets for investment funds other than ETFs (the ones listed on the stock exchanges), stock markets, and bond markets by analyzing their development. In the case of the investment funds other than ETFs, the development of the ETFs markets in Europe was proven to boost their turnover. Taking into account the analysis of the determinants of the diffusion of ETFs, it may be concluded that while the role of the other investment funds for the development of ETF markets in Europe is generally insignificant, in the case of the other side of the relationship, some positive influence may be noticed, implying their complimentary nature. For the next part of the financial system, we have found evidence for the positive impact of ETFs on both the size and liquidity of the stock markets; however, in the case of the high values of the assets of ETFs (i.e., high level of diffusion) their role for the development of the equity markets appeared to be neutral; it may be concluded that apparently all possible strengthening effects took place earlier. Due to the lack of convincing evidence for the impact of the stock markets on the diffusion of ETFs, it may be claimed that the impact of ETFs on the development of the stock markets was (at least to some degree) positive while there was no such influence on the other side of this relationship. However, it must be stressed that the results obtained for the influence of ETFs on the stock markets were less convincing than in the case of the relationship with the other investment funds as shown, in particular, by the panel models applied to study the determinants of the capitalization of the stock markets. Finally, in the case of bond markets, their development was proxied by the bond turnover; an indicator for many reasons inferior to the value of the outstanding debt securities yet applied in this context due to the fact that ETFs can be expected to affect, above all, the turnover of bonds (due to, e.g., transactions related to the creation/redemption mechanism) rather than the primary bond markets and due to data availability. Our analysis uncovered that the impact of ETFs on the turnover on the bond markets was positive for the lower levels of the development of both ETFs and bond markets and neutral in the case of the higher levels. The overall effect can be briefly described as mostly neutral and, to conclude, it may be stated that our study has provided support that ETFs affect more strongly the equity markets than the bond markets due to, in particular, their prevalent equity exposure.

The final examined issue was the possible impact of ETFs on the stability of the financial systems in the countries in our sample. In that part of the study, due to considerable between-country differences, we focused exclusively on country-level evidence. Results of our analysis can be summarized briefly as confirming the conclusions of Amenc, Ducoulombier, Goltz, and Tang (2012) who showed that most potential threats posed by ETFs to the European financial systems are vastly exaggerated. Our analysis did not uncover convincing evidence for the possible negative impact of ETFs on the financial instability in the European countries; ETFs markets in Europe have developed most rapidly in the period of decreased financial stress, that is, in the years after the 2008 global financial crisis and Eurozone sovereign debt crisis. The main reason is the still very low assets of ETFs in comparison to the whole financial systems or their key segments—even the leading European ETFs markets are quite small. Interestingly, in the case of the most-developed ETFs markets in Europe, their diffusion was positively related to financial stability (i.e., negatively to the level of financial stress) thus it may be stated that they could have actually be one of the stabilizing factors. However, it must be emphasized that the applied research approach has severe limitations as we considered the stability of the entire financial system and ETFs could have affected, to at least some extent, the particular segments of the financial sector; still, the financial stress indicator that we used covered the parts of the financial system that are potentially most strongly linked to the ETFs markets. The analysis was supplemented by the examination of the structure of the European ETFs in terms of the replication method due to the potential threats linked to the synthetic funds and is broadly recognized in the literature. As we showed, based on the empirical evidence and by referring to the previous studies of Amenc et al. (2012), Amenc, Ducoulombier, Goltz, and Le Sourd (2015), and Amenc et al. (2017), the contribution of the synthetic ETFs to financial instability can be assessed as negligible due to, for instance, the high regulatory coverage of these funds.

## 6.5 SUCCESS AND FAILURE OF EXCHANGE-TRADED FUNDS IN EUROPE: SELECTED CASE STUDIES

Apart from the main stream of our discussion, we also analyzed some European countries separately using the case studies convention. Our analysis covered Poland, Italy, and Germany. Poland was examined as an explicit example of the failure of ETFs to become an important part of the local investment industry or, more broadly, the Polish financial system. Despite the apparently favorable economic environment and high level of financial stability (even during the most recent global financial crisis), the Polish ETFs market has remained among the smallest in Europe (of course, ignoring the countries with no ETFs markets), with only one fund that was primary listed on the local stock exchange. Possible explanations may be their unfavorable position in the dominating distribution channels and insufficient awareness of potential investors. However, it does not mean that the Polish financial system has no linkages to the global ETFs market as Polish assets are held by many ETFs listed and traded outside Poland. The second case study covered Italy, the European ETFs market for which examination of the actual development level and the degree of the diffusion of ETFs is hindered by the position of the Italian stock exchange within a group of trading venues. Therefore, this market was studied separately (as the only one) with the turnover indicators as using values of assets was problematic. Results of the analysis imply that substantial development of the Italian ETFs market in terms of turnover has been observed and may be expected to continue in the future. In the final, third case study we analyzed one of the leading European ETFs markets, that is, Germany. The success of innovative funds is evidenced not only by the increasing assets of ETFs, but also by the emergence of the other types of exchange-traded products: exchange-traded commodities (ETCs) and exchange-traded notes (ETNs). Consequently, we did not concentrate exclusively on the local ETFs that were covered within the preceding analysis of their diffusion, but rather on the less-known ETCs and ETNs, showing the substantial diversification of this section of the German investment industry. Still, the role of both ETCs and ETNs has remained marginal in comparison to ETFs.

## 6.6 FUTURE RESEARCH DIRECTIONS

After presenting the most crucial empirical findings concerning the development of the European ETFs markets, we demonstrate their possible implications and recommendations that may be useful for, firstly, entities with the most direct interest in the ETFs markets: investors and financial companies (in particular companies that manage these and other types of investment funds or consider entering the ETFs market), and, secondly, for the other entities that need to consider the possible diffusion of ETFs and their linkages to the financial system: regulatory authorities and policy makers (considered jointly).

In our empirical discussion we did not focus on the attributes of the European ETFs that may be perceived as being of key significance for the investors that consider including the shares of innovative funds in their portfolios, such as their returns or tracking errors, mostly because they were examined in a vast number of different studies (although the number of studies on the US ETFs is incomparably higher). Moreover, it would be impossible to formulate such conclusions in the case of our research sample that includes a few thousand individual funds, data from which were aggregated on the country level for the 12 European economies. Nevertheless, regardless of these stipulations, our analysis led to some conclusions that should be taken into account by the current and potential investors in the European ETFs. The first reason is related to our examination of the development (diffusion) levels of particular European ETFs markets, its results showing which ETFs market may be chosen by prospective investors and which remain underdeveloped, with no predicted growth. Generally, in the case of the largest European financial systems it may be stated that ETFs are slowly becoming increasingly more important (see, for instance, the example of the United Kingdom); for the remaining countries the results are, at best, mixed which indicates that investors interested in the European ETFs should continue to focus on the group of countries with the most-developed ETFs markets and funds whose shares are primary listed on their stock exchanges. Secondly, even though the key aspect of ETFs considered by investors is the risk/return profile of their shares, investors should also pay attention to the general trends on the ETFs markets. In our study we showed the main changes that have been taking place in Europe, together with projections; we also scrutinized the determinants of these processes that could affect ETFs not only at the level of the aggregate country or regional market, but also the particular funds; therefore, they should not be neglected by the holders of the shares of ETFs. Finally, portfolios of most investors consist of various classes of assets. We showed that there are significant linkages between ETFs markets, stock markets, bond markets, and markets for investment funds other than ETFs; these relationships need to be accounted for in the portfolio management decisions.

The results of our analysis may also have some important consequences for financial companies; obviously, companies from the asset management industry are the group most directly affected by the changes that take place on the ETFs markets, yet they are not the only group as various types of commercial banks should also take into account both the trajectory of the diffusion of ETFs and its factors and consequences. Key implications are parallel to the ones formulated with regard to the investors: further development of the biggest ETFs markets seems unavoidable, spurred by some financial factors and adoption of new technologies. In particular the latter group of determinants should be taken into account in the business strategies of the financial institution that compete in the financial sector—we showed clearly that their role is undeniable. The growing popularity of ETFs in European countries with the largest economies and biggest populations means that financial institutions need to be ready to deal with the expectations of customers that are interested in innovative funds, even though that may lead to substantial transformation of the advisory and distribution networks (sometimes linked to substantial negative financial consequences). To some extent, in the European Union such changes are already taking place as the consequence of the EU-level regulations that are aimed at increased transparency. ETFs seem to be one of the main beneficiaries. One of the main challenges for the asset management industry is adapting to the low-cost and high-accessibility investing model proposed by ETFs.

The third group of entities that may find the results of our study useful are various bodies and institutions responsible for regulating and setting the policy for the financial system. Above all, the results of our diffusion analysis imply that, at least in case of the leading European economies, ETFs may not be ignored and should not be neglected as their assets may reliably be predicted to continue to grow—unless some unexpected developments take place, related to, for instance, regulatory and technological issues; however, currently they seem to boost the diffusion of ETFs rather than being a barrier. It means, among others, that regulatory authorities should be ready to tackle various issues resulting from the growing assets of the innovative funds (e.g., linked to the problems faced by the investors in the shares of ETFs). Results of our analysis shed some light on the issue of factors that can be accelerators or barriers to the development of the ETFs markets. Bodies responsible for setting and exercising strategies concerning the financial system may accordingly account for such determinants if they aim to initiate or boost the development of ETFs markets. The results of our analysis of the impact of the diffusion of ETFs on the development of financial systems show quite unambiguously that innovative funds can be a positive factor. A very important conclusion of our analysis concerns the identified relationships between ETFs markets and other parts of the financial system which further underline the necessity to carefully oversee the spread of innovative funds—maybe these interdependencies are currently still rather weak, yet they can be potentially growing with the spread of ETFs. However, the analysis of the possible contribution of the diffusion of ETFs to the financial instability in Europe led to the conclusion that previously raised concerns about the potential systemic risks of ETFs were overstated and could not be identified, at least with regard to the countries in the research sample. Obviously, such threats cannot be ignored as they may substantially increase in the wake of the growth of the currently still small ETFs markets. Another interesting, yet up to now mostly ignored, possibility is using ETFs to reach the aims of the monetary policy, for instance through the operations of the central bank performed with the shares of ETFs. This application would be new in Europe, but is not groundbreaking on a global scale as the actions of Bank of Japan illustrates (Abner, 2016; Fueda-Samikawa & Takano, 2017). It may be considered a possibility worth consideration in the wake of possible ineffectiveness of the other tools and taking into consideration the growing ETFs markets in the largest European economies.

In spite of the fact that we designed our study to be a comprehensive examination of the previously unaddressed issues concerning European ETFs markets in order to fill some of the substantial gaps in this stream of economic research, there are still many issues that require further analysis as (for various reasons) they remained outside the scope of our study. They not only show directions for future research, but also indicate some fundamental questions concerning the outlook for ETFs.

Firstly, future studies could focus on further explanation of the reasons behind the high level heterogeneity of the development of the European ETFs markets by considering the potentially important issues such as close examination of the differences in the legal and regulatory environments in particular countries, structures of the local financial system with the particular focus on the asset management industry and various costs and incentives linked to the distribution of the shares of ETFs versus other investment funds (Hill, Nadig, & Hougan, 2015) or, in the broader perspective, following the burgeoning field of economic research by evaluating the role of the institutional framework. Nonetheless, one of the main barriers that hinder analysis in any of these areas is the lack of sufficient and consistent data in order to study them using a comparative perspective. From a methodological perspective, application of the regression models to examine some of those factors is hindered by the problems with their quantification.

Moreover, even though we analyzed the possible linkages between ETFs and the development of financial systems (considered as a whole or its selected particular segments) as well as financial stability, and identified these relationships in case of the European countries, the unanswered albeit interesting question concerns the exact mechanism through which diffusion of the innovative funds can affect, for example, development of the stock market (and, obviously, the same applies for the reverse relationship). There are increasingly more studies devoted to the examination of the impact of ETFs on the liquidity of the underlying or tracked assets, but they are still far from being conclusive and are highly idiosyncratic; they provide evidence valid for particular funds (or their group) and rarely offer generalizations. The question remains whether such generalizations can be reached.

Finally, some interesting and very significant questions were not covered in our study simply because it is still too early for their robust analysis. Probably, one of the examples that are most worth mentioning in this context is the impact of the new technologies on the ETFs markets—not only basic types of ICT that can be quantified and were accounted for in our analysis (e.g., access to the Internet) but also various new developments such as data science. A related question is the future role of robo-advising (or, more generally, digital advising), strongly linked to the ETFs markets, with the potential to deeply transform the asset management industry; a change that, although in a limited scale, already takes place in the United States. The long-term effect of robo-advising and, indirectly, the consequences of the diffusion of ETFs, could be increased financial inclusion (OECD, 2017; Schwinn & Teo, 2017).

# References

Abner, D. (2016). *The ETF handbook. How to value and trade exchange-traded funds* (2nd ed.). John Wiley & Sons.

Amenc, N., Ducoulombier, F., Goltz, F., & Le Sourd, V. (2015). *The EDHEC European ETF survey 2014*. Nice: EDHEC-Risk Institute.

Amenc, N., Ducoulombier, F., Goltz, F., & Tang, L. (2012). *What are the risks of European ETFs?* EDHEC-Risk Institute.

Amenc, N., Goltz, F., & Le Sourd, V. (2017). *The EDHEC European ETF and smart beta survey*. EDHEC-Risk Institute.

Blitz, D., & Huij, J. (2012). Evaluating the performance of global emerging markets equity exchange-traded funds. *Emerging Markets Review, 13*, 149–158.

Calamia, A., Deville, L., & Riva, F. (2013). Liquidity in European equity ETFs: What really matters? *GREDEG working paper series, 10*, 1–26.

Edde, J., & Vaghela, V. (2017). *MiFID seen sending European ETFs over trillion dollar mark.* <https://www.bloomberg.com/news/articles/2017-08-10/mifid-seen-sending-european-etfs-over-the-trillion-dollar-mark> Accessed 18.02.18.

Foucher, I., & Gray, K. (2014). Exchange-traded funds: Evolution of benefits, vulnerabilities and risks. *Bank of Canada Financial System Review*, December, pp. 37–46.

Fueda-Samikawa, I., & Takano, T. (2017). *BOJ's ETF purchases expanding steadily—How long will the BOJ hold risky assets with no maturity? Japan Center for Economic Research.*

Gastineau, G. L. (2010). *The exchange-traded funds manual*. John Wiley & Sons.

Hill, J. M., Nadig, D., & Hougan, M. (2015). *A comprehensive guide to exchange-traded funds (ETFs)*. CFA Institute Research Foundation.

Hull, I. (2016). The development and spread of financial innovations. *Quantitative Economics, 7*(2), 613–636.

ING. (2017). *Mobile banking—The next generation. How should ways to bank and pay evolve in future?*

Jackson, O. (2018). Mifid II prompts shift from traditional funds to ETFs. *International Financial Law Review*. Available from http://www.iflr.com/Article/3790630/Mifid-II-prompts-shift-from-traditional-funds-to-ETFs.html.

Lannoo, K. (2018). MiFID II will profoundly affect the portfolio management business. *European Capital Markets Institute Commentary, 47*, 1–4.

Lechman, E., & Marszk, A. (2015). ICT technologies and financial innovations: The case of exchange traded funds in Brazil, Japan, Mexico, South Korea and the United States. *Technological Forecasting and Social Change, 99*, 355–376.

Madhavan, A. N. (2016). *Exchange-traded funds and the new dynamics of investing*. Oxford University Press.

Marszk, A., & Lechman, E. (2018). New technologies and diffusion of innovative financial products: Evidence on exchange-traded funds in selected emerging and developed economies. *Journal of Macroeconomics*, in press.

OECD. (2017). *Robo-advice for pensions.*

Schwinn, R., & Teo, E. G. (2017). *Inclusion or exclusion? Trends in robo-advisory for financial investment services, Handbook of blockchain, digital finance, and inclusion* (Vol. 2, pp. 481–492). Academic Press.

# Methodological Annex

## METHOD 1: TECHNOLOGY DIFFUSION MODELS, LOGISTIC GROWTH MODEL AND BI-LOGISTIC GROWTH MODEL

Mathematically, the logistic growth function is broadly applied to study technology diffusion and originates from the exponential growth model, and when written as an ordinary differential equation is as follows:

$$\frac{dY_x(t)}{dt} = \alpha Y_x(t). \tag{A.1}$$

If $Y(t)$ denotes the level of variable $x$, $(t)$ is time, and $\alpha$ is a constant growth rate, then Eq. (A.1) explains the time path of $Y(t)$. If we introduce $e$ to Eq. (A.1), it can be reformulated as:

$$Y_x(t) = \beta e^{\alpha t}, \tag{A.2}$$

with notation analogous to Eq. (A.1) and $\beta$ representing the initial value of $x$ at $t = 0$.

The simple growth model is predefined as exponential, thus, the "resistance" parameter was added to Eq. (A.1). This modification introduces an upper "limit" to the exponential growth model, which instead gives the original exponential growth curve a sigmoid shape. The modified version of Eq. (A.1) is the logistic differential function:

$$\frac{dY(t)}{dt} = \alpha Y(t)\left(1 - \frac{Y(t)}{\kappa}\right), \tag{A.3}$$

where the parameter $\kappa$ is the imposed upper asymptote that limits the growth of $Y$. We define $\left(1 - (Y(t)/\kappa)\right)$ as a "slowing term" (negative feedback), which is close to 1 as $Y(t) \ll \kappa$, but if $Y(t) \to \kappa$ then $\left(1 - (Y(t)/\kappa)\right) \to 0$. By adding the slowing-down parameter to exponential growth generates an S-shaped trajectory.

The 3-parameter logistic differential equation—see Eq. (A.3)—can be rewritten as a logistic growth function, taking non-negative values throughout its path:

$$N_x(t) = \frac{\kappa}{1 + e^{-\alpha t - \beta}}, \tag{A.4}$$

where $N_x(t)$ stands for the value of variable $x$ in time period $t$.

The parameters in Eq. (A.4) are:

- $\kappa$—upper asymptote: shows the limit of growth ($N(t) \to \kappa$), also labeled "carrying capacity" or "saturation"
- $\alpha$—growth rate: shows the speed of diffusion
- $\beta$—midpoint: shows the exact time ($T_m$) when the logistic pattern reaches $0.5\kappa$.

To ease the economic interpretation, we replace $\alpha$ with a "specific duration" parameter, defined as $\Delta t = \ln(81)/\alpha$, that allows approximating the time needed for $x$ to grow from $10\%\kappa$ to $90\%\kappa$.

The logistic growth model defined in Eq. (A.4) generates logistic growth patterns, which resembles S-shaped trajectory. The S-shaped trajectory may be divided into three characteristic phases: Phase 1 during which growth is spasmodic and no radical changes are observed; Phase 2 during which examined variable grows exponentially; Phase 3 during which the system head toward full saturation and maturity.

In Eq. (A.4), we have 3-parameter logistic function, but for estimates of the asymmetric responses 5-parameter logistic functions are applied, which follows:

$$y = f(x;p) = d + \frac{(a - d)}{\left[1 + [x/c]^b\right]^g},$$

(A.5)

where $p = (a, b, c, d, g)$, $c > 0$ and $g > 0$. If we restrict $g = 1$, a 4-parameter logistic function is generated.

Growth processes are decomposable into sub-processes; hence the standard logistic growth model can be transformed into a multiple growth "pulses" model. If we have two growth pulses, this gives rise to the formula:

$$N_x(t) = N_1(t) + N_2(t).$$

(A.6)

where, $N_1(t)$ and $N_2(t)$ are: $\left[\left(\kappa_1 / \left(1 + \exp\left(\left(\frac{\ln(81)}{\Delta t_1}\right)(t - T_{m_1})\right)\right)\right)\right]$ and $\left[\left(\kappa_2 / \left(1 + \exp\left(\left(\frac{\ln(81)}{\Delta t_2}\right)(t - T_{m_2})\right)\right)\right)\right]$ respectively. The model defined in Eq. (A.6), is a bi-logistic growth equation.

The generalized version of Eq. (A.6) for multiple ($\to$ 'z') logistic growth sub-processes follows the *z-component* logistic growth model:

$$N(t) = \left[\frac{\kappa_1}{1 + \exp\left((\ln(81)/\Delta t_1)(t - T_{m_1})\right)}\right] + \ldots + \left[\frac{\kappa_i}{1 + \exp\left((\ln(81)/\Delta t_i)(t - T_{m_i})\right)}\right] = \sum_{i=1}^{z} N_i(t),$$

(A.7)

if:

$$N_i(t) = \frac{\kappa_i}{1 + \exp(-\alpha_i(t - \beta_i))}.$$

(A.8)

# METHOD 2: INEQUALITY MEASURES—GINI COEFFICIENT, ATKINSON COEFFICIENT, AND LORENZ CURVE

*Lorenz curve* is used to graphically represent the relative size distribution of a variable, e.g., income or wealth. Technically speaking, if $x$ represents income and $F(x)$ is its distribution that explains the proportion of individuals who have incomes less than or equal to $x$. The first moment distribution function may be defined as $F_1(x)$, and $F_1(x)$ explains the proportion of total income that was earned by individuals who have incomes less than or equal to $x$. In that case, the Lorenz curve demonstrates the relationship between $F(x)$ and $F_1(x)$. The area below the Lorenz curve is widely used to calculate the value of the Gini index (coefficient) (Gini $\to$ one minus twice the area below the Lorenz curve). The generalized Lorenz curves are commonly labeled "concentration curves" and are broadly used as a tool to consider different aspects of distribution in economic analyses.

*Gini coefficient*, as one of the common inequality measures derived from the Lorenz curve, measures inequality of income distribution, while 0 corresponds to perfect income equality, and 1, i.e., total inequality. The Gini coefficient is proportional to the area between the 45° line and the Lorenz curve line for a given variable. The further the Lorenz curve from the 45° line, the higher value of Gini coefficient is reported, which suggest higher inequality.

For a given population attributed to values $y_i$, $i = 1 \ldots n$, and if $(y_i \leq y_{i+1})$, the general formula for Gini coefficient is defined as: $= 1/n \left(n + 1 - 2 \left(\sum_{i=1}^{n} (n + 1 - i) y_i / \sum_{i=1}^{n} y_i\right)\right)$ (Gini, 1912). Graphically, value of Gini coefficient measures twice the surface between Lorenz curve, which shows the cumulative distribution of variable in the sample, and the line presenting totally equal distribution.

Gini coefficient ranges from 0 to 1. Perfect equality would yield a value Gini coefficient of 0; while perfect inequality is 1.

*Atkinson coefficient* (Atkinson, 1970), also labeled inequality aversion parameter, was developed within a class of inequality indices designed to explicitly introduce value judgments into the inequality measurement. Atkinson coefficient with inequality aversion parameter $\varepsilon$ included, has a general form: $A_\varepsilon = 1 - \left[1/n \sum_{i=1}^{n} [y_i / \bar{y}]^{1-\varepsilon}\right]^{1/(1-\varepsilon)}$, where $\bar{y}$ stands for average income of each individual in the sample, $y_i$ is the income of an individual, $n$ is the number of individuals in the sample. The $\varepsilon$ parameter represents the degree of inequality aversion. Atkinson coefficients demonstrates high sensitivity to the value of $\varepsilon$; introducing different $\varepsilon$ may generate different trends in value of Atkinson coefficient, and even produce different rank orders among countries/individuals, if studied. If $\varepsilon = 0$ this suggest no aversion to inequality; if $\varepsilon = \infty$ which shows infinite aversion to inequality.

## METHOD 3: KERNEL DENSITY ESTIMATIONS

Kernel density estimators belong to a class of nonparametric density estimators. Opposing to parametric estimators they have no fixed structure and depend on the data points that are supposed to be reached by the estimate. In other words, Kernel density estimations may be claimed as a nonparametric method of estimating the probability density function for continuous random data. This highly useful nonparametric technique allows visualizing the underlying distribution of a continuous variable and Kernel density curves are generated.

Kernel density curves that are plotted by adopting a nonparametric estimation of the probability density function holding the form:

$$f(x) = \frac{d}{dx}F(x), \tag{A.9}$$

where $F(x)$ explains the continuous distribution of random variable $X$. The density curves that were generated by the kernel density estimator are continuous and show an "empirical" distribution of variables. To estimate density $f(x)$, we use its discrete derivative, and so the kernel estimator takes a general form:

$$f(x) = \frac{1}{nh}\sum_{i=1}^{n}k\left(\frac{X_i - x}{h}\right), \tag{A.10}$$

where $k(u)$ is a kernel function that satisfies $\int_{-\infty}^{\infty}k(u)du = 1$. In our case $f(x)$ shows the percentage of observations located near $x$. If many observations are located near $x$, then $f(x)$ is large, and the opposite otherwise.

In our study we apply Kernel Epanechnikov, holding a general form:

$$\frac{3}{4}\frac{(1 - u^2)}{(|u| < 1)}. \tag{A.11}$$

## METHOD 4: PANEL REGRESSION MODELS

Fixed effects regression, which allows for heterogeneity across countries, follows the general form:

$$\Psi_{i,y} = \alpha_i + \beta(x_{i,y}) + u_{i,y}, \tag{A.12}$$

where $\alpha_i$ is unknown intercept for each entity (country), $\Psi_{i,y}$ denotes depended variable; $\beta$ is the $L \times 1$ and $x_{i,y}$ stands for the $iy$th observation on $L$ explanatory variables. The subscripts $i = \{1, \ldots \ldots N\}$ stand for entity (country) and $y = \{1, \ldots, T\}$ for the time period. In Eq. (A.12), the $u_{i,y} = \mu_i + \nu_{i,y}$, while the $\mu_i$ accounts for the unobservable and time-invariant country-specific effect, which is not captured in the model, and $\nu_{i,y}$ is the remainder disturbance (the observation-specific errors).

Fixed effects models can be alternatively presented using binary variables for entity fixed effects, so Eq. (A.12) becomes:

$$\Psi_{i,y} = \beta_0 + \beta_1 X_{1,iy} + \ldots + \beta_k X_{k,iy} + \vartheta_2 E_2 + \cdots + \vartheta_n E_n + u_{i,y}, \tag{A.13}$$

with notation as in Eq. (A.12), and where $E_n$ is the entity $n$ (with $n - 1$ entities included in the model), $\vartheta_2$ is the coefficient for the binary regressors.

If time fixed effects are added to Eq. (A.13), the time and fixed effects regression model holds the form:

$$\Psi_{i,y} = \beta_0 + \beta_1 X_{1,iy} + \ldots + \beta_k X_{k,iy} + \vartheta_2 E_2 + \cdots + \vartheta_n E_n + \gamma_2 T_2 + \ldots + \gamma_y T_y u_{i,y}, \tag{A.14}$$

with notation as in Eq. (A.13), where $T_y$ is time binary variable (dummy) (with $y - 1$ time periods included in the model) and $\gamma_y$ is the coefficient for the binary time regressors.

To control for the possibly of emerging heteroskedasticity or within-panel serial correlations, robust standard errors should be specified and reported.

Alternatively, if some differences across examined entities (countries) may have influence on depended variable, we specify random effects model that holds a general form:

$$\Psi_{i,y} = \alpha + \beta(\grave{x}_{i,y}) + u_{i,y} + \varepsilon_{i,y}, \tag{A.15}$$

With notations as in Eq. (A.12), however where $u_{i,y}$ explains between-entity error, and $\varepsilon_{i,y}$—within-entity error.

## METHOD 5: LOCALLY WEIGHTED POLYNOMIAL SMOOTHER

Locally weighted polynomial smoother is a nonparametric method used to graphically fit the curve displaying relationship between two variables. This method of analysis is useful and widely adopted as it allows relaxing rigid assumptions of conventional parametric analysis and regressions, and thus no assumption regarding the form of the relations is made. A huge advantage of using the LOWESS method is that it is outlier resistant and thus no disturbances in results are introduced.

We approximate the function having a general form:

$$f(.), \tag{A.16}$$

under assumption that all errors $e_i$ generated by the model are identically zero. Having defined $x_i$ as one of the covariates we can estimates the $f(.)$ by using the multivariate polynomial form where respective $x_i$ is chosen to extrapolate:

$$y_i = f(x_i^*), \tag{A.17}$$

if $i = 1, \ldots, k$, in the $k$-nearest neighborhood of $x^*$, with underlying assumption that $f$ is the locally a smooth function.

## References

Atkinson, A. B. (1970). On the measurement of inequality. *Journal of Economic Theory*, 2(3), 244–263.

Gini, C. (1912). Variabilità e mutabilità. In E. Pizetti, & T. Salvemini (Eds.), *Reprinted in Memorie di metodologica statistica*. Rome: Libreria Eredi Virgilio Veschi.

## Further Reading

### *Method 1*

Geroski, P. A. (2000). Models of technology diffusion. *Research Policy*, 29(4), 603–625.

Karshenas, M., & Stoneman, P. (1995). Technological diffusion. *Handbook of the Economics of Innovation and Technological Change*, 265–297.

Kucharavy, D., & De Guio, R. (2007, November). Application of S-shaped curves. In *7th ETRIA TRIZ future conference* (pp. 81–88).

Kwasnicki, W. (2013). Logistic growth of the global economy and competitiveness of nations. *Technological Forecasting and Social Change*, 80(1), 50–76.

Metcalfe, J. S. (Ed.), (2004). Ed Mansfield and the diffusion of innovation: An evolutionary connection. *The Journal of Technology Transfer*, 30(1-2), 171–181.

Meyer, P. S. (1994). Bi-logistic growth. *Technological Forecasting and Social Change*, 47(1), 89–102.

Meyer, P. S., Yung, J. W., & Ausubel, J. H. (1999). A primer on logistic growth and substitution: the mathematics of the Loglet Lab software. *Technological Forecasting and Social Change*, 61(3), 247–271.

### *Method 2*

Gastwirth, J. L. (1971). A general definition of the Lorenz curve. *Econometrica: Journal of the Econometric Society*, 39, 1037–1039.

Mehran, F. (1976). Linear measures of income inequality. *Econometrica: Journal of the Econometric Society*, 44, 805–809.

Shorrocks, A. F. (1983). Ranking income distributions. *Economica*, 50(197), 3–17.

Wolff, E. N. (2009). *Poverty and income distribution*. Blackwell Pub.

### *Method 3*

Hall, P., Sheather, S. J., Jones, M. C., & Marron, J. S. (1991). On optimal data-based bandwidth selection in kernel density estimation. *Biometrika*, 78(2), 263–269.

Sheather, S. J., & Jones, M. C. (1991). A reliable data-based bandwidth selection method for kernel density estimation. *Journal of the Royal Statistical Society. Series B (Methodological)*, 53, 683–690.

Silverman, B. W. (2018). *Density estimation for statistics and data analysis*. Routledge.

Terrell, G. R., & Scott, D. W. (1992). Variable kernel density estimation. *The Annals of Statistics, 20*, 1236–1265.

Wand, M. P., & Jones, M. C. (1994). *Kernel smoothing*. Chapman and Hall/CRC.

## Method 4

Baltagi, B. H. (1995). *Econometric analysis of panel data* (Vol. 2). New York: Wiley.

Maddala, G. S., & Lahiri, K. (1992). *Introduction to econometrics* (Vol. 2). New York: Macmillan.

Greene, W. H. (2003). *Econometric analysis*. Pearson Education India.

## Method 5

Diggle, P., Diggle, P. J., Heagerty, P., Heagerty, P. J., Liang, K. Y., & Zeger, S. (2002). *Analysis of longitudinal data*. Oxford University Press.

Fan, J. (2018). *Local polynomial modelling and its applications: monographs on statistics and applied probability 66*. Routledge.

Royston, P. (1992). Lowess smoothing. *Stata Technical Bulletin, 1*(3), 7–9.

Shumway, R. H., & Stoffer, D. S. (2011). *Time series regression and exploratory data analysis. Time series analysis and its applications* (pp. 47–82). New York: Springer.

# Index

Printed in the United States
By Bookmasters